TERRITORIAL IMPLICATIONS OF HIGH-SPEED RAIL

Transport and Mobility Series

Series Editors: Richard Knowles, University of Salford, UK and Markus Hesse, Université du Luxembourg and on behalf of the Royal Geographical Society (with the Institute of British Geographers) Transport Geography Research Group (TGRG).

The inception of this series marks a major resurgence of geographical research into transport and mobility. Reflecting the dynamic relationships between socio-spatial behaviour and change, it acts as a forum for cutting-edge research into transport and mobility, and for innovative and decisive debates on the formulation and repercussions of transport policy making.

Also in the series

Sustainable Transport, Mobility Management and Travel Plans
Marcus Enoch
ISBN 978 0 7546 7939 4

Transition towards Sustainable Mobility
The Role of Instruments, Individuals and Institutions
Edited by Harry Geerlings, Yoram Shiftan and Dominic Stead
ISBN 978 1 4094 2469 7

Integrating Seaports and Trade Corridors
Edited by Peter Hall, Robert J. McCalla, Claude Comtois and Brian Slack
ISBN 978 1 4094 0400 2

International Business Travel in the Global Economy
*Edited by Jonathan V. Beaverstock, Ben Derudder, James Faulconbridge
and Frank Witlox*
ISBN 978 0 7546 7942 4

Ports in Proximity
Competition and Coordination among Adjacent Seaports
Edited by Theo Notteboom, César Ducruet and Peter de Langen
ISBN 978 0 7546 7688 1

Railways, Urban Development and Town Planning in Britain: 1948–2008
Russell Haywood
ISBN 978 0 7546 7392 7

For further information about this series, please visit www.ashgate.com

Territorial Implications of High-Speed Rail

A Spanish Perspective

Edited by

JOSÉ M. DE UREÑA
University of Castilla La Mancha, Spain

Routledge
Taylor & Francis Group

LONDON AND NEW YORK

First published 2012 by Ashgate Publishing

Published 2016 by Routledge
2 Park Square, Milton Park, Abingdon, Oxon OX14 4RN
711 Third Avenue, New York, NY 10017, USA

Routledge is an imprint of the Taylor & Francis Group, an informa business

British Library Cataloguing in Publication Data
Territorial implications of high-speed rail : a Spanish
  perspective. -- (Transport and mobility series)
  1. High-speed trains--Spain. 2. Railroads--Location--
  Spain. 3. Railroads--Spain--Passenger traffic. 4. Urban
  transportation policy--Spain. 5. Local transit
  accessibility--Spain. 6. High-speed trains--Europe.
  I. Series II. Ureña, José M. de.
  711.7'5'0946-dc23

Library of Congress Cataloging-in-Publication Data
Ureña, José Maria de.
  Territorial implications of high-speed rail : a Spanish perspective / by
José M. de Ureña.
  p. cm. -- (Transport and mobility)
  Includes bibliographical references and index.
  ISBN 978-1-4094-3052-0 (hbk)
  1. High-speed trains--Spain. 2. Railroads--Spain. I. Title.
  HE3195.U74 2011
  385.3'120946--dc23

                                                                    2011052186
ISBN 9781409430520 (hbk)
ISBN 9781138274914 (pbk)

Contents

List of Figures   vii
List of Tables   xi
List of Contributors   xiii
Foreword   xv
    Gabriel Dupuy
Preface   xix
    José M. de Ureña

1   High-Speed Rail and its Evolution in Spain   1
    José M. de Ureña

2   High-Speed Rail – The European Experience   17
    Roger Vickerman

3   Territory and High-Speed Rail: A Conceptual Framework   33
    Severino Escolano

4   Demographic and Socio-economic Context of Spatial
    Development in Spain   55
    Pedro Reques, Olga de Cos and María Marañón

5   Accessibility Evaluation of the Transportation Network in Spain
    during the First Decade of the Twenty-first Century   83
    Ángel Pueyo, Jorge A. Jover and María Zúñiga

6   Mobility Characteristics of Medium-Distance High-Speed
    Rail Services   105
    José M. Menéndez, Ana Rivas and Inmaculada Gallego

7   Territorial Implications at National and Regional Scales of
    High-Speed Rail   129
    José M. de Ureña, José M. Coronado, Maddi Garmendia
    and Vicente Romero

8   The High-Speed Rail in Spanish Cities: Urban Integration and
       Local Strategies for Socio-economic Development   163
       Carmen Bellet, Pilar Alonso and Aaron Gutiérrez

9   High-Speed Rail and Regional Accessibility   197
       Ángela de Meer, Cecilia Ribalaygua and Elena Martín

10   Economic Assessment of High-Speed Rail in Spain   217
       *Vicente Inglada, Pablo Coto-Millán, José Villaverde
       and Pedro Casares*

11   Afterthoughts: High-Speed Rail Planning Issues and Perspectives   241
       José M. de Ureña

Bibliography   *251*
Index   *277*

List of Figures

1.1 HSR systems 3
1.2 Spanish conventional rail network 8
1.3 Spanish HSR network in corridors that also maintain a conventional line 9
1.4 Mixed HSR-conventional services in Spain 11
1.5 Spanish conventional rail infrastructure, upgraded or rebuilt 12
1.6 Comparison of all new HSR and conventional upgraded infrastructures in operation or being built with the HSR plan (PEIT 2005–20) 13

2.1 European HSR network 23
2.2 Passengers carried on HSR 29

3.1 Elasticity of space-time and transport technologies 43
3.2 Some relationships between HSR, territory and individuals 45
3.3 Spatial structure of accessibility 48
3.4 Potential impact of HSR in some perceptual domains of the shell 'region' and 'nation' 52

4.1 Population density in Europe in 2010 59
4.2 Territorial demographic imbalances, urban system, rural space and HSR in Spain in 2010 61
4.3 Population density and HSR in Spain in 2010 62
4.4 The demographically dynamic Spain 64
4.5 Economic activity, territory and high-speed rail in 2010 agrarian versus industrial and tertiary areas of Spain 67
4.6 Employed persons who spend more than 60 minutes travelling from residence to workplace 69
4.7 Employed persons who work in Madrid and officially live in a different municipality 72
4.8 Employed persons who work in Barcelona and officially live in a different municipality 73
4.9 Employed persons who work in Seville and officially live in a different municipality 74
4.10 Employed persons who work in Ciudad Real and officially live in a different municipality 75

4.11   Population that works in another municipality different from
       that of official residence: North of Spain and Andalusia   78

5.1   Absolute potential accessibility in 2010 by highway, airplane
       and HSR   92
5.2   Accessibility improvements due to the addition of the HSR to the
       2010 transportation network   93
5.3   Accessibility according to route factor in 2010 by highway,
       airplane and HSR distances   95
5.4   Accessibility according to route factor and population in 2010 by
       highway, airplane and HSR distances   97
5.5   Percentage improvement of accessibility according to route factor
       accounting for municipal population in 2010   98
5.6   Improvement of the population potentials using the HSR network   101

6.1   French HSR network   107
6.2   Passengers-km carried on European HSR networks   108
6.3   Passengers carried on intermediate relationships of Madrid-Seville
       HSR corridor (2000)   110
6.4   Medium-distance HSR services in Spain   111

7.1   Understanding processes and effects of new HSR lines   133
7.2   Spanish HSR network and city system   139
7.3   Alternative HSR connections for small cities located close to
       a metropolis   148
7.4   Air and HSR transport between metropolitan areas   153
7.5   Zaragoza, Córdoba, Lille and Brussels HSR networks   154
7.6   The Ciudad Real-Puertollano transportation node   158

8.1   Current state and plans for the implementation of the HSR
       network in Spain   167
8.2   The HSR in Figueres and Guadalajara   174
8.3   The railway network in Camp de Tarragona   176
8.4   The HSR in Zaragoza and Valladolid   179
8.5   The HSR in Barcelona and Madrid   181
8.6   The HSR in Lleida and Málaga   185
8.7   Socio-economic and territorial effects of HSR over time   187

9.1   Transformation process along the arrival of the HSR   199
9.2   HSR accessibility models: tangential in Ciudad Real and radial
       in Segovia   204
9.3   Technological park near the station of Valence, France   206
9.4   Use of HSR by companies located near a HSR station   209

9.5   Comparison of the types of activities according to the HSR
      stations locations   210

10.1 HSR benefits for passengers transferred from trains and coaches 225
10.2 Evolution of costs and profits in relation to demand   236

11.1 A model of the Iberian Peninsula urban areas and of the
      concentration/decentralisation processes   244
11.2 Regional systems of small cities connected to HSR   245

List of Tables

1.1 Years when new HSR lines began to operate   10

2.1 HSR networks   21
2.2 Passenger density on HSR (million pass/km)   30

3.1 Fordism versus flexibility: Space   40

4.1 Areas of influence of HSR stations through their concentric
corridors   76
4.2 Numbers of potential commuters between municipalities with
HSR stations in 2001   77

6.1 Evolution of Passenger Traffic on Paris South-East   106
6.2 Medium-distance HSR services, passengers (2009) and travel time
for different modes   112

7.1 HSR trip purposes and passenger profiles   131
7.2 HSR station locations in Spanish cities (with more than 10,000
inhabitants)   136
7.3 Characteristics of the cities with HSR at about one hour from
Paris or Madrid   143
7.4 HSR services through big intermediate cities in 2008
(Madrid (Md), Seville (Se), Córdoba (Co), Málaga (Ma),
Barcelone (Ba), Zaragoza (Za), London (Lo), Lille (Li),
Brussels (Br), Paris (Pa))   156

8.1 Location of the HSR stations and demographic size of the
urban areas   168
8.2 Level of transformation of the railway system and urban change
in HSR Spanish cities   172

9.1 Differential factors of the functional structure   203

10.1 Evolution of the frequency of trips on the Madrid–Seville route   221
10.2 Motives for choosing HSR in terms of other alternative transport
modes. Madrid–Seville route (% of the long-distance segment)   222
10.3 Discriminating factors of the Madrid-Barcelona HSR submarkets   224

10.4   Categories of costs and benefits considered in the evaluation of a
       prototypical HSR project   227
10.5   Travel times on the Madrid–Barcelona route   231
10.6   Assumed Time Values (Euros 2002 per passenger and hour)   231
10.7   Monetary costs of the various modes of transport, Madrid–
       Barcelona route (Euros 2002)   232
10.8   Marginal external social costs per transport mode (Euros 2002)   234
10.9   Minimum volume of demand for HSR profitability (million
       equivalent passengers)   237

List of Contributors

Pilar Alonso, Universitat de Lleida, Spain

Carmen Bellet, Universitat de Lleida, Spain

Pedro Casares, Universidad de Cantabria, Spain

José M. Coronado, Universidad de Castilla La Mancha, Spain

Olga de Cos, Universidad de Cantabria, Spain

Pablo Coto-Millán, Universidad de Cantabria, Spain

Gabriel Dupuy, Université Paris 1 Panthéon-Sorbonne, France

Severino Escolano, Universidad de Zaragoza, Spain

Inmaculada Gallego, Universidad de Castilla La Mancha, Spain

Maddi Garmendia, Universidad de Castilla La Mancha, Spain

Aaron Gutiérrez, Universitat Rovira i Virgili, Spain

Vicente Inglada, Universidad Complutense de Madrid, Spain

Jorge A. Jover, Universidad de Zaragoza, Spain

María Marañón, Universidad de Cantabria, Spain

Elena Martín, Universidad de Cantabria, Spain

Ángela de Meer, Universidad de Cantabria, Spain

José M. Menéndez, Universidad de Castilla La Mancha, Spain

Ángel Pueyo, Universidad de Zaragoza, Spain

Pedro Reques, Universidad de Cantabria, Spain

Cecilia Ribalaygua, Universidad de Cantabria, Spain

Ana Rivas, Universidad de Castilla La Mancha, Spain

Vicente Romero, Universidad de Castilla La Mancha, Spain

José M. de Ureña, Universidad de Castilla La Mancha, Spain

Roger Vickerman, University of Kent, United Kingdom

José Villaverde, Universidad de Cantabria, Spain

María Zúñiga, Universidad de Zaragoza, Spain

Foreword

Gabriel Dupuy[1]

A short while after the opening of the first French High-speed rail line (TGV) between Paris and Lyon, our reaction to the event was summed up with the following words: '… these new trains are not a sideline to the existing railway system, rather they come as the currents carrying deeper, structural changes' (Dupuy et al., 1985). It is more: high-speed trains have been the only real innovative addition to public transportation in over half a century, a breach engulfing modernity, innovation, urban renewal, land management, all of which have acted as harbingers of profound social significance. Regarding Spanish High-speed rail, this book edited by José-Maria de Ureña has aptly summed up the extent and significance of these changes.

Nonetheless, as the author of the book's second chapter, entitled 'High Speed Rail – The European Experience', concludes '… in most cases objectives are obscure, optimum bias common …' These new technologies, undeniably, require considerable investments (as well as high maintenance costs). Without a healthy dose of optimism many high-speed lines would never have been built. But in the end, reality always returns to the operators, and even more pertinently, to the political leaders. Trains have to be filled, the main lines need high levels of traffic and the latter must be sought wherever it exists.

In all the countries which adopted it, High-speed rail (HSR) owes a large part of its success to the network effect. As for other types of networks (electricity, telecommunications, etc.) a high-speed railway network can only find its equilibrium by combining a diversified clientele, servicing varied locations, offering multiple services which can positively reinforce the network effect and move beyond the most strictly logical profitability scenarios. In the early days of the French HSR (TGV) lines, French National Rail (Société Nationale des Chemins de Fer Français – SNCF) had settled on the following slogan: 'Le progrès ne vaut que s'il est partagé par tous', or 'For progress to truly be progress, it must benefit everyone'. The outcome successfully demonstrated that these words were not just empty sloganeering! It is particularly true in Spain, where in order to share the benefits of high-speed lines it was first necessary to overcome the gauge gap. The choice of a European gauge standard for the Spanish HSR might have made it into a network with no connection to the 'classic' Spanish rail network, which would have seriously hindered the network effect. This was also true for *HSR*

---

1   University of Paris 1 Panthéon Sorbonne.

medium-distance trains. Even though the traffic between Puertollano and Ciudad Real typically rarely surpasses the number of students being transported by bus to/from a big French high school, the *HSR medium-distance* (AVANT) service is genuinely innovative and manages to strengthen the network effect.

Capitalising on the network effect seems much less certain at the international scale. While European integration has truly made great strides in many fields, with regard to high-speed rail the national borders are still a considerable obstacle to the network effect. Plans for the Lyon-Turin line have hardly budged in the last 20 years. The HSR link between Germany and France via Strasbourg is not really ready. From Madrid, the HSR will soon reach Perpignan, but how long until the high-speed Spanish line will reach Montpellier? In general, when will European high-speed rail manage to overcome the obstacles of borders which its cousin the highway system has long managed to level out?

Despite the undeniable successes of high-speed rail, a success story which the authors of this book have knowledgeably and carefully analysed, the battle is not yet won. In most countries, Spain being no exception, the uneven price schedule, the new exploratory HSR services, the occasional surprising choices of station location, all belie an attempt to overcome a certain generalised fragility. For example, the pricing for HSR commuter traffic is still in search of itself. What is most needed: cheaper rail passes to ensure full trains or rather higher prices serving to make space for more economically empowered ridership? All countries face the same issues. The responses vary over time and in space. Regarding the tracing of new lines, uncertainty is also an issue. The HSR services (TGV) linking Le Havre-Roissy-Strasbourg which opened two years ago has now shut down. It was initially presented as an innovation, an unusual East-West line that avoided Paris while providing a stop-over at the gigantic airport hub of Roissy Charles de Gaulle. But the actual sales figures did not bear up. The average traffic was ... 72 riders per day!

In light of the above, there is still much work to be done until HSR comes into its own. Most importantly, it is vital to make HSR into an outgrowth of airlines and road transportation, two modes of transportation which have undergone enormous growth since the idea of high-speed rail first appeared in Europe. Despite scattered reports on modal traffic, their average growth rate has hardly been impacted by HSR, therefore they must be entered into the equation.

The question of external effects and land management are also dealt with in this book. The difficulty of showing evidence of effects that are specific for the HSR has been confirmed, especially in the large Metropolitan areas. But at the lower end of the urban hierarchy there has definitely been a 'tugging' effect: when the arrival of high-speed rail is accompanied by urban planning which is streamlined with the rail network, a definite drawing effect may be observed, one which generates virtuous circles.

As suggested by the authors in Chapter 8, it is also necessary to rethink rail stations in the age of high-speed. Certain French HSR (TGV) stations outside the urban centres are swamped by cars, overflowing from immense parking lots which were nevertheless designed with the expectation that a greater percentage of persons will arrive through public transport means, not by car, which make heavy demands on land to enlarge those parking lots, preventing the commercial or residential developments that were planned near the stations. When it comes to using former central stations for high-speed lines, the image (and the value to urban planning) of the old underused stations is often difficult to change.

Providing an in-depth analysis for the manifold features of Spanish HSR, this book is much more than a situation report. It offers truly insightful thoughts on the spatial coherence of networks in relation to innovations in the areas they cross. José-Maria de Ureña is a long-time observer of his subject. He has managed to coalesce around himself and his publication a remarkable team. The author of this foreword hopes that the readers, like him, will appreciate the quality of the book.

Preface

José M. de Ureña[1]

Thirty years ago the first European new High-speed rail line started operating. Since then this new transportation mode has proven to be useful for a variety of travelling distances, passengers and purposes.

This transportation mode has been the subject of a variety of monographic studies, most of them shortly after the first lines were opened, many based on particular cities and often undertaken from a specific scientific disciplinary point of view.

The main contents of this book are the result of 10 years of research undertaken by several Spanish universities and including professionals from different scientific disciplines (Architecture, Economics, Geography, Transport Engineering and Urban & Regional Planning). The objective of the book is to present a broad understanding of the implications of this new transport mode. The final manuscript was completed in April 2011, thus HSR developments after this moment are not included.

Nowadays many European, Asiatic and American countries are engaged in creating some type of High-speed rail network. The experience gathered together in this book is certainly of interest for all these countries, since the creation of the High-speed rail infrastructure should not be considered the end objective, but rather the initiation of a long process of developing actions and strategies to enhance its effects.

Most of the contents of this book were produced within the framework of two research projects from the Spanish National R+D+I Plan, references TRA2007-68033-C03 and T98/2006, financed by the Spanish Ministry of Science and Innovation (*Ministerio de Ciencia e Innovación*) and the Spanish Ministry of Public Works (*Ministerio de Fomento*). These two projects have jointly financed Chapters 1, 5, 6, 7, 8, 9 and 11. The first project financed Chapter 10, and the second financed Chapters 3 and 4. Chapters 1, 7 and 11 have also received the financial support of a third project, reference number TRA2010-20749-C03-0 1.

The authors would like to acknowledge our gratitude to all those passengers and managers who have answered our questionnaires and to those public servants that participated in in-depth interviews with us. The information they gave us has been irreplaceable in developing our understanding of the implications of the

---

1   University of Castilla La Mancha.

High-speed rail. We acknowledge also our thanks to the Spanish statistical (INE) and railway (ADIF and RENFE) authorities for supplying the required data.

Finally the authors would like to thank the work undertaken by Marta Buitrago, who revised the final typescript of the book, and by Eva García-Villaraco, who drew the figures for several chapters.

Chapter 1

High-Speed Rail and its Evolution in Spain

José M. de Ureña[1]

1.1 The First High-Speed Rail Lines

High-speed rail (HSR) is only one of the numerous transport innovations that can be observed over the last 200 years (Knowles, 2006) and was designed as an alternative to inter-metropolitan transport systems, many of which were functioning close to their maximum capacities with growing traffic demand (Vickerman, 2009). Thus, governments have been urged to develop alternatives to tackle this increased demand.

During the 1950s, the main Japanese inter-metropolitan rail line Tokyo–Osaka was already functioning at its maximum capacity. To alleviate this problem, the design of a bullet train, Shinkansen, began in 1958 (the idea was introduced just before World War II). The Tokyo–Osaka HSR line started operation in 1964, just before the Tokyo Olympic Games and six years before the Osaka World Exhibition, and covered 400 km, reaching a maximum commercial speed of 210 km/h (see Chapter 2).

In 1971, the French government approved the HSR Paris–Lyon line, which began operation in 1981 as the first HSR line established in Europe, reaching a maximum commercial speed of 260 km/h. The surplus electrical energy in France and the petroleum crisis of the 1970s prompted the French government to choose an HSR alternative to cope with the increase in inter-metropolitan traffic demand using their own energy, while an air alternative would had have increased dependency on foreign energy sources.

These HSR services in operation, along with new special HSR tracks in both Japan and France, rapidly improved their maximum commercial speeds to about 300 km/h.

The first Spanish HSR line started operation in 1992. What was initially going to be an improvement of the conventional Madrid–Seville rail line became the first HSR line, with a maximum commercial speed of 300 km/h. Spanish accession to the European Economic Community was of great relevance for inducing this change.

The commercial speeds of the HSR services were approximately twice the commercial speeds of the existing conventional rail services. For instance, the best Spanish conventional rail services since 1986 had a maximum commercial

---

1   University of Castilla La Mancha.

speed of 160 km/h, while the first HSR services reached a 300 km/h maximum commercial speed.

Recently, several countries have discussed the possibility of increasing the maximum commercial speed of their HSR. Greater speeds allow for the possibility of running efficiently over larger distances, but they also mean higher energy consumption and maintenance costs. The present speed of 300/350 km/h is sufficient for distances up to 600/700 km (see Section 1.3 and Chapter 7) and thus for most European countries' inter-metropolitan connections. However, these speeds may not be sufficient for internal inter-metropolitan relations in larger countries, such as China or the USA, or for trans-European lines.

1.2 High-Speed Rail Systems

The three HSR lines described in the previous section were based on a new rail infrastructure that differs from the conventional and uses a new type of HSR rolling material. Nevertheless, one of the objectives for the French HSR lines is to connect them with conventional rail networks such that HSR services can continue at lower speeds along these conventional tracks.

At the same time, other European countries, including Britain, have begun to establish faster rail services along conventional lines, although their maximum commercial speed was much lower than 300 km/h, generally 200 km/h in the best conventional rail tracks. These other fast rail services were established even earlier than the French or Spanish HSR in some cases. For example, Britain's Intercity 125, which was intended for the UK's main lines, such as the East Coast Mainline, entered service in 1976.

With globalisation and transport innovations Knowles (2006) indicates that many researchers have mistakenly assumed a simplistic and uniform shrinkage in the time and cost of travel and some models of spatial development have incorrectly assumed cost-distance relationships to be linear. Murayama (1994) showed that the introduction of HSR in Japan increased the accessibility of most cities but also increased the differential between HSR cities and peripheral non-HSR ones, the first ones gaining the highest location advantages.

Progressively, HSR has been defined as rail services having a certain minimum commercial speed, depending on whether they use special rail infrastructure (300-km/h maximum commercial speed) or conventional standard or improved infrastructure (200-km/h maximum commercial speed) (see Chapter 2 and Charlton and Vowles, 2008). This definition, together with the possibility of HSR services using the conventional rail infrastructure and of traditional rail services using the special new HSR infrastructure, has led to a more diversified concept of HSR (Campos and de Rus, 2009b).

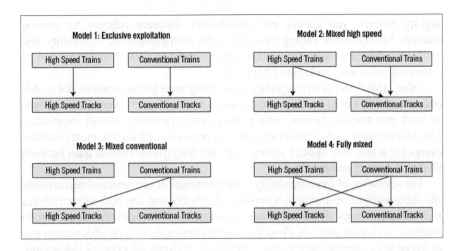

Figure 1.1 HSR systems
Source: Campos and de Rus (2009b).

A HSR classification based on the relations between HSR and conventional rail services and infrastructure is adequate to understand the spatial implications of the HSR. As it will be indicated in Chapters 7, 8 and 9 of this book, these implications are deeply dependent upon elements that can be highlighted by HSR and conventional rail services and infrastructure relations. These elements are the number of possible stops (stations) and their location in relation to each specific city (central, peripheral, etc.), the number and timetable of services, the speed, fare, comfort and reliability of HSR services and the intermodality between HSR and traditional rail (and other means of transport), and most of them are well discriminated if HSR uses conventional or new infrastructure and if HSR and conventional services are mixed or separated.

Conceptually, there are four models of HSR infrastructure and services with improved commercial speed, and how they relate to conventional rail infrastructure and slower rail services (Figure 1.1).

The first model consists of two independent infrastructure networks used by two independent types of rolling material (see Model 1 in Figure 1.1), with the HSR infrastructure used exclusively for passenger services. In this model, new HSR tracks are normally built for very high speeds, 300 km/h or more, and they have adequate slopes (not exceeding 0.2% to 0.4%), curvature radii (7-km radius for horizontal curves and 14-km radius for vertical curves) and very few stations (about one every 100 km). The new HSR infrastructure also normally incorporates other improvements, such as security and management systems.

In general, new HSR infrastructures that use metal tracks and HSR rolling materials that use metal wheels and electric or petrol engine traction have some level of interoperability with traditional rail systems, even though they may use slightly different rail gauges and considerably different voltages for electric traction. Special HSR rolling materials with multiple-voltage operability and with some degree of automatic gauge-change capacity allow both systems to be somewhat interchangeable (see Chapter 2).

Other HSR systems envisaged for developing even greater commercial speeds (more than 400 km/h) based on magnetic levitation require a very different type of track and traction system, which makes interoperability almost impossible. The development of these other systems has been almost halted in most countries except for a few very special settings, i.e., the magnetic-levitation train between Shanghai Airport and the city.

The relevance of interoperability with traditional or conventional rail services and infrastructure, resulting in a number of services that use both infrastructures and transport many passengers, has undoubtedly influenced this reduction in magnetic-levitation projects. From the very beginning the French HSR system was designed to be compatible with the existing conventional rail network (Menerault, 1998). Thus, HSR trains can run on a much wider network than just the dedicated HSR lines.

The second HSR model consists of two connected networks, a newly built HSR network and the conventional one, which are connected only in one sense. The first network is used exclusively by HSR, almost always for passenger trains, and the second is used both by traditional rolling stock for all types of transport (passengers and freight, long distance, regional and suburban) and by HSR rolling material (see Model 2 in Figure 1.1).

This is the HSR model used in most countries. In France, the interoperability of HSR rolling material is complete in all electrified conventional rail infrastructures, as in many other countries. However, in Spain and a few other countries, interoperability is not complete, but it is becoming easier; the conventional rail tracks are slightly wider (about 0.2-m difference), and the improvement of the guage-changing mechanism in passenger HSR rolling material allows the change to be made at 20 km/h in about nine places in Spain (Japan also has a different HSR gauge to its conventional railway gauge). Railway services using both gauges (HSR and conventional) account for around 15% of total HSR services[2] (see Section 1.3).

This second HSR model can be subdivided into two sub-models based on the number of new HSR lines employed. In the first case, the HSR rolling material uses mainly new HSR infrastructure, and conventional infrastructure is only used to serve places without the new infrastructure. In the second case, the HSR rolling material mainly uses conventional tracks, which have been improved in some cases, and only occasionally uses the few HSR infrastructures that have been built in special areas (e.g., congested corridors). In the first sub-model, most HSR services do not coexist with conventional rail services, thereby assuring punctuality and better service, while in the second sub-model, HSR services are

---

2   Based on the Madrid-Seville HSR line.

often affected by other rail services, and become less reliable (because they are subject to conventional rail service incidences). The first sub-model resembles the situation in France and Spain, while the second better resembles the situation in Germany (see Chapter 2).

The third HSR model also consists of two connected networks, a newly built HSR network and the conventional one, but they are connected only in the reverse sense, as in model two (see Model 3 in Figure 1.1). This model is rarely used. One exists in Spain near the Spanish–French frontier, where new HSR tracks are going to be prepared to admit conventional freight trains towards the harbours of Barcelona and Bilbao.

The fourth HSR model is a combination of the second and third (see Model 4 in Figure 1.1). HSR networks that were initially composed of a few lines, often independent of conventional rail infrastructures, are progressively evolving into complex networks of model four, combining all possibilities.

HSR models consisting of new HSR infrastructure with the initial objective of connecting distant metropolitan areas only needed a few stations. Therefore intermediate stations were only built if major cities were along the route, or for security reasons. Stations were established every 150/200 km whereas conventional rail networks have stations approximately every 15/30 km. Under these conditions HSR networks based on new infrastructure and independent services (Model 1) do not serve a great percentage of the intermediate places between metropolitan areas, thus reinforcing polarisation in a few places and increasing its 'tunnel' effect (Plassard, 1991). Whereas HSR models based on conventional lines (Model 3) would have stations much closer to each other, even though conventional rail services may stop in more stations than HSR services. Currently HSR networks based on new HSR infrastructure have stations approximately every 100 km.

1.3 High-Speed Rail Services

The initial objective of HSR services was to substitute and/or compete with air transport between metropolitan areas 400 km to 600 km apart, or between two and three hours of travel time (not including pre- and post-travel by HSR) in 300-km/h HSR maximum commercial speed services, or slightly shorter distances at 200-km/h maximum commercial speed.

In Europe HSR is being used intensely for four travel times intervals. The first one has been around 2.5 hours, the second type of travel time to appear was around 1 hour travel time, the third one was around 4 hours and the last one was around half an hour. Nevertheless HSR is also used for personal reasons and on occasions for shorter and longer travel time intervals (see Chapter 6 and 7 and Charlton and Vowles, 2008).

The first HSR use was for professional reasons between 2 and 3 hours travel time since it allowed day return travel. Ureña et al. (2009d) showed that, for travel times of 2 to 3 hours, HSR captures important numbers of air-travel passengers, namely between 50 and 80% of professional travel (calculations were undertaken with the Madrid-Seville line). The advantages of travelling by HSR as opposed to air travel for these time distances rely not only on a simple comparison of total travel time and price but also on a wider combination of factors that include reliability, comfort and use of total travel time.

HSR services are more punctual than air services, and the percentage of HSR services cancelled for a variety of reasons (e.g., weather, technical reasons, or congestion) is substantially smaller than that of air services. Moreover, the total travel time, including checking, security controls, waiting for departure, access/ departure to/from plane/train and main travel, results in a greater percentage of unusable time when travelling by air than when travelling by HSR. This means that, even in cases when the total travel time is longer by HSR than by air, travelling by HSR may allow more time for working or relaxing than when travelling by air. The total travel time by air for these distances includes more time spent in pre- and post-plane travel, while the total HSR travel time includes much less time spent in these pre- and post-activities and more time in the train. The professional use of time while in planes is also much less efficient than that in HSR trains. This results in greater efficiency of total travel time. This efficiency is even greater for HSR travel if one considers that most professional travel has a metropolitan centre as its final destination, where most office activities and metropolitan HSR rail stations are located (see Chapter 8).

The overall comfort along these 400- to 600-km distances, summing all travel activities, is also better for HSR travel than for air travel.

This initial type of long-distance HSR services (two to three hours of HSR travel time) was soon complemented by others, as HSR has not only demonstrated efficiency in capturing passengers over those distances but also over longer and shorter routes. HSR has demonstrated its efficiency for one-hour commuting travel and for more than three hours of professional and personal travel.

The second type HSR usage was for commuting reasons between 0.75 and 1.5 hours since it allows commuting and opens labour opportunities over longer distances. HSR has also demonstrated its capacity to capture between 50 and 80% (Ureña et al. 2009d) of passengers from rail and road commuting, for between 0.75 and 1.5 hours of HSR travel time (not including pre- and post-main travel by HSR), i.e., between 150-km and 250-km distances for 300-km/h maximum commercial speed HSR. This use of HSR for commuting purposes has been achieved by attracting passengers from other transportation means and also by inducing new commuting activities at longer distances (Ureña et al. 2005a), thus generating new mobility patterns and passengers (see Chapters 6 and 7).

While the 2- to 3-hour HSR services inter-connect metropolitan areas, these medium distance 0.75- to 1.5-hour HSR services connect other types of cities: small cities with metropolises, medium-sized cities with metropolises and small settlements with medium-sized cities. Moreover, these 2- to 3-hour and 0.75- to 1.5-hour HSR services are not only used for professional and commuting purposes but also increasingly for personal purposes, both generating new travel and capturing passengers from other transportation means.

The reverse process also occurs when persons who had travelled on conventional rail services no longer travel on the equivalent HSR services but start to use bus services. This is due to a substantial increase in fares when comparing conventional rail services to the equivalent HSR ones. It also happens because some or many equivalent conventional rail services are cancelled when HSR services are established along a corridor. In this situation, passengers whose priority is cost management rather than timesaving transfer to travelling by bus. There are signs of this phenomenon in the Madrid–Córdoba route in Spain, where a direct bus service Madrid–Córdoba was established at the same time as the HSR.

Third, in addition to the above-mentioned two- to three-hour-long distances, there is increasing demand for HSR travel for greater distances (e.g., Barcelona–Seville) of up to 4 hours of HSR travel time for professional and more so for personal and leisure purposes. Zembri (2005) confirmed this demand for the Paris–Marseille route.

The fourth and last type of HSR service to be introduced in Europe occurs over shorter distances, between 70 km and 150 km in metropolitan environments (around half an hour travel time), as a new type of suburban or metropolitan transportation mode for the outer parts of some metropolitan areas, such as London and Madrid (see Chapters 6 and 7 and Ureña et al. 2010).

Interoperability between the new HSR network and conventional rail networks, the different length of HSR services and the increasingly web-like character of the HSR network, result in the rather complex character of HSR services and users. What was initially thought of as a metropolis-to-metropolis service is now a complex system of services between all types of cities.

In general, HSR has produced a substantial increase in total travel, not only attracting passengers from other transport means but also inducing new travel (an increase of between 10 and 30%).

1.4 The Development of High-Speed Rail in Spain

In Spain there are two rail networks with different gauges: conventional and HSR. The conventional network (Figure 1.2) with the Iberian gauge[3] (1.668 m) built over two centuries has a spider-web form with many interconnections. Nevertheless, the lines that link the main cities have better technical characteristics (electrified double tracks) and maintenance procedures, while others that connect less relevant areas or run along complex topographic areas are not as well equipped (e.g., single tracks not electrified). All of the 47 mainland Spanish provincial capitals are connected to this network.

---

3   The line along the northern Spanish coast has another gauge, a one-meter gauge.

Figure 1.2 Spanish conventional rail network
Source: Author based on data from ADIF.

Very different types of rail services use this network: passenger and freight, long distance, regional and suburban. They have different speeds, 50 to 150 km/h, and different numbers of stops, more frequent for regional and suburban services and less frequent for long-distance services. Single-ticket fares for regional and suburban services are about 0.09 €/km (2010). At present the only conventional rail services running frequently are the suburban ones, while many long-distance services along this conventional rail network have been cancelled and progressively substituted by HSR services along the new HSR infrastructure.

The new HSR network with the standard international gauge (1.435 m), maintaining the conventional rail line along similar corridors, has a radial tree-shaped structure with its centre at Madrid (Figure 1.3). This new network began to be built only in the 1980s (see Table 1.1), and most of it has similar high standard technical characteristics: double track, electric traction and 300/350-km/h design speeds.[4] This network is being extended, maintaining its basic radial tree-shaped

---

4　In the Basque region, due to its complex topography, the design speed is 250 km/h.

structure, mainly towards the north (Figure 1.3). At present, only 16 of the 47 provincial capitals are connected to this network. In the near future 12 more will be connected, reaching a total of 60% of the provincial capitals (28 out of 47).

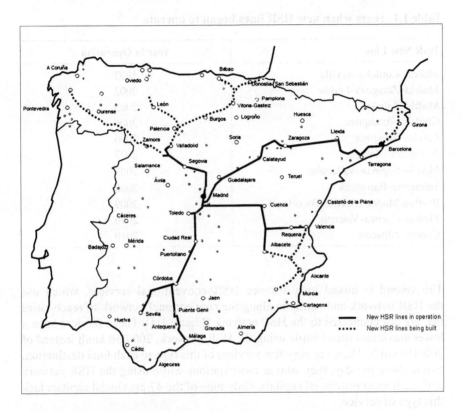

Figure 1.3 Spanish HSR network in corridors that also maintain a conventional line

Source: Author based on data from ADIF.

Three types of HSR services use this new infrastructure. The first is pure long-distance HSR services, which correspond to the initial objective of HSR. They exclusively use the new HSR infrastructure and connect the main cities, with single-ticket fares that are twice the cost of conventional rail services, roughly 0.19 €/km (2010). Fares of conventional air trips are between 0.40 and 1.10 €/km, while low cost air trips are around 0.10 €/km.[5] Some stop at intermediate cities (more in the larger ones than in the smaller ones), and there are frequent

---

5 Based on the Madrid-Seville relation.

journeys between major cities, about 15/20 per day (30/40 both ways). Maximum commercial speeds are 300–350 km/h, and average speeds are 200–250 km/h.

Table 1.1 Years when new HSR lines began to operate

HSR New Line	Year in Operation
Madrid–Córdoba–Sevilla	1992
Madrid–Zaragoza–Lérida	2003
Madrid–Toledo	2005
Córdoba–Antequera	2006
Lérida–Tarragona	2006
Antequera–Málaga	2007
Madrid–Segovia–Valladolid	2007
Tarragona–Barcelona	2008
By-Pass Madrid (Sevilla–Barcelona)	2009
Madrid–Cuenca–Valencia	2010
Cuenca–Albacete	2010

The second is mixed long-distance HSR–conventional services, which use the HSR network and continue along the conventional network to reach cities that are not connected to the HST network (Figure 1.4). These services have a lower maximum speed while using the HSR network, 200/250 km/h instead of 300/350 km/h. There are very few services of this type to each final destination, two to three per day, they stop at most stations while using the HSR network and reach most provincial capitals. Only nine of the 47 provincial capitals lack this type of service.

In Spain these mixed HSR-conventional services require special trains, which automatically change their gauge at particular points where they transfer from the HSR infrastructure to the conventional one.[6] These services are less punctual than the pure HSR services, mainly because of the inconveniences encountered in using the conventional tracks due to their technical characteristics and their use by freight, suburban and regional conventional services. Single-ticket fares costs are between those of conventional and pure HSR services, around 0.12 €/km (2010).

---

6   In most countries with the same gauge, this can be done in more places. In particular, in France, there are about twice as many places than in Spain where HSR services can change from the new HSR tracks to the conventional ones (Ureña 2009b).

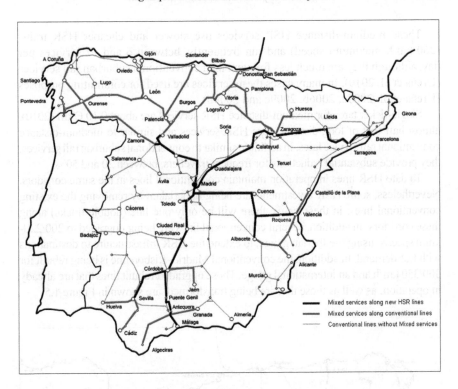

Figure 1.4 Mixed HSR-conventional services in Spain
Source: Author based on data from RENFE.

Finally, the third type is medium-distance HSR services, which connect a few regional city systems and some small and medium cities with metropolitan areas. All of these services cover distances of up to 200/350 km. These services were first established in Spain (Ureña et al. 2009d) and they use only the new HSR network.[7] There are only six services of this type, using approximately half of the new HSR network. The first to be established was of a metropolitan type: Madrid–Ciudad Real–Puertollano. The second was also of this type: Madrid–Toledo. The third was of a regional type in Andalucía: Seville–Córdoba–PuenteGenil–Antequera–Málaga. The other three have a mixed character: Madrid–Segovia–Valladolid, Zaragoza–Calatayud and Barcelona–Tarragona–Lleida. Figure 1.4 includes the names of all of these cities.

---

7   These services are called AVANT or LANZADERA. There is one such service that has not been included in this type of HSR service, the Jaen–Córdoba–Seville–Cádiz service. This exclusion is because it has only two services a day and because it partially uses the conventional network. This service has been included in the mixed HSR-conventional type, although its fares are of the medium-distance HSR type of service.

These medium-distance HSR services use slower and cheaper HSR trains (260-km/h maximum speed) and run frequently, between 6 and 12 services per day, although they are much less frequent than conventional suburban rail services (Ureña et al. 2010). In many cases these services are used for commuting purposes (Ureña et al. 2005a, 2006b, 2009c and 2009d).

Single-ticket fares for medium-distance HSR services are about 0.10 €/km (2010), almost half that of long-distance pure HSR services and similar to medium-distance conventional rail service fares. In addition, similar to conventional suburban rail services, they provide substantial reductions for frequent travellers, between 20 and 50%.

To date HSR lines in operation maintain conventional lines in the same corridors. Nevertheless, some HSR investments are being undertaken by removing the existing conventional lines; in these cases, there will be only one line (double tracks) along these corridors. In addition, several conventional lines are being upgraded to 200/220-km/h speeds, using the Iberian gauge, to extend the HSR infrastructure to destinations with less demand. In addition, the conventional Madrid–Lisbon line is being rebuilt for 300/350 km/h and an international gauge. Those upgraded/rebuilt lines that are already in operation, as well as those that are being transformed, are shown in Figure 1.5.

Figure 1.5 Spanish conventional rail infrastructure, upgraded or rebuilt
Source: Author based on data from ADIF.

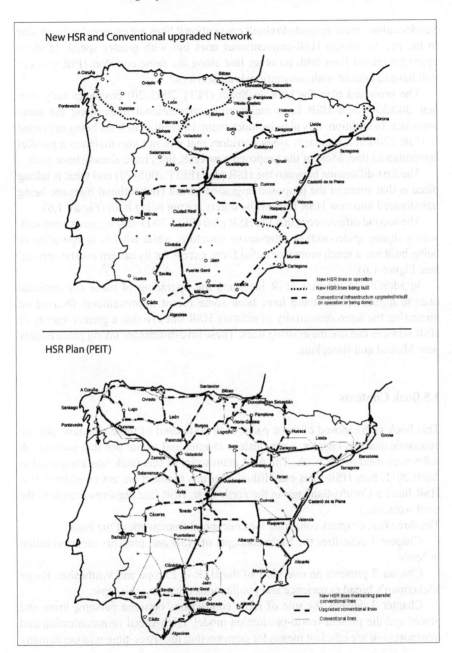

Figure 1.6 Comparison of all new HSR and conventional upgraded infrastructures in operation or being built with the HSR plan (PEIT 2005–20)

Source: Author based on data from ADIF.

Services along these upgraded/rebuilt conventional lines are expected to be similar to the present mixed HSR-conventional ones but with greater speed. In these upgraded/rebuilt lines with no other line along the same corridor, HSR services will have to coexist with conventional rail services.

The proposed plan for HSR in Spain (PEIT 2005–20) envisages only four new 300/350-km/h HSR lines maintaining conventional lines along the same corridors. In addition, this plan includes many conventional lines being upgraded to HSR 220-km/h standards along corridors that will not also maintain a parallel conventional line. Most of the proposed new HSR lines have already been built.

The first difference between the HSR plan (PEIT 2005–20) and what is taking place is that some of the proposed upgraded/rebuilt conventional lines are being transformed into new HSR lines while others are not being built (Figure 1.6).

The second difference is that the HSR plan (PEIT 2005–20) suggests a network with a strong spider-web or interwoven structure, while what is in operation or being built has a much more tree radial form, except for its eastern coastal section[8] (see Figure 1.6).

In addition to the new HSR lines and the upgrading of some conventional ones to higher speeds there have been some recent improvements focused on increasing the interconnectivity of existing HSR lines so that a greater variety of HSR services can use the existing lines. These investments are taking place mainly near Madrid and Barcelona.

1.5 Book Contents

This book is composed of three parts, each composed of three chapters, plus an economic analysis chapter, a conclusions chapter and a final one that includes all references used in the book. The final manuscript of this book was completed in April 2011, thus HSR lines established after this moment are not considered (i.e. HSR line La Coruña-Santiago in the north-west, HSR line Figueres-France in the north-east, etc.).

The three first chapters constitute the conceptual framework of the book:

Chapter 1 describes the basic concepts of HSR and presents their evolution in Spain

Chapter 2 presents an overview of the HSR in Europe and synthesises Roger Vickerman's broad experience and publications regarding this topic.

Chapter 3 debates the role of rapid connections between persons, firms and places and the present world-production model. High-speed communication and transportation are efficient means for compressing the space-time relation in many

---

8   It was expected that there would be an HSR connection between the Madrid-Zaragoza-Barcelona line and the Madrid-Valladolid-Vitoria line, which would generate an interweaved structure in this part of the HSR network, but so far, there are no concrete plans to do so.

production and social processes. This compression accelerates the economic flow of persons, goods and information, which in turn accelerates the capital's rate of return, influences regional development and changes the experience that people have of the geographical space.

The next three chapters provide the socio-economic and transportation framework of the book:

Chapter 4 debates the spatial distribution of population and employment in Spain and compares it with the present layout of the HSR infrastructure. It also describes the overall pattern of residence-work trips in Spain, using the individual mobility data of the 2001 census.

Chapter 5 describes changes in accessibility in Spain achieved by using road, rail and air transportation networks. It analyses the regions that have experienced greater improvements in global accessibility, in particular those regions that have already received the new HSR infrastructure.

Chapter 6 analyses the characteristics of HSR passengers and synthesises the authors' experience obtained through several sets of interviews with HSR passengers.

Chapters 7–9 make up the core of the book and debate the territorial implications of the HSR in Spain, using examples from other European countries:

Chapter 7 presents the inter-urban implications of HSR, showing the creation of new city-to-city relations, the connection of cities to inter-metropolitan relations and the reinforcement of existing ones. The chapter emphasises the HSR implications in intermediate cities along the HSR lines.

Chapter 8 debates the urban implications of HSR. It shows the strategies and projects developed locally to reinforce the opportunities opened by HSR. The first change taking place is the physical and spatial transformation that accompanies the introduction of the HSR service, which becomes an instrument of urban planning.

Chapter 9 discusses functional structure modifications associated with the arrival of the HSR and the strategies used to expand the accessibility of the limited number of HSR stations to wider areas in more-or-less polarised and inhabited territories. The authors review the impact that HSR station locations may have on the manner that a particular area functions, both in the reorganisation of transport and in the strategy of attracting activities.

Chapter 10 provides an economic evaluation of the HSR in Spain. Starting with a review of studies carried out for the Madrid-Seville and Madrid-Barcelona cases, it concludes that it would be difficult for the HSR to be economically viable in Spain. The minimal level of demand required to make this type of project viable in Spain is determined using cost-benefit analysis. Finally, the chapter assesses whether the minimum threshold can be reduced using the economies of the network.

Chapter 2
High-Speed Rail – The European Experience

Roger Vickerman[1]

European experience with high-speed rail (HSR) is 30 years old in 2011. The first stage of the first dedicated HSR line between Paris and Lyon was opened to traffic in 1981. Since that first 430 km link the development of four major routes centred on Paris, with interconnecting links around Paris, and the first transversal link have created a network of 1200 km of high-speed lines in France. This network has also been connected internationally to the United Kingdom (via the Channel Tunnel), to Belgium and most recently to Spain. Since the trains using this network can also run on existing 'classic' rail lines international links are also possible to the Netherlands, Germany, Switzerland and Italy. The French network has become the most developed in Europe and for geographical reasons sits at the centre of a growing European network, one of the designated Trans-European Transport Networks. Although Germany, Italy, Belgium, the Netherlands and the United Kingdom have also invested to a lesser extent in HSR using purpose built dedicated track, only Spain has developed a network on the scale of that in France.

In this Chapter we pose the questions: why has high-speed rail claimed such a central role in the development of European transport networks; why have there been different approaches to HSR development in different countries; how has the HSR concept changed over the past 30 years; and what are the consequences for its future development?

2.1 A Short History of High-Speed Rail[2]

The first country to exploit HSR technology on dedicated new track was Japan in the 1960s. At this time, countries like the United Kingdom were finding ways of raising speeds on historic nineteenth-century rail networks, initially to 200 km/h through the diesel High Speed Train. Japan was constrained by having a historic network largely based on 1067 mm track gauge rather than what had become the more normal standard gauge of 1453 mm. Rapid economic growth was placing pressure on the existing network where capacity constraints were becoming severe. The tight curvature possible with the Japanese gauge network was seen as inappropriate for future development and thus the decision was taken to build

---

1   University of Kent.

2   A more comprehensive recent history is contained in Gourvish (2010).

new lines where new capacity was needed. These would be on new alignments to the standard 1435 mm gauge and allow speeds of up to 250 km/h although initial service speeds were 210 km/h. The first of these lines, the *Tokaido Shinkansen* between Tokyo and Osaka, opened in 1964 and was rapidly followed by other lines to complete a network linking Tokyo to all the major cities.

France had pioneered raising speeds on parts of the classic network using electric traction, reaching speeds of over 330 km/h in 1955. However, as in Japan, it was not the objective of speed alone, but capacity constraints which led France to develop its first *ligne à grande vitesse* (LGV). The key route between France's two largest cities, Paris and Lyon, was becoming heavily congested due to the growth in both passenger and freight traffic in the economic boom of the 1960s. Enlarging capacity through additional tracks was not feasible due to the constraints of the twisting route along the Yonne and Saone valleys. A new route was the solution and it thus seemed sensible to construct this avoiding tight curves and hence providing the possibility of faster speeds. Moreover by taking a more direct route, more than 100 km could be saved between Paris and Lyon. Thus by raising speeds to a possible 300 km/h (initial service speeds were 270 km/h) a headline two-hour end-to-end journey time could be achieved, a saving of 1 hour 45 minutes on the previous best Paris–Lyon timings. The first section of the new route was opened in 1981 and gradually extended until eventually new high-speed track had been built for the entire route from Paris to the Mediterranean. This was followed by the key routes to the South-West, the North and the East.

As in Japan a key to the concept of the new LGV routes was that they were dedicated to fast passenger traffic only (although the French did also build some high-speed postal trains); all trains would maintain the same speed profile thus maximising capacity. Exploiting new technology, the vertical profile of the French lines was also more extreme with steeper gradients avoiding the need for as many expensive tunnels and viaducts. Unlike Japan, however, as the new *trains à grande vitesse* (TGV) used the same track gauge as the classic network, they could also serve the existing terminal stations in city centres avoiding the need for very expensive new infrastructure and could serve destinations off the LGV network. The TGV network thus penetrates all the major cities of France. The construction of a series of links around Paris also enabled faster province to province journeys without passengers needing to change trains in Paris. Thus the network capacity is exploited to the full.

Whilst Italy followed broadly the same principles as France in developing a network of new dedicated lines serving the main cities, progress was much slower. Germany, however, took a rather different approach (see Chapter 1). This was to some extent dictated by a different geography, but also by the then political division of Germany. West Germany, separated from the historic capital of Berlin, had re-oriented traffic flows on a north-south axis. In this area there was no one single dominant city in the way that Paris dominated traffic flows in France. Moreover north-south flows between the northern industrial cities of Hamburg and the Rhine-Ruhr and the fast growing southern cities such as Munich and Stuttgart had to follow rather tortuous and capacity-constrained routes along the Rhine Valley or through the Mittelgebirge highlands. As in France the solution to the capacity constraints was seen to be completely new routes. In Germany, however, the general view was that these should be mixed traffic routes allowing for faster freight. This constrained construction parameters and involved many more tunnels and hence the new lines were more expensive. In practice mixed use has not been common. The other difference was that Germany did not rely on completely new city to city lines, but rather a mix of new construction to deal with geographical constraints, *Neubaustrecken* (NBS), and where possible improvements to existing routes, *Ausbaustrecken* (ABS). The exception to this was the Frankfurt–Köln line which was designed much closer to French principles taking a route which minimised expensive physical infrastructures and, significantly, was built to serve the airports of the two cities.

The reunification of Germany in 1990 led to a necessary reorientation of the developing network to incorporate Berlin including the development of a new main railway station for the city where a reinstated north–south route crossed the existing east–west cross-city route. The development of the German network has however been rather more patchy than that in France. Increasing costs, where costs per kilometre were already significantly higher, have delayed many projects. However, as in France, the compatibility of trains with the classic network allowed the development of a national network of InterCity Express (ICE) services.

Both the French and German networks were also designed to extend to international as well as domestic traffic. European Union interests were thus shown initially with the so-called PBKAL (Paris–Brussels–Köln–Amsterdam–London) or north-European HSR network. These cities were all in the 400–600 kilometre range which was seen as ideal for exploitation by HSR since the resulting two- to three-hour city centre-to-city centre timings would be highly competitive with both air and road alternatives (see Chapters 1 and 7). This would be likely to produce sufficient traffic for viability and also contribute to the increasing pressure for more sustainable transport networks. International rail traffic in Europe had suffered from the greater ease with which air and road could cross international borders within the EU; rail continued to be hindered by nineteenth century differences in national standards which affected loading gauge, (even where standard track gauge was used), electrification standards and signalling systems, not to mention the restrictions on working practices imposed by a highly unionised sector. These differences had persisted into the development of HSR technology with France and Germany developing their own highly specific new trains in the TGV and ICE respectively. With a growing interest in HSR worldwide French and German railway manufacturing interests also had an eye on the export potential and hence showed reluctance to compromise on a European standard.

To some extent the difficulties of varying working practices were resolved by setting up joint ventures to exploit the Paris/Brussels–London services (Eurostar) and Paris–Brussels–Amsterdam/Köln services (Thalys). Both of these were dominated by French influence and use derivatives of the standard TGV trainset.

Genuine competition was however restricted to relatively few sections of route, for example Brussels–Köln. Even here technical problems of compatibility between infrastructure and train have caused problems.

The late entrant to the European HSR development was Spain. Development here followed a slightly different route. As in Japan, Spain's main railways had been developed with a different track gauge from the standard 1435 mm, but here it was a broad 1670 mm gauge. There was also a substantial network of narrow gauge railways. The different track gauge made connections with the rest of the European network more difficult although a fleet of specially developed coaches with variable gauge axles was built for international services. Spain saw the development of HSR as an opportunity to renew what had become a very run down railway system, but also to construct this to standard European gauge to facilitate international connections without the need for a gauge change, and also to enjoy the benefits of being able to purchase standard rolling stock rather than having to develop this separately. As in France, the urban geography of Spain also appeared to offer advantages to HSR with the main cities at distances of 500–600 kilometres. The need to impose a different track gauge did however imply the need for new routes into the major cities and limited the scope for serving destinations off the main routes without the need for a gauge-change. The Spanish development is remarkable for four features. First, it grew extremely quickly to create the largest network by length of route in Europe. Secondly, it employed a variety of competing train designs so that derivatives of all the main HSR traction technologies can be compared. Thirdly, it provided the opportunity for mixed use by allowing conventional broad gauge trains using gauge changing technology to benefit from the more direct routes provided by the new lines but enabling access to places off the new network. Fourthly, by creating direct routes previously not really served by an effective train service, it had impacts on travel and commuting patterns in the Greater Madrid area as well as on longer distance travel to cities such as Sevilla and Barcelona (see Chapters 6 and 7).

If the speed of development in Spain appeared fast, it was soon overtaken by that in China. China spent time experimenting with alternative technology such as developments of the German Maglev system, *Transrapid*. Germany planned a Maglev link between Hamburg and Berlin but this was eventually abandoned on cost grounds, not least the need to duplicate infrastructure into the heart of major cities rather than using existing track. China developed one link, that to Shanghai's new Pudong airport, using Maglev, but reverted to conventional steel wheel on rail technology for the emerging HSR network (see Chapter 1). China, like Spain, although on a much larger scale, had an ideal urban geography of major cities situated 500–600 km apart. In China however the sheer scale of these urban areas was sufficient to generate viable traffic volumes from the very start. As Table 2.1 shows, China has rapidly become the major user of HSR.

Table 2.1 HSR networks

Network length (m)	Built	Under construction	Planned	Total
France	1,163	186	1,626	2,975
Spain	993	1,379	1,058	3,430
Germany	799	235	416	1,450
Italy	463	82	245	790
Netherlands/Belgium	108	97	0	205
UK	70	0	0	70
Japan	1,524	367	362	2,253
China	742	5,611	1,803	8,156
Taiwan	214	0	0	214
S Korea	205	51	0	256

Source: UK Department for Transport (2010).

This very brief history of the major HSR systems identifies a number of key issues
for discussion in later sections:

- The choice between dedicated passenger and mixed traffic systems affects
  the construction costs, operational simplicity and the underlying economics
  of HSR;
- Whilst the original concept was as a substitute mode for road and air in the
  range 400–600 km, HSR has also had impacts on much shorter journeys
  where it has opened up new markets. It has also become increasingly a
  complementary mode with HSR serving airports as a feeder service rather
  than a competitor;
- HSR has the potential to have impacts on land use in both the major urban
  areas served and on intermediate places, but these impacts will depend
  largely on the implementation of accompanying polices and cannot be
  guaranteed;
- The development of international HSR services has been slow in Europe
  and effective competition between HSR operators minimal.

2.2 High-Speed Rail in European Union Transport Policy

Although a Common Transport Policy was established in the Treaty of Rome, apart
from various attempts to develop a common market in transport services by various
modes very little progress was made on using policy to shape the development of
European transport networks until the late 1980s. In the early years the policy did not
even include shipping or aviation and efforts focussed first on trying to harmonise
the various national regulations affecting road haulage, mainly in place to protect
state-owned railways, to ensure fair competition. This was done initially through

elaborate harmonisation of regulations, but later through increasing liberalisation. On the railways the main interest was in ensuring a common approach to the public service concept justifying public subsidy to public transport modes. There was little thought given to an overall strategy for transport in the EU with the exception of some recommendations on common approaches to transport investment appraisal.

The emphasis changed considerably with the production of the first White Paper on a Common Transport Policy in 1990. This was the first time that a strategic overview of the whole transport sector was taken against the background of increasing concerns on environmental impacts and sustainability. Moreover significant EU funds were being used on transport projects, not under the auspices of any transport policy, but largely as part of the growing Structural and Cohesion Funds. Poor transport infrastructure was seen as a major constraint on the development of lagging regions in the EU whilst the congestion problems of the core regions were arising from increasing concentration of activity in the areas with the better developed, if often inadequate, infrastructure. Whilst much of the emphasis was on trying for the first time to ensure a level playing field for competition between the modes, it was also thought desirable to try and define transport networks with a European significance. Thus the concept of Trans-European Transport Networks (TENs) was developed. The problem was that although the TENs could be defined at an EU level, within the context of an overall strategy for transport, the responsibility for implementing policy lay with the member states. In particular, EU funding for TENs was also largely limited to funding for studies and not for their development. Hence national priorities and national constraints on funding for new investment determined actual development of the TENs. Nevertheless considerable emphasis has been placed on identifying a Europe-wide network of both high-speed (180–250 km/h) and very high-speed (more than 250 km/h) lines (Figure 2.1).

The TENs concept has two major potential flaws. First, it developed separate networks for each mode (including separate networks for HSR and conventional rail). This failed to provide for a strategic decision on the relative priorities for the different modes. Lobbying by regions to be on TENs, and typically on more than one TEN, implied considerable duplication of networks. Secondly, there is an inbuilt bias in most national transport priorities towards investment in new construction. Rarely is there consideration of alternative solutions, for example, the capacity constraint of many conventional rail networks is not the amount of track available, or even its configuration, but the traction and signalling systems employed. For these reasons HSR networks have largely been built independently of any consideration of the classic rail network, not least as to how the two networks complement each other. Ironically more attention has been devoted to the complementarity between HSR and the two networks with which it was initially expected to compete with; HSR is now being seen as an important connector to airports providing a substitute for short-haul air feeder services and intermediate stations on HSR networks are typically built out-of-town with large scale provision for park and ride. This is exacerbated where the HSR service is provided by a different company from classic rail.

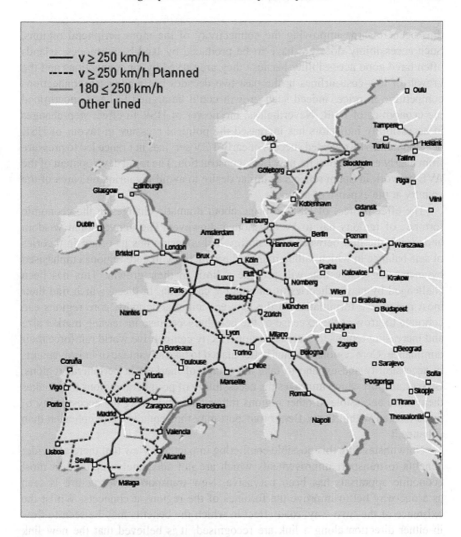

Figure 2.1 European HSR network
Source: UIC (2009) (in UK Department for Transport 2010).

Part of the problem with the focus on HSR has been the emphasis placed on reducing disparities in accessibility in policies towards cohesion. The EU's poorer regions are to a large extent those in more peripheral locations. Accessibility is usually measured with respect to time, to reflect the extent to which higher quality infrastructure will sustain higher speeds and hence more distant locations with a less well-developed infrastructure will have lower levels of accessibility than more central regions (Vickerman et al. 1999a). Since accessibility is generally positively correlated with economic performance, a central tenet of cohesion policies has thus been towards improving the connectivity of the more peripheral regions. Such accessibility does not have to be produced by land-based modes. Islands often have good accessibility because they are served by air connections and the growth of low-cost airlines in the past two decades has made such connections competitive in price, indeed such growth could be argued to have undermined the economics of HSR. Nevertheless, the power of HSR to effect step-changes in accessibility indicators has increased the political pressure in favour of HSR development. The revealed success of early TGV services in France led to pressure from nearly every region for new LGV construction. The rapid development of the AVE network in Spain reflects a similar desire to avoid favouring one area of the country at the expense of another.

The effectiveness of HSR to bring about dramatic changes in the economic fortunes of regions has to be questioned, however. The conventional wisdom underlying the link between accessibility and cohesion has its origin in theories of self-balance in which falling marginal productivity in core regions emphasised by increasing congestion will provide a limit to their growth. This has been challenged by newer theories of cumulative causation. In these, which find their most persuasive formulation in the new economic geography, core regions can continue to grow at the expense of the periphery because increasing market size and increasing returns to scale in an imperfectly competitive world reinforce their dominance. Core regions are thus better placed to take advantage of improvements in accessibility and expand to take advantage of markets in peripheral regions. Better transport which improves the accessibility of peripheral regions thus makes them more accessible to other regions rather than improving the accessibility of firms located within them. Better transport may thus equally harm cohesion than enhance it.

Notwithstanding this possible conflicting impact, the view that there are wider benefits to transport improvements which are not adequately captured in most economic appraisals has been pervasive. New transport infrastructure is seen as a one-way bet to improve the fortunes of the regions it connects. Whilst the existence of the 'two-way' road effect in which the benefits may be seen to flow in either direction along a link are recognised, it is believed that the new link must generate sufficient additional benefits through reduced transport costs in the economy as a whole to have net additional impact. This is supported by recourse to the general theory of agglomeration: reduced transport costs increase the size of a market, evidence suggests that larger markets (particularly large cities) are associated with higher levels of productivity; these higher levels of productivity benefit all activities in the region, but are not captured in the willingness to pay of individual transport users. This argument was reinforced by the large number of studies which followed the initial attempt by Aschauer (1989) to measure the productivity of public infrastructure. These studies, which did not produce totally consistent results and often demonstrated that other forms of infrastructure were more effective in achieving these benefits than transport, were mainly based on highly aggregate data at the level of states, regions or even countries. What they did not show was that any particular transport link would automatically generate benefits at the level implied by the aggregate results.

The evidence from studies which have investigated these effects in more detail is inconclusive. Whether improved accessibility works in favour of peripheral regions or against them is essentially an empirical matter which depends on existing industrial structures and market size, the importance of transport costs, and the magnitude of any change. The fact that HSR is mainly about passenger traffic and not freight does not make this analysis irrelevant. Labour is one of the major costs faced by firms in most sectors, the contribution of HSR to enlarging labour markets has an important impact on both costs and productivity. The increased importance of the service sector, particularly in major metropolitan areas reinforces this point. Graham (2007, 2009) found that the elasticity of productivity with respect to labour market size in London was significantly higher than that for manufacturing industry. Even within manufacturing the role of transport costs in such activities as sales and marketing depends on personal transport and since it is likely to be more time-sensitive may be a more important factor in enlarging market areas than the costs of delivering goods. Evidence from the early TGV lines in France suggested two factors at work. There was little evidence of overall concentration of activity from provincial cities towards Paris (or vice versa), although there was some evidence of internal restructuring within firms. On the other hand there was evidence of intra-regional concentration towards the main centres which had the best accessibility to the new infrastructure and to Paris. Thus we might argue that HSR networks lead to a greater concentration of activity towards the networks (strictly towards the points of access to the networks) than along those networks.

There is one effect which may be felt along an HSR network, though one which is consistent with the effects noted above. HSR networks typically do not affect accessibility in the same way as classic rail or road networks in that they are not continuous. The need to take maximum advantage of the speed possible reduces the potential for intermediate stops. HSR is thus more like air travel focussing on end-to-end passengers. Not only may it have little impact on the performance of peripheral regions, it may also help to create pockets of reduced relative activity in intermediate locations along the line of route. This creates a potential area of conflict. Intermediate regions may incur many of the costs imposed by new HSR lines, destruction of the environment, visual intrusion, noise but fail to gain any potential benefits from improved access. In fact access could deteriorate if existing conventional rail services are reduced with the advent of HSR (Vickerman 2008). Intermediate stations are often provided as an apparent compensation for such regions, but train operators are reluctant to sacrifice the time benefits for the great majority of end to end passengers for the benefit of intermediate stops. Stopping high-speed trains is costly both in terms of energy and time. Generally therefore only infrequent services are provided and this fails to make much impact on the effective accessibility of such locations. The evidence suggests that very few of these intermediate stations have been a success. The exceptions are those where the stations are well integrated into the regional rail network and where accompanying land-use policies have encouraged development around the stations.

An exception to this is a recent study of the impact of the Köln-Frankfurt line on the intermediate stations of Limburg and Montabaur which suggests positive impacts on the local economy (Ahlfeldt and Feddersen 2010). This is, however, more likely to be a commuting effect given the way the impact has been measured using labour market data, which is similar to the way that some intermediate points on Spanish lines have had profound impacts on commuting patterns around Madrid (see Chapters 6 and 7). This raises a new dimension outside the conventional view of HSR in transport policy, HSR as an intra-regional tool to exploit changing labour market and commuting patterns.

2.3 Changing Nature of High-Speed Rail

HSR was initially seen as a means of providing modern rail competition to road and air modes over medium distances of 400–600 km. The rationale for its introduction was primarily one of increasing capacity, but exploiting higher speeds created in effect a new mode. That initial objective has largely been maintained in Japan, and to a certain extent in France, where the spacing of the major urban areas and the stability of labour market areas has kept the main use to that of longer distance business and leisure travel. In Germany, the rather different urban structure, with major cities at rather shorter distances from one another, and the lack of development of new inter-city infrastructures has led to the ICE network being a substitute for the earlier IC network of regular trains, interconnecting at major hubs, benefitting from some acceleration but not changing the fundamental nature of inter-urban or intra-regional movements. The one exception to this is the Köln–Frankfurt ICE noted earlier, which has had a more significant impact on all three dimensions of inter-city connections, wider regional commuting and airport links.

The role of HSR as a competitor to air has been modified in a number of cases, notably in France and in the German case of Köln–Frankfurt noted above, to one of a complementary mode. Direct links to airports have enabled rail to be substituted for short-haul feeder air movements. This benefits airlines by releasing slots at congested airports for reallocation to more profitable long-haul flights and carries with it a potential environmental benefit. Following the original interchanges at Paris Charles de Gaulle and Lyon St Exupéry, the Köln–Frankfurt line serves both Frankfurt and Köln-Bonn airports. Frankfurt Flughafen in particular is well integrated into the ICE network with direct connections to most major German cities. New lines are increasingly being designed with such connections in mind. Amsterdam Schiphol, like Frankfurt Flughafen, is both on the new Dutch high speed line and a major interchange point with direct services to most Dutch cities. There has been considerable debate over the plans for the UK's planned second high speed link from London to Birmingham not to serve London Heathrow directly, despite being used as a rationale for cancelling a proposed third runway and new terminal at the airport. The argument here depended on the relative sizes of airport and London bound traffic and the time penalty which a longer (and expensive) route via the airport would impose on the majority of end to end passengers. Interestingly neither of the French examples cited above provides a direct connection between the airport and the city centre as both are on by-pass lines for trains avoiding Paris and Lyon respectively.

The other major change has been in the increasing use of HSR for shorter distance commuting journeys (see Chapters 1, 6 and 7). The spacing of German cities has implied that significant use of the ICE network has always been used for shorter distance, less than 200 km, journeys, but the NBS and ABS of the German network have been mainly shorter improvements to constraints on the classic network rather than the largely separate new networks characteristic of the French and Spanish cases. In Spain, however, the construction of the new lines has opened up new opportunities for shorter distance and commuting journeys of up to 200 km around Madrid. Previously the relatively poor quality of rail services outside the immediate Madrid metropolitan area had limited the commuting potential but HSR has enabled a number of locations to become within one hour of central Madrid and this has had significant potential for changing labour market areas. Interestingly, as with the observed impacts of French lines over longer distances this has had a two-way effect with both labour markets benefitting. A feature of the development of the Spanish services to meet this demand has been an increasing differentiation of the product with separate trains and differentiated pricing.

This market segregation has occurred most obviously in the case of the first British dedicated high-speed line between London and the Channel Tunnel. In this case the construction of the line required government backing which depended on its use for regional services in Kent as well as the international Eurostar service between London and Paris and Brussels. Since the Eurostar services are not allowed to carry local passengers within the UK for reasons of both security and protection of the UK domestic rail franchises, regional services were granted to the local operator Southeastern Trains. These are thus a completely separate operation with their own operator and trains distinct from the international Eurostar services. Although these regional services are providing 225 km/h services between London and various towns in Kent at a distance of 100–130 km from London, including services which run off the high-speed line to a variety of destinations, the experience is distinct from that in Spain (see Chapter 7 and Ureña, et. al. 2010). Here the services are a direct substitute for existing commuter services into London – the biggest gain is that for Ashford where typical journey times were reduced from 70–80 minutes to just 37 minutes. An initial survey of users showed that some 94 per cent of Ashford originating passengers would switch from other rail services and only 2 per cent were newly generated travellers (quoted in *Modern Railways*, February 2011). The Kent service seems unlikely to change commuting patterns but rather to reinforce existing labour market areas, albeit there could be some readjustment of property markets as a result.

Ashford itself is an interesting case of an intermediate station on a high-speed inter-capitals line, served by five regional rail lines, which has not fulfilled its promise of delivering local economic development on the back of improved accessibility. Levels of service have been compromised by the presence of other intermediate stations and the absence of a comprehensive development strategy designed to integrate the HSR service into local land-use policies and other regional rail services has prevented effective exploitation of the accessibility changes. It remains to be seen whether adding the regional HSR services to the international will change that perception. In this case the new service is provided to a different London terminus from the traditional commuter services, but which also provides a better cross-London connection for destinations to the north of London.

This phenomenon of shorter distance HSR commuting has not been so obvious in France. The absence of obvious commuter towns served by the TGV network, which has tended to avoid urban areas in the Greater Paris catchment area and rely on stations in greenfield locations, close to but not in urban areas, has meant that there has been little such development. In relatively few cases have these intermediate TGV stations been integrated into the regional rail network.

2.4 The Economic Case for High-Speed Rail

Many claims have been made for the benefits of HSR, both the direct benefits for users and the wider benefits that are assumed to flow from the resulting increased accessibility (see Chapters 10 and 11). Similarly objectors, especially those concerned at the environmental impact of new construction, have made conflicting claims citing in particular the optimism bias often present in scheme appraisals (Flyvbjerg et al. 2006). As the evidence accumulated in De Rus (2009) shows, there is no universal rule which can determine the likely return to HSR investment. Construction costs per kilometre vary significantly both within and between countries over a range from less than €10 million to around €40 million depending on land costs, on the terrain and resulting engineering costs and on the environmental protection needed. A positive rate of return appears to require a minimum first year demand of six million passengers in the most favourable circumstances of low construction costs and a low discount rate; as construction costs rise a minimum of at least nine million passengers seems likely to be needed. In the least favourable circumstances this figure could rise towards 20 million.

Total traffic levels have risen as route length has increased as Figure 2.2 shows for the four largest networks. But this does not look so encouraging if we look at the trends in traffic on HSR services (passengers per km) relative to the length of HSR track as shown in Table 2.2. Here it can be seen that increases in the length of the network have not always been matched by an increase in the number of passengers. Only in France has the density of demand kept pace with the growth of the network and the fast growth of the Spanish network has not been matched by a commensurate growth in traffic.

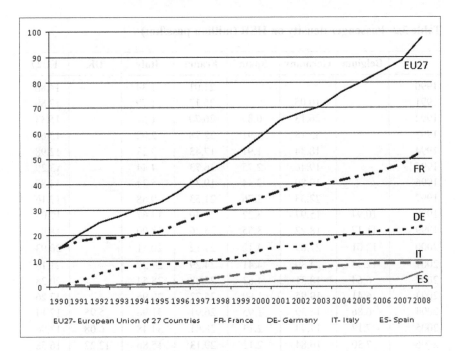

Figure 2.2 Passengers carried on HSR (thousand millions)
Source: Author based on data from DG Move.

Table 2.2 has to be interpreted carefully as it includes all passenger-km in HSR rolling stock relative to the length of HSR track, but it does give an indicative view of both trends and comparative traffic densities. The French case, and to a lesser extent the German case, shows the benefit of an HSR network which maximises the use of dedicated HSR track by providing services which use conventional track.

Even in France, however, with the exception of the original TGV-Sud Est, rates of return have not met expectations. TGV-Atlantique was forecast an internal rate of return of 12 per cent but yielded 7 per cent whilst TGV-Nord was forecast 12.9 per cent and only achieved 2.9 per cent (RFF, 2005). In the latter case this was mainly because traffic only reached 50 per cent of the forecast level with the biggest shortfall (64 per cent) in traffic to and from the UK, but even French domestic traffic was 40 per cent below expected levels. It would seem that the enthusiasm with which the first TGV line was greeted led to significant over-optimistic forecasts for newer routes. Much more cautious approaches have been taken with respect to more recent extensions of the network.

Table 2.2 Passenger density on HSR (million pass/km)

	Belgium	Germany	Spain	France	Italy	UK	EU27
1990				21.01	1.34		14.86
1991		10.05		25.17	1.79		17.89
1992		26.13	0.85	26.70	1.61		15.33
1993		35.18	1.91	22.78	2.02		15.63
1994		18.34	1.91	17.43	3.23		12.98
1995		19.46	2.75	16.73	4.44		13.29
1996		19.80	2.34	19.35	5.24		14.87
1997		22.53	2.76	21.53	9.68		17.16
1998	10.94	15.97	3.22	23.40	14.67		17.05
1999	11.17	18.22	3.55	25.26	18.00		18.83
2000	12.01	21.89	4.12	27.12	20.51		20.93
2001	12.35	24.39	4.41	24.29	27.27		21.18
2002	6.64	18.31	4.63	25.88	28.54		20.28
2003	6.41	19.95	1.90	25.72	29.96		17.26
2004	6.86	16.39	1.95	26.91	31.96	5.95	17.14
2005	7.17	17.44	2.13	28.01	34.48	6.08	17.96
2006	7.30	16.84	2.12	29.13	15.86	12.22	16.58
2007	7.43	17.06	1.71	25.62	15.69	12.32	15.41
2008	7.88	18.16	3.44	28.08	11.93	8.79	16.22

Source: Author based on data from DG Move.

One of the major issues which is not always addressed clearly is the impact of traffic abstraction from the classic rail network. We have already noted that the introduction of an alternative HSR service in the UK has drawn most of its custom from existing rail services which have been scaled back as a result. The success of TGV in France and its claimed profitability needs to be set against the increasing losses of the classic Grande Lignes railway leading to widespread withdrawal of such services. The planning for a possible second high-speed line in the UK has highlighted the benefits derived from less intensive use of the commuter networks for longer distance traffic thus yielding increases in capacity, but also identifies that certain locations will suffer a reduced level of service in terms of lower frequencies and longer journey times.

We have not explored appraisal techniques in any detail here (see Vickerman 2007, 2010 for more detailed discussion). What is clear, however, is that in most cases objectives are obscure, optimism bias is common and there is a failure to apply consistent tests to projects across the transport sector.

2.5 Conclusions

The analysis in this chapter has shown how the concept of HSR has changed from the renewal of rail as a medium distance competitor to air and road to one of asserting its complementarity to other modes whilst also becoming an instrument for changing the pattern of commuting and land use around large metropolitan areas. Much of this has been the result of unintended consequences and reflects the largely ill-thought out way that transport policy evolves at all levels, not least at the EU level where it features strongly as aiming to meet various objectives from improving competitiveness and cohesion to reducing the carbon footprint of transport. At the same time the economics of HSR is also being challenged both at the project level as to whether it meets the usual tests for an acceptable social rate of return and at the macro level as to whether it promotes the rate of growth and economic development more generally. It would appear that HSR development in Europe has often been achieved on little more than a promise. Nevertheless, HSR has caught the public imagination and achieved a momentum of its own in several countries where significant networks have been established. The aftermath of the economic crisis means that such large projects are under more serious scrutiny as to whether they actually deliver many of the benefits claimed. What is clear is that promoters will have to be much more careful in specifying exactly what they expect a particular scheme to achieve and there is significant scope still to improve the appraisal methodology used for such projects.

Chapter 3
Territory and High-Speed Rail: A Conceptual Framework

Severino Escolano[1]

3.1 Introduction: Transport, Communications, Society and Territory

Anyone who examines a medium- or large-scale map, even if it is about a less developed area, will immediately notice peculiar shapes formed by the lines representing the transport and communication systems that link regions within countries. This cartographic evidence is a reflection of the extraordinary importance of transport and communication in the activities of individuals, businesses and institutions.

Furthermore, the introduction of transportation systems beyond the local scale is an inherent part of the development of human relations because such systems materially support the flows of goods, people and information. It follows from this observation that structures and forms of transport grow in parallel with the general development of a society.

The effects associated with the historical development of transport and communications, i.e., their deployment in societies and territories, have been studied using different approaches. For Anderson (1986), the slow and continual changes in logistics (transport and communications) have promoted structural changes in production and location systems that account for a succession of revolutionary regional economic transformations, although the author also accepts the 'interdependence' between transport infrastructure and the 'nodal production capabilities'. In contrast, transport and communication are essential to Innis (1950), who suggests that historical changes can be attributed to innovations that affect the spread and persistence of information and knowledge in space and time.

The most widely accepted approaches and those most consistent with available empirical data and scientific knowledge argue that the interactions between transportation systems and socio-economic actors and sectors of a given territory and society are neither simple nor linear. In contrast, this interdependence has a systemic and nonlinear character: it may present contradictions in time and space and produces numerous externalities (Dobes 1998) that are difficult to measure accurately. In every historical period, the means and organisation of transport and communications have specific configurations (structure, complexity, inherited

---

1   University of Zaragoza.

networks) that mediate the relations of those systems with economic activities, technology, political ideas, physical characteristics of the territory and finally, the culture of each era. At the same time that transportation systems acquire a certain structure and level of development, they also condition the future decisions of social partners and of individuals. This is part of the scope of the emerging 'new mobilities paradigm' (Urry 2007).

Why have transport and communications become so important in society? There are many answers to this question. We will discuss only a few explanations that consider productive and territorial factors.

One of the main reasons for the importance of transportation and communications is the fact that their role has strategic importance for production and consumption, especially for systems of production that move high volumes of goods, people and information over medium and long distances. Systems of communication and transport maintain connections and coherence among different parts of the socio-economic system of increasing 'fluid societies' (Bauman 2000).

The uneven development of infrastructure and transportation services makes particular locations more or less accessible. The accessibility (see Chapter 5) of a given location is a standard dimension that is typically used to measure spatial resistance (friction) in terms of distance, time, economic potential, movement cost or the energy invested to recover that cost and, generally speaking, to assess the complex relationship between transport and the 'changing geography of opportunity' (Shen 2000). The level of accessibility of a territory is a fundamental property that affects both its potential for development and people's everyday lives.

In turn displacement, transport and communications become the main means of defining the social time-space relation of each mode of production. This relationship is one of the most influential forces shaping a territory and affects people's perceptions and experiences of it.

In addition the material translation of transport and communication activities into various types of infrastructure, facilities, technical means and land use that are specific to the area and to the activities performed there characterise the landscape of particular urban and rural areas. 'Landscapes of the road' (*roadscapes*) or 'railroad landscapes' (*railroad-scapes*), typical of the American Great Plains, are notable for their dark, straight lines edged with telephone or electricity poles and their great works of engineering (e.g., bridges, tunnels). The landscapes associated with ports, airports and logistics platforms are also examples of the immense power of transport and communications to transform and define the landscape.

Consequently, the appropriate context for interpreting the functions, effects and dynamics of transport and communications in contemporary societies and in territorial terms is formed by the interactions among global socio-economic, technological and spatial processes on one hand and the unique structures of a given area, produced as a result of its development through history, on the other. The former processes, which act on a global level, include, among other agents and means, the forces driving the transformation of productive and spatial systems related to the increasing internationalisation and mobility of economic activities, people and, especially, capital and the increased spatial competitiveness in the production and search for new markets at all levels. At the other end, at the national, regional and local levels, other factors, such as the specific economic, social and territorial conditions and the political-institutional framework of each political unit, form a very important platform for the development of transport. These factors are even more fundamental in the context of decentralised political and administrative organisations, such as Spain's semi-federal political framework of *the Autonomous Communities* (regions).

In the following paragraphs we expand on these ideas with a focus on transport, particularly High-speed rail (HSR). The argument is organised into three parts. The first presents the general socio-economic processes most relevant to the development of transport and communications. In the second, focus is directed to transport systems in general and HSR in particular to demonstrate their great ability to alter space and time and how they are understood as socio-economic and territorial categories essential to a mode of production. The discussion then moves to identifying some possible HSR relations with particular places and the spatial behaviours of individuals that are derived from changes in accessibility and in the location strategies of socio-economic activities induced by transport. Finally, the third part provides some general observations and conclusions.

3.2 Transport in the Context of Recent Socio-Economic Restructuring

Most transport studies carried out in the social sciences, use a static approach that views transports, and in particular movement, as an effect caused and explained by other social processes (Sheller y Urry 2006).

This approach, which relegates transport to the category of passive agents and subordinates, can explain the demand for transport services but does not account for the advantages that transportation systems confer for economic activity and the population's spatial and temporal experience.

The feedback of the relations between society and both transport and communication is of even greater relevance at the current stage of capitalist development. This stage is characterised by the acceleration of almost all processes of production, circulation and consumption as a way of increasing the rate of capital return.

The following highlights some general aspects of the recent social restructuring process that surrounds the development of transport and then expands on some discussions related to the inclusion of transport in the emerging economic and spatial system.

3.2.1 The Emergence of a Regime of Flexible Accumulation

Since the mid-1970s, intensive general socio-economic restructuring has taken place worldwide. This process manifests itself in all key dimensions of social organisation: the economy, culture, the relations between states, consumption patterns and many other dimensions that make up the matrix of social life where people and businesses operate.

Superimposed on the array of studies that address these changes and beyond the *post*-names that have been coined in each academic discipline (post-modernism, post-structuralism, post-industrial, post-Fordism, etc.), there persists the idea of the global, fragmented and interrelated character of these changes, of their worldwide scope and of the prominent role of economic forces in the process of change.

Although it is difficult to establish temporal boundaries and define the contents and features of each economic period, it is possible to identify the context and the set of basic relationships that define each particular stage.

The integration of previous trends with new ones is one way in which social structures change. In this sense, after a transition period where both coexist, the integration yields a different model. In this view, the process of economic restructuring has been interpreted as an expansion of forces identified in the Fordist economic mode, along with other, hitherto unrecognised, factors related to technological advances and information.

Many studies of these transformations since the mid-1970s in multiple socio-economic dimensions agree in interpreting those changes as particular manifestations of a single, consistent process of restructuring in both the 'regime of accumulation' and the 'socio-institutional structure of accumulation' (Aglietta 1982, Boyer and Mistral 1983, Lipietz 1986, Harvey 1989). The 'regime of accumulation' refers to the types of economic growth and the sectoral composition of an economy, to the economy's consumption patterns, to the organisation and production techniques, and to the ways of organising work that become dominant in a given period. The 'socio-institutional structure of accumulation' refers to all institutions that regulate social and economic relations, including market mechanisms, policy and economic interventions involving accumulation and the legitimisation of states, and physical and social infrastructure.

However, there is no unanimous agreement on the nature of the emerging regime of accumulation, which has been tagged with such terms as post-Fordist, post-industrial, informational, service (Bell 1973, 1979), post-modern, and globalised, and as the extended expression of 'flexible accumulation':

> I broadly accept the view that the long postwar boom, from 1945 to 1973, was built upon a certain set of labour control practices, technological mixes, consumption habits, and configuration of political-economic power, and that this configuration can reasonably be called Fordist-Keynesian. The break-up of this system since 1973 has inaugurated a period of rapid change, flux, and uncertainty. Whether or not the new systems of production and marketing, characterised by the more flexible labour processes and markets, of geographical mobility and rapid shifts in consumption practices, warrant the title of a new regime of accumulation, and whether the revival of entrepreneurialism and neo-

conservatism, coupled with the cultural turn to postmodernism, warrant the title of a new mode of regulation, is by no means clear. (Harvey 1987, 1989: 124)

Yet, whatever the denomination may be, certain fundamental features of the mode persist in all approaches: flexibility (of production and work), increasing mobility (of information, capital, resources and people), weakening economic power of states, and the spatial restructuring of the socio-economic system and its integration into global systems. All of these features are closely related to the services they produce or facilitate with regard to transport and communications, namely high mobility and speed, connection and interaction.

3.2.2 Main Processes of Flexible Accumulation in Relation to Transport

Since the first scientific understanding of the system of 'flexible accumulation', scholars have assigned crucial importance to the inseparable triad of technology, information and services, not only as components and engines of modern capitalism but also as factors driving social and territorial change (Gershuny and Miles 1988, Illeris 1989, Coffey and Bailly 1992, Moreno and Escolano 1992, Daniels 1993).

Technological innovations, particularly those related to progress in microelectronics, have been shown to be the main drivers of socio-economic changes in terms of depth and diversity since the mid-1970s. For this reason, for some authors, technological development, especially that associated with information, is the distinguishing quality of the new mode of production and even of a new social system (Castells 2000).

The impacts *of* new technologies are not limited to any particular activity or aspect of social life. Through capillary action, they have reached, to varying degrees, all corners of societies and territories. Although the cluster of activities related to scientific research and its applications constitutes one of the most expansive and dynamic economic sectors, the most momentous contribution *of* new technologies has been to enable a radical renewal of the technical procedures and modes of organisation of production, transport and communications, provision and procurement of services, and consumer activities. The spread of new technologies has produced substantial improvements in production efficiency and has markedly influenced changes in the localisation patterns of many socio-economic activities (Mandeville 1983, Castells 1995, Moss 1998) as well as post-modernising lifestyles in general.

The growing importance of services is a hallmark of modern capitalism, manifested in their high share in the valuation of national and regional production, in the large volume of people employed in the sector and in their strong presence in the development of society and individuals.

This strength is due, *inter alia*, to the rampant growth of demand from individuals, businesses and institutions for the renewal of methods and organisation of production and to the action of technological innovations, the global restructuring of certain markets (Daniels 1985, Noyelle 1985, Illeris 1989, Rada 1989), and the overlap between the services and production activities that generated a single, integrated and continuous goods-services production process (Barcet et al. 1984, Bailly and Coffey 1994). This increased flow causes sectorial specialisation to fade or blur and encourages movement towards functional specialisation, defined by spatial clustering of certain economic functions (Duranton and Puga 2002, Halbert 2005).

Within the service sector, *business services* are of special relevance. Their distinguishing feature lies in their focus on the middle market. In short, their output is incorporated as an input in the production process, either within the same company or after acquisition by another.

This direct connection to production units turns this type of service, especially *advanced services to production* (research, insurance, legal, auditing, etc.), into an indispensable element in the improvement of the competitiveness of enterprises by increasing their territorial significance (Bailly and Maillat 1989, Daniels 1991, Moreno and Escolano 1992).

De-industrialisation, re-industrialisation and new industrialisation characterise the transition to the new regime of flexible accumulation, with immediate implications for transport. Since the beginning of the 1970s, capital restructuring of entire industries, such as mining and metallurgy, has reached an unprecedented scale. These actions, carried out at the international level, have focused on streamlining and improving production efficiency and have increased the importance of multinational enterprises. Their effects have resulted in the loss of industrial activity and jobs (which have declined deeply across entire regions), drastic changes in sectors and the creation of new industrialisation areas (Scott 1988; Faust, Voskamp and Wittke, 2004).

This confluence of forces has promoted other intense territorial restructurings at all levels with logic and procedures that differ from those of the previous stage. Their effects are neither linear nor expressed simultaneously, and they can be mixed in time and space. This baroque set of activities, which combines functional and spatial centralisation with the decentralisation of activities, exhibits such complexity that it can only partially be apprehended through a plethora of neologisms and semantics: *suburbanisation, post-city, post-metropolis, metapolis, post-urbanisation, diffuse, global city, world city, urban archipelago*, etc. All of these descriptors refer to new urban and territorial entities composed of fragments arranged in grid systems, the functionality and connectivity of which are maintained through transport and communication networks.

Horizontal changes are one of many aspects of spatial reorganisation in the transition to a regime of flexible accumulation. Another consists of the 'vertical' integration of local systems at various levels of hierarchy, which wields great influence in shaping flows of all types and affects the environments and daily practices of most people worldwide. It should be remembered that the emergence of a global system is not a separate physical entity or a mere externality, but the combination of many agents that work together on a global scale.

The consequences of the more comprehensive coupling of small socio-economic systems to constitute others of greater size are abundant and diverse. On one hand, the rise in material and information flows is inevitable, as is the increased complexity of the means to organise them. On the other hand, the different organisational levels of the territorial mosaic, traditionally built as a function of distance and gradients, are recomposed from other logics that consider not only continuity and contiguity but also connectivity and accessibility.

In this movement of globalisation, cities have an important role as key elements of the territorial reconfiguration process. Arranged in complex networks, they are the nodes that articulate different levels of territorial organisation and their respective, sometimes contradictory, logics.

Finally, to complete the framework of forces that strongly interact with transport, it is relevant to refer to the post-modernisation of consumers and consumption. The generalisation of methods such as the micro-segmentation of markets and products, the timing of obsolescence of products and services so that their duration is transient, the association of values related to personal image and prestige with consumption activities, increasing sales of goods and cultural services in the market, and the staging of consumption have all triggered an increased volume of consumption and changed its social nature (including the use of HSR). Also relevant here are residential dispersion and new ways of marketing products and services.

This complex network of social, economic and territorial changes exerts pressure on transport and communications to meet the new and growing demands.

In this context, transport and communications are the vectors necessary to maintain the spatial and temporal coherence of the socio-economic system at the global and local levels. In short, the above changes and others have produced socioterritorial system more complex and mobile, more integrated and interdependent, configured as interconnected networks of variable size, geometry and topology, which connect all places worldwide.

Therefore, transport and communication manifest constant adjustments and revolutions of their methods of operation and of the technical means that make them precise systems capable of mobilising the growing demand for flows of people and goods at faster speeds and cheaper prices and from further afield. Almost all regional, national and international strategies for the recovery of areas in crisis or the enhancement of socio-economic development provide for the creation or improvement of infrastructure and transport and communications systems as basic conditions for maintaining or gaining competitiveness (Janssen and Hoogstraten 1989, Tira et al. 2002, Spiekermann and Wegener 2006).

3.3 Transport and Communications, Space and Time in the Transition to a Regime of Flexible Accumulation

The formation of a flexible regime of accumulation is evident not only in the renewal of the modes of organisation of production and in adjustments in the relations between capital and labour but also in the performance of its own modes of conception, creation, control and use of social space and time. Because space and time define social, economic, cultural and territorial futures, many of the forms and practices of the activities of these areas have been transformed, sometimes remarkably.

Table 3.1 lists the characteristics of space in the flexible accumulation regime, taken from a summary prepared by Albrechts and Swyngedouw (1989) of the properties of economics, politics, space and ideology in the Fordist versus flexible accumulation modes.

Table 3.1 Fordism versus flexibility: Space

Fordism	Flexibility
-Spatial decentralisation -Spatial division of labour -Homogenisation of regional labour markets (spatially segmented labour markets) -Worldwide sourcing of components and subcontractors -Organisation of consumption space through suburbanisation	-Spatial clustering and agglomeration -Spatial integration/division of labour -Labour market diversification (In-place labour market segmentation) -Spatial proximity of vertically quasiintegrated firms -Organisation of consumption space through urban centres

Source: Albrechts and Swyngedouw (1989).

Many of the spatial characteristics of the flexible production model (and of Fordism) originate in the acceleration of material and information flows enabled by networks of transport and communications. These networks also serve as material links connecting economic activities and human relations in general.

These connecting functions are relevant in at least three aspects of the construction of social space and time. First, they enable the seamless integration of space and time with production processes and their use as means of social control. Second, they have been, and continue to be, a source of radical change in the practices and experiences of individuals in social space-time. Finally, they have inspired original ways of thinking and reasoning about the relations among society, space and time.

3.3.1 Space and Time as Categories of Social Evolution

Space and time are two fundamental dimensions that underlie both the material organisation of activities and elements of human life as well as the development of ideas and means to represent the world. Space and time also guide many 'territorial' actions.

In fact, every event that affects people in which social and natural processes are deployed happens on specific spatial-temporal scales, with possible ranges extending from micro-events (e.g., buying a newspaper) to planetary-scale events (e.g., climate change).

Space and time are historical categories with conceptualisation, measurement, value and other properties that are specific to the socio-economic system in which they operate. Companies and individuals generate physical, regulatory and other kinds of resources to develop their activities in specific time-space coordinates. Among these resources, technology is noteworthy for its vast capacity to alter inherited space-time concepts and practices.

Knowledge of the nature of interactions among society, space and time is a recurring theme in Western thought that arguably has its roots in classical antiquity. Innerarity (2004) asserts the following about space: 'Almost all the categories we use to explain certainty and confusion are spatial in nature.'

This work is not the appropriate forum to provide a detailed summary of the issue, but it is worth mentioning some theories that explain and formalise the ties among society, space and time. Some of them come from the field of social theory, whereas others come from space theory and have been developed within such disciplines as sociology, economics, political science, history, geography, urbanism and architecture. For example, some major conceptual streams that feed the debate on the issue are represented in the 'theory of structuration' (Giddens 1984), 'space syntax' (Hillier and Hanson 1984), and the 'production of space' (Lefebvre 1974) and subsequent research (Soja 1989).

Each of these theories takes a different approach to defining the concepts of *society, space* and *time* and to articulating their interactions. However, in all cases, the theory explicitly recognises the crucial importance of space, both as an abstract category and as a physical entity, in the structuring of society and everyday practices of individuals.

Likewise, most studies describe and explain, the vagaries of space and time as part of a broader set of socio-economic changes, and granted to transport systems a major role in the recent transformations of the social and individual space-time.

3.3.2 Time-Space Compression: 'Time is Money'

The consolidation of the regime of flexible accumulation represents a new twist on the historical process of time-space compression, which several authors, such as Harvey (1989) and Virilio (1991), have placed in the foundations of postmodernity.

Because the implementation of any particular activity takes time and space, space-time coordinates form the framework for all social and economic activities: 'There is no unspatialized social reality' (Soja 1996). Thus, socio-economic systems possess specific forms of regulation of space and time. In capitalism, these systems operate by the old adage, *time is money*. This maxim has become one of the most unique and enduring qualities of the regime of flexible accumulation. According to Altvater (1994), 'To shorten the circulation time of capital is a principle inherent in capitalist development, as a way of increasing the rate of accumulation'.

In general, efforts to achieve this goal have promoted the convergence of social *time* and *space*; in turn, these efforts have produced devastating effects on earlier forms of the space-time relation. Time, understood as duration, is separated from human activities and becomes an entity external to them, measurable with great precision, fragmented in homogeneous units and interchangeable in the market (Altvater 1994). Physical space has been adapted to reduce the durations of economic activities, usually by removing or easing barriers to the movement of flows, with the consequence that space is also robbed of its qualities and meanings and reduced to abstract, standardised units.

Flexible actions to overcome the rigidities of Fordism, especially with regard to capital, meanwhile, have prompted and accelerated time-space compression. One of the most effective options for resolving the crisis of over-accumulation inherent in capitalism, along with other traditional measures (such as regulation and monetary policy), consists precisely of the dispersion of surplus in time and space:

> The absorption of over-accumulation through their temporal and spatial displacement provides, in my judgement, a much richer and longlasting, but also much more problematic, terrain upon which to try and control the overaccumulation problem. (Harvey 1989: 182)

The erosion of the 'friction of space' has been so overwhelming that the timespace relation has reached infinitesimal values, to the extent that some authors have referred to the 'end of geography' (O'Brien 1991, Morgan 2004) or the 'Death of Distance' (Cairncross 2001). Technological innovations applied to production processes to 'dematerialise' products and services (for example, the editing and printing of books and journals) and the spectacular advances in telecommunications and transportation systems and its convergence, are the fundamental means of implementing this space-time implosion.

Transport and communications have historically been the primary means of changing the relation between space and time. Change was achieved through selective diffusion, from the standpoint of social and territorial cohesion, of technological innovations that have steadily increased the speed of the flow of goods, people and information (Knowles 2006).

This convergence is often represented by space-time generalisations of a shrinking globe as transport and communications gain speed. However, this image, made famous by Dicken (1986), is misleading because it ignores regional differences in the provision of infrastructure and means of transport and communications (unequal accessibility) and social inequalities in access to transport and communications (unequal mobility).

Figure 3.1 shows the general space-time variation for different means of transport and telecommunications. The figure illustrates the 'elasticity' of space-time in relation to the means of transportation. The horizontal lines represent the radius of the distance travelled per time unit; the position on the vertical axis represents the number of time units required to cross a space unit. The point of comparison is the relationship between the space (distance) covered and the amount of time spent by a person walking at a normal pace. The relationships expressed are qualitative. It is clear that the gains in speed (space-time convergence) condense two opposing effects: space 'contracts' (space-time compression) and time is 'expanded'.

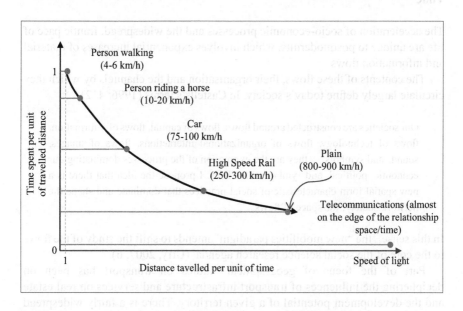

Figure 3.1 Elasticity of space-time and transport technologies
Source: Author.

The reduction in the degree of convergence of space-time produced by various means of transport has accelerated dramatically since the nineteenth century. HSR is one of the modes that have made a significant contribution to compressing the space-time relationship, at least in Europe (Spiekermann and Wegener 1994; ESPON 2010). If, as indicated by Bleijenberg (2002) and Metz (2004), the time spent on personal mobility is almost constant (1.1 hours per day on average),[2] the range of distances travelled per person has risen rapidly in the last 50 years, especially in terms of transport by rail and air (about 5 km/hour/year and about 10 km/hour/year, respectively).

As a result, space has been subsumed in time to the point that, for many actions and decisions, the world has *shrunk* so much that it looks like a single place that can be traversed with relative ease, homogeneous and different at the same time.

Very few aspects of today's world have been marginalised as a result of this process. The majority of economic activities, places and everyday practices of individuals and their associated areas have been affected by space-time compression to some extent.

3.4 High-Speed Rail, Territorial Organisation and the Experience of Space-Time

The acceleration of socio-economic processes and the widespread, frantic pace of life are unique to postmodernity, which involves exponential increases of material and information flows.

The contents of these flows, their organisation and the channels by which they circulate largely define today's society. In Castells's terms (1996: 412),

> Our societies are constructed around flows: flows of capital, flows of information, flows of technology, flows of organizational interactions, flows of images, sounds and symbols ... they are the expression of the processes dominating our economic, political, and symbolic life. Thus, I propose the idea that there is a new spatial form characteristic of social practices that dominate and shape the network society: the space of flows.

In this sense, 'the "new mobilities paradigm" intends to shift the study of the flows to the core of the social science research agenda' (Urry, 2007, 6).

Part of the focus of geographical studies on transport has been on deciphering the influences of transport infrastructure and services on real estate and the development potential of a given territory. There is a fairly widespread consensus about the positive relationship between the provision of facilities and transport infrastructure and the general level of development of countries and

---

2   In Spain, the average per person duration of all commuting is 61 minutes, whereas the time spent commuting to work is 24 minutes (Ministerio de Fomento 2007). In Britain, the average time taken to commute to work was 24 minutes in 2002 (Office for National Statistics, Labor Force Survey). In the US, this duration increased from 20.4 minutes in 1983 to 25.1 minutes in 2009 (U.S.: Census Bureau, American Community Survey).

regions, although the nature and forms of that relationship are not understood with precision.

Transport networks develop in a socio-economic framework with social, political and economic issues, along with the features of the terrain that influence the deployment of transport. Therefore, mutual interdependencies among transport, society and territory are neither automatic nor simple; they depend on the scale on which they are studied. The political, economic and social factors involved are sometimes very volatile; those factors, in turn, are also affected inexorably by the supply of transport services.

In any case, economic policies on transport, and especially European (for example, the Trans-European Networks, TEN) and US (U.S. Department of Transportation) policies, assume that the existence of transport networks of high quality is a necessary precondition for economic development and for improving territorial cohesion.

Transport (and communications) also conditions practices and experiences that individuals have of space as it limits or facilitates the movement around and accessibility of a territory.

Consequently, high speed affects, directly or indirectly, places and territorial configurations as well as individuals' range of space-time (Figure 3.2).

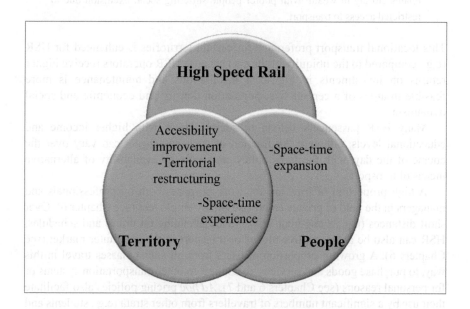

Figure 3.2 Some relationships between HSR, territory and individuals
Source: Author.

3.4.1 Some Specific Socio-Territorial Features of High-Speed Rail

The social and territorial integration of HSR has unique features (compared to conventional rail or automobiles) that derive in part from technical and economic requirements of their infrastructure and operations (see Chapters 1 and 2). These peculiarities also make socio-territorial impacts different. We highlight the following three of many effects.

One aspect is manifested in the highly selective nature of the territories in which networks are deployed and of the users of the services.

Despite the great historic expansion of transport networks across all latitudes and the reduced friction of distance for the implementation of transport systems that are faster and cheaper and that have accelerated the convergence of time/space (Janelle 1969) and cost/space (Abler 1975), density and access to transport use are far from uniform regardless of the considered scale (Ohnmacht et al. 2009). Knowles (2006: 408) maintains that,

> ... the differential collapse in time/space which has always been very uneven spatially, economically and socially. This has created a misshapen world in terms of travel time, accessibility and personal mobility. Transport consumption relates closely to wealth with poorer people suffering social exclusion due to restricted access to transport.

This locational transport preference for certain territories is enhanced for HSR (e.g., compared to the ubiquity of the car) because HSR operators receive higher returns on investments in high-cost installations and maintenance is more feasible in areas of a certain size, population density and economic and social dynamism.

Many HSR passengers belong to social classes with higher income and educational levels, although the fraction of such passengers can vary over the course of the day, with the fares policy, and with the availability of alternative means of transport.

A high proportion of trips are for work purposes both by professionals and managers in the field of private enterprise and by employees (see Chapter 6). Over short distances (e.g., a one-hour drive), and depending on prices and schedules, HSR can also be a competitive means of transport in the commuter market (see Chapters 6). A growing proportion of users from all social classes travel in this way, to purchase goods and services, to connect to other transportation systems or for personal reasons (see Chapters 6 and 7). *Ad hoc* pricing policies also facilitate their use by a significant numbers of travellers from other strata (e.g., students and pensioners).

Another differentiating factor lies in the loose configuration of networks and the strong polarity of the nodes.

The spatial structure of HSR networks is built from markedly linear forms with few segments and very much polarised node patterns that evolve into more or less spider-web-shaped and hierarchical forms. Furthermore, the nature of the system requires a certain minimum distance between stations (nodes) that is significantly longer than that for conventional railways. High-speed is very efficient for contracting the space/time relation, but it is very restrictive in terms of the number of places that can be connected (see Chapters 7, 8 and 9).

This network design makes a high-speed connection to a given territory very different, perhaps substantially so, from the analogous connection formed by conventional rail and other ground transportation systems.

High-speed trains dramatically shorten travel time between nodes that are directly connected and the areas around them. These travel times will generally be low, but this advantage comes at the expense of the rest of the territory that these trains traverse. It is as if the train passes through a tunnel (Plassard 1991). High-speed lines connect points that are relatively far apart, using the territory in between merely as support. Roads with very dense networks that access almost all populated settlements, in contrast, allow a mode of territorial organisation that is almost continuous. In return for this selective coverage, the gain in speed afforded by HSR trains allows workers to commute daily over distances of 200–300 km and still put in full working days (see Chapter 7).

The third of the traits, which derived from the previous two, is the significant change in the spatial distribution of accessibility (Murayama 1994, Gutiérrez 2001) for the nodes of the network (see Chapter 5). The network alters the relative positions of all centres of a territorial system in terms of conditions, benefits and opportunities to engage in socio-economic activities (Shen 2000).

The HSR alters the traditional pattern of accessibility, organised in gradients of road transport systems and conventional rail, to create islands of high accessibility to the surrounding territory (see Figure 3.3). This model of accessibility is ground transport itself, but it bears some resemblance to aviation and maritime transport. The effect of HSR on the landscape of accessibility is complex and goes beyond simply reducing the travel time between two points (L'Hostis 2009). This effect of 'fragmentation' of the spatial dimension by HSR is symmetrical to that exercised over time, which is termed by Klein (2004) as 'fragmented time'.

In short, the implementation of HSR is likely to trigger or intensify socio-economic polarisation processes in favour of nuclei connected by HSR, a development that exacerbates social inequalities and spatial accessibility, deepens existing socio-spatial ruptures and creates new ruptures.

3.4.2 High-Speed Rail and the Restructuring of Territory

Transport and communications systems are the basis of the diversification of spatial strategies of many socio-economic activities because they allow, from technical and economic standpoints, the physical separation of productive activities from tasks associated with management and direction.

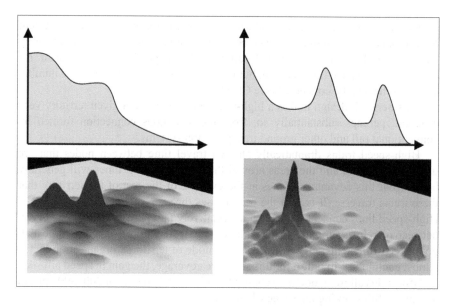

Figure 3.3 Spatial structure of accessibility
Note: Left: surface and gradient accessibility of ground transportation systems. Right: surface and accessibility profile of indention produced by HSR.
Source: Author.

Numerous empirical studies have presented evidence regarding the formation of new patterns of location and operation of productive activities relating to service, residential, consumer and social relationships. These analyses found that the spatial structures of many economic activities result from a double articulation: one defined by the dialectics of centralisation and decentralisation of functional organisation and the other, symmetrical with the previous articulation, characterised by a concentration-dispersion opposition of the locations of activities (Biggiero 2006).

Furthermore, urban systems recompose their hierarchies at all scales (global, national, regional), highlighting the presence of 'global cities'. At the same time, models of urban land use are fragmented and dispersed, especially for residential uses, while the great centres of leisure and consumption locate along the fuzzy borders of cities. Such a configuration generates (and requires) voluminous and diverse spatial and functional flows of people, information and goods, necessitating corresponding means of transport and management.

High-speed rail lines are important distinguishing features from a territorial point of view, allowing quick and efficient movement of people between the nodes (cities) that are connected. This benefit changes, to some extent, the existing functional and space framework in which individuals, companies and institutions exist. Indeed, the availability of HSR allows some companies to decentralise (or reorganise) their production units in cities with HSR stations if the profits so obtained (e.g., in land prices or labour costs) outweigh the disadvantages of physical separation. In the same sense, new businesses can be created in these cities because they provide easy access for face-to-face meetings. The greater accessibility of cities served by HSR extends local companies' potential markets for goods and services but also increases competition (Willigers 2008) (see Chapters 7 and 9).

Therefore, the entry into service of HSR lines adjusts the economic and territorial scenarios, at various scales, in which individuals, companies and institutions are developed. However, it is hard to separate territorial impacts attributable solely to HSR because, as noted, it requires joint action by many factors and local contexts. Nevertheless, it is possible to observe and explain the modes of influence and the strength with which high-speed processes were initiated or are conducted.

At a local level, outside of the footprint of the HSR facilities in the urban landscape, the main impacts arise from the high-speed services offered and from the impact of the central focus that is generated at the stations and their surroundings (see Chapters 7 and 8).

On one hand, civil construction, especially of the stations, is part of the emblematic image of cities. On the other hand, institutions and other local agents (especially employers) view the provision of modern HSR services as an important advantage, providing new opportunities for the development of economic activities and human relations in general. Therefore, HSR services are incorporated into the competitive strategies of cities and into urban marketing plans.

At sub-national, national and international levels, HSR simultaneously triggers or intensifies processes of articulation and disarticulation according to the socio-economic structure, relationships and distance between connected areas.

The effects of HSR can be significant at medium and large scales (national, sub-national) and even on the international scale (continental, EU), although the latter effects are more likely to fade into the mainstream of other forces working in this field. On a national scale, the socio-economic relations of cities with HSR stations are reinforced, which can trigger movements of competence, specialisation and complementarities of uneven range depending on the proximity and relative size of each city, its dominant economic activities and the efficiency of competing transport systems. The action of these forces is likely to leave its mark in the form of changes in urban hierarchies on the sub-national and national scales and in new functional specialisations.

As a hypothesis and final generalisation, it can be argued that HSR helps to consolidate and extend a spatial order that, by analogy with the 'archipelago city' or 'discontinuous metropolisation', consists of the coherent and complementary functioning of the cities connected by HSR, which, in turn, are situated in a nearly empty space.

3.4.3 High-Speed and the Space-Time Experience

Researchers have created several theoretical and analytical frameworks for the modern geographical study of the practices and experience of space-time. One of the most developed frameworks began with the pioneering work of Hägerstrand (1978). The targeted individuals are agents with time-space trajectories that can be accurately recorded and represented by lines and other symbols in a prism defined by three orthogonal axes: latitude (y), longitude (x) and time (z). The technique allows the tracing of the spatial-temporal signature of each individual and, from its analysis, derives the principles of spatial behaviour. Taking into account some basic conditions (e.g., indivisibility of the individual, duration of activities, limited capacity of space), it identifies the spatial-temporal patterns that characterise the time occupied by activities (work, social relationships and encounters, travel) and where those activities occurred (home, business, equipment) in relation to the structure of physical space (transport network, roads, *attractors,* etc.).

This methodology is useful for visualising the daily schedules of individuals, but critics (Giddens 1984, Harvey 1989, Rose 1993) have raised concerns about its failure to explain the predominance of certain space-time configurations and their social, personal, economic and territorial implications. Researchers have criticised its reductionist view of individuals, who are considered, in practice, merely as moving, interchangeable points that populate a volume (Adams 1995).

In addition to the classic contributions of space-time geography, notions such as *extensibility* and others from phenomenology and the theory of social structure form a framework for the study of changes in the experience of space and time caused by high-speed trains.

The concept of *personnel extensibility* refers to the opportunities and capabilities of an individual or a group to deal with the friction of distance using means of transport and communications: 'Human extensibility is conceptually the reciprocal of time-space convergence' (Janelle 1973: 11). Improved transport and communications have increased the *extensibility* of individuals and broadened the horizons of human interaction. However, there are great differences in personal extensibility among social classes, locations, ages, genders and other significant socio-economic categories.

The phenomenological approach places the individual *(me)* in the centre *(here point)* of a set of concentric zones, or *shells,* in which the experiences related to the formation of its identity and of their places are distributed and ordered and refers to the acquisition of an idea of the world:

> ... the nature of these shells that man builds around him and represent a profound social psychology, too often ignored by the developer, the vectors of his appropriation of space.

> These shells appear under two aspects: one topological aspect and another ontogenetic aspect linked to human development, methodical connection between the development of the personal and culturized space. (Moles and Romher, 1990: 93)

The theory of social structure distinguishes between two categories of human interaction: one that occurs *face to face* between co-present individuals and another that occurs between physically separated people through media. The first is called 'social integration' and the second 'time-space distancing' (or 'system integration'). Social integration is 'the reciprocity of practices between actors in circumstances of copresence, understood as continuities in and disjunctions of encounters', whereas 'system integration' is 'the reciprocity between actor or collectivities across extended time space, outside conditions of copresence' (Giddens 1984). These two notions articulate the relations between individuals and social systems. Space and time are essential to organisation and social integration mainly because of direct contact between people: 'space is not an empty dimension along which social groupings become structured, but has to be considered in terms of its involvement in the constitution of systems of interaction' (Giddens 1984).

With the above concepts we can articulate the following hypothesis, which needs further verification: HSR has selectively expanded the extensibility of individuals to significantly increase the spatial extent of co-presence in human relations.

Some consequences of this expansion are obvious and immediate, whereas others are more subtle and appear over time. Both groups rarely occur in isolation, but combine with effects from other means of transport and communication to power very complex processes. For example, the complementarity between high-speed rail and telecommunications is evident in the heavy use travellers make of mobile phones and the Internet during trips, but it has been found that the transport and telecommunications sectors are mutually reinforcing (Thrift 1996, Gaspar and Glaeser 1998).

High-speed rail is a very powerful vector capable of removing and deforming, disproportionately, the limits of the *shell* 'region', i.e., the corresponding area of the maximum daily distance, without an overnight stay, from the 'here point'. It has also greatly expanded the boundaries of the shell 'nation' and, to a lesser extent, the 'wide world' area that requires overnight stays. Virtually all perceptual domains located in the 'region' and the 'nation' are affected upwards or downwards as the frequency and interaction time in these areas, as well as the effort to access them, vary substantially when crossed by the HSR (see Figure 3.4).

However, the strong alteration of some territorial rings not only influences perceptual variables but also disturbs the overall balance of the structure of the topology of space-time experience. It is possible that certain practices in areas of the environment located close to the subject could become so weak that they eventually disappear. Some shells may collapse and then merge with the 'region' or the 'nation' or the 'region' may be incorporated into the nearby rings. Even the 'nation' becomes more similar to the 'wide world' if connections by air are taken into account.

Undoubtedly, HSR has a high potential to modify the traditional experience of space-time for individuals and thereby may influence modes of integration and social structure. The degree of actual change depends on many factors related to general economic and technological contexts and on the income, educational level, occupation, age, sex and other characteristics of individuals.

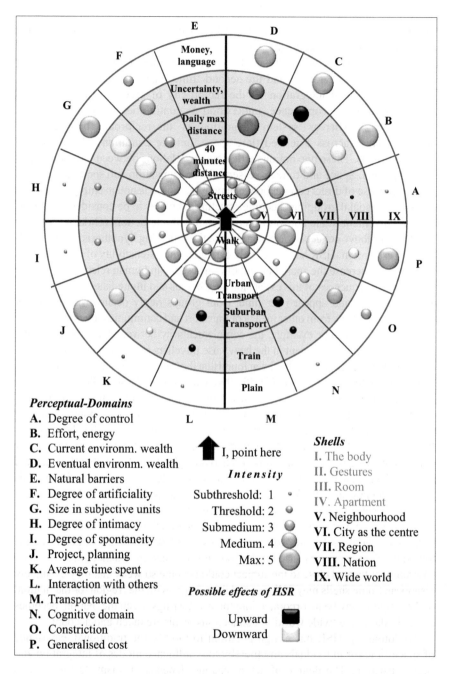

Figure 3.4 Potential impact of HSR in some perceptual domains of the shell 'region' and 'nation'

Source: Author based on Moles and Romher (1990).

3.5 Final Considerations

Since the mid-1970s, there has been particular interest in actions in socio-economic systems aimed at accelerating the processes of production, transport, communications and consumption and at softening the relations between capital and labour as effective ways of shortening the period for return on investment.

Technological innovations applied to all areas of society, production, methods of organisation, style, consumption patterns and cultural creation facilitate the setting of countless socio-economic fragments in a hyper-complex and fluid system fed by massive and increasing flows of people, information, capital and goods.

A multitude of self-organising or concerted actions have created one of the fundamental conditions of the flexible accumulation regime, namely, the drastic change in the traditional space-time relation. Geographical hypermobility requires that the physical, qualitative and historical characteristics of space be changed. It is necessary to reduce the friction that it exerts when crossed, usually through the mass deployment of technology; space should also be mixed and subjected to a specific mode of regulation and control. In other words, the production of space and its enhancement are two aspects of a single process.

High-speed rail fits consistently in certain geographical and social contexts in which it provides fast and comfortable passenger transportation over average and longer distances.

The introduction of HSR lines alters the existing supply of accessibility in favour of cities that are part of the network. These cities acquire advantages that can be significant for attracting companies or developing activities that can benefit from greater accessibility. For residents of these cities, HSR can potentially expand the horizons of space-time experience.

The spatial effects of HSR depend on its scale and on the general socio-economic environment in which it is implemented. Locally, the impacts are concentrated in cities with stations. In these places, the spatial distribution of accessibility is directly related to the degree of development and efficiency of transport systems. At the supra-regional level, HSR may promote unprecedented movement of competence, complementarity and functional specialisation among cities, which may lead to adjustments in national, regional and urban hierarchies.

One final consideration is that the spatial effects of ground transportation should be differentiated from those of communications. With the former, HSR has had a strong impact on geographic space-time, although its deformations of the earth's surface are subject to a spatial order imposed by the routes and the geographical locations of cities. Of course, the intervening and barely seen space that is crossed does not benefit from improved accessibility. In communication networks, by contrast, the connections determine the positions of nodes in an abstract and organised space around domain names and other topologies from which geographic coordinates have vanished.

Chapter 4
Demographic and Socio-economic Context of Spatial Development in Spain

Pedro Reques, Olga de Cos and María Marañón[1]

4.1 Introduction: Justification and Objectives

The study of demographic-territorial structures is unavoidable in transport infrastructure planning processes. Issues such as population dynamics, peopling, density or spatial inequalities in the characteristics of the population should condition proposals, justify the existence of these infrastructures, determine their routes and aid decision-making processes.

Moreover, infrastructures in general, and High-speed rail (HSR) in particular, play a decisive role in urban growth. HSR services promote mobility, transform the concept of distance both in terms of time and of costs, and act as a driving force in socio-economic and territorial dynamics.

In post-industrial societies, such as that of Spain in the twenty-first century, the population–land relations are characterised by a certain complexity, a multilateral nature and the increasing importance of the time function: space and time must be analysed jointly to understand the relations between society and the geographical space (see Chapter 3).

In these societies, new life spaces have appeared, and the traditional idea of urban sprawl, that is, with spatial relations of continuity and adjacency, has gradually been replaced by ideas of geographical discontinuity, multiple territorialities, and the fragmentation of each activity into different territories. All of this development has been facilitated and favoured by the development of the transport and communications networks, giving rise to ever more complex and spatially and temporally segregated life spaces.

At the same time, a close relationship has been identified between the routes of the HSR lines and spatial accessibility (Taede et al. 2003, Monzón de Cáceres et al. 2008, Campos and de Rus 2009b) and between the HSR lines and the locations of qualified tertiary employment, the relocation decisions by companies (Willigers et al. 2005, Willigers 2006) and the reconfiguration of internal labour markets (Kingsley 1997, Fröidh 2008). Finally, the development of double residency (maintaining a residence in two places at the same time) has been boosted by the reduction in rail transport time (Beauvais et al. 2007, Willigers 2006).

---

1 University of Cantabria.

The HSR lines make large contributions to land development (Gutiérrez and Urbano 1996, Gutiérrez 2001, Schäfer and Victor 2000, Bellet et al. 2010a) and to urban development (Kiyoshi and Makoto 1997, Roger 1997, Blum et al. 1997, Garmendia et al. 2008, Borzacchiello et al. 2010) (see Chapter 8) as well as other matters, such as territorial – regional or provincial – restructuring (Komei et al. 1997, Blum et al. 1997, Kwang 2000, Ureña et al. 2006a, Martínez and Givoni 2009, Stanke 2009) or the intensification of and changes in land use (Geurs 2006), are also related to HSR (see Chapter 7).

High-speed rail also has diverse implications for the movement possibilities of persons, especially around the main nodes (such as towns where there is an HSR station) (Calvo 1998, Garmendia et al. 2008, Bellet et al. 2010a). Thus, the transport and communications network acts as an articulating element of a set of spatial connections that has the population as its actor and the territory (that is, the space or environment) as the reference scenario. In this new territory, new mobility schemes are organised, with the nodes of the network acting as an attractive force, the axes as the main channels of communication and the access links between them.

As a consequence of all of the above mobility has become a mass phenomenon and the multiterritoriality of the population a social norm. The places to which an individual is linked through work, study, residence, leisure, second-home ownership, supply, administration, and so on produce a complex grid of life spaces. In these areas, the transport and communications networks play a decisive role both in consolidating existing trends and in generating new links and new spatial mobility patterns and, together with these, new forms of spatial organisation.

The development of means of transport and of information and communications technologies that so favour the contraction of space-time have increased the possibilities of mobility and allow the simultaneous use of different spaces as well as an increase in the space-time available for the development of individuals' life-projects (Knowles, 2006). At the same time, they also contribute to the generation of a space-time of variable geometry and increasing dimensions as regards their destination (see Chapter 3). Interstitial gaps, like *tunnel-spaces*, can bring the individual closer to the farthest territories (destinations) and cause him or her to ignore the closest territories (routes), leading to what some authors have defined as the *archipielagisation of the land* (Dollfus 1995). Modern communications do not eliminate space but rather create new spaces of a spatial and temporal nature (Pueyo et al. 2009).

Space and time form two closely integrated concepts, and their relation is articulated as the fundamental conditioning factor of population mobility patterns. If they are analysed from the point of view of everyday movement, which finds its maximum expression in commuting, these two concepts are inversely related so that the individual capacity to reach ever more distant places depends on the progressive reduction in the travel time to access them.

Within this theoretical framework, the first part of the present chapter presents the analysis, at a municipal and settlement scale, of the spatial population distribution patterns in Spain as well as its demographic dynamics and its economic activity.

The second part analyses inter-municipal commuting in Spain. The potential demand for means of transport comes from different types of travellers, including professionals and students who travel daily between their places of residence and work or learning (commuters), business travellers, and recreational travellers. Among these groups, commuting for working purposes is of special relevance.

Commuting for working purposes is the one type of travel that is most heavily influenced by the conditioning brought about by transport infrastructures. Thus, the spatial relations between the places of residence and of work of the Spanish working population, highly conditioned by travel times, can be seen as a complex system of relations established between the municipality of residence and that of work and of a daily or less frequent reiterative nature.

4.2 Sources and Methods: The Importance of Official Population Statistics and Geographic Information Systems

The spatial analysis of the population often depends on the availability of suitable statistical sources as regards both the appropriateness of the variables and the geographic reference entities for which these statistics are provided.

Statistics are produced by the National Institute of Statistics (Instituto Nacional de Estadística – INE) on this basis for the analysis of the spatial patterns of the population distribution in Spain, its demographic and economic activity structures and their inter-municipal commuting for working purposes. The sources used, which were updated on commencing the study, are the municipal population and housing census or partial census and the municipal population and housing data undertaken at the settlement level (called Nomenclator in Spain). Settlements in Spain are eight times more numerous than municipalities.

These sources allow the analysis of the population dynamics and structures in great detail, especially through the use of micro-data, i.e., individualised data, which are essential for obtaining information on commuters' level of education, professional situation, and socio-economic status or field of activity by economic sector. Furthermore, these sources provide data on matters concerning both the daily mobility related to travelling to the workplace (e.g., number of daily trips, travel time, intermunicipal relation between places of legal residence and of workplace) and the means of transport used, with the possibility of combinations of several means. In short, these micro-data provide insight into all of the main variables characterising commuting patterns in Spain.

The analysis of population territorial patterns and commuting in Spain undertaken in this research involved very large volumes of data: over one million individualised records, more than 65,000 settlements and more than 8,000 municipalities, characterised by over one hundred variables gathered for each unit of analysis. Therefore, from a methodological viewpoint, one of the most important phases of the research was the integration of the statistical sources and the cartographic bases. The two environments, statistical and cartographic, are interrelated through a geographic information system: the common coding of geographical elements and statistical elements allows the linking of the relevant variables with the most adequate entities for population data of each settlement and each municipality. Several cartographic techniques were used, the most important of which is vectors.

Geographic information systems' capacity for population spatial analysis and for land development decision-making, such as that represented by the launching of new HSR lines in Spain, make these systems the most adequate technical-methodological instrument available.

4.3 Settlement System, Human Occupation of the Territory and Transport Infrastructures: Territorial Imbalances

The analysis of the population distribution over the territory is one of the most important dimensions not only of the analysis of economic and social aspects but also of the study of transport infrastructures. It acts as both a cause and an effect. Moreover, the relation between the population and the land on which it settles must always be understood as dynamic (De Cos 2004), which explains the importance of the analysis of space-time processes (Cheyland 2007), especially concerning the development of transport networks in general and the HSR network in particular.

In the European context (Le Bras 1996), Spain has a comparatively low population density (Figure 4.1) and one of the most geographically imbalanced population distributions. At the same time it boasts a relatively high number of HSR lines, whether measured relative to land area or population. From a European demographic point of view Spain is a country of extremes: it has evolved from having some of the highest natural growth to having among the lowest and from being one of the youngest and most traditional nations in demographic and social terms to being one of the oldest and most modernised.

The current distribution of the population is the result of a long historical process in which natural and economic factors and resulting infrastructure factors, mainly transport (e.g., road, rail) have been decisive or, at least, highly conditioning.

In Spain the last few decades have seen great changes in the use of territory. The main aspects of the Spanish population territorial distribution model that changed during the second half of the twentieth century were laid down in the 1960s and 1970s, with strong urban industrial and tertiary development combined with a rural exodus and profound social and economic changes. In the last two decades, this classic model of rural areas in decline and growing urban centres has broken down, leading to an accelerated process of urban-metropolitan decentralisation and, thus, of peri-urbanisation. The individual transport revolution and the development of public urban and metropolitan transport have contributed enormously to this phenomenon.

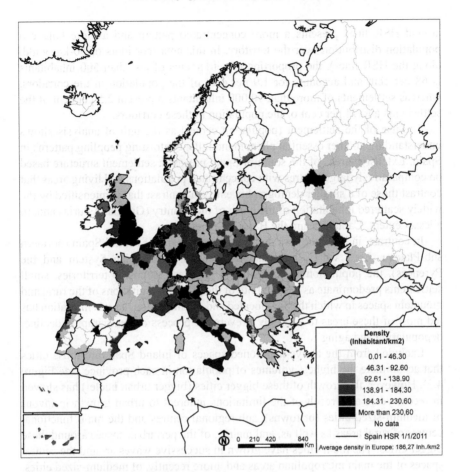

Figure 4.1 Population Density in Europe in 2010
Source: Authors, based on EUROSTAT.

From the point of view of human land use, there are two essential scales of analysis: the settlement, which is the minimal spatial unit considered from the statistical point of view in relation to peopling, and the municipality, which facilitates understanding the use of the territory through the indicator of population density (inhabitants per square kilometre). The population density in Spain shows significant territorial imbalances (see Figure 4.2).

The distribution of the Spanish population across settlements is highly imbalanced: 90 per cent of the settlements have lessrthan 500 inhabitants and account for only 6.7 per cent of the country's population. In contrast, settlements of more than 10,000 inhabitants, which constitute only 0.5 per cent of the settlements, make up 55 per cent of the national population, demonstrating the weight of the urban and semi-urban settlements in Spain. However, the population around HSR lines presents a more concentrated pattern and a more balanced population distribution over the territory. In this area (corridors of 50-km width along the HSR lines), the proportion of settlements of less than 500 inhabitants is 68 per cent and accounts for 1.9 per cent of the population in the corridors, whereas settlements of more than 10,000 inhabitants represent 2.5 per cent of the settlements and 74 per cent of the population in these corridors.

The use of the settlement (population centre) as the unit of analysis allows understanding another essential phenomenon: the contrasting peopling patterns in Spain. Extensive areas of the south of Spain present a settlement structure based on comparatively large centres with concentrated populations and living areas that contrast those of a smaller demographic entity, a contrast that is intensified by the widely scattered inhabitation of the north of the country (Galicia, Asturias and, to a lesser extent, Cantabria and the Basque Country).

In contrast, in both northern and northeastern parts of central Spain (northern sub-Plateau, Ebro Valley, mountainous areas of the Iberian System and the Pyrenees), the population is concentrated. In these extensive territories, small settlements predominate as a result both of the physical limitations of the rural and mountain spaces in which they are located and of emigration. Rural emigration has led most of these areas to a largely irreversible process of demographic decline, depopulation and aging.

Excluded from the above-mentioned spaces of inland Spain are those cities that accumulate the highest volumes of population in each province (see Figure 4.2). However, the growth of these bigger cities (bigger urban nuclei) has slowed in recent years as a result of the limitations inherent to urban growth in favour of medium-sized cities (or towns), sub-regional centres and the main functional centres of rural areas as well as, and mainly, of the periurban spaces around these bigger cities. The main cities have grown in successive waves around the central spaces of the main metropolitan areas and, more recently, of medium-sized cities, which also experience internal expansion induced by the recent change from a traditional Spanish high-density residential pattern to a low-density one.

In short, the analysis of the Spanish population's spatial distribution confirms the strong demographic development of the urban nuclei, located predominantly on or near the coast and in the south of the peninsula, with the exceptions of Madrid, Valladolid, Zaragoza and a few other provincial capitals of both central Spain plateaus. These spaces (cities and peri-urban adjoining areas) which are experiencing positive changes in their demographics, are in sharp contrast with the rural nuclei, which are characterised by regressive natural dynamics and by a slow and continual decline in population. This process of movement of the Spanish population towards the coast has been ongoing since the 1950s and has accelerated in recent years thanks to foreign immigration through both the so-called *gerontoimmigration* (Echezarreta 2005), or immigration of a residential nature from central and northern European countries (Rodríguez and Warnes 2002), and work-related immigration from the rest of the world, which is largely complementary to the former (Gil and Domingo 2006).

These circumstances explain the unequal human use of the territory and the coastal character of the Spanish population, as can be observed in Figure 4.2. This map shows the settlements of more than 2,000 inhabitants that form part of the Spanish urban system.

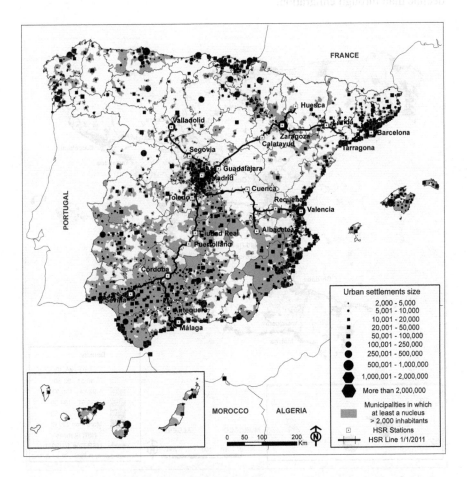

Figure 4.2 Territorial demographic imbalances, urban system, rural space and HSR in Spain in 2010

Source: Authors, based on National Institute of Statistics Municipal Census 2008.

The current population density by municipality (Figure 4.3) also illustrates some of the above-mentioned phenomena. The relative emptiness of inland Spain is the result of a high number of small municipalities with critical densities lower than 25 inhabitants/km². The traditional economic frailty of these areas, resulting from the limitations of the physical environment and the urban-based spatial model imposed by the economic development, together with a municipal demographic history strongly affected by emigration processes of the 1950s and 1960s and the consequent demographic aging and decline, have led to the increasing depopulation of rural inland Spain (Reques and Rodríguez 1998), more through demographic decline than through emigration.

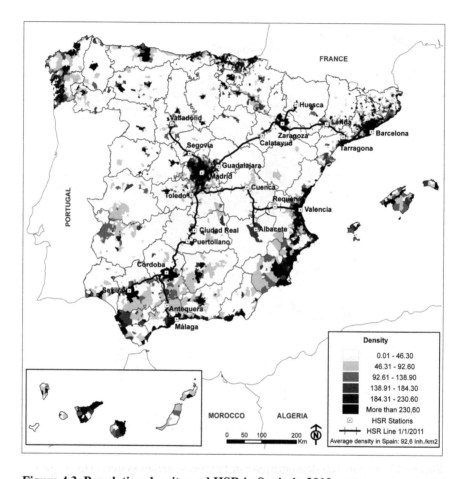

Figure 4.3 Population density and HSR in Spain in 2010
Source: Authors, based on National Institute of Statistics Municipal Census 2008.

These spaces are in sharp contrast with the coastal municipalities and their neighbours, with densities that are double or even triple the average density nationwide, which is 90 inhabitants/km². However, this value is still a low density in the European context.

Madrid and its functional metropolitan space constitute the most outstanding counterexample to the low density found in inland Spain. Madrid has expanded along the main transport corridors over a range that even surpasses the region's territorial administrative bounds. This expansion is a consequence of the process of peri-urbanisation of the capital of Spain, of the extension of this area of influence due to the improvement in communications, of the development of new economic activities and of the transformation of secondary residences into primary ones.

Further examples of exceptions to this context of low density can be found in the provincial capitals and even in some larger regional centres: these municipalities do not form a spatial continuum but rather a scattered distribution. The transfer of population from other regions and the return of Spanish emigrants to Europe since 1975 have also contributed to their growth. The population has also increased through the dynamics of production, linked to industrial and service activities of an urban nature, in municipalities that at present tend to extend their influence over their adjoining environments in the form of small metropolitan areas.

Other examples of medium or high densities in inland Spain are provided by the municipalities of the main valley areas of the south (Guadalquivir, Tajo and Guadiana valley plains) and also in the east (the Ebro valley plains), with horticulture and irrigation agriculture accounting for this relatively high population density.

The higher density of the coastal area, meanwhile, is normally associated with high levels of urbanisation, industrial, commercial and service activity and, above all, tourism. The tourism activities and the consequent urban expansion account for the density in the coastal regions of eastern and southern Spain and the Balearic and Canary Islands.

4.4 Recent Demographic Dynamics and High-Speed Rail: An Analysis at a Municipal Scale

The cartographic and statistical analysis at a municipal scale of the demographic dynamics in Spain over the last two decades offers an overall perspective representative of the recent process of metropolitan growth and peri-urbanisation in Spain.

The decision-making processes regarding place of residence, which are not necessarily connected to the workplace, lead to increasing daily travel flows, the analysis of which, based on the profile of the population involved, is fundamental in the study of the relation between HSR, the population, and the land. This importance is explained by the fact that HSR in Spain is so closely linked to the organisation of the geographical space; it connects areas of medium and high densities and contributes decisively to the restructuring of the national territory.

Beginning in 1991 (the year before the first HSR line between Madrid and Seville started operating) and ending between 2001 and 2007 (the years in which the lines to Malaga in the south and Barcelona in the northwest, respectively, started operating) (see Chapter 1), the demographic dynamics of the Spanish municipalities underwent a pronounced polarisation: the part of Spain that was growing did so progressively and the Spain that was in decline accentuated its regression. At present, the new HSR infrastructure connects five important, demographically expansive or progressive areas: Greater Madrid, including several cities around 70 km away and others up to 200 km away, the northeastern coast (Barcelona–Tarragona), the South, along or near the coast (Seville and Malaga), the central part of the eastern coast (Valencia) and the three main inland cities, Zaragoza to the northeast (in the central Ebro Valley), Valladolid to the northwest (at the centre of the northern sub-plateau) and Córdoba to the south (at the centre of the Guadalquivir valley) (Figure 4.4).

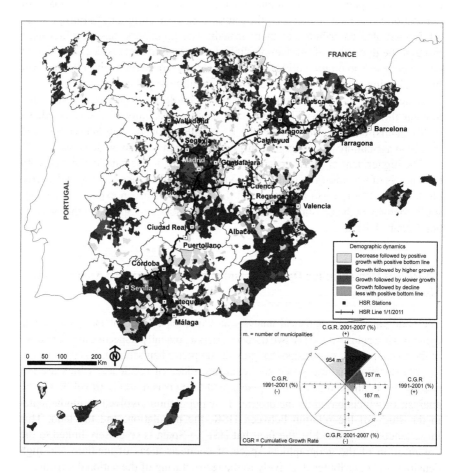

Figure 4.4 The demographically dynamic Spain
Note: Types of demographic growth of the Spanish municipalities between 1991–2001 and 2001–2008 and HSR in Spain in 2010.
Source: Authors, based on National Institute of Statistics Population and housing Census of 1991, 2001 and Municipal Census of 2008.

The territorial distribution of the demographic growth in Spain at the municipal level is a consequence of a set of relatively rapid processes of spatial expansion and functional change, which have shaped territorial models closely related and conditioned by the metropolitan dynamism and the improvement and expansion of the transport infrastructures. In this sense, as indicated previously, the demographic evolution of the urban municipalities has transformed their adjoining peri-urban environments, going beyond the municipal administrative boundaries to generate functional cities of supra-municipal dimensions (metropolises or conurbations and urban agglomerations). These metropolitan processes have led to the separation of the place of residence from that of work and, consequently, to an increase in commuting.

The urban and metropolitan municipalities constitute extraordinarily complex spaces, protagonists of a demographic and functional expansion that cannot be constrained inside the administrative boundaries in which they are located. These municipalities organise highly dynamic areas of influence in their surroundings articulated from the axes of transport, fed by daily return movements to and from the conurbation centre town for purposes both of work and study and of supply and leisure. These new metropolitan type environments, with their vague and changing bounds, are of varying sizes often proportional to the magnitude of the central municipality.

The cartographic representation of the population growth from 1991 to 2008 and of the inter-annual growth rates allows the identification of the phases of incorporation of the different Spanish municipalities to the urban and metropolitan dynamics, in keeping with what Vries (1987) classified as 'demographic urbanisation'. It is thus possible to establish, on the basis of the municipal administrative unit, territorial corridors with relatively homogeneous behaviours regarding the indicator of the annual growth rate and type of growth dynamics. The defining features of the urban structure in Spain are the existence of a greater number of metropolitan areas in which the residential function and the development of new centres of supply and leisure appear in the peripheral nuclei, which leads to a great intensity of daily return movements between places: the residence, the workplace and the administrative centres. Madrid and Barcelona are the most advanced environments, while other large or medium-sized cities have undergone the same processes, though with less intensity and range, and with a chronological delay of about a decade.

Territorially, those parts of Spain with continued economic growth between 1991 and 2007 are structured by two great transport networks, the HSR lines and stations and the main highways and motorways, which constitute not only important communication corridors but also significant demographic growth corridors as a consequence of the virtuous circle of economic growth à population growth à better communications à economic growth.

In contrast, the depopulating regions of Spain correspond to the rural areas (in the northwest, together with wide areas of rural Extremadura and the municipalities of the Iberian System, essentially the provinces of Soria, Teruel and

Cuenca and those of the Betic and Panibetic mountain ranges). All of these areas have accentuated their tendencies towards depopulation, though at far slower and decelerated paces between 2001 and 2008 than between 1991 and 2001. The explanation for this change is that the process of emigration and transfer of population from the primary sector to the secondary and tertiary sectors and from rural territories to urban and metropolitan ones seems to have come to an end.

Rural, inland and mountainous Spain (with the exception of the Pyrenees), meanwhile, has seen its process of depopulation intensified, though at a slower pace between 2001 and 2008 than between 1991 and 2001. In short, the axes of communication and transport (national road and rail, and singularly, dual carriageways and motorways) always play contributing, if not decisive, roles in geo-demographic processes.

4.5 Economic Activity and Territory: Agrarian Spain Versus Industrial and Tertiary Spain

The final aspect to analyse concerning the parallelism between the settlement pattern and the layout of the HSR network in Spain is the distribution of the working population by economic sector, taking the municipality as the unit of analysis and the average values for Spain as a reference. Figure 4.5 constitutes a synthesis cartography in which the available information has been broken down into the three economic sectors (primary, secondary and tertiary) and their possible combinations to obtain a representative typology that will facilitate its geographic interpretation.

The analysis of the working population economic profile verifies the strong presence of municipalities in which the primary sector is dominant or is combined with the secondary and tertiary sectors. Agriculture is still the main economic activity in many municipalities of inland Spain (Galicia, Asturias and, to a lesser extent, Cantabria, the Duero basin, the Iberian mountain range and rural Extremadura and Andalusia).

The secondary sector is geographically dominant in the traditional industrial zones and has the spatial form of an inverted lambda (Reques and Rodríguez 1998). Particularly prominent is the presence of the industrial municipalities of Barcelona and its area of influence, far outreaching the province itself. The Basque Country is another zone with a strong industrial presence, especially in its central area. This area also links up with the well-connected spaces of the Ebro Valley, which, although they do not form a continuous corridor, seem to be influenced by the economic flow derived from the Basque Country.

The third industrial space is made up of the municipalities to the south and east of the metropolitan area of Madrid, while the municipalities to the west and north show no particular industrial relevance. In contrast, the industrial expansion from Madrid farther to the south (Toledo) and northeast (Guadalajara) owes much to the communications system, confirming that communication links play a decisive role in the design of this model of industry-based territorial articulation.

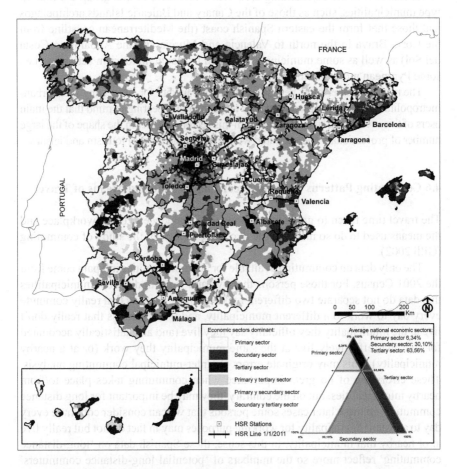

Figure 4.5 Economic activity, territory and high-speed rail in 2010 agrarian versus industrial and tertiary areas of Spain

Source: Authors, based on National Statistics Institute Population and Housing Census of 2001.

The last great industrial zone is the Valencia zone, with the identifying feature of the duality between large and medium establishments and scattered and diversified small industry producing toys and shoes.

The rest of the industrial municipalities are spread over diverse regions.

The predominantly tertiary municipalities present a heavily scattered spatial distribution model, as might be expected from the function they fulfil. These municipalities correspond to the big cities and some large municipalities in their surrounding areas, provincial capitals or other regional centres and nuclei with an urban function in the surrounding area. Other members of this group are tourist-type municipalities, such as those of the Canary and Balearic Islands archipelagos and those that form the eastern Spanish coast (the Mediterranean coastline from the Costa Brava in the north to Valencia and Murcia and the Andalusian Costa del Sol) as well as some municipalities linked to mountain tourism activities (i.e., some Pyrenean mountain municipalities).

The new HSR lines must be justified by their capacity for connecting great urban-metropolitan clusters of a predominantly tertiary nature, bearing in mind that the main users of this means of transport come from this sector, whether in the shape of the large number of professionals and educated workers or in the form of tourism and leisure.

4.6 Commuting Patterns in Spain According to Time and Means of Travel

The travel time taken to go from one's place of residence to one's workplace and the means used to do so make up the two basic aspects of the study of commuting (Gilli 2002).

The only data on commuting available for all municipalities in Spain come from the 2001 Census. For those persons that live and work in different municipalities this data do not separate two different realities: those persons that really commute every day to work to a different municipality, and those persons that really don't live at the municipality they officially say they live (and are statistically accounted for) but that effectively live at the same municipality they work (or at a nearby municipality). This may originate errors for inter-municipal commuting analysis. These errors are of no great importance when commuting takes place to/from nearby municipalities, but on the contrary, they may be important for long distance commuting. In these later cases some persons that we can consider commute every day to a distant municipality for working purposes may in fact do not but really live at or nearby that municipality. In this sense, these Spanish data on 'long-distance commuting' reflect more so the numbers of 'potential long-distance commuters' than the actual effective long-distance daily commuters. This has to be taken into consideration in this section as well as in Sections 4.7 and 4.8.

The following analyses use these data, and thus, in section one, only the HSR lines that existed in 2001 or earlier are considered (see Chapter 1) to enable comparison with the available commuting data.

a) Commuting and Travel Time

The time factor plays a major role in a large number of commuting patterns. Hence, the journey's duration often conditions the number of daily trips for the working population with split shifts (morning and afternoon work); it may even condition the possibility of returning to one's place of residence in the same day.

The statistical analysis of the travel time of the residents of different municipalities reveals some highly significant behaviour patterns.

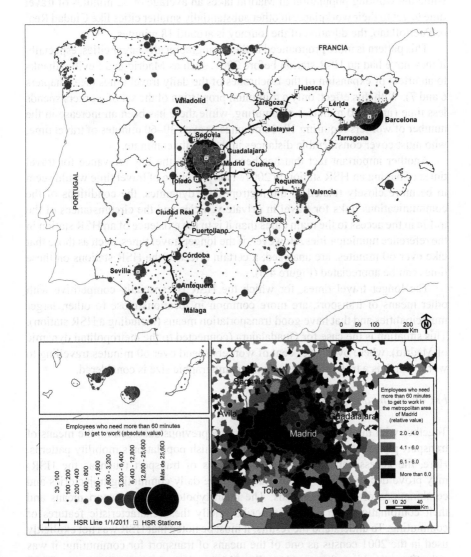

Figure 4.6 Employed persons who spend more than 60 minutes travelling from residence to workplace

Source: Authors, based on National Statistics Institute Population and Housing Census of 2001 and Municipal Census of 2008.

The first feature is the direct correlation between the demographic size of the municipalities analysed and the time dedicated to the residence-workplace journey: while the working population of Madrid takes an average of 32 minutes of travel time to get to their workplace, in other substantially smaller cities like Ciudad Real or Puertollano, the duration of the journey is around 18 minutes.

This pattern is more pronounced in the demographically larger cities, especially if they have had an HSR station before 2001, such as Madrid and Seville, thanks to an effect of expansion of the isochrones of the daily travel times (see Chapters 6 and 7). With this effect, only a minimum proportion of the set of workers spends less time (under 10 minutes) commuting, while there has been an increase in the number of workers requiring 10–30 minutes or even 30–60 minutes of travel time, who must cover considerable distances in their daily commute.

Another important fact that has been verified is the low relevance for travel times of having an HSR station in 2001. This prototype of travel time would seem to be more closely related to the metropolitan dynamics, the conditions of the communications links for travel in private vehicles and the circumstances of the traffic in the access to the main cities than it is to the existence of an HSR station in the reference municipalities. However, if the longer travel times, such as those that take over 60 minutes, are analysed, a certain effect of the HSR stations on these times can be appreciated (Figure 4.6).

The longer travel times, for which the HSR is especially competitive with other means of transport, are more common in locations close to other, larger municipalities and that have good transportation means (including a HSR station). This situation is the case for Guadalajara (connected to the metropolitan dynamic of Madrid), where over 7 per cent of workers spend over 60 minutes travelling to work, which is a truly high ratio if only demographic size is considered.

b) Commuting and Means of Transport

Together with the time factor analysed in the previous sub-section, the means of transport plys a fundamental role in thhe Spanish population's mobility patterns. Here, the access capacity to a certain means of transport (such as the HSR) may prove decisive in the configuration of the daily commuting trajectories and combinations of transport means. The main typologies of transport means and their combinations are used to describe briefly these characteristic features of commuting. To understand the results, it must be noted that HSR was not explicitly used in the 2001 census as one of the means of transport for commuting; it was rather integrated into the generic 'railway' category.

With the exception of the large urban or metropolitan municipalities and those located in the immediate surroundings or in the heart of a metropolitan area, private transport is the overwhelmingly preferred means, with percentages of over 90 per cent. However, none of the municipalities with an HSR station in 2001 reached such high proportions.

In general terms, the second most widely used means is the bus, with values ranging from 10 to 20 per cent on average. The position occupied by the bus in the set of means of transport also presents exceptions in the main Spanish metropolitan systems of Madrid and Barcelona, where the metro is the second most widely used means. This difference underlines the importance of the choice of means of transport and, above all, of the suitability of this means of transport in the larger urban-metropolitan areas.

The railway shows little statistical significance in all of the municipalities that have an HSR station.

Bus-metro, bus-railway and railway-metro combinations have only marginal importance, with the exceptions again of Madrid and Barcelona, for which these combinations represent 16 per cent and 10 per cent of residents' commuting means, respectively.

Thus, travel using the train as the means of transport is subject to the orientation of stations of departure towards certain destinations, in which this system takes on a greater representation in the links with the main urban-metropolitan systems, with the combinations of different means of transport being relegated to positions of scarce statistical relevance.

4.7 Commuting and Employment Basins: Movements of the Working Population towards Destinations with High-Speed Rail Stations

The analysis of the employment areas and areas of influence generated around the municipalities with an HSR station in 2001 is based mainly on the cartographic representation of the working population's mobility vectors and on the municipal ratios of the workers who travel to work in another municipality (Figures 4.7, 4.8, 4.9 and 4.10). The methodology applied to create a meaningful and sufficiently representative depiction of the patterns analysed is based on the intersection of three criteria:

1. A maximum radius of influence (in Euclidian distance) of 200 kilometres is considered for municipal centres of metropolitan areas of over 500,000 inhabitants (such as Madrid, Barcelona and Seville) and 100 kilometres for those of smaller demographic sizes (such as Ciudad Real).
2. Percentage of employed persons who travel to work in the central municipality with an HSR station compared to the total number of employed persons from each municipality included in the potential maximum area of influence as defined above.
3. Representation of travel vectors (employed persons who travel in absolute terms) from each municipality in the potential maximum area of influence, as defined above, to the central municipality with an HSR station.

On the basis of the above, four examples are considered representative: Madrid, Barcelona, Seville and Ciudad Real, corresponding to different models of urban systems. Madrid is a large metropolitan area with a national scope of influence and had a HSR station in 2001. Barcelona has a supra-regional range of influence and did not have a HSR station at the time. Seville acts as an articulating node of a metropolitan area of a regional scope of influence and had a HSR station. Finally, Ciudad Real is an example of an urban area with a provincial scope of influence, also with a HSR station.

The results obtained allow the following conclusions to be drawn (take into consideration what was mentioned at the beginning of Section 4.6):

The area of influence of Madrid (Figure 4.7) extends significantly over eight provinces and to a lesser extent over six more corresponding to its own region and three other regions (Castilla La Mancha, Castilla and León and Extremadura). In total, 777 municipalites with at least one person travelling to Madrid for working purposes, which adds up to an area of almost 75,000 km² (15 per cent of the total Spanish surface).

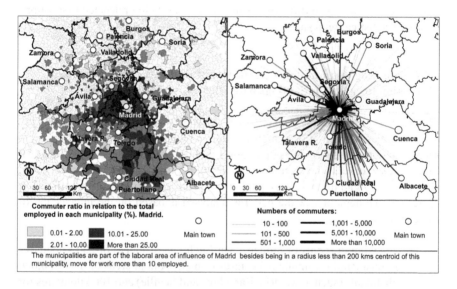

**Figure 4.7 Employed persons who work in Madrid and officially live in a
           different municipality**

Source: Authors, based on National Statistics Institute Population and Housing Census of 2001.

The total number of employed persons who travel in the defined area of influence is over 450,000, a volume that represents, in relative terms, 18.6 per cent of the employed persons in the employment area without taking into account those living in the Madrid municipality. Moreover, considering the ratio of employed persons who travel to Madrid to work, there is a great asymmetry in its area of influence. There is a greater percentage of the working population arriving from farther south than from farther north. In fact, while the connection to Madrid in the northern area is discontinuous, the area to the souty shows a strong connection, with ratios of at least 10 per cent of employed persons travelling to Madrid in practically all cases. This patternthappens across the provinces of Toledo and Ciudad Real and in parts of other provinces and clearly forms a broad area of employment of supra-regional dimensions.

The area of influence of Barcelona (Figure 4.8) covers more than 50,000 km² (10% of Spain), grouping together the four provinces of the Catalonian region and extending over the nearest parts of the neighbouring provinces. This area of employment covers 1,083 municipalities. There are around 250,000 employed persons who travel to work towards the municipality of Barcelona (without considering the population resident in this capital), which represents just over 30 per cent of the total number of employed persons who work in this area.

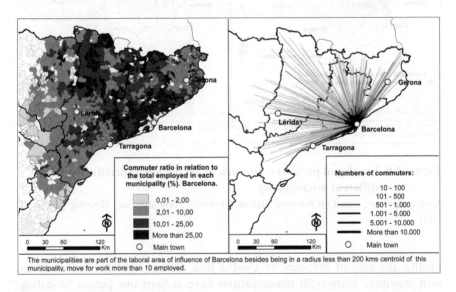

Figure 4.8 Employed persons who work in Barcelona and officially live in a different municipality

Source: Authors, based on National Statistics Institute Population and Housing Census of 2001.

The area of influence of Seville (Figure 4.9) extends over the province of Seville and into substantial parts of the adjoining provinces towards the south and west (Cadiz and Huelva), to a lesser extent towards the north and east (Córdoba and Badajoz) and marginally over others located farther away (Jaen, Malaga, Granada and Caceres). There are 230 municipalities with at least one person travelling to Seville, summing up around 43,000 km^2. The total number of employed persons travelling from these municipalities to Seville is around 82,000 (nearly 5 per cent of the total number of employed persons in the area of employment of Seville, excluding the municipality of Seville itself). If the ratio of employed persons who travel to the total number of employed persons of each municipality is considered, the area of influence of Seville can be classified at a supra-provincial level.

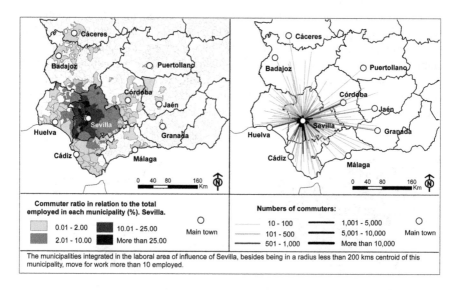

Figure 4.9 Employed persons who work in Seville and officially live in a different municipality

Source: Authors, based on National Statistics Institute Population and Housing Census of 2001.

Finally, the area of influence of Ciudad Real (Figure 4.10) is limited to its own province. Sixty-eight municipalities have at least one person travelling to Ciudad Real, covering an area of around 15,000 km^2. The total number of employed persons travelling from these municipalities to Ciudad Real is slightly over 7,000 (4% of the total number of employed persons in the employment area of Ciudad Real, without taking into account Ciudad Real itself). Considering the ratio of the employed persons who travel to the total number of employed persons in each municipality, the area of influence of Ciudad Real forms an employment area of provincial or infra-provincial dimensions, given the lack of representation in this area of some of the municipalities of the south and southeast of the province.

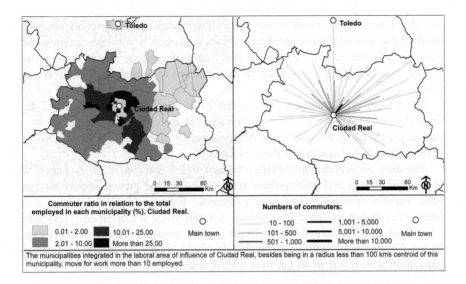

Figure 4.10 Employed persons who work in Ciudad Real and officially live in a different municipality

Source: Authors, based on National Statistics Institute Population and Housing Census of 2001.

Considering the network of HSR lines and stations in Spain in 2010, it is possible to establish a hierarchy of stations that essentially correspond to three main types (in relation to their employment areas calculated as above with the 2001 Census) according to their locations: stations in large metropolitan areas, stations in large cities and provincial capitals and stations located in urban centres that are not provincial capitals.

These types of stations and their areas of influence can be differentiated according to the following parameters see Figures 4.7, 4.8, 4.9 and 4.10):

- First-level stations located in large metropolitan areas. Thion is the case of Madrid and Barcelona, from which concentric corridors or buffers of 15 km, 30 km and 60 km are defined.
- Second-level stations located in large cities and provincial capitals. This type accounts for most stations: Toledo, Ciudad Real, Córdoba, Seville, Malaga, Valladolid, Cuenca, Albacete, Valencia, Zaragoza, Huesca, Lerida and Tarragona. From each location, areas of influence in the form of concentric buffers of 10 km, 20 km and 40 km can be identified.
- Third-level minor stations located in urban centres that are not provincial capitals, such as Puertollano, Antequera, Calatayud and Requena, with concentric corridors of 5 km, 10 km and 20 km.

The above-mentioned corridors and areas allow certain spatial discontinuities to be identified around the metropolitan stations that reach beyond the autonomous community in the case of Madrid and that intercommunicate in a continuum the area of influence of Barcelona from all three stations of Barcelona, Tarragona and Lérida.

Other features of interest are the singularity of the regional set made up of the three stations of Aragon (Calatayud, Huesca and Zaragoza) and the polycentric pattern presented by the southern Córdoba–Seville–Malaga line (with additional HSR stations in Antequera and Puente Genil).

The study of the distribution of the whole set of HSR stations (in 2010) connected to the main urban and metropolitan systems reveals the greater opportunity of HSR access to residents below certain threshold distances (Table 4.1). Thus, it is noteworthy that nearly 10 million people in Spain reside at a distance of less than 5 km from an HSR station, nearly 40 per cent of residents already live less than 20 km from an HSR station and, if this threshold is doubled, nearly half of the population lives less than 40 km from a HSR station.

Table 4.1 Areas of influence of HSR stations through their concentric corridors

Distance of corridors from HSR stations	N° municipalities	Resident population	% over total population
Under 5 Km	86	9,891,836	21.9
Under 10 Km	268	12,383,237	27.4
Under 20 Km	760	16,904,210	37.3
Under 40 Km	2,006	21,054,378	46.5

Source: Authors, based on National Statistics Institute Municipal Census of 2009.

In addition to analysing the HSR stations according to their areas of influence, it is also important to consider the patterns of integration of the various municipalities in which they are located according to the volume of exchange of commuting travellers. The working population living in one municipality with an HSR and working in another is shown in Table 4.2.

In absolute terms, it is the Madrid–Toledo link that stands out, with nearly 1,200 employed persons living in Madrid and working in Toledo and nearly 1,000 people living in Toledo who work in Madrid. Second, and far less numerous, are the Sevilla–Madrid link, with almost 950 employed persons travelling in this direction (and one fourth in the opposite), and Cordoba–Madrid, with more than 700 workers (and only one tenth in the opposite). If we consider these last two cases, and taking into account that these HSR stations were operational prior to the 2001 Population Census, it is possible to advance the importance of the Madrid–Seville line for these links.

Table 4.2 Numbers of potential commuters* between municipalities with HSR stations in 2001

Municipality of departure	Municipality of destination							Comm.
	CR	CO	M	MA	Pt	SE	TO	
C. Real (CR)	-	24	687	9	422	7	116	1,265
Córdoba (CO)	43	-	738	391	30	716	16	1,934
Madrid (M)	261	65	-	138	104	211	1,190	1,969
Málaga (MA)	7	84	580	-	1	294	4	970
Puertollano (Pt)	495	21	525	13	-	14	53	1,121
Seville (SE)	8	388	949	370	6	-	17	1,738
Toledo (TO)	40	3	992	4	5	1	-	1,045
Comm.	854	585	4,471	925	568	1,243	1,396	10,042

Note: *See argument at the beginning of Section 4.6.

Source: Authors, based on National Statistics Institute Population and Housing of 2001.

4.8 Commuting, Main Nodes of Attraction and Areas of Influence: The Examples of Andalusia and the Northern Regions of Spain

The vectorial cartography representing commuters (or potential commuters, see argument at beginning of Section 4.6) in Spain may be understood focally, as in the examples presented above that are focused on analysing one single node, such as Madrid, Seville or Ciudad Real, but can also be used to analyse networks of interrelations between the different nodes of a regional or supra-regional system. The regions of northern Spain (Asturias–Cantabria–Basque Country) and the region of Andalusia will be analysed in this way.

Based on these two reference cases, the 2001 Census micro-data analysed in this study are shown to highlight possible new spatial patterns of mobility (or potential mobility, see argument at the beginning of Section 4.6) and new modes of connection for a network that is fundamentally balanced in the case of Andalusia and a more polarised, dual system with two sub-networks, in the case of the northern regions.

The representation of the mobility vectors of the regions of northern Spain (Asturias–Cantabria–Basque Country) highlights the existence of a polarised network with four major areas of concentration (Figure 4.11): one to the west in Asturias composed of the urban system of Oviedo–Gijón–Avilés, another in the centre at Cantabria and composed of the urban area of Santander-Torrelavega and, finally, two more to the east in the Basque Country around the cities of Bilbao and San Sebastian. A fifth centre of less importance can be identified to the south of the last two, around the city of Vitoria.

In addition to showing that the network closely follows regional boundaries, the vectorial cartography highlights a strong link between two of the autonomous communities concerned. This is the case of the eastern area of Cantabria and the western part of the Basque Country, which, with its focal point in Bilbao, acts as a major node for daily commuters who live in the east coast of Cantabria.

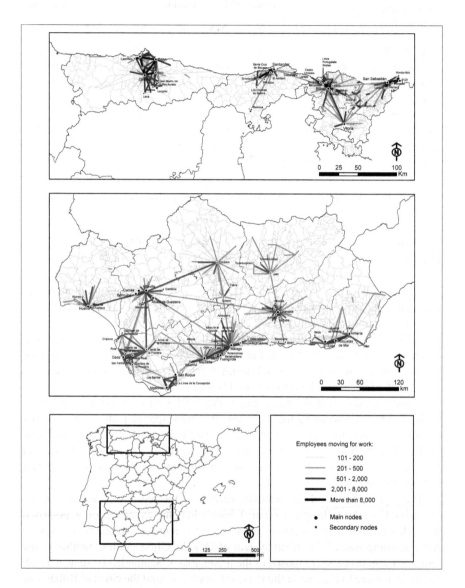

Figure 4.11 Population that works in another municipality different from that of official residence: North of Spain and Andalusia

Source: Authors, based on National Statistics Institute Population and Housing Census of 2001.

The commuting network in Andalusia (Figure 4.11) can be broadly described as balanced; in fact, almost all of the provincial capitals maintain some linking vector with neighbours of varying size, normally with more than 500 commuters per day.

As regards these inter-provincial links, the most noteworthy node is Seville, featuring strong mobility vectors towards all adjoining provinces (Cadiz, Huelva, Cordoba and Malaga). On top, there is an important commuting network in five of the eight provinces of Andalusia. The weakest one is Granada, with a mainly provincial influence, which maintains weak connections with other provinces such as Jaén and Almeria as well as Málaga. These vectors are the only ones that manage to integrate the city of Granada into the balanced network described above.

In addition to considering the network as a whole, it is possible to extract some particularly pronounced commuting patterns in cities near the coast, mainly in Marbella–Fuengirola–Malaga and, to a lesser extent, Almeria–Roquetas–El Ejido to the east and around Cadiz to the west.

4.9 Conclusions

The spatial analysis of the Spanish population characteristics at municipal and settlement scales demonstrates the relations between demography, economy, territory and transport infrastructures. This chapter does not include the most recent period of time in which Spain is suffering a profound economic and land development crisis.

With the exception of Madrid and a few inland urban centres, the population of Spain is distributed, regarding its economic activity and demographic growth, according to a functional schema and a spatial model that offer a sharp contrast between inland and the coastline, with quite different economic bases and demographic-territorial structures and dynamics.

The population distribution in Spain was conditioned by the natural dynamics from the beginning of the century until the late 1950s, by an extraordinary development of migratory mobility and by a concentration of the population in urban and metropolitan areas in the 1960s and 1970s, and by a process of urban de-concentration and peri-urbanisation in the 1980s and 1990s. This model is at present undergoing an additional strong urban-metropolitan readjustment characterised by the occupation of city centres by the immigrant population and of the various metropolitan rings by the autochthonous population. These factors explain the current geographic configuration of the population density and the occupation of the land in Spain.

Pueyo et al. (2009) point out that urban expansion resulting from the development of the low-density residential model currently makes the growth in the urban use of land in Spain exceed the population growth. The inhabited spaces and living centres are articulated around increasingly complex networks facilitated by the development of transport and telecommunications. This fact has given rise to important processes of suburbanisation and decentralisation of cities towards their peripheries, de-urbanisation of large cities, recovery and transformation of historic city centres through gentrification, and recovery of degraded central areas through foreign immigration and counter-urbanisation or the return of the population to the rural world (phenomenon of neo-rurals). The post-metropolitan hypotheses (Soja 2009) that suggest the end of the separation of the rural world from the urban world is imposing itself as a theoretical framework in Spain.

From a demographic perspective, the progressive dynamics in the Mediterranean, coastal and urban Spain contrast with the regressive dynamics of the northwest and the mountain areas. From the peopling perspective, the Spain of the micro-settlements and of the sparsely populated northern area contrasts sharply with the concentrated medium and large settlements of the south. From an economic perspective, the agriculture-based Spain (increasingly less extensive both in land and in economic importance) contrasts with the economically dynamic industrial and tertiary Spain. This chapter shows that the integration of transport and communications in Spain into a single model is not possible or desirable. It is essential to respond to the specific needs and the spatial-demographic identity of each territory.

In short, any sectorial or regional planning policy (financial, equipment, infrastructure, transportation) must take into account the demographic-territorial factor and the conditions it induces. Undoubtedly, transport, and particularly HSR, unites the territories, but they are neither homogeneous nor equally balanced. As the Spanish case shows, transport infrastructure and particularly HSR, although a factor of territorial cohesion, may also have unbalancing effects as far as the population and the territory are concerned and may promote a not always desirable effect of 'archipielagisation' of economic activity and population growth.

The chapter has also shown the usefulness of commuting studies in the planning of transport systems.

Furthermore, this chapter has served to delineate the areas of influence of the major urban centres, configured with the current transportation system and the current commuting patterns in Spain, and to identify the nodes of attraction and their areas of influence both for balanced and for more polarised areas, closely related to forms of peopling.

It has also demonstrated the importance of the factor of choice of mode of transport and, especially, the suitability of HSR in large urban-metropolitan areas both to consolidate the metropolitan links between the main and secondary nodes and to incorporate new, more remote nodes that would remain outside of the metropolitan systems without the HSR link.

In short, commuting patterns in Spain should not be interpreted as fixed or unchangeable. The existence of new travel opportunities (such as new HSR routes) may open up new spatial relationships and new opportunities that go beyond the scope of this work and that must be studied once the new 2011 Census is available. Rather, the main contribution has been the analysis of the demographic and territorial conditions and of the patterns of commuters, both of which must form the basis for planning new high-speed rail routes and for the assessment of the regional impacts of existing ones.

Chapter 5

Accessibility Evaluation of the Transportation Network in Spain during the First Decade of the Twenty-first Century[1]

Ángel Pueyo, Jorge A. Jover and María Zúñiga[2]

5.1 Importance and Evaluation of Accessibility in Territorial Studies: Previous Considerations

Accessibility is understood in territorial studies as the nearness of a node compared to all others based on the minimum distance, cost or time of travel. It depends to a great extent upon each point's location with respect to the group of nodes that constitutes the system (Calvo et al. 1997, Gutiérrez et al. 1998, García 2000, Harris 2001, Bavoux et al. 2005). Other studies measure accessibility by the quality of the path of each element of the transportation infrastructure. Accessibility is also measured by the opportunities that each group of people has, at a certain location in space, to participate in certain activities by identifying the net benefit obtained. Thus, this form of measurement approximates the concept of spatial rent (Mérenne-Schoumaker 2008a, Alonso and Bellet 2009, Brocard 2009). Still other studies suggest as an optimum measure of accessibility the cost of minimising travel times and thus the difficulty of the journey. Some of these approaches correspond to a macroeconomic vision as they fit into the usefulness theory applied to the transportation system. In summary, researchers have broadened the concept of accessibility as a way of explaining the interrelations between human activities,

1   This study was carried out with the technical and human support of the Cartography Area of the National Atlas of Spain, the General Subdirection of Geographic Applications of the National Geographic Institute (NGI) and the Census Registration Subdirection of the National Institute of Statistics (NIS).

Funding for this work was received from the Spanish Research and Development Plan for project n° CSO2010-16389 'HGISe: a platform for the analysis of transportation, population and socio-economic data of Europe (1850–2010). A case study of England, Wales and the Iberian Peninsula'.

Also collaborating on the project are J. L. Calvo, J. M. Jover, D. Mora, D. Ballarín, M. Sebastián, S. González, L. A. Castellano, E. Sánchez, C. Loscertales, S. Valdivielso and J. Repollés.

2   University of Zaragoza.

the transportation network and the transportation systems (García 2000, Monzón de Cáceres et al. 2005, Gutiérrez et al. 2006, Brocard 2009).

Currently, in addition to improving the infrastructures, spatial planning is recognised to be crucial to enhance accessibility (Gutiérrez et al. 2010). With all of this information in mind, the accessibility indicators are useful in the following situations:

- For integration with cartographic tools and geographic information systems, as they help to evaluate the value and quality of and the access to transportation infrastructure.
- For studies of the ideal strategic locations for public equipment because of their communications and privileged position.
- As an aid in planning and decision-making processes and as a tool for prioritising actions, especially when they are strongly linked to the transportation network (Moreno and Escolano 1992, Calvo et al. 1997, Baradaran and Ramjerdi 2001, Crozet and Musso 2003, Mérenne-Schoumaker 2008a, 2008b).

Thus, these indicators must be valued as aids to decision-making in the policies re-establishing territorial equilibrium and those related to the location of public equipment (Calvo et al. 1997, Haesbaert 2004, De Mattos et al. 2005). Therefore, depending on the quality of the transportation network, regions far from natural resources or from large consumption centres can benefit if they are near in space-time to human resources with a high-quality socio-cultural and/or environmental background. This fact suggests that an area can be more or less peripheral depending on its infrastructure connections to the basic transportation networks, benefiting from the nearness to centres of innovation, of economic development and of population growth (Vickerman 1995b). From this perspective, transportation networks can be considered as structural elements of the territory (Hagget 1972) and as the effects that these actions have on the space and its activities (Escalona 1989). It must not be forgotten that transportation systems are crucial for the socio-economic structure of the modern world (see Chapter 3). They provide a structure to the territory and reflect the imbalance that exists between the urban system and socio-economic activities (Calvo et al. 1997, Nogales and Gutiérrez 2002).

However, it should be noted that researchers have interpreted the concept of accessibility in different ways (Hägerstrand 1967, Dalvi and Martin 1976, Gutiérrez et al. 1998, García 2000, Monzón de Cáceres et al. 2005, Bavoux et al. 2005, Gutiérrez et al. 2006, Mérenne-Schoumaker 2008a, Brocard 2009, Gutiérrez et al. 2010) such as the following:

- A characteristic of a point, a line, a network or a surface of geographic space. In this sense, it approaches the notion of geographic location and of the measurements that determine it.

- A factor in spatial perception and behaviour.
- A structuring factor of space influencing the organisation of intra- and inter-urban socio-economic activities.
- A spatial measure of the economic performance and profitability of the transportation system. In this case, accessibility focuses on the analysis of the fluidity and the improvement of the productive activity of a territory.
- A form of redistribution and social arbitration. It refers to the offer and demand of equipment and services to the community. It changes the concept of distributive justice to rights justice. It must not be forgotten that, in developed countries, there is an implicit social commitment to equality from which public authorities must ensure a minimum fulfilment of services (e.g., health, education, and social assistance), guaranteeing quality for the entire population, wherever it may be located.

All of these meanings of accessibility must be considered in societies that have experienced a strong growth of telematic communication networks and of transportation modes in the past decades. This development of transportation has brought the spaces of demand and consumption of equipment and services closer to the points of production and supply. The European Union intends to follow this development and produce rapid communication means (e.g., airports, highways, high-speed railways, intermodal transportation centres, and broadband communication networks) that favour the availability of qualified labour, access to equipment and services and proximity to entrepreneurial research and to innovation centres, all within a high-quality cultural, physical and environmental medium (Comisión-Europea 2001, OECD 2002, Tapiador et al. 2008).

A new organisation of space is rising, based more on networks than on hierarchies. Good accessibility (i.e., the ability to connect to networks) plays an important role in the development and establishment of services and equipment for the population. It is true, however, that sometimes the main centre does not reach the demand thresholds that are suggested for the location of the equipment (Bavoux et al. 2005, Mérenne-Schoumaker 2008a, Brocard 2009).

5.2 Goals of the Analysis of Intermodal Accessibility in Spain

Considering the geographic characteristics of the Spanish transportation networks and the distribution of the population by municipalities,[3] the present work has

---

3 The accessibility study considered as spatial reference units the municipal capital and the exact locations of stations and airports. On this basis, the changes between the networks and the differences in conditions between these units and the reference cities are

integrated different indicators of accessibility into an intermodal model in which the road and airport networks are combined with high-speed rail (HSR). These indicators are used to accomplish the following:

- Evaluate the respective impacts of the aerial connections and HSR and the degrees to which they complement the road network.
- Analyse those zones with deficient mobility, which are in greater need of transportation services.
- Compare the accessibility results that account for the various means of transportation and the synergy produced among them.
- Evaluate the impact of actions on this matter.
- Present the results of the accessibility indicators with a thematic cartography that favours understanding the impact of the transportation infrastructures.

Because it is a determining parameter when evaluating the location of activities, it is appropriate to study accessibility from different perspectives. However, all of the proposed indicators of accessibility measure the separation of activities and of human settlements that are interconnected by a transportation system. Thus, the basic elements that have been considered are as follows:

- The way in which the separation between two or more points (e.g., by time, cost, distance, or friction) is measured.
- The valuation of the relations created with a transportation system that connects two points, of the effort required, and of the activities that can be developed. For this purpose, it is necessary to establish the correspondence between the indicators of accessibility and the demographic variables. If the fit is adequate, it will help to quantify the territorial effects caused by improvements of the network.
- The calculation of the minimal distances between the nodes in the network that will contribute to the development of the accessibility models. For this purpose, it is necessary to work with algorithms that optimise the critical pathway (or minimum distance), such as Ford and Bellman-Kalaba's algorithms (Kaufmann and Desbazeille 1974). This research has chosen the algorithm suggested by Floyd (1962) and Warshall (1963), which has the advantage of speed and agility in the calculation of times and distances and allows for the calculation of these pathways, in time or distance, without storing the connection itineraries.
- The diversity of cases and formulations. The same concept can be measured in different ways, and even though the results cannot be extrapolated, they

---

considered. This situation is the case for the majority of airports in Madrid and Barcelona, which are located in the outskirts of their municipalities, and for some of the HSR stations, such as those in Segovia, Antequera, and Camp de Tarragona, which are uncharacteristic of these population centres.

help to evaluate the different spatial effects of the transportation network at the national and regional levels (Calvo et al. 1997, Gutiérrez et al. 1998, García 2000, Harris 2001, Ajenjo and Alberich 2005, Bavoux et al. 2005, Gutiérrez et al. 2006, Raux et al. 2008).

5.3 Selection of the Ground Infrastructure Network and Representation of the Accessibility Results

As mentioned in the previous section, the road, railway and aerial infrastructure network constitutes the basis for the calculation of the accessibility indicators. This research has obtained results on the national and regional scales that, although very similar in methodology, often vary in the degrees of disaggregation of information and in the final goals of the reference units:

*   At the national scale, the intra- and interregional relationships between the municipalities are of interest, while the study of the local relationships is less relevant.
*   At the regional scale, the local and regional connections prevail, requiring a much more detailed network that includes the valuation of the population distribution and/or the characteristics of the settlements.
*   Initially, the only transportation network that was to be used for the model was the General Interest Government Network (in Spanish, Red de Interés General del Estado-RIGE), as it was done for the model of the General Highway Plan 1984–91 and the Strategic Transport Infrastructures Plan 2004–20 (Gutiérrez et al. 1998, MOPTMA 1994, García 2000, Ministerio de Fomento 2005, Gutiérrez et al. 2006). Nevertheless, this RIGE network neglected a large part of the second-order regional network. The RIGE required that the two work scale models be combined incorporating the conception and selection of information for both the network and the population centres (Calvo et al. 1997).

The RIGE network, with better conditions than the rest of the road network, focused on high-volume connection axes between urban centres and neglected rural areas with poor accessibility, from which the results of a few selected points were extrapolated. Thus, more than 70 per cent of the municipalities in Spain were not considered. This study worked from the premise that a good territorial analysis and plan should consider the different spatial scales and the national-regional-provincial-urban relations and therefore a greater number of elements of transportation networks.

A large part of the research (Gutiérrez et al. 1998, García 2000, Gutiérrez et al. 2006) as well as the studies carried out for the last Infrastructure Plan (in Spanish, *Plan Estratégico de Infraestructuras y Transporte*, PEIT) (*Ministerio de Fomento* 2005) have focused on a final road network totalling some 80,000 kilometres in length with more than 12,000 arcs and approximately 8,000 nodes. Population groups or urban conglomerates of more than 75,000 inhabitants, as well as provincial capitals, were identified as activity spaces (Ministerio de Fomento 2005, Monzón de Cáceres 2005, Gutiérrez et al. 2006, Gutiérrez et al. 2010). This analysis requires the extrapolation of the results of the selected urban spaces to their surrounding areas. Many of them are depopulated and have deficient connection networks compared to the selected road and HSR systems. According to these parameters, it was again proposed that, for this research, the road network must meet the following requirements:

- Classification in three levels to facilitate the analysis of both national and regional traffic:
  - High-capacity roads such as motorways. For these roads, each junction was evaluated, along with its connections with the lower-level network. This evaluation was necessary because these roadways are accessible only at these junctions and improvements in accessibility will materialise only at these connection points.
  - First-order highways encompassing the rest of the RIGE and the first-order regional highways. At this level, the second-order regional roads were also considered, especially old provincial roads.
  - Local roads that link some important routes, allowing for the closing of circuits of the network or the connection of relevant centres.
- This analysis entailed the modelling of a network that approximates the real one as closely as possible to recreate the connectivity model existing in peninsular Spain, which has great disparities in the quality and number of connections. This network differentiates levels of accessibility that could have been masked by a homogeneously distributed network. The network finally considered spans more than 105,000 km and has more than 200,000 vertices, 56,000 arcs, and 20,000 nodes.
- Linking the 8,037 municipalities of the Iberian Peninsula to the network, with their importance prioritised by the municipal population.[4]

For the airport network, the 35 airports of the Iberian Peninsula were considered as nodes. Arches with travel times representing regular aerial connections were also considered. For this work, only HSR was considered as constituting the rail network. Conventional railways, with the exception of some national lines and local connections, take longer to travel compared to highways and

---

4   It is true that assigning all of the population to the municipality produces certain gaps in the regions of Cantabria and Galicia, where the population is distributed across smaller entities called parishes. However, this research focused on the national and regional levels; thus, an excessive disaggregation would not substantially improve the results. This accessibility analysis did not consider the Spanish islands and the African cities of Ceuta and Melilla.

motorways. As in the case of motorways, the values of accessibility of the HSR network are considered only at the stations, which in this network function as nodes of the system.

For the calculation of the indicators, two possible scenarios were evaluated:

- A simple model that exclusively accounts for the road network and that allows comparing the indicators of accessibility with the results of studies carried out by the Research Development Ministry and other studies performed in Spain (Gutiérrez et al. 1998, Ministerio de Fomento 2005, Monzón de Cáceres 2005, Gutiérrez et al. 2006, Gutiérrez et al. 2010). In addition, in a society that is starting to value and foster intermodality between transportation systems, it was considered essential to develop accessibility indicators accounting for the multiplicity of travel modes.
- A perfect intermodal model that integrates the air, HSR, and highway networks. This model allows the evaluation of the effects produced when time frictions are avoided along with economic costs incurred in the development of the transportation system. The model also selects the arc that allows the fastest travel by path coincidence.

Before calculating the accessibility indicators, it was necessary to design a working procedure that could manage the information in the model, which has more than 200,000 vertices, 56,000 arcs, 20,000 nodes and 8,037 peninsular municipalities, by performing intermediate computation and valuation of mean travel times. Considering the population potential studies (Calvo et al. 1997) and based on the extrapolation of the accessibility indicators to other gravitational-type studies (Calvo et al. 2008c); a regular 207-by-174 grid was used to represent the peninsula with 5-by-5-kilometre cells. The following steps were used:

1. Calculation of an origin-destination matrix containing the mean travel times from each of the points of interest (municipalities, nodes and vertices) to all other points.
2. Linking of each cell on the grid to one or more points of interest, accounting for the following considerations that help to prioritise them according to the importance of the point or points of interest:

- Type I: The municipalities of the Iberian Peninsula (located in 6,352 cells, 31.4 percent of the total of the matrix).
- Type II: Nodes without settlements that correspond to the endpoints of the transportation modes and changes and effective crossings between them, including airports, HSR stations and motorway exits (2,332 cells, 11.5 percent of the total).
- Type III: The vertices of an arc (excluding those of motorways and HSR)

that affect a cell. In this case, the two nearest nodes to the vertices of an arc that are found in the cells of the matrix are accounted for (5,956 cells, 29.4 percent of the total).

- Type IV: Cells that do not have any arc or cells that contain a highway, motorway or HSR line but do not offer a real connection. They can be classified into three sub-types:

    - Less than 5 kilometres from the nearest vertex (4,337 cells, 21.4 percent of the total).
    - Between 5 and 10 kilometres from the nearest vertex (1,015 cells, 5.1 percent of the total).
    - More than 10 kilometres from the nearest vertex (251, 1.2 percent of the total).

3. Calculation of the different accessibility indicators by pairing each of the cells of the grid with each one of the points of interest, selecting the best of the values for each of the intermediate calculations.

The accessibility indicators were coded in visual variables according to the general principles of semiology of graphics with the use of cartographic and infographic tools (Brewer 1989, Chapelon and Cicille 2000, Suchan and Brewer 2000, Eicher and Brewer 2001, Cauvin et al. 2007, Zúñiga et al. 2010). The resulting maps are intended to make it easier for the reader to understand accessibility in peninsular Spain. All of them have been mapped, taking advantage of the raster matrix used for the calculation of the indices.

5.4 Basic Indicators Used for the Study of Intermodal Accessibility in Peninsular Spain

Initially, three types of basic indicators were selected that do not account for the effects of congestion and that help to evaluate the general accessibility levels and the changes that the incorporation of a HSR transportation system can entail. According to the indicators proposed in the literature, the goals of the study, the criteria for the selection of the road and railway network and the cartographic representation model, the work was carried out with the following formulations:

- Absolute Potential Accessibility (APA)
- Route Factor (RF)
- Population potential models (PPM)

Absolute Potential Accessibility

$$APA_i = \frac{\sum_{j=1}^{n} dm_{ij}}{n}$$

Absolute Potential Accessibility (APA) captures the sum of the distances (dm_{ij}) from each cell i to all municipalities of peninsular Spain (j) following the shortest itineraries, represented by travel time and divided by the total number of considered municipalities (n).

Because of the difficulty of obtaining the travel times for all of the arcs and the particular nature of the traffic in the metropolitan areas and their surroundings (in which the mean values mask a complex and divergent reality depending on the hour, day and time of the year), the average speed assigned by Spanish General Direction of Traffic for each type of roadway was used (250 kilometres per hour for HSR, 120 for motorways, 80 for first-order roads, 70 for second-order roads and 60 for local roads). The Spanish Airports and Aerial Navigation webpage was referenced to determine the mean travel times of the regular connections between the airports. As mentioned previously, congestion effects were not accounted for because there is not enough disaggregated information for the entire road network. Similarly, in studies that account for all of the connections of all municipalities in Spain, the availability of alternative networks neglects the implicit limitations of traffic jams in large metropolitan areas at certain times of the day. Also, as this effort constitutes an analysis at the national-regional scales, the time calculation parameters proposed by the Research Development Ministry were used (*Ministerio de Fomento* 2005).

This accessibility indicator favours central nodes as pseudopods according to the characteristics of the road, HSR and airport network, although it is affected by the following peculiarities of the Spanish network:

- An asymmetry in the density of the network that facilitates the connectivity of the northern part of central Spain.
- The existence of a greater number of nodes in the northern region.

Mapping the results (see Figure 5.1), the values demonstrate better accessibility in the northern part of Central Spain because of the existence of the Valladolid and Segovia HSR stations and the proximity of Madrid (airport and HSR) and Guadalajara (HSR), thus generating significant accessibility in all of the outskirts of Valladolid and Segovia. It is also worth noting that there is high accessibility toward the east in Valencia, in the Ebro River Valley and in the southern part of Spain.

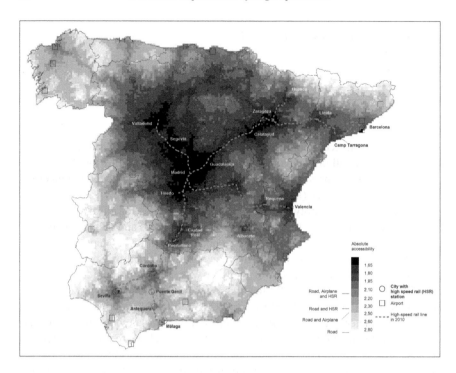

Figure 5.1 Absolute potential accessibility in 2010 by highway, airplane and HSR
Source: Authors based on data from Ministerio de Fomento, IGN, INE, GEOT.

Because it is a perfect intermodal model, accessibility substantially improves in all of the surrounding spaces because it combines all of the advantages of airport connections, HSR, and the conventional high-capacity road network. This network provides high potential connectivity in the Madrid–Guadalajara–Calatayud–Zaragoza–Huesca and the Madrid–Toledo hubs, in which there are not only HSR stations but also several motorways. In addition, the Madrid–Barajas airport is located nearby, with connections to nearly all of the peninsular airports.

Nonetheless, the effects upon accessibility of the addition of the HSR networks (see Figure 5.2) show a positive impact of the Madrid–Ciudad Real–Puertollano–Cordoba, Cordoba–PuenteGenil–Antequera–Malaga, Lleida–Tarragona–Barcelona, Madrid–Cuenca–Albacete, and Madrid–Segovia HSR lines. To a lesser degree, there is an increase in accessibility in the spaces along the Segovia–Valladolid, Cuenca–Requena–Valencia, Madrid–Guadalajara–Calatayud–Zaragoza, and Cuenca–Requena–Albacete lines that, despite having lower levels of accessibility, presents some instances of improved variations of accessibility above the mean.

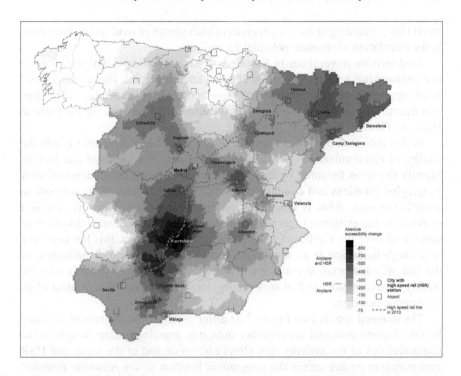

Figure 5.2 Accessibility improvements due to the addition of the HSR to the 2010 transportation network

Source: Authors based on data from Ministerio de Fomento, IGN, INE, GEOT.

Route Factor

For both distance and time, the route factor (RF) is one of the clearest indicators to measure connection quality provided by a particular transportation infrastructure. In this case, the best accessibility is directly related to the infrastructure pathway, being optimal for the user when the itinerary used to minimise travel time coincides with the shortest route and has an adequate level of service (e.g., high-speed travel, road quality, absence of mountain ports, and good pathways).

$$RF_i = \frac{\sum_{j=1}^{n} \dfrac{dm_{ij}}{de_{ij}}}{n}$$

To quantify the quality of transportation or route factor (RF_i) from a cell i to the municipalities of peninsular Spain (j), it is necessary to obtain the path with the minimum travel time (dm_{ij}) following the shortest itinerary and valuating it, in travel time, according to the weight given to each stretch of road, as has been done in the calculation of absolute potential accessibility.

To determine travel times in Euclidean distance or along a fictional straight-line pathway (de_{ij}), an average speed of 64.44 km/h was used. This average speed is still applied in the Spanish Research Development Ministry studies. This value was determined as the mean velocity in the entire road network for the General Highway Plan of 1994 (MOPTMA 1994).

In this indicator, the lower the value of (RF_i), the better the pathway and the quality of communication between the two nodes. The indicator can help to identify the areas favoured by the transportation network independent of their geographic locations and can indicate global quality deficits of the network in a particular area. What is labelled as an accessibility deficit in this case is a response to the existence of an unbalanced network with estimated distances or times well over the Euclidean values. On several occasions, this has been due to a rough landscape (e.g., mountains and swamps), inadequate pathways, or the lack of transportation pathways in one of the directions, which is why the quality of accessibility to that area is considerably worsened independent of its geographic position.

The mapped results (see Figure 5.3) differ greatly from the results obtained by the absolute potential accessibility indicator, granting greater weight to the characteristics of the network that affect each node and to the aerial and HSR transportation modes versus the geographic location of the Absolute Potential Accessibility (APA). The spaces with the best accessibility, measured by the route factor, are Galicia in the northwest of the Iberian peninsula, western and coastal Andalusia in the southwest, all of the eastern coastal region, especially in the southeast, the Lleida–Tarragona–Barcelona corridor and its extension throughout the northeastern coast, the metropolitan surroundings of Madrid–Toledo, and the Ciudad Real–Puertollano and Zaragoza–Huesca corridors. In all cases, the combined presence of airports, HSR stations and a good road transportation network facilitates intermodality and connectivity with even the most distant nodes.

To a lesser extent, but with significant values because of the presence of HSR stations, the surrounding areas of Valladolid (and its connections with the north of Spain), Segovia, and the Calatayud–Zaragoza and Madrid–Cuenca corridors stand out. This result suggests that, when efficient intermodal systems are in place, HSR can generate positive effects beyond the locations of the stations by supporting rapid transportation pathways or the use of different transportation modes (Tapiador et al. 2008 and see Chapter 9). The induced effects from Valladolid to the northeast (Palencia) or the northwest (Leon) must not be neglected. Currently, this intermodal capacity is being used in the overall railway network with the use of interchangers between HSR and conventional rail (see Chapter 1).

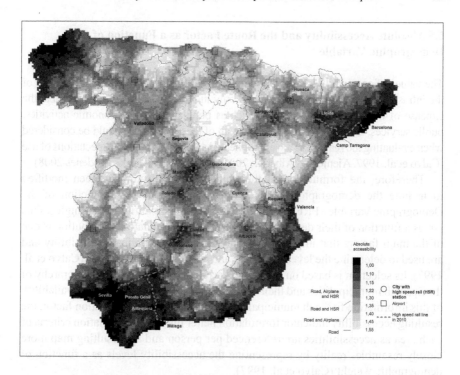

Figure 5.3 Accessibility according to route factor in 2010 by highway, airplane and HSR distances

Source: Authors based on data from Ministerio de Fomento, IGN, INE, GEOT.

Other effects of the airport network where there is good accessibility are observed in several regions of northern Spain (Asturias, Santander, Basque Country and Pamplona) and in the western portion of the peninsula in Badajoz, all of which, for the most part, have aerial connections.

Areas with a rough landscape have low levels of accessibility and are isolated because of a scarce and inefficient transportation network that greatly limits their connectivity with population centres, airports and HSR stations. Following the assumptions of the generated isolation, polarisation and tunnel effects reported by some authors (Vickerman 1995a, Gutiérrez 2004), white or very light grey maps are the norm for the isolated areas in the Iberian, Central, Penibetic and Cantabric mountain systems.

5.5 Absolute Accessibility and the Route Factor as a Function of the Demographic Variable

The values of accessibility, considering exclusively the location and characteristics of the infrastructures, must not be measured only in terms of geometry or friction at the expense of other territorial variables, such as population, socio-economic activities, public services, and natural spaces. Rather, all of these variables should be considered when evaluating the real use of a well-connected area and its greater expectations of use (Calvo et al. 1997, Ajenjo and Alberich 2005, Gutiérrez et al. 2006, Módenes 2008).

Therefore, the formulation of the route factor indicator has been modified to include the demographic variable (the Route Factor as a function of the Demographic Variable –PRF) by considering the municipalities not as single points but as a function of their demographic weights. The population distribution is one of the main factors that improve the analysis of intermunicipal accessibility and are used to determine the levels of access and congestion in a territory (Calvo et al. 1997). Its selection is based on the strong correlation between the real hierarchy of the Spanish municipalities and their effective demographics and on the availability of this information for each municipality. By introducing the population factor, the resulting accessibility indicator formulation better fits the differentiation criteria of each area as accessibilities are referenced per person and the resulting map more closely resembles reality by representing the accessibility levels as a function of demographic weight (Calvo et al. 1997).

Thus, the place of residence of the users is what determines the use of geographical space, giving reduced priority to the longest distances. In addition, the assumptions made in other research works that have used gravitational models are maintained. This research uses this research team's more than two decades of experience with population potentials analysis, of which the study of accessibility is a part (Calvo et al. 1997, Ajenjo and Alberich 2005, Gutiérrez et al. 2006, Calvo and Pueyo 2008a).

$$ PRF_i = \left[\sum_{j=1}^{n} \left(\left(\frac{dm_{ij}}{de_{ij}} \right) \times P_j \right) \right] \times \frac{1}{\sum_{j=1}^{n} P_j} $$

In this formulation, PRF_i is the quality of transportation of each cell i of the matrix when it relates to all of the municipalities (j) of peninsular Spain; dm_{ij} corresponds to, as in the formulation of the route factor, the minimum distance between i and j along the transportation network according to the mean travel time; de_{ij} represents the length of the fictional Euclidian distance time between i and j; and P_j represents the population of each of the municipalities of peninsular Spain. When the population j is within the cell i, the ratio (dm_{ij}/de_{ij}) is given the value of 0. Thus, the methodological coherence is maintained as in those formulations undertaken for the potential population maps developed by road distance (Calvo et al. 1997).

The introduction of population to the maps has consequences because it gives a better interpretation of accessibility (see Figure 5.4) since it reinforces the routes and corridors that interconnect important population centres, especially in those areas in which there is an airport and/or a HSR station (Morellet and Marchal 1997, Menerault and Stransky 1999, Hammadou and Jayet 2002, Facchinetti-Mannone 2005, Beyer 2008, Zembri 2008, Alonso and Bellet 2009). Thus, the incorporation of the population components better reflects the importance of the relationship supported by the Madrid-Zaragoza–Lleida–Barcelona and the Madrid–Segovia–Valladolid–Peninsular Northwest corridors, as is perfectly captured by the map (see Figure 5.4) that now fully depicts the HSR network and its effects beyond the network itself, making use of highways and roads. The same situation is found in the Valladolid–French border, Ebro River Valley–Basque Country and coastal zone of northern Spain (Asturias and Cantabria) corridors due to the positive indirect effects of the airports-railways-highways-municipalities combination in areas with populations above the national mean.

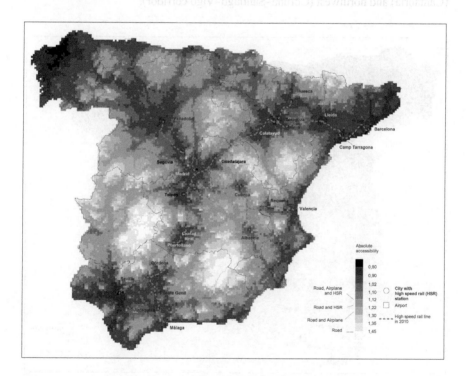

Figure 5.4 Accessibility according to route factor and population in 2010 by highway, airplane and HSR distances

Source: Authors based on data from Ministerio de Fomento, IGN, INE, GEOT.

In contrast, in regions with natural areas and small populations, such as those southwest of Antequera and in the surrounding areas of Doñana in the southwest of Sevilla, the accessibility values decrease considerably because of the combination of transportation problems and the existence of small settlements. The areas that show minimal changes are mountainous areas that have poor communications and are sparsely populated.

It is interesting to evaluate the changes in this indicator. For this purpose, a map was made (see Figure 5.5) comparing the route factor accessibility results including and not including the population. In general, when the demographic weight of each municipality is accounted for, the spaces nearest the transportation nodes with good railway accessibility and high populations are reinforced. The entire northern portion of central Spain improves substantially, with induced effects in areas of the north, such as central Asturias and the communities of La Rioja and southern Navarra, which are well connected with Zaragoza. The most significant improvements are found in the areas surrounding the Valladolid, Segovia, Guadalajara, Calatayud, and Zaragoza HSR stations, as well as in the vicinity of the airports in the north (Cantabria) and northwest (Coruña–Santiago–Vigo corridor).

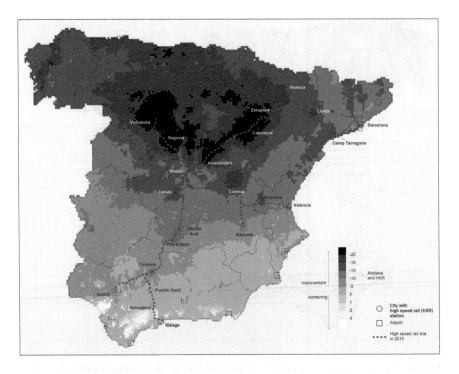

Figure 5.5 Percentage improvement of accessibility according to route factor accounting for municipal population in 2010

Source: Authors based on data from Ministerio de Fomento, IGN, INE, GEOT.

Moreover, peripheral areas with poor connectivity and a road network that is less dense than average and of inferior quality demonstrate values that are below the mean or negative. These areas are found west of the central Iberian peninsula (Extremadura) and in the southeast (Andalucía). Central peninsular areas such as Castilla–Leon or the Ebro River Valley corridor have much better communications.

Thus, in the valuation of the results of accessibility indicators based on route factor and population, the particular geographic nature and the specific pattern of the transportation network are highly influential for the following reasons:

- The fostering of the radio-concentric relationships due to the irregular morphology of peninsular Spain, which is much broader in the north.
- The favourable topography in northern central Spain.
- The greater development of the HSR network in northern Spain, with stations that can function as intermodal centres for more isolated areas.
- The smaller number of municipalities and the population concentration in coastal areas.

5.6 Population Potentials: Valuation of the Gravitational Effects

Until now, analyses have focused on the infrastructures constituting the transportation network and their relations with demographics. However, the inverse analysis can also be carried out based on the population and the potential use of the transportation infrastructure. The analysis can be attempted using indicators of aggregated measures of gravity that measure the interrelation of the population with the transportation network (Boursier-Mougenot et al. 1993, García 2000, Ajenjo and Alberich 2005, Monzón de Cáceres 2005, Gutiérrez et al. 2006, Calvo et al. 2008c, Calvo et al. 2008b).

In this sense, the studies of population potentials constitute one of the more fruitful contributions of physics to the field of geography. In the middle of the nineteenth century, Carey (1858) mentions that the sphere of influence of a population is proportional to its demographic effects and proposed that the influence decreases as distance increases. Reilly, Stewart and Zipf developed this concept to analyse the interactions between a wide range of social phenomena and to develop different ways of calculating them and assigning potential values (Camagni 2005, Calvo and Pueyo 2008a). The cartographic representation of the gravitational models, including the population potentials, details the visualisation of the spatial interactions with a large 'explicative weight' because they graphically recast population, activity and distance in absolute values (Isard et al. 1971, Grasland 1991, Boursier-Mougenot et al. 1993, Faiña et al. 2001, López-Rodríguez and Faiña 2006, Calvo and Pueyo 2008a).

Among other positive aspects, population potential allow the visualisation of geometries that vary with time and that perfectly reflect 'life basins' that are transforming the relations between humans and the area in which they live (Vinuesa 2005, Calvo et al. 2008c). In modern society, the individual divides his or her activities into different spaces and times, often depending on information and communication technologies. The administrative footprint of each citizen always covers at least one municipality (Torres 2003). The cartographic representations of population through population potentials meet the characteristics and dimensions of the territory in which they are inserted. They also account for the real values of population, transportation networks, use of space and trends in geographic dynamics.

A variant of the gravitational model has been used for this work, with the same calculation formulation and the same 207-by-174 matrix for the indicators of accessibility (Calvo et al. 1997, Calvo and Pueyo 2008a):

$$POT_i = \sum_{j=1}^{n} \left(\frac{P_j}{dr_{ij}^{2}} \right) + P_i$$

Where POT_i is the population potential accumulated in the cell i, P_j are the polled inhabitants in each of the remaining cells, and P_i is the number of inhabitants of the cell i, whereas dr_{ij} is the distance following the shortest itineraries (according to the calculation system developed for the accessibility indicators and route factor) valuated in travel time between each of the cells of the matrix.

Therefore, the cartographic values of POT_i are equal to the corresponding values for its resident population (P_i) in addition to those inferred or derived from the rest of the system as a consequence of their position in the group. These values were obtained by the sum of the population values of P_j divided by their distance (dr) from each accountable cell (j) with respect to (i) and raised to an exponent, in this case 2, coinciding with the gravitational formula proposed by Newton and adapting itself to the proposed problem and the expected results in relation to what is known in reality (Díez 1970).

The results of the population potentials that account for transportation networks yield significant variations in the models of potentials that do not consider only Euclidean distances. The introduction of highway, HSR and airport transportation favours those spaces affected by improvements in the network, bringing outlying areas closer to urban centres, altering the neighbouring spaces and influencing relations between cities. These changes turn the model into an optimal tool to analyse the effects of population diffusion and its sphere of influence with respect to the variations of transportation and intermodal systems. Basically, the model of potential by distances implies the following:

- Improvement of the valuation of the spaces near urban centres;
- Empowerment of the spaces in which there is a good transportation network that connects with the most populated areas;

- Signalling of those isolated territories that are poorly connected and removed from population centres.

The highest population potential values are clearly seen in the urban centres of Madrid, Barcelona, Valencia, Sevilla, Malaga–Costa del Sol and Bilbao, which can be considered authentic urban regions. There are also high metropolitan areas that complete the hierarchy of large urban areas: Oviedo–Gijon–Aviles in the northern Cantabrian coast region; Zaragoza and Alicante–Elche in the East; and Cadiz–Jerez in the southwest.

It must also be underscored that the inclusion of HSR networks and aerial links reinforces the relations between population centres at the mercy of these infrastructures. These spaces provide important advantages for the location of equipment and services because they combine good accessibility with high thresholds of population potential. It is essential to remember that besides the activation of the infrastructures, other factors such as innovation are also necessary.

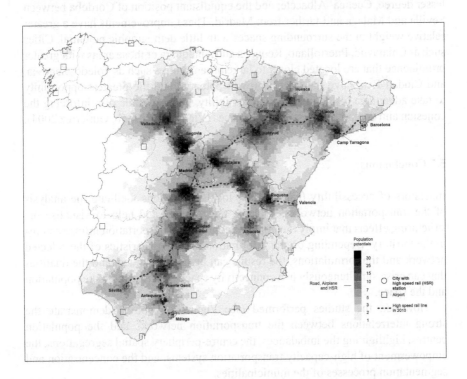

Figure 5.6 Improvement of the population potentials using the HSR network

Source: Authors based on data from Ministerio de Fomento, IGN, INE, GEOT.

Differentiating the various modes of transportation in the potential calculations, improvement is feasible due to the HSR network versus aerial and terrestrial transportation (see Figure 5.6). The cartographic results illustrate how the potential population growth occurs in those areas surrounding the municipalities with HSR stations. These areas are essentially those mid-size and small cities that are located within a 200-km radius of large cities such as Madrid (Segovia, Guadalajara, Toledo, Cuenca, Ciudad Real and Puertollano), Barcelona (Lleida and Tarragona), Valencia (Requena), Sevilla (Cordoba), Malaga (Puente Genil and Antequera), and Zaragoza (Huesca and Calatayud).

Similarly, the interaction of mid-size cities in the HSR network and in the transportation network also generates potential growth corridors. This is the case for Aragón, where important growth has been induced in the centre of the region because of the presence of railway stations in Calatayud, Zaragoza, and Huesca; the border effects of Lleida, Valladolid–Segovia, and Cordoba–PuenteGenil–Antequera–Malaga; the effects between Cuenca–Requena–Valencia, and, to a lesser degree, Cuenca–Albacete; and the equidistant position of Cordoba between Sevilla and Malaga and farther from Madrid. These improvements have a greater relative weight in the surrounding spaces with little demographic potential. Cities such as Calatayud, Puertollano, Requena and Antequera or those areas with greater prominence that are located closer to large urban centres such as Toledo, Segovia, and Ciudad Real have the largest growth potential and the greatest opportunity to take advantage of the improved accessibility, being capable of reinforcing the cohesion and competitiveness of these spaces (Vickerman 1995b, Gutiérrez 2004).

5.7 Conclusions

Indicators of accessibility that consider local populations facilitate the analysis of the transportation networks, evaluate their impact and help to visualise the structuring effects that imply the improvement of the transportation infrastructures in the territory. Depending on the information, the characteristics of the selected network and the formulations, the results can be used to understand the dualities that can arise simultaneously in a connectivity space with respect to the population and the space.

However, the studies performed (see Figure 5.6 above) demonstrate the strong interrelations between the transportation networks and the population centres, highlighting the imbalances, the centre-periphery spatial segregations, the empowerment of high-capacity transportation systems, and the concentration and segmentation processes of the municipalities.

These indicators specifically highlight in space:

- The great expectations and the potential for small and mid-size cities near Madrid, such as Toledo, Segovia and Guadalajara. This finding is also true of other cities farther from Madrid that are incorporated into HSR hubs, such as Calatayud, Ciudad Real, Cuenca and Puertollano. Finally, places near large cities such as Malaga (Puente Genil and Antequera) and Valencia (Requena) can be highlighted. The policies and territorial strategies that are developed are essential for taking advantage of the synergies of the modes of rapid transportation (Gutiérrez 2004).

- The positive, albeit smaller, effects in the urban spaces of large cities such as Valladolid, Zaragoza, Huesca, Lleida, Camp de Tarragona, Valencia, Albacete, Sevilla and Malaga. Because these cities are larger, the positive effects will always be qualitatively smaller than those experienced in the smaller surrounding areas, provided that there is an optimum intermodal system in place, although the accessibility indicators are quantitatively more important (see Figure 5.4). The larger urban spaces can best take advantage of the enhanced accessibility in the peninsular context (Alonso and Bellet 2009).
- The low impacts in Madrid and Barcelona due to the sizes of their populations. This result suggests that the impact of HSR on these large cities will have to be analysed more in terms of the functional aspects, specialisation aspects, and services and upper range activities because, from the start, they present the best chance to capture and reinforce their upper and mid-range activities in an economic context of strong concentration and polarisation of the activities (Vickerman 1995a).
- The loss of position of the peninsular spaces in the north that do not already have a high HSR connection (Basque Country, Galicia or Asturias); those that have good aerial connectivity; and those western areas (Extremadura) that will remain isolated until a HSR connection is made between Madrid and Lisbon.

The positive effects of intermodality on the rural areas are also confirmed when the population variable is modified, and a true intermodality system is generated that is supported by the secondary networks (Gutiérrez 2004). The true beneficiaries could be rural spaces that actualise an increase in their inferred values both for the growth of urban centres and for the improvement of the infrastructure networks as long as the intermodality policies are real and efficient (see Chapter 9). Unfortunately, the lack of judgement and investment are reinforcing the tunnel effect, wasting an opportunity to bring balance back to the territory.

In conclusion, accessibility and potential maps, when the demographic variable is introduced, are valid and useful instruments for evaluating the effects of the infrastructures. In addition, they allow modelling of future scenarios and can be of great interest for decision-making in the planning of transportation infrastructures.

Chapter 6
Mobility Characteristics of Medium-Distance High-Speed Rail Services

José M. Menéndez, Ana Rivas and Inmaculada Gallego[1]

6.1 Introduction: Travel Demand on the First European High-Speed Rail Lines

The high-speed rail Paris–Lyon (called TGV South-East, see Figure 6.1), the first in Europe, was implemented in 1981 and significantly increased the number of trips available by train in that corridor. The increase from 1980 to 1985 was above 50 per cent, which reflected an 11.1 per cent average annual increase. The French rail company (SNCF) estimated that without this high-speed rail (HSR), growth would have been limited to 2 per cent per year (Plassard and Cointet-Pinell 1986). Nonetheless, this increase was not homogeneous in all the cities served by the HSR; the increase was greatest in those cities with poorer accessibility to Paris. Between Paris and Lyon, the travel time was reduced by half to two hours, and the number of trips doubled (see Table 6.1).

However, the most significant increase in the number of trips by train was between Paris and Le Creusot (see Table 6.1 and Figure 6.1), which is a small city of 45,000 inhabitants that benefited the most from the reduced travel time to Paris (over 70 per cent). On the new HSR line, travel time to Paris is less than 90 minutes. Prior to 1981 this city was served by a transversal secondary line, which had a stop in Dijon. Because of the HSR line the number of travellers increased 7.2-fold in the first four years of operation (Plassard and Cointet-Pinell 1986, Bonnafous 1987). From the city of Chalon-sur-Saône, which is served only by a mixed HSR line/service (see Chapter 1), the travel time to Paris was reduced by 28 per cent, but the effects on mobility were the opposite of what was experienced at Le Creusot. Not only did the journeys by train not increase, but Chalon-sur-Saône's role as a significant railroad stop diminished with the new infrastructure because the conventional Paris–Lyon rail line passed through Dijon and Chalon-sur-Saône, while the new HSR did not (Mannone 1995) (see Figure 6.1).

---

1   University of Castilla La Mancha.

Table 6.1 Evolution of Passenger Traffic on Paris South-East

Paris-City (both sense)	1980*	1981*	1983*	1984*	Growth Factor
Lyon	1466	1731	2834	3668	2,5
Saint Étienne	205	232	334	410	2
Bourg-en-Bresse	73	75	113	160	2,1
Valence	212	214	323	396	1,6
Chambery	119	123	171	185	1,5
Annecy	191	201	258	295	1,5
Dijon	851	854	903	1042	1,2
Le Creusot	51	102	296	368	7,2
Mâcon	135	146	216	259	1,9
Chalon	180	188	152	167	0,9
Total 10 Cities	3483	3866	5600	6950	2
Total Paris-South East	12240	12730	15670	18360	1,5

Note: *Thousands of passengers.
Source: Authors based on data from Plassard and Cointet-Pinell (1986).

Throughout the first 10 years of the Paris–Lyon HSR service its performance was similar to that of the Japanese *Shinkansen*: the number of trips by railroad increased three-fold on both lines (Beauvais 1992).

Given the experience gained from the Paris–Lyon HSR, it was expected that implementing the second French HSR line, called the TGV-Atlantique (see Figure 6.1), would also generate a significant increase in railroad traffic. Although this expectation was fulfilled, the effects of the TGV-Atlantique on mobility presented unexpected peculiarities (Troin 1995). For example, although the number of trips by train increased, the increase was not as high as expected based on the performance of the first HSR line. In this case, the aspects of traffic evolution that were extrinsic to the HSR system itself were very relevant, including the economic crisis that occurred at the time this second HSR line opened. Other aspects were related to SNCF management, such as the need for reservations and the excessive cost imposed on the fares (Klein and Claisse 1997a).

The implementation of the third French HSR line, called TGV-Nord Paris–Lille (see Figure 6.1), which allowed for journeys of 220 km in 60 minutes, immediately increased the amount of traffic in that corridor. During the first three years the mobility in this corridor grew 11 per cent, reaching a railroad market share of 27 per cent (Houée 1999). This effect was expected because of the implementation of the new high-speed infrastructure. However, the noticeable effect of the TGV-Nord was different from that of the TGV Sud-Est and TGV-Atlantique, the two previous HSR lines, because the railroad traffic growth was mainly generated through the development of commuter trips and the increased mobility of a population that was already travelling before the implementation of the new HSR; the demand was generated by an increase in trip frequency in this corridor.

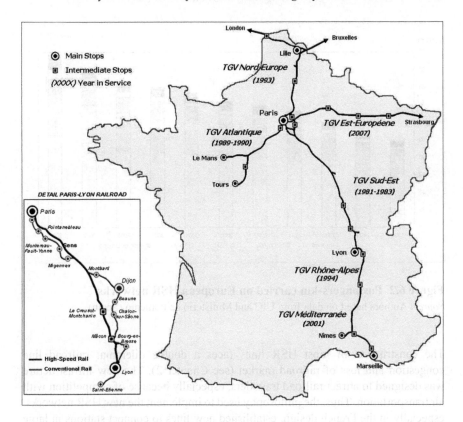

Figure 6.1   French HSR network
Source: Authors.

New HSR infrastructures in other countries, particularly in Spain, demonstrated similar behaviours in attracting travellers. Between Madrid and Seville, which is the route served by the first Spanish HSR line, the number of railroad trips in 1991, the year prior to the implementation of the HSR line, was 400,000, whereas a year later, with the new HSR infrastructure, that number was three times higher. It was feared that the initial success of the HSR in Spain was associated with the 1992 World Exhibition in Seville and the 'novelty effect' (Inglada 1994). However, the high-speed train continuously increased its market through the years, and in 2000, ten years later, six million travellers were attracted to the Madrid–Seville HSR (Guirao 2000). This number of travellers has been maintained with no significant variation.

Over the last decade the HSR traffic evolution in Europe has followed the trends mentioned above. The number of travellers per kilometre continues to grow in Europe and in every country with an HSR network (see Figure 6.2).

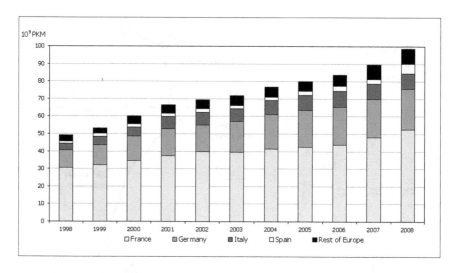

Figure 6.2 Passengers-km carried on European HSR networks
Source: Authors based on data from UIC and Ministerio de Fomento (Spain).

The construction of most HSR lines faces a double dilemma: railroad line congestion and loss of railroad market (see Chapter 2). The new infrastructure was designed to attract railroad travellers, especially because of competition with air transportation. Thus, the philosophy used to implement the new HSR networks, especially in the French design, established new lines to connect stations in large cities or metropolises that are far apart and to travel in the least time possible and with high frequency (Auphan 2002). Thus, fewer stops are available between these large cities or metropolitan areas. The best distances for this system are those with a travel time between two and three hours (400 to 700 kilometres, see Chapter 1) (Plassard 1988, Klein and Claisse 1997a).

Given these premises a theory was developed to suggest that the mobility in other intermediate cities along the HSR line, particularly in the small cities, would not vary with the presence of the new HSR system. Klein (1997c) suggested that new mobility behaviours in those intermediate cities was not possible because the travel opportunities offered by the HSR were not new for trips of 200 to 250 kilometres (around one hour), as these trips were already feasible by private automobiles prior to the introduction of the HSR. For the small cities, the expected success was even smaller when considering the short distances to larger cities and the limited travel demand, which was estimated as a function of population (Muller et al. 1987, Plassard 1988, 1989).

Nevertheless, the Spanish experience with the 'medium-distance HSR' suggests that the relationships for short trips (travel time less than 75 minutes) are similar to those observed for trips between metropolises (travel time of two or three hours) (Rivas and Coronado 2005). This new 'medium-distance HSR' service generates an extraordinarily high number of railroad trips even when the HSR stations are located in small cities (Menéndez et al. 2002a, Rivas et al. 2006) (see Section 6.2).

This chapter aims to characterise the effects of medium-distance HSR mobility according to the mobility patterns that have been identified and the parameters that influence travel demand. The final part of this chapter is dedicated to characterising HSR connection types, which depend on travel time and the socio-economic characteristics of the cities. In particular, two travel time thresholds are considered: between 45 and 75 minutes (175 to 250 kilometres) and less than 30 minutes (100 kilometres). In addition, the different relationships are analysed within these travel time thresholds: small cities/metropolises and medium-size cities/metropolises within 45 to 75 minutes and small cities/small cities within 30 minutes.

6.2 The 'Medium-Distance' High-Speed Rail Service[2]

A few months after the opening of the first Spanish HSR line, called the Madrid-Seville, a new service that had never been used in any other European HSR network was offered on this line: the 'medium-distance' HSR service in the Madrid–Ciudad Real–Puertollano axis (see Figure 6.4). This was called the '*AVE Lanzadera*' or '*AVANT*' and had a tremendous effect on mobility. This service not only reduced travel time by almost two-thirds compared with an automobile trip but also showed improved characteristics such as high frequency and low fares (Menéndez et al. 2002a).

The medium-distance HSR service was undoubtedly the most peculiar aspect of the HSR in Ciudad Real and Puertollano if we consider the small population of each of those cities (approximately 60,000 inhabitants in 1992) (Rivas et al. 2002). The *AVE Lanzadera* service started in November 1992 and began as a result of the great demand of passengers in these two cities. This important travel demand, which was almost totally based in Madrid, was unexpected and created an imbalance on the long-distance Madrid–Seville HSR line (Menéndez et al. 2004). The long-distance Madrid–Seville HSR trains were full until they reached Ciudad Real, and a significant number of seats remained unused until the trains reached Seville. Passengers who wanted to travel between Madrid and Seville could not find available tickets because seats were already sold through to Ciudad Real and Puertollano. Therefore the traffic on the medium-distance Madrid–Ciudad Real–Puertollano route was separated from the long-distance Madrid–Córdoba–Seville demand, and HSR shuttle services were offered. This service was opened with a high frequency, which currently consists of 20 daily services, and with an important fare reduction to stimulate the separation of traffic (0.10 Euros/km for

---

2   See also section 7.4.1. of Chapter 7.

the shuttle versus 0.19 Euros/km for the long-distance trains; medium distance commuting fares are not subsidised; see Chapter 1).

This medium-distance HSR is unusual in two respects: it is more similar to a high-speed suburban train than a long-distance train, and it was the first HSR line in Europe in which the traffic flows were clearly separated (Menéndez et al. 2004).

The number of trips with the medium-distance HSR service has noticeably increased. Although the existing data do not provide accurate information about the increase produced by the implementation of this service, it is possible to estimate the amount by which travel demand increased throughout the whole corridor: the number of trips in 1993 on HSR services (the first year that this medium-distance HSR service was offered) compared with those taken in 1987 on the conventional long-distance rail services increased by at least three-fold. In 1998, this increase was four-fold, and 10 years after the Madrid–Seville HSR line was opened, the number of annual trips by medium-distance HSR services in the Madrid–Ciudad Real–Puertollano corridor was at least five times higher than that in 1987. In 2003, the number of trips by medium-distance HSR trains in this corridor was 1.7 times higher than that in 1993. The number of trips has remained stable since then (Rivas 2006).

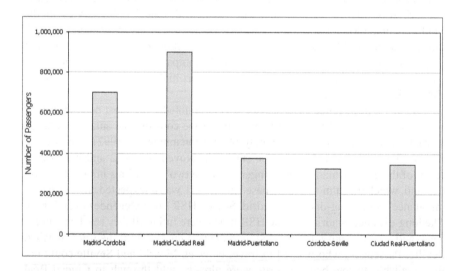

Figure 6.3 Passengers carried on intermediate relationships of Madrid-Seville HSR corridor (2000)

Source: Authors based on data from Renfe.

The effect of the medium-distance HSR service is more evident when evaluating the number of trips on the AVANT Madrid–Ciudad Real–Puertollano connection compared with the trips of the same HSR line between metropolises and medium-size cities, e.g., Madrid–Córdoba–Seville, which are not served by the medium-distance HSR service during the comparison year (see Figure 6.3). The travel demand between Madrid and Ciudad Real was clearly higher than that between Madrid and Córdoba, and additionally, the travel demand between Ciudad Real and Puertollano, which are separated by 40 kilometres and whose total number of inhabitants did not reach 120,000 in 2000, was slightly higher than that for the Córdoba–Seville connection, where the total number of inhabitants was 12 times larger (more than 1.5 million people) and the travel distance four times longer (150 kilometres).

Recently, new medium-distance HSR services were opened in Spain: Madrid–Toledo, Córdoba–Seville–Malaga, Zaragoza–Calatayud, Madrid–Segovia–Valladolid, and Lérida–Tarragona–Barcelona (see Chapter 1, Figure 6.4 and Table 6.2). The implementation of these services is generating mobility effects that are in some respects similar to those described in the Madrid–Ciudad Real–Puertollano corridor (Martínez et al. 2010).

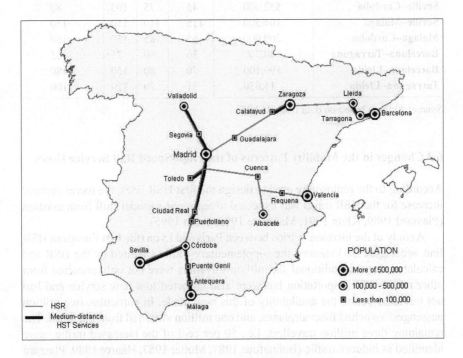

Figure 6.4 Medium-distance HSR services in Spain
Source: Authors.

Table 6.2 Medium-distance HSR services, passengers (2009) and travel time for different modes

	AVANT Passengers (2009)	Travel Time (minutes)			
		AVANT	Car	Bus	Conventional Train
Madrid–Ciudad Real	895,700	53	120	180	160
Madrid–Puertollano	320,250	73	135	195	203
Ciudad Real–Puertollano	294,050	14	30	45	34
Madrid–Toledo	1,513,000	30	55	55	-
Madrid–Segovia	512,000	27	75	75	115
Madrid–Valladolid	400,500	65	120	135	160
Valladolid–Segovia	37,000	37	70	90	-
Zaragoza–Calatayud	45,000	30	45	70	80
Seville–Cordoba	532,000	45	75	105	80
Seville–Malaga	104,500	115	110	150	150
Malaga–Cordoba	209,000	65	85	150	160
Barcelona–Tarragona	40,700	36	60	75	85
Barcelona–Lleida	190,100	70	80	150	180
Tarragona–Lleida	15,650	31	70	120	100

Source: Authors based on data from RENFE.

6.3 Changes in the Mobility Patterns of the High-Speed Rail Service Users

According to the philosophy used to design the first HSR lines, the travel demand increase for the HSR trains was expected to represent a modal shift from aviation (Plassard 1989, Klein 1991, Mannone 1995, Troin 1995).

A study of the increase in trips between Paris and Lyon (the first European HSR line, see Figure 6.1) showed the supplementary traffic captured by the HSR and calculated that the additional six million travellers were not only attracted from other modes of transportation but were also attracted to a new service and had not travelled before the availability of this new mode. In particular, two million passengers switched from airplanes, and one million switched from the roads. The remaining three million travellers, i.e., 50 per cent of the increased traffic, were identified as induced traffic (Bonnafous 1987, Muller 1987, Hanrot 1989, Plassard 1989). Likewise, the HSR increased its market share in the Atlantique corridor (the second French HSR line, see Figure 6.1) after the new HSR infrastructure opened. HSR trips increased by 13 per cent, whereas air traffic decreased from 21 per cent to 12 per cent. Road traffic remained at the same level. However, the modal shifts were not the sole cause of the increased traffic in this corridor. The induced traffic was equally noticeable in this axis. Consequently, these numbers suggest that the second French HSR line impacted those zones situated between two and three hours from Paris, which is the area where the greater HSR system effects were expected and is an area similar to that covered by the Paris–Lyon HSR line (Klein 1997c).

The third French HSR line TGV-Nord (see Figure 6.1), as indicated, presented the peculiarity of joining two metropolises (Paris and Lille) that are separated by a smaller distance (200 kilometres) in a significantly reduced travel time of only one hour. Thus, Paris and the region of Lille in the HSR system are considered to be suitable for the development of commuter trips. The daily home-to-work journeys, rather than a modal shift, explained the increase in travel demand in this third French HSR corridor (Houée 1999).

The implementation of Madrid–Seville, the first Spanish line, produced effects on mobility similar to those described in the first and second French cases. The air traffic between the cities decreased by approximately 60 per cent in the first year, and the traffic generated by the HSR essentially arose from a modal shift (Inglada 1994, Guirao 2000).

Studies of different HSR axes undertaken primarily in France and Spain confirmed what was mentioned above: a new mode of transportation generates remarkable transformations in travel patterns. The change in mobility behaviours is defined by modal shifts and induced traffic. (Plassard 1988, Klein 1991, Inglada 1994, Mannone 1995, Troin 1995, Guirao 2000). As a result of both, the travel demand by railroad increased.

Therefore, whereas the shift of air travellers to the HSR and the induced traffic explain the increase in railroad trips in the connections established between distant metropolises (Paris–Lyon, Madrid–Seville or Madrid–Barcelona), the increase in travel demand as a consequence of the HSR service in the medium-distance connections is due neither to the modal shift nor to the induced traffic. The emergence of the home-to-work translocations (commuters) justifies some of the significant increase in traffic on the medium-distance connections. (Rivas and Coronado 2005, Rivas 2006).

The modal shift and the increase in travel frequency that were defined as the new mobility patterns and mainly occurred for connections between big cities and for travel time between two and three hours are not relevant in the case of medium-distance connections. The mobility patterns developed for these connections have different origins. The increase in demand in these cases was not due to a modal change; it was generated by induced traffic, especially by 'new users', i.e., travellers who did not travel in the corridor prior to the opening of the HSR infrastructure (Rivas et al 2004).

The concept of pendular translocation has been traditionally considered a travel purpose. This concept includes professional travel characterised by very high travel frequencies (practically every day). On the other hand, pendular trips are not present every time a new connection is implemented in a transport infrastructure. Certain conditions must be offered, such as travel time, available railroad service, and particularly frequency and fare. Moreover, this type of translocation emerges if one of the centres is attractive because of its socio-economic characteristics (Rivas 2006).

Pendular translocations, e.g., home-to-work (commuting trips), can be considered a type of mobility generated by a change in the types of transportation available, in particular by the implementation of an HSR train service for the medium-distance connections.

The high number of translocations by commuters in the medium-distance services has been confirmed on all of the lines implemented in Spain (Martínez et al. 2010). They all have reduced the travel time to below 60 minutes, which is the upper threshold for the development of pendular trips from home to work.

Commuters find medium-distance HSR connections to be beneficial for three reasons: first, reduced travel time; second, the frequency of trains that serve a specific corridor; and third, the fare, which can be a determinant either for or against the use of the service (Rivas 2006). The medium-distance HSR services offer a special fare for frequent users, which reflects a greater economic incentive with a greater number of trips within a month; the fare is 0.06 Euros/km if the monthly translocations reach 50 compared with 0.1 Euros/km for the regular ticket fare (see Chapter 1).

However, all of the medium-distance HSR services in Spain are characterised by a significant effect on mobility, which is fundamentally based on high demand and on a high number of commuters, and these values differ substantially between corridors. For instance, the travel demand between Madrid–Ciudad Real and Madrid–Puertollano on the same line, where the travel times are 53 minutes and 73 minutes, respectively, has similar characteristics: service frequency, fare expressed in Euro/km, and number of inhabitants. The Madrid–Puertollano link has an almost three-fold lower total demand than that of Madrid–Ciudad Real (see Table 6.2), and the number of commuters between Madrid and Puertollano is almost four times less than that between Madrid and Ciudad Real (Rivas 2006).

Therefore, the different behaviours in these connections, although they use a similar HSR service, allow us to assume the existence of factors other than the transportation itself that explain these discrepancies. Such remarkable differences are not solely the result of changes in travel time and ticket fares.

6.4 Mobility Parameters

Parameters related to railroad service, including travel time, fare, and frequency, are considered critical in mobility studies; however, they do not provide an adequate explanation for the demand described above for medium-distance HSR connections. The socio-economic indicators of the city, the station location in relation to the urban centre, and the area of influence of HSR station also influence the mobility changes in practice. Finally, other parameters that are not commonly considered in studies of demand may be relevant for HSR stations in medium-distance axes (Rivas 2006).

The parameters that impact mobility can be divided into three groups: parameters that are related to the HSR service that are rendered to the station, parameters related to certain characteristics of the city where the station is located, and parameters related to other means of transportation that are coincidental or complementary to the HSR system.

The first set of variables that directly relate to the HSR service includes travel time, fare, and frequency. The influence of these variables on the demand for short trips is confirmed because the services that capture the highest number of users are those with travel times below the 60-minute threshold. The most important differences between these connections in terms of demand result from the numbers of commuters.

The annual demand in medium-distance HSR connections is considered to be lower than the annual demand in long-distance HSR connections (between two metropolises), but the presence of commuters in the medium-distance trains determines their increase in travel demand, as each commuter makes a great number of journeys yearly. Therefore, the difference in mobility between some medium-distance HSR connections and others is strongly linked to the number of commuters.

Similarly, the fare impacts the user's choice of the HSR mode, although its influence is not as remarkable as the travel time. It is important to highlight that the fare in terms of Euro/km is not appropriate as a variable to explain mobility; rather, the absolute travel price is a much better explanatory variable. On the other hand, the existence of fares adjusted with a monthly bonus granted to the frequent/ daily travellers is a necessary element to attract commuters (Rivas 2006).

The travel frequency parameter, which is considered by several authors as a key factor to describe mobility, is not as important in this type of service. Some clear examples overestimate the numbers of daily service, and the increase in travel frequency does not affect demand.

The threshold of between six and eight daily services indicates the minimum needed to attract relevant demand, considering that the scheduling of these trains is suited to making return trips on the same day to facilitate pendular translocations. In summary, travel frequency itself should not be considered a determinant parameter; instead, a proper report of the services offered that allow home-to-work routes during different periods of the day is necessary (Rivas 2006).

The effect on demand of the parameters related to certain characteristics of the city is conclusive (see Chapter 7). Tertiary cities with certain types of facilities, especially university centres, hospitals, or public administration, attract a higher number of HSR users (Menendez et al 2002, Rivas 2006). Furthermore, the ideal location of a station in a small city is at the edge of the urban centre. This location keeps the main advantages of the central stations because the different urban transportation lines are available to serve the HSR station, whereas access on foot or by bicycle is possible for a great number of users (Fröidh 2003). This location is also advantageous because users from other surrounding locations who use private automobiles can arrive faster and avoid traffic problems, which are common to urban centres (see Chapter 8). The inconvenience of stations that are several kilometres from the cities, as in the French network and some Spanish cities, sometimes results in the need for intermodal services such as shuttle buses between the urban centre and the station which coincide with the departures and arrivals of each train. However, these intermodal services are difficult to maintain due to the concentration of the demand at certain times – by commuters who are medium-distance HSR passengers (Menéndez et al 2006, see also Chapter 7).

The last parameter, which is related to the other modes, establishes the area of influence. In this case, intermodality is a key factor in the growth of mobility because it considerably increases the population that potentially uses the HSR station (see Chapter 9).

In summary, all of these parameters are, on a large scale, favourable to commuters. They differ from those usually used to estimate the demand for long-distance connections established between metropolises at the ends of each HSR line. However, they are valid for medium-distance HSR connections established between small cities and a metropolis. In particular, these parameters have explained the difference between the numbers of users in the Madrid–Ciudad Real and Madrid–Puertollano connections, previously described. The travel time (over 60 minutes) and the characteristics of the city (Ciudad Real has a university and services, and Puertollano has industry) explain why the commuter numbers between Madrid and Puertollano are almost four times lower than those of Madrid–Ciudad Real and why the travel demand is three times lower (Rivas 2006).

6.5 Mobility Characterisation and High-Speed Rail User Profile for Different Medium-Distance Connections

The recent implementation of different HSR lines in Spain that included medium-distance services shows the similarities and differences between distinct connections in terms of demand (see Table 6.2). Finally, mobility can be characterised and segmented as a function of the travel time and socio-economic characteristics of the cities that are interconnected with the HSR system.

Based on these parameters two possible types of HSR connections for travel times between 45 and 75 minutes are presented: small city-metropolis and medium-size city-metropolis. For travel times of less than 30 minutes, suburban HSR connections between a metropolis and a small city have been analysed. In this case, Ciudad Real-Puertollano illustrates how small cities less than 15 minutes apart are connected by an HSR system.

The characterisation of these types of connections has been determined from passenger surveys of different medium-distance HSR connections.

6.5.1 Connections with Travel Times between 45 and 75 Minutes

The HSR travel time between 45 and 75 minutes represents the connections in which the travel time reduction is the most remarkable when comparing the previous situation with the new HSR infrastructure. The time saved by taking the HSR compared with the road system or the classic railroad is over 50 per cent and reaches approximately 70 per cent in those cases where there is no motorway. This aspect, together with the characteristics of the medium-distance HSR service, generates a remarkable improvement in the accessibility of these connections (Ureña et al 2005a).

The Spanish HSR service is not the same for the two connections (small city-metropolis, medium-size city-metropolis) in the 45–75-minute travel time interval. In the case of translocations between a metropolis and a small city, AVANT is offered, which, as already described, is characterised by a high frequency of trains distributed through the different time bands of the day; moreover, the AVANT service offers tickets that are markedly less expensive than those for the long-distance translocations. Additionally, for the connections between a metropolis and medium-size cities, a long-distance service is offered[3]; the tickets for that service are more expensive, and there are no special discounts for frequent travellers, especially commuters (Menendez et al 2002).

A) Connections between metropolises and small cities The increase in the number of trips produced as a result of replacing the conventional railroad with the medium-distance HSR system can be understood by the emergence and the progressive growth of the home-to-work pendular translocation (commuting) in this new connection, which represents approximately 30 per cent of the total HSR travel demand (Menéndez et al 2002b, Rivas et al 2002, Rivas 2006). However, this mobility pattern does not completely explain the number of trips for this type of translocation. The introduction of the AVANT trains has induced new users who did not previously use these routes, thereby increasing traffic. For those who travelled prior to the HSR service implementation, the travel frequency change is clear and can be defined as the increase in the number of frequent translocations, especially by those who travel once a month to twice or more per week (Rivas 2006). With respect to pendular movements, there has been a transition from the occasional use frequency to the commuter frequency.

These new mobility patterns introduced by the HSR system are described in the previous section: home–work pendular translocations, modal shifts, and induced traffic divide the demand generated by new trips and the demand generated by an increase in travel frequency (Rivas and Coronado 2005). The quantification of these mobility patterns shows that for these connections, between 20 and 30 per

---

3   After completing the research for the medium distance HSR connections a new AVANT service was introduced between Madrid and Valladolid which is not considered in this book.

cent of users are commuters, 20 to 25 per cent come from the modal shift, and approximately 60 per cent correspond to induced traffic, whereas the number of new users is higher than the number of those who increased their travel frequency (Rivas et al 2004).

The increase in travel frequency, which is considered an induced traffic category, may overlap with the modal shift. Former travellers may shift their mode of transport and also increase the frequency of their trips when faced with the new service offered. In cases where the classic railroad is replaced by the HSR system, the former users switched to the new system.

Many of those who changed their mode of transportation previously used a private vehicle. More than 60 per cent of HSR users previously used their automobiles to travel (Fröidh 2003, Rivas 2006). The rest of them used the conventional railroad or buses prior to the implementation of the HSR system.

The quantification of the new mobility patterns for this type of connection can be complemented by analysing some aspects related to mode choice in terms of the users' motivation to travel on the HSR and their level of loyalty to this service in their trips.

The users' reasons to travel with the AVANT and not with any other mode of transport become more interesting when the motivations of the new travellers were compared with those who switched modes. The speed of the HSR service was the most favourable element for the former, whereas security was the main motive for the latter.

The users of the AVANT system are very loyal, as determined from the percentage of translocations each traveller made in the HSR system. More than 75 per cent of the travellers used the HSR system for at least three-quarters of their trips (Rivas 2006).

If this HSR shuttle service did not exist, 65 per cent of the travellers would have kept to their plans and made the trip, and approximately half of them would have travelled by car (Rivas 2006).

An evaluation of the transportation modes that would be used by those who travelled before the HSR service was implemented, if the AVANT service did not exist, demonstrates that although a private vehicle is the alternative mode that would be used on the highest scale, the percentage of travellers that would use it is remarkably smaller than the percentage of those who previously used an automobile (50 per cent compared with 65 per cent). Additionally, many passengers would have used the long-distance HSR services, but this mode of transportation is significantly more expensive than the AVANT.

Similar behaviours have been observed in studies conducted in Sweden. The long-distance HSR service would attract certain users from medium-distance HSR if service ceased, which was explained by Fröidh (2005) as arising from the users prioritising their travel time, partly because of their income level. If the AVANT operation stopped, these users would choose faster transportation despite the higher cost.

Most users who travel amongst these connections do so for work (commuters and business trips). Approximately 50 per cent of the users travelled for work, whereas 45 per cent travelled for family reasons; such travel mostly occurred over the weekend. One-fourth of the travellers in these connections are technicians (middle-level or senior). Travellers with more lucrative occupations, such as directors, executives or the self-employed, represented 20 per cent of the total. It is important to highlight the remarkable presence of students, who made up approximately 15 per cent of the passengers. Students frequently use the medium-distance HSR but are not part of the profile of the long-distance HSR trains because of their higher cost.

Increased travel time (from 45–75 minutes), especially for times exceeding 60 minutes, translates into lower demand and increased discrepancies in terms of the number of commuters. This effect is more relevant in industrial cities. In these cases, there is a significant increase in the number of passengers who are travelling for personal reasons in parallel with a decrease in the numbers travelling for professional purposes. Both aspects can be interpreted as the first indication of different mobility patterns in these connections compared with those connections with shorter travel times (55 minutes).

In general, the new travel patterns amongst the connections where the travel times are slightly over one hour have some similarities to the case previously described (travel time below 60 minutes). The translocations associated with the induced traffic dominate those associated with a modal shift and home-to-work pendular commuting; however, the percentage of the modal shift is slightly higher if the travel time is over 60 minutes. On the other hand, the varying number of commuters is the most remarkable difference between the connections of the AVANT with a travel time over 60 minutes and those with a shorter travel time. Consequently, there are also some differences with respect to the travel purpose. When the travel time exceeds 60 minutes, the number of commuters decreases along with the reasons for business travel (work and business), and trips for family or personal reasons are more relevant (Rivas and Coronado 2005, Rivas 2006, Rivas et al 2006).

B) Connections between metropolises and medium-size cities[4]   The medium-size cities (those with more than 300,000 inhabitants) show mobility characteristics that are opposite to those of small cities. The diverse services available in medium-size cities make business trips the main reason for translocations. In these cases, the HSR service offered in Spain, when comparing the long-distance HSR services with the AVANT trains, significantly influences both the mobility patterns and the

---

4   This section was writen before the AVANT services were introduced between Madrid and Valladolid and is based on the results of the project *Alta velocidad, intermodalidad y territorio: Caracterización de viajeros, empresas usuarias de la alta velocidad y oportunidades urbanas.* TRA2007-68033-CO3-03/MODAL (Spanish Ministry of Science and Technology).

user profile. The number of daily trains in these connections is very high and is even higher than the frequencies offered by the AVANT trains. However, the main difference between these services is the fare (Euro/km), which is significantly higher on the long-distance HSR services.

Both the socio-economic characteristics of the city and the railroad services establish that the majority of the translocations are made for professional travel purposes. More than 60 per cent of the travellers who use the HSR trains between a metropolis and intermediate cities for journeys of no more than 75 minutes travel for that reason. However, the commuters are practically non-existent; they represent only 1 per cent of the travel. This is because of the lack of discounts for frequent travellers.

The remaining users who do not travel for professional reasons travel for family or leisure reasons; almost no users travel for reasons other than the three mentioned above: professional (between 65 per cent and 70 per cent of the travellers), family, and leisure (between 20 per cent and 25 per cent). Translocations are characterised by returns that happen on the same day (30 per cent) or within half of a day (30 per cent).

The frequency of travel between a metropolis and a medium-sized city is in accordance with the reasons given above. The frequency is not like that of the commuters and is concentrated on translocations that occur once every month or quarter. A very small percentage of users travel twice or more each week, and these are mainly weekend pendular travellers. Thus, these are travellers who work in one of the cities during the week, especially the metropolis, but live in a medium-sized city at the weekend.

Most of the users of these connections are directors, senior executives, and businessmen (30 per cent) who perform their business in different cities and who do not care about the fare. Senior or medium-level technicians also use these connections (30 per cent).

The implementation of long-distance HSR services between a metropolis and medium-size cities attracts important demand to the railroad and reflects a modal shift from the private vehicle. The modal shift accounts for more than 70 per cent of the total travellers, and induced traffic accounts for the remaining 30 per cent. The changes in mobility patterns introduced by the HSR are similar to those seen in the connections amongst the metropolises (Madrid–Seville or Madrid–Barcelona) compared with the connections served by the AVANT, although the travel time is closer to that of the latter.

The number of translocations generated by residents of medium-sized cities is slightly higher than the number generated by residents of a metropolis (60 per cent compared with 40 per cent). However, there are no substantial differences in the profiles of the users as a function of their hometown. The most remarkable differences in the analysis separating the origin and destination are the mobility patterns generated as a result of the introduction of the HSR system. Both cases basically result in a modal shift that is motivated by distances that are not too far and essentially include travellers who make professional trips and who had travelled previously. Nevertheless, the proportions of the modal shift and induced traffic (60 per cent compared with 40 per cent) are very close if we consider the metropolis to be the origin, whereas if we consider the medium-sized city to be the origin, then the modal shift is remarkably more prevalent than the induced traffic (75 per cent compared with 25 per cent) because the quality of the HSR services, i.e., speed and comfort, increases the translocations of executives from the metropolis to the medium-sized city.

6.5.2 Connections with a Travel Time up to or Less than 30 Minutes[5]

Two specific cases of translocations on the HSR for travel times up to or less than 30 minutes are presented in this section: small cities close to a metropolis that can be called 'suburban connections' and connections between small cities with a travel time of less than 15 minutes. In the latter case, it seems that the HSR emphasises the distance from one city to another, and the characteristics of the translocations, such as travel frequency and travel purpose, are completely different from those of the other cases analysed.

A) Suburban connections between a metropolis and small cities Within the existing cases of suburban connections (less than 30 minutes) between metropolises and small cities in Spanish HSR network (see Figure 6.4 and Chapter 7), there are three different connections that are going to be examined: Madrid–Toledo, Madrid–Segovia, and Madrid–Guadalajara (the other possible cases such as Barcelona-Tarragona, Valancia-Requena and Málaga-Antequera have only been in operation for a short number of years). These three cases have similar populations, which range from 56,000 in Segovia to 84,000 in Guadalajara, and a priori, the effect produced by the three HSR connections could be assumed to be the same. However, the characteristics of the HSR service in each case (AVANT services in the two first cases and long-distance in the second) together with the means of transportation that compete with the HSR in those journeys (the existing conventional suburban conventional trains that are fast and very efficient between Madrid and Guadalajara, which do not exist for the two other connections) suggest that the annual HSR translocations are relevant in the first two cases and irrelevant in the third. In this last case the trips between the metropolis and the small city are made by conventional suburban services. Consequently, the AVANT medium-distance HSR service compared with the long-distance HSR and the absence of other modes that can compete with the travel times of the HSR service in Segovia and Toledo are the determinants for the use of the HSR.

---

5   This section is based on the results of the project *Metodología de evaluación de los efectos provocados por la aparición de la alta velocidad en ciudades de tamaño mediano. Análisis ex-ante y ex-post de 6 ciudades españolas representativas.* (Spanish Ministry of Public Works).

The implementation of HSR services between a metropolis and small cities with reduced travel times and appropriate frequency and cost can immediately generate an increase in translocations by rail; many more annual translocations may occur in such connections than in the connections between larger cities.

The interchanges between cities of this type tend to have typical numbers of users before the implementation of the HSR due to their proximity. There are translocations from small cities to the metropolis for work and study reasons. However, the arrival of the AVANT service tremendously increased the number of annual trips by railroad due to the modal shift of more than half of the users and the increase in the number of users who now travel. Regarding the modal shift and the difference that occurs in the connections where the travel time is longer and where the automobile was the most used mode of transportation before the opening of the HSR, the shift in very short connections (30 minutes) occurs from the use of public transportation (bus or conventional railroad depending on the quality of service). If the AVANT train stopped working users would continue to make the same trips using the transportation they had employed prior to the existence of the HSR.

The low travel times in these cases for those travelling by car or conventional railroad (between one hour and one hour and a half) allowed the existence of commuters before the implementation of the HSR services. However, the characteristics of the new service, including faster journeys, comfort, and punctuality, increase the number of daily travellers by up to 50 per cent compared with the situation without the HSR service. Commuters make up more than half of the users of these connections. Other significant travel purposes include business (15–20 per cent), family (12–15 per cent), and study (10 per cent).

The job profile of the travellers in these suburban connections is more similar to that of travellers who ride trains that operate between a metropolis and a medium-sized city than to that of travellers who ride trains that connect a metropolis to a small city with longer journey times (between 45 and 75 minutes). In these latter two cases, the existence of commuters is the most relevant aspect (Rivas 2008); however, other travel purposes are also present. In summary, when the distances are longer and there is a lack of other transportation options that can compete in terms of travel time with the AVANT services, most of the translocations, regardless of the purpose, are made on these trains. When the distances are shorter, the AVANT services are used for professional reasons (commuters and business) and by users who place a high priority on time. The remaining travel purposes (family and personal) for using other modes of transportation may be economic.

When separating the set of translocations according to metropolis or small city, there are interesting differences. First, the number of users who travel from the small city to the metropolis is three times greater than the number of users that travel in the opposite direction. More than 80 per cent of the commuters live in a small city compared with 20 per cent who live in the metropolis.

The connection between Madrid and Toledo presents a particularly interesting case because Toledo is a city with a significant tourism industry. The AVANT trains are the ideal means of transportation for tourists because they can go out and return on the same day, or within half a day (Guirao et al 2008). The HSR service used during peak hours by commuters is also valid for tourists at certain times of the day, and thus, the occupation level of the HRS services is high at all times of the day. In this case, 30 per cent of travel demand is due to tourists.

B) Connections between small cities that are less than 15 minutes apart   The AVANT services between Ciudad Real and Puertollano (see Figure 6.4) establish a 'peculiar' connection because they do not connect an important city, country capital or regional metropolis with a medium- or small-sized city; instead, they connect two small cities with a similar population (Menendez et al 2002b).[6] Additionally, the time spent in transit between both cities is just over 15 minutes (other similar cases such as Puente-Genil and Antequera have been in operation only for a short time, see Figure 6.4).

This service between Ciudad Real and Puertollano emerged as an opportunity to fill seats that remained empty at Ciudad Real, and that success was due mainly to low fares.

Given that the HSR connection Ciudad Real–Puertollano is an exceptional case, no general conclusions can be reached from its analysis. However, as already discussed, it is a situation that has been documented, and therefore, it is interesting to show the mobility effects that the HSR service has generated on this origin-destination connection, which is considered very 'atypical'.

First, for this connection, the travel demand that results from the service offered (mainly with respect to high frequency and reduced tariffs) reaches numbers similar to those obtained in other connections that are implemented in cities with larger populations and greater distances such as Córdoba–Seville or Madrid–Puertollano (Figure 6.3). Second, as a result of the remarkable socio-economic differences between both cities (Puertollano is essentially industrial, whereas the service sector dominates in Ciudad Real), Ciudad Real represents an attractive centre to Puertollano, which is suggested by the imbalance in the commuter percentages (70 per cent of the translocations are from Puertollano to Ciudad Real, whereas 30 per cent are from Ciudad Real to Puertollano) (Menéndez et al 2002a). The HSR service has reinforced the capital status of Ciudad Real compared with Puertollano as a result of the service facilities offered, particularly the existence of a university campus in Ciudad Real. Third, the travel purpose of the users of the AVANT services in that connection has no precedent in any other European HSR connection and is associated with the imbalance in translocations between the cities, which results from the service sector in Ciudad Real. Of the travellers who commute between Ciudad Real and Puertollano, 44 per cent are students who live in the industrial city and travel daily using the HSR service to the university campus in Ciudad Real.

---

6   It has to be indicated that data for this relation is only available prior to the existence of a motorway between both cities.

The HSR connection between Ciudad Real and Puertollano is similar to a local train for students but is a punctual and comfortable service, unlike typical urban transportation (Menénedez et al 2004). The implementation of the new infrastructure with AVANT services, which reduced the travel time between these two cities by around 60 per cent, has mainly attracted new users (40 per cent of the total) who did not travel between the cities prior to its implementation (1992). The modal shift from the use of private vehicles to the HSR system surpassed 20 per cent of the translocations during the initial implementation of the infrastructure. About 30 per cent of the translocations were commuters who had new mobility patterns. The remaining 10 per cent included induced traffic by users who already travelled but increased their travel frequency as a result of the availability of the HSR service (Rivas et al 2006).

Users of the AVANT services between Ciudad Real and Puertollano make high-frequency trips: almost 50 per cent of them travel two or more times per week. However, the introduction of the HSR service changed the travel frequency between Ciudad Real and Puertollano; prior to 1992 users who travelled one or more times a week were only somewhat relevant to the change in mobility. This is an expected effect considering the short distance between the two cities. However, there has been an increase in the percentage of users who travel more frequently. Before the implementation of the AVANT services, this group comprised 50 per cent of the total users who travelled between Ciudad Real and Puertollano; with the HSR service, the percentage increased to 70 per cent. In addition, it is important to highlight that prior to 1992, 20 per cent of the users between Ciudad Real and Puertollano declared that they would not travel on a regular basis; this number decreased to 4 per cent with the implementation of the HSR shuttle train service (Rivas 2006).

The reasons mentioned by the users who travel between Ciudad Real and Puertollano by AVANT are different from those expressed by users of the other, longer connections in the Madrid–Seville corridor (travel time between 55 and 75 minutes). Time and comfort are taken into account by the users of the AVANT route between Ciudad Real and Puertollano, whereas these reasons comprise a marginal percentage of the responses from those who take trips with travel times between 55 and 75 minutes. According to Fröidh (2003), the comfort and image of the new trains are important factors in attracting demand, and this new demand is reflected in the Ciudad Real–Puertollano connection, where comfort and punctuality are considered important factors in the election of this mode of transportation.

Most of the users of the AVANT in the Ciudad Real–Puertollano connection use this service for almost all of their translocations between these two cities; 82 per cent of the clients on these trains between Ciudad Real and Puertollano make at least 75 per cent of their trips on the shuttle.

The last quantifiable aspect that is different is the number of users who would continue to travel even without the AVANT. These users represent a high percentage: 82.5 per cent. These results are expected considering two aspects:

commuters comprise an important proportion of the ridership, and the distance that separates both populations is small (42 kilometres), which allows daily pendular translocations on the road (by private car or bus) (Rivas 2006).

If the AVANT services were not available, the commuters' primary form of transportation would be the bus, which would accommodate 41 per cent of the customers. These customers would rather keep to their plans and travel because buses regularly operate between these two locations, with eight daily services in each direction. A private vehicle would be used by 39 per cent of the users; the conventional railroad would be used by 12 per cent and the long-distance HSR services by 6 per cent.

6.6 Conclusions

The new HSR lines generate significant increases in rail traffic and significant changes in mobility patterns. These include modal shifts and induced traffic with two components: new passengers and an increase in individual mobility for those who already travel.

These 'direct' effects, which occur almost immediately after the implementation of the new infrastructure, have been identified for all HSR lines and appear in varying degrees depending on the level of access.

Cities that are located at intermediate points on the HSR lines tend to improve their levels of accessibility to a greater extent than that achieved by metropolises, which occupy the endpoints of the lines. This is because the new infrastructure brings these cities very close to the metropolises; the travel time to the closest metropolis does not normally exceed 90 minutes because the desired connections between metropolises are less than three hours (between the start and end of the line). The reductions in travel time are greater in the case of intermediate cities such that accessibility is improved in areas where there was previously no high-speed or capacity transit infrastructure. In these cases, changes in mobility can be expected, and these changes can be qualitatively and quantitatively more significant, particularly when the intermediate cities are small, than those changes at the ends of the line.

However, the existence of an HSR station in an intermediate city does not guarantee that high levels of travel demand will be satisfied. The cases of the Spanish medium-distance and European HSR networks suggest that the parameters that explain the characteristics of mobility when travel time is reduced can be determined.

Three parameters are involved in HSR service, and these are related to the rail service that is being provided: the specific characteristics of the city, the presence of other transportation services and whether the HSR is complementary to or competitive with the train.

Travel time, service frequency and fares are the three key parameters necessary to understand the use of HSR services. In connections shorter than

75 minutes, the travel time determines the routes of travel and the presence of commuters, whose numbers significantly decrease when a time period of 60 minutes is exceeded. The frequency, which is defined as the distribution of service provided during different time frames to permit a round trip within a day or half a day, also influences the number of commuters. The train frequency is a key factor that determines users' reasons for choosing a method of travel. The lack of targeted discounts to frequent (almost daily) users results in far fewer train commuters.

Cities with tertiary facilities generate more trips than those that are not dominated by service-based socio-economic activities; however, the availability of other transportation services that compete with HSR is important, especially for very short distance trips of approximately 30 minutes.

The aforementioned parameters explain the mobility patterns and user profiles in various medium-distance connections that have been analysed in the Spanish network for travel of different time intervals and different socio-economic conditions of the cities served.

For travel times between 45 and 75 minutes, the medium-distance HSR service that is offered in Spain at high frequencies and reduced fares, particularly those aimed at commuters, generates values of served demand that are much greater than those that could be expected based on the size of the population. Combined with attractive fare policies and service where competitive means of transportation do not exist (road travel is twice as popular as railroads), the HSR trains are used not only for work purposes (commuting and business trips) but also for other travel purposes (family, personal and student travel). In these cases, the induced traffic exceeds the modal shift, and it is worth noting that commuters form new transportation habits given the faster travel times of the HSR in comparison with previous modes of transportation. The level of demand served by the HSR is significantly different if the travel time is increased to over 60 minutes because the number of commuters falls dramatically under such conditions. Family, personal and study travel purposes are considered to be similar to work travel purposes.

As fares rise, the number of commuters and work, family, personal and student journeys falls, and HSR trains are used mostly for business travel. This effect is reinforced if the city that houses the station is medium-sized. The increased demand for the HSR services in these cases can be explained by the modal shift in medium-sized city users and by induced traffic of users from the metropolis who, because of the new services provided (mainly speed and comfort), take business trips that they did not make previously or increase the frequency of the trips that they were already making.

For travel times not exceeding 30 minutes, service characteristics play a major role in the competitiveness of the HSR. Although the HSR is efficient, its effects on transportation mobility are virtually zero due to previously existing local services and the high cost of the HSR. Another reason is that although the demand served is high, those served are mostly commuters. Finally, the lack of effect by the HSR on mobility could be caused by the behavioural shift from business travel because users who travel for other reasons may prefer to continue using other means of transportation that are more economical even if the travel time is twice as long (between 60 and 75 minutes).

Chapter 7
Territorial Implications at National and Regional Scales of High-Speed Rail

José M. de Ureña, José M. Coronado,
Maddi Garmendia and Vicente Romero[1]

7.1 Introduction

The reduction of travel times, or, equivalently, the gradual expansion of areas affected by improved accessibility, is nothing new. Classical geographers such as Wolkowisch (1973) and Potrykowski and Taylor (1984) have affirmed the relations between improvements in transport and urban and socio-economic development. Moreover, transport's link with economic growth was demonstrated throughout the last century, as affirmed in the macroeconomic analysis of Bell and McGuire (1997), even though some authors, such as Plassard (1991), started to question whether there was such a direct or automatic relationship between accessibility improvements and economic development in the beginning of the 1980s.

The traditional capability of roads to create activity in intermediate areas of adjacent corridors underwent a significant change with the arrival of motorways and the reduction of their access points. This fact creates large communication possibilities for the network at particular nodes and, therefore, focuses activities on these points while the rest of the territory remains free of activity. The idea of 'tunnels' in the territory makes clear the situation of the areas in which there is no exit, and thus, in principle, no attraction for activity. The concept of the 'tunnel effect', presented in the studies of Plassard (1991) in the 1980s, summarises the territorial relations between the new high-speed infrastructures (airplane, motorway, and high-speed railway) and the territory. This idea was a new concept as, in contrast to the activity that accompanied the route of traditional infrastructures, the limited number of access points to the infrastructure meant that the activity became concentrated at these privileged points, while the rest of the territory lost importance. The intermediate space became less competitive for attracting activities that must make intensive use of the high-capacity infrastructures.

Despite the similarities with other modes of transport, the phenomenon of high-speed rail (HSR) is relatively new in its social and physical repercussions on cities. It cannot be considered a 'plane with wheels' or a 'fast local train', it is a

---

1   University of Castilla La Mancha.

new transportation mode that, due to its infrastructure and service characteristics, is unique in the impact that it can have on urban and territorial structures.

The initial HSR objective was to facilitate contacts between metropolises that were 500 to 700 km apart (two to three hours' HSR travel time), reducing dependency on air transport and reinforcing quaternary activities. The Spanish urban system seemed optimal for HSR because of the central and coastal structure of its major cities and the distance between them (see Section 7.4 and Figure 7.2). Nevertheless, pressures from local communities to establish stations in smaller cities and evidence of traffic over shorter distances opened up new perspectives.

After 19 years of HSR in Spain and several studies on the topic, the purpose of this chapter is to synthesise the research results on HSR-territory interaction in Spain that go beyond direct transport impacts. To achieve this purpose, the chapter is divided into two parts. The first part (Sections 7.1 and 7.2) sets out the current status of the issue, while the second (Sections 7.3 and 7.4) focuses on findings from empirical analysis. These findings are described according to general conclusions and supported by specific Spanish examples.

Section 7.2 describes the factors to be considered in determining the spatial implications and reviews the scientific literature. Section 7.3 debates the importance of the HSR station's location for attracting activities. Section 7.4 examines impacts at an interurban scale regarding new relations between metropolises, medium-sized and small cities. The conclusions consider the spatial implications of HSR and their possible use for spatial planning.

Considering the existing HSR network and projects, the Spanish HSR network in the near future (see Figure 1.6 in Chapter 1) will be composed of six new 300/350 km/h HSR lines (only for HSR services, keeping existing lines running in parallel) and a few lines improved to 200 km/h. The latter will have Spanish gauge and offer all types of rail services. It will play intra-regional roles, although they will not cover the whole of Spain (Ureña 2009b).[2]

As described in Chapter 1, the congestion of the main traditional Madrid–Andalucía line (south of Spain) and the impossibility of duplicating it along the Despeñaperros mountain pass led to the idea of new railway access to the south. This new railway line between Madrid and Seville was finally designed for trains running at a speed of 300 km/h with the European gauge (Menéndez et al. 2002a) and led to the birth of Spanish HSR in 1992. Seven months later an unexpected travel demand appeared between two small cities (Ciudad Real and Puertollano) and Madrid, 200 km apart from each other, which led the Spanish railway operator (Renfe) to segregate this medium-distance traffic from the long-distance routes by establishing new specific services in what has been called a substitution strategy (Ureña et al. 2009d). These medium-distance HSR services, which are used mainly for commuting purposes (see Chapter 6), have changed the concept of

---

2   The French HSR model has new 300/350 km/h lines only for HSR services, while the German model has improved traditional lines to 200/250 km/h and a few new 300/350 lines, both with the same gauges.

HSR in Spain (Menéndez et al. 2002a, Ureña et al. 2005a) and have started to be considered for other networks (France, the Nord–Pas de Calais region; see also Chapters 1 and 2).

Furthermore, during the period between 1992 and 2008, the technology that allows trains to transfer between different rail gauges improved substantially. The new rolling stock can transfer from conventional to high-speed lines without stopping, spreading the mixed HSR services and expanding the benefits of HSR lines to an increased number of places (see also Chapter 1). These mixed services are mostly used to connect Madrid and Barcelona with important cities where the HSR infrastructure has not yet been built. Nevertheless, connections between the HSR and traditional infrastructure are more numerous in France, where no gauge change is needed, than they are in Spain.[3] Currently, the Spanish HSR infrastructure is used by three types of services: pure long distance, pure medium distance and mixed long distance (see Chapter 1).

In Spain, until now, HSR has been used mainly for work and business trips for highly educated workers, especially over long distances (see Table 7.1 and Chapter 6).

Table 7.1 HSR trip purposes and passenger profiles

Relation	Trip Purpose		Passenger profile	
	Work and business related passengers	Most important other purpose	With University degrees	Passengers (both directions)
Long distances (above 500 km)				
Madrid–Seville	61%	21% tourism	69%	2.5 million
Madrid–Barcelona	61%	-	69%	2.7 million
Medium distance (below 250 km)				
Madrid–Ciudad Real and Madrid–Puertollano	46%	22% family	58%	1.4 million
Madrid–Toledo	42%	37% tourism	66%	1.5 million
Madrid–Segovia	62%	15% tourism	72%	0.8 million

Source: Authors, based on data from RENFE.

---

3   Around 20 connections in France but only around nine in Spain, see www.renfe.es.

7.2 Understanding Spatial Implications of High-Speed Rail: Key Factors

High-speed rail leads to changes in accessibility and travel time, which induce changes in modal share and new transport demands (see Chapter 6). These changes are called the 'transport' effects of HSR (Givoni 2006) and are directly based on the space/time relations (Spiekerman and Wegener 1994). The literature on the transport effects of HSR has focused on accessibility and modal share changes (Vickerman 1997, Gutiérrez 2001, Fröidh 2005, Willigers et al. 2007,) and on new mobility patterns characterising passengers and inter-city relationships (Klein and Claisse 1997a, Menéndez et al. 2002a, Ribalaygua et al. 2002, Klein and Million 2005). The latter has focused on metropolitan integration processes and new commuting patterns (Garmendia et al. 2008) and tries to shed light on the 'uneasy' relationship between mobility and spatial dynamics (Priemus et al. 2001).

These accessibility improvements facilitate changes in economic activities, but these changes take more time to happen and usually are more difficult to assess. Research on these economic effects has developed models to establish the contributions of HSR to national, regional and local development (De Rus and Inglada 1993, 1997, Vickerman et al. 1999a,). The economic effects of HSR have been classified as temporary (related to the infrastructure construction), permanent at the location of economic activities (Quinet and Vickerman 2004) and permanent for economic activity in general: greater diffusion of innovations, wider access to goods and services, enlargement of market areas and greater competition (Plassard 1991). Permanent economic impacts are related to the use of HSR and may affect development and location strategies (Blum et al. 1997).

Finally, the literature has identified 'psychological' or intangible effects on investors and entrepreneurs, which can boost investment strategies. First, 'announcement' or advance effects are identified (Serrano et al. 2006, Bazin et al. 2007, Garmendia et al. 2008), which have been also observed for motorways (Zembri and Varlet 1999, Boarnet and Charlempong 2001). Second, 'perception' effects have been described (Burmeister and Colletis-Wahl 1996) when entrepreneurs or citizens state a positive HSR impact on development even though no tangible effects can be measured. Third, an 'image' effect can be observed, which improves the status of HSR cities or neighbourhoods (Plassard and Cointet-Pinell 1986, Mannone 1995, Pol 2002, Willigers et al. 2005).

Altogether, these mobility, economic and intangible HSR effects have indirect and long-term impacts on territorial development (see Figure 7.1), giving rise to complex and difficult-to-assess spatial implications (SETEC 2004). These spatial implications can be summarised in three different processes: changes in functional integration of HSR cities, spatial and urban hierarchy reorganisation, and city re-structuring. The first two have a large territorial scope and are studied on regional, national and even international scales (Varlet 1992, Vickerman 1997, Gutiérrez 2001, Zembri 2005, Ureña et al. 2006b). The latter, on a local scale, are usually analysed by comparative studies (Van den Berg and Pol 1997, Bertolini and Spit 1998, Ureña et al. 2009d).

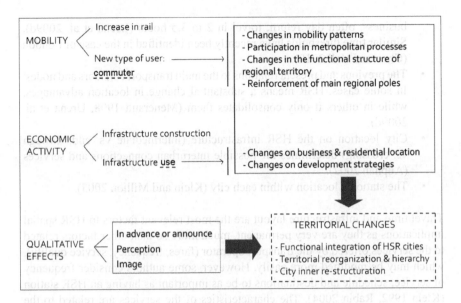

Figure 7.1 Understanding processes and effects of new HSR lines
Source: Authors.

The urban role of HSR is related to the double identity of the stations established by Bertolini and Spit (1998) as both a transport node and a place. The HSR station may become the city gate, improving the integration of the station area with the rest of the city (Mannone 1997) and with other HSR cities (Garmendia et al. 2008). Furthermore, each scale (station surroundings, local, regional, national and international) interacts with and influences the others (Ureña et al. 2009d).

The literature argues that HSR almost never generates new processes but rather accelerates or consolidates existing dynamics and strategies (Plassard 1991, Offner 1993, Givoni 2006, Ribalaygua 2006b) and highlights the necessity of strategies to maximise the HSR benefits and dim its negative effects (Van den Berg and Pol 1997, Bazin et al. 2006) (see also Chapter 9). Given the different characteristics of cities, HSR networks, and regional/national contexts, there is no recipe to ensure research success, but the sum of empirical studies comparing the effects on various case studies leads to a set of general criteria. These criteria can be synthesised in two spatial factors to understand the roles and challenges of HSR: the territorial and infrastructural factors and the city or agglomeration factors.

The key territorial and infrastructural factors are as follows:

- The HSR cities' locations in relation to metropolises (or other cities). Travel time is a key factor (Klein, 2004) because HSR allows the appearance or consolidation of certain interurban relations, such as commuting in one hour (Klein and Claisse 1997a, Fröidh 2005, Ureña et al. 2005a) and

> business, often day return, travel in 2 to 3.5 hours (Ureña et al. 2009d). Similar time thresholds have recently been identified in the case of London (Chen and Hall 2010).
> • The previous and present relations to the main transport corridors and nodes. In some cases, HSR means a substantial change in location advantages, while in others it only consolidates them (Menerault 1998, Ureña et al. 2009d).
> • City location on the HSR infrastructure (intermediate vs. end, through vs. crossing) determines the possible interurban connections and services (Auphan 2002).
> • The station's location within each city (Klein and Million 2005).

Travel time and infrastructure layout are the most relevant factors to HSR spatial implications as they are very permanent, much more so than other factors related to the services offered by the transport operator (fares, frequency, service quality), which may be modified more easily. However, some authors consider frequency of service, schedule and destinations to be as important as having an HSR station (Klein 1992, Rabin 2004). The characteristics of the services are related to the size of the cities (the bigger the city, the higher the frequencies will be) and also to its social and economic characteristics and its location on the HSR network. Travel time and infrastructure layout (which may include the station location, see Chapter 8) are very permanent because substantial changes are not expected in terms of HSR speeds and because changes in HSR infrastructure requires major investments.

The key city or agglomeration factors are as follows:

> • Each city's economic base. Tertiary cities have more synergies with HSR than industrial ones do (Burmeister and Colletis-Wahl 1996).
> • The existence of administrative, office and singular services: regional capitals, business headquarters or universities (Kobayashi and Okumura 1997).
> • The quality of public and private services (Ureña et al. 2006b), environment and culture (Troin 1995).
> • The city's local entrepreneurship environment (Van den Berg and Pol 1997, Bellet et al. 2010a).

If some of these features are combined with custom-made local or regional strategies and an adequate situation of the station, they will be synergic to the HSR. As mentioned earlier, the literature has considered HSR as a necessary, though not sufficient, condition for economic and urban dynamics.

Taking into account these territorial/infrastructural and city/agglomeration factors, and considering previous debates on spatial implications of HSR, its impacts and challenges can be classified into two groups: those related to the HSR station within the city, or agglomeration (see Chapters 8 and 9), and those related to changes in inter-city relations.

To understand the local framework in which HSR appears and the synergies that may exist between HSR and the urban dynamics, HSR studies have considered four spatial scales: the station surroundings, local, regional and national (international). In reality, each scale interacts and influences the others. This chapter deals with the interurban scale, which covers the regional and national scales, whereas Chapters 8 and 9 deal with smaller territorial scales. It is important not to forget that the local scale, including the stations' surroundings, the city and the urban agglomeration, may also be critical when analysing the role of a city linked by HSR to a complex urban system.

7.3 Evidence of Inter-Urban Implications of the Locations of High-Speed Rail Stations

According to their urban location, HSR stations have been classified as central or peripheral, although this classification is subject to abundant nuances (Auphan 1992, Zembri 1992, Troin 1995, Mannone 1997, Klein and Million 2005, Santos 2007). More detailed classifications are used in Chapters 8 and 9.

The convenience of central and peripheral stations has been debated profusely in cases such as Ashford in the UK (Vickerman and Norman 1999b), Lille in France (Menerault 1996) or Lleida in Spain (Bellet and Llop 2005). Decisions on whether a station will be central or peripheral are usually related to a balance between infrastructure/service benefits and urban/social benefits: shorter HSR lines between metropolises and thus peripheral stations in intermediate cities or longer HSR lines with more detours to reach central parts of intermediate cities.[4] The HSR station location debate is crucial for small cities because they often have peripheral HSR stations that are not connected to traditional rail, while combined central stations are more frequent in big cities (see Table 7.2 and Chapters 8 and 9).[5]

Research methodologies to understand inter-urban implications of the HSR station's location are based on the following data:

- Surveys of HSR passengers about their travel origin and destination and transport modes used to access the stations (see also Section 7.4). In Spain, 20,000 passengers travelling from/to HSR stations in small cities medium-sized and large cities were surveyed. Ciudad Real and Puertollano in 2000, see Menéndez et al. (2004); Guadalajara in 2006, see Ribalaygua et al.

---

4   To balance competitive route times with servicing intermediate city centres, some HSR lines have city by-passes and detours to the centre (Zaragoza or Lleida).

5   No small Spanish city has two HST stations. This situation does happen in France, with a peripheral station on the HSR line offering most HSR services and a central station on the traditional line offering some HSR services (Facchinetti-Mannone 2009).

(2006a) and Burckhart et al. (2008); Toledo and Segovia in 2008 and 2009, respectively, see Menéndez and Rivas (2010); and Madrid, Zaragoza, Lleida and Barcelona in 2006, see Burckhart et al. (2008).

- A household survey in Ciudad Real (70,000 inhabitants and 900 survey responses) on residential decisions and the roles of the HSR station and other single urban elements in these decisions (Garmendia et al. 2008).
- In depth interviews of each city's economic sector representatives (see Section 7.4).
- Urban Plans and Projects: sub-regional plans, city plans and plans around the HSR station (Bellet and Gutiérrez 2011) and land use maps.

Table 7.2 HSR station locations in Spanish cities (with more than 10,000 inhabitants)

City	Size of urban area (thousand inhabitants)*	HSR station	Rail connection of traditional and HSR stations
Madrid	6000	Central	Same station
Barcelona	5000	Central	Same station
Valencia	1500	Central	Same station
Seville	1000	Central	Same station
Malaga	930	Central	Same station
Zaragoza	740	Edge of centre	Same station
Valladolid	400	Central	Same station
Tarragona-Reus	380	10 km from cities	Unconnected
Córdoba	330	Central	Same station
Albacete	170	Edge of centre	Same station
Lleida	160	Central	Same station
Guadalajara	150	8 km from city	Unconnected
Toledo	115	Edge of centre	No traditional rail
Ciudad Real	88	Edge of centre	Same station
Segovia	72	6 km from city	Unconnected
Cuenca	56	3.5 km from city	Unconnected
Puertollano	52	Central	Same station
Antequera	45	17 km from city	Unconnected
Requena	34	6 km from cities	Unconnected
Puente Genil	30	6 km from city	Unconnected
Calatayud	22	Central	Same station

Note: *According to Atlas Digital de las Áreas Urbanas (Spanish Ministry of Public Works).
Source: Authors, based on data from INE and RENFE.

A very different situation occurs when travelling towards an HSR city as most passengers do not have a car at the destination. It is also a very different situation regarding attracting new tertiary activities as offices in most Spanish cities, especially in small ones, have central locations, and it is easier to increase their quantity around existing ones. Therefore, a central station is better for people who are travelling towards cities and for business development in these cities (especially small ones).

Surveys of HSR passengers show that peripheral HSR stations in small cities are used less by people from other places travelling towards them and more (on the order of three times as frequently) by local people travelling from them, e.g., Guadalajara and Segovia.[6] This disequilibrium is smaller in small cities with central HSR stations, with outbound travel happening only up to twice as frequently (e.g., Ciudad Real, Puertollano or Toledo).

When the connection between places is improved by transport, some people and firms may relocate to either of the places. When this happens between equally strong places (in terms of quantity and diversity of inhabitants and economic activities), there is normally a balance of flows between them. But when differently sized places become connected, it always means that persons and activities flow and/or change locations in both directions, generally in an unbalanced way. The imbalance may manifest in terms of quantity (more in one direction than the other) or in terms of quality (movements and/or flows towards the big cities are different from those towards the small ones), so the differences between the two places may increase or decrease. For example, between Ciudad Real and Madrid, commuting profiles are unbalanced, with about three times as many commuters travelling to Madrid, but these commuters are less educated than those travelling towards Ciudad Real (Menéndez et al. 2006).

As will be described in the next sections, HSR has created new relations between big and small cities that force them to start competing in a common market. Small cities may lose high-level economic activities to the big cities and gain low-level ones or vice versa. The location of the HSR station is not neutral in this competition, and the Spanish experience tends to indicate that central locations in small cities help their competitiveness, although many other factors are also important, such as economic profile, administrative ranking, and tertiary relevance.

In the case of Spain, five out of the 11 smallest HSR cities have central or edge-of-centre HSR stations, while the other six have peripheral ones. Nevertheless, on the most recent Madrid–Valencia line, the two stations in small places (Cuenca and Requena) are peripheral (see Table 7.2).

In other countries, the locations of the HSR stations often depend on the overall HSR system type (see Chapter 1). In the French case, which is the prototype for the mixed HSR system, with abundant new HSR infrastructure and full accessibility of HSR services to conventional rail infrastructure, there are many

---

6   This situation also happens in Vendôme (France) (Rivas 2006).

cases of peripheral HSR stations that are not connected to the conventional central ones or were recently connected to the conventional rail network. In the case of Germany, where most HSR services use improved conventional rail infrastructure, most HSR stations are conventional stations in central locations that have, in some cases, been improved.

Peripheral HSR stations (outside of urban areas and amongst several settlements) have generally led to new sub-regional agglomeration initiatives. When an association of municipalities existed prior to the HSR, its arrival increased the association's activity, but when it did not exist previously, the arrival of the HSR meant the creation of such an association (e.g., *Communautés Creusot-Montceau* and *du Pays de Vendôme* in France). In general, the activity of these associations is directed at three territorial themes: sub-regional public transport, including the HSR station, technology parks, mainly located by HSR stations, and tourist developments (Colin and Zembri 1992, Troin 1995).

In Spain, the processes are similar, with some peculiarities. The sub-regional leadership is often undertaken by the smaller municipalities rather than by the larger ones (e.g., Segovia; Bellet et al. 2008) because they expect to benefit most from the peripheral station, all the other public services being concentrated in the biggest sub-regional municipality. There are still few sub-regional plans in Spain, although places with peripheral HSR stations tend to prepare them (e.g., Segovia and Tarragona).

In summary, the location of the station is not neutral regarding the relations between cities that the HSR generates or facilitates. Peripheral locations, which are typical in small cities, makes the integration of HSR into the dynamics of these cities difficult; moreover, in Spain, these cities are usually compact and do not easily benefit from a station isolated on the periphery. On the other hand, central stations more rapidly consolidate the effects that the HSR can provide, more rapidly finding synergies with existing activities in the city (e.g., public transport, business, facilities). Chapter 8 analyses these issues in greater detail.

7.4 Evidence of New Inter-Urban Territorial Processes

The most important HSR territorial effects are not derived from changes in modes of transport (from air to HSR) or from reinforcements of existing relations (more trips between metropolises), which were the initial objectives of HSR, but from new relations between cities where HSR has produced major transportation changes, not just marginal ones (Vickerman et al. 1999a). Currently, research has pointed out that the main advantages opened up by HSR for cities (and their adjacent territories) are derived from facilitating two types of contacts: more intense or new contacts between distant cities (Garmendia et al. 2008) and involvement in flows between other big distant cities (Ureña et al. 2009d).

The Spanish city system is composed of a populated geographical centre, a populated band by the coast and an emptier area in between with few big cities.

In this sense, HSR is appropriate to connect the centre and the coast, a distance of 400 to 600 km (see Chapter 5 and Figure 7.2):

- Two metropolises of 5 to 6 million, Madrid in the centre and Barcelona on the coast, separated by 600 km.
- Six one-million-inhabitant metropolises or conurbations, all on or near the coast: Seville, Malaga (with the Costa del Sol tourist area), Murcia-Alicante, Valencia, Bilbao and Oviedo-Gijón-Avilés.
- Four medium-sized cities or conurbations of 400,000 to 800,000 inhabitants: Zaragoza and Valladolid-Palencia inland and Coruña-Santiago and Pontevedra-Vigo on the northwest coast.

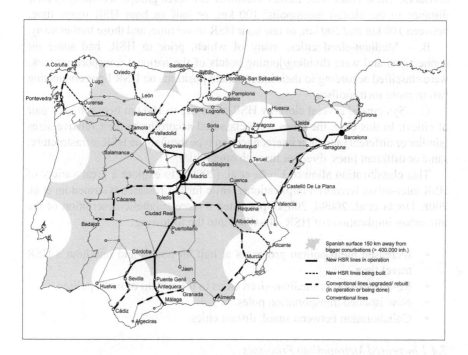

Figure 7.2 Spanish HSR network and city system
Source: Authors, based on data from ADIF, INE and RENFE.

Figure 7.2 combines this general urban settlement pattern with the current configuration of the rail network, both conventional and HSR, including partially completed lines. The figure also highlights the areas far from bigger cities and conurbations.

Half an hour, one hour, and two to three hours' HSR travel time are thresholds for allowing certain types of relations, such as commuting (1 hour) and business, often day return, travel (2–3 hours), and will be critical in understanding the new possibilities opened up by HSR. These new possibilities will also depend on how each city is situated in relation to other cities and how it is connected to the major transportation infrastructures (not only HSR). The HSR services available in terms of frequency and fares may also be very restrictive, making only certain types of relations possible: e.g. commuting is only possible with early morning and afternoon trains of sufficient frequency.

Ureña et al. (2006b) analysed the Spanish HSR experience, classifying the HSR cities according to their size and distance to metropolises and to other similar cities:

A. – Small cities, most of which, prior to HSR, did not have good (or any) air connections, some of which were not located near the main national transportation corridors. These cities were further classified into three groups according to their distance to the closest metropolis: 100 km, or half an hour HSR travel time, between 100 km and 200 km, or one hour HSR travel time, and those farther away.

B. – Medium-sized cities, many of which, prior to HSR, had some air connections and were dividing/joining points of the national transport network, were classified according to their intermediate positions on HSR lines connecting two or more metropolises.

C. – Systems of several close-by HSR cities (up to 100 km between each pair of cities). In this case, the cities were classified according to their relative sizes (similar or different) and their interconnection type through the HSR infrastructure: same or different lines, direct or through other cities.

This classification allowed Ureña et al. (2006b) to explore a great variety of HSR inter-urban territorial implications, while further research (Garmendia et al. 2008, Ureña et al. 2009d, 2009c) presented a more synthetic description of the interurban implications of HSR, classified into the following:

*   Increased metropolitan processes at half an hour's and one hour's HSR travel time.
*   Re-articulation of medium-sized cities to the system of metropolises.
*   New isolated transportation poles.
*   Collaboration between small, distant cities.

7.4.1 Increased Metropolitan Processes

Research on small cities shows that HSR is facilitating a double metropolitan growth process: a discontinuous expansion of small cities at up to one hour's HSR travel time (around 200 km), with surrounding areas not necessarily being integrated into the metropolis (Ureña et al. 2005a), and a reinforcement of the existing continuous metropolitan integration of small cities at up to half an hour's HSR travel time (around 100 km) within areas already integrated into the metropolises (Ureña et al. 2009d).

This renewal of transport infrastructures generated by the HSR takes place within a context of social and territorial renewal in which the conception of a metropolis has undergone major changes. Authors such as Soja (2000) have described the pattern of the new metropolis by giving it the name 'flexopolis', relating it to the new post-Fordist production systems and the decentralisation of activities. The new metropolitan conception has some features that have already been stated, such as the trend toward spatial expansion of economic activity locations, which are added to the fragmentation of company working patterns (Gutiérrez 2004).

a. *Discontinuous metropolitan expansion at one hour's high-speed rail travel time*[7] The new mode of transport (HSR) brings together two types of areas that have different and complementary characteristics. While metropolises have a high cost of living, abundant professionals and high-quality services, small cities are comparatively cheaper, with a small number of highly qualified professionals and plenty of available land. These now-accessible cities are, therefore, investment attraction points and a reasonable expansion area for certain activities linked to the metropolises.

The arrival of the HSR in small French and Spanish communities has also led to an historic change. Specifically, there has been a reduction in travel times to small cities located around 200 km from a large metropolis of around 60 per cent, which means, suddenly, the possibility of being incorporated into the metropolitan processes. Furthermore, there are small cities along the length of the HSR lines between metropolises that have through stations and, therefore, in addition to connecting with the closest metropolitan area into which they will integrate, they are connected to other, farther away places.

Plassard (1991) defines four characteristics that differentiate the HSR system from other modes subsequently assumed by other authors: speed, frequency, capacity and cost for the user. In comparison with other modes of transport, HSR offers some specific characteristics in terms of its impact on small cities and their ability to be incorporated into the metropolitan area.

First, the distance of 200 km as the boundary of the possibility of relations between the metropolitan capital and the small city is produced in a fluid and quick way thanks to HSR, although this distance means certain rigidity in the type and frequency of possible relations.

Second, in small cities, the arrival of the HSR means a major increase in accessibility, which means that the incorporation of a new HSR network involves a major step up in the hierarchy of national cities. These communities, which historically had remained at a modest hierarchical level, suddenly find themselves in a privileged position as an access point to the new HSR network.

Lastly, and in part derived from the previous point, given that these small communities lived in partial isolation (relative to their current situation on the HSR network), with this new rapid transport, small cities can offer the metropolises such advantages as land and labour prices and an environmental

---

7   See also section 6.2. of Chapter 6.

quality that has a great attraction for metropolitan demands. This unbalanced situation also occurs in the opposite case: the metropolises, which are now less than one hour away, offer a wider spectrum of work, academic and personal possibilities of all kinds.

In conclusion, there is evidence that discontinuous metropolitan expansion is happening in small cities with an HSR station within one hour's HSR travel time (200 km) from the centre of metropolises. This partial metropolitan integration happens although other places closer in distance to the metropolis do not experience it. The integration is partial because HSR does not offer freight transport, and thus only some activities and citizens can take advantage of it. In these cases, the cities are intermediate on HSR lines that connect major cities, and they always have through HSR stations. The combination of these two facts means that these cities have more HSR services than local demand would strictly justify because some extra long-distance HSR services between major cities stop there. Previous important administrative activities and cheap medium-distance (suburban type) HSR fares plus high frequencies between these cities and the metropolis have allowed new long-distance commuting in both directions, which was impossible before the HSR (see also Chapter 6, section 6.2).

This situation is happening, for example, in the bi-polar Ciudad Real–Puertollano sub-region, which has two HSR central stations at 200 km from Madrid (see Table 7.3), and in Lerida in relation to Barcelona (178 km). It could also happen in Cuenca, at 160 km from Madrid (Figure 7.2), although in this case, the absence of cheap fares restricts commuting possibilities. In France (see Figure 6.1), long-distance HSR commuting also happens in cities such as Vendôme (180 km south of Paris on the southwest HSR line) and Montchanin (in the Le-Creusot and Montceau-les-Mines bi-polar sub-region, 250 km southeast of Paris on the southeast HSR line), although metropolitan processes in France are taking place at a slower pace because of the small cities' characteristics, lack of regional or provincial public administration and distances to Paris (see Table 7.3).

Table 7.3 Characteristics of the cities with HSR at about one hour from Paris or Madrid

	Municipal Population	Population within 30 km of station	Motorway and distance to it	Economy and university existence	Station location	Distance to metropolis	Travel time to metropolis	Frequency daily each direction	Prices* single and monthly	Year in service
France										
Montchanin	5,600	100,000	No, 35 km	Industrial/No	5 km from centre	320 km	80 min	6	58.9 €/ 287.2 €	1981
Vendome	18,000	70,000	No, 50 km	Rural and Industrial /No	4 km from centre	180 km	42 min	4	40.3 €/ 276.4 €	1990
Spain										
Ciudad Real	72,000	150,000	No, 50 km	Services/Yes	City edge	170 km	55 min	20	16.7 €/ 342.0 €	1992
Puertollano	50,000	80,000	No, 50 km	Industrial/No	Central	200 km	73 min	20	20.3 €/ 418.0 €	1992

Note: *Average single tourist class ticket prices. Monthly tourist class tickets supposing 22 days of round trip travel.
Source: Authors.

- Montchanin has 5,600 inhabitants, although it is located within a homogenous area of 88,000 inhabitants, with a multi-community territorial structure and two main cities (or large towns) of around 30,000 inhabitants, located at 15 and 25 kilometres from the HSR station (Le Creusot and Montceau-les-Mines). Only one of them offers some undergraduate university studies (without research). It is a region in recession, traditionally dedicated to metallurgy and mining. Before HSR, the area was not very well connected to Paris, being 40 km from the Paris-Lyon motorway (at 351 km from Paris and 190 km to Lyon). The HSR station, located 5 km from the centre of Montchanin, was the first to give service to a small city, which is why it has been studied by various authors, such as Pietri (1990), Plassard (1991), De Courson et al. (1993), Mannone (1995), and Bavoux (1997).
- Vendôme has 18,000 inhabitants and is the most important town in a rural area of 70,000 inhabitants. It has several large industrial plants. Located on the traditional road from Paris to Spain, it is now some 50 km from the motorway. The station is located 5 km from the centre of Vendôme. For more details, see the works of Bellanger (1991), Colin and Zembri (1992) and Troin (1995, 1997).
- Ciudad Real is a provincial capital of 72,000 inhabitants with a modern university specialising in engineering and social sciences. It is located 50 km from the southern train and road corridor that connects Madrid to the South. The station is next to the dense urban part of the city.
- Puertollano is an industrial urban area of 50,000 inhabitants, just 35 km to the south of Ciudad Real and is based on a large petrochemical plant. It is located 50 km from Spain's southern rail and train corridor. There is no provincial public administration, and the HSR station is in the centre. The Ciudad Real-Puertollano conglomeration has 230,000 inhabitants.

These two cities were the first small Spanish cities to have HSR, so Ciudad Real and Puertollano have been extensively studied since 1992 by such researchers as Tau (1993), Fariña et al. (2000), Bellet (2000b), Menéndez et al. (2002a), Ribalaygua et al. (2004), Ureña et al. (2005a), Rivas (2006), Serrano et al. (2006), Garmendia et al. (2011).

The lessons from this discontinuous HSR metropolitan process can be summarised as follows:

- Previous important administrative activities in these small cities have proven to be crucial for the process. In the French cases, Vendôme and the bi-polar sub-region of LeCreusot–Montceau-les-Mines, which do not play any important roles in public administration (none of them are provincial or regional capitals), the effects of HSR are less intense than in Ciudad Real, which is a tertiary and university city and capital of its province.
- Travel time, abundant services, cheap fares and comfort are crucial to provide for new high professional-level commuting. In these cases, the

HSR connection facilitates new residential and labour strategies, allowing people who would have migrated to work in the metropolis to continue living locally and people who want to live in the metropolis to expand their job possibilities (Menéndez et al. 2002b). In the cases of Ciudad Real and Puertollano, their proximity and the segregation of medium-distance from long-distance HSR traffic have allowed higher frequencies of travel to Madrid than would have existed if each city had had independent services. The opposite is happening in Cuenca, where, due to its small population (55,000 inhabitants), it has not been necessary to segregate medium-distance from long-distance HSR traffic. Only long-distance trains stop at Cuenca, and the fares are higher than in other medium-sized Spanish cities with medium-distance HSR.

- Metropolitan integration is unbalanced. Commuters who travel towards the metropolis are more numerous and of a lower professional level than the reverse (Menéndez et al. 2002a). Commuting is more unbalanced in cities without administrative or university roles: in Vendôme, with no university or public administration role, four fifths of the commuters travel to Paris, while in Ciudad Real, with a research university and being the provincial capital, two thirds of commuting is towards Madrid. In 2000, 84 per cent of those commuting from Madrid to Ciudad Real had a university degree, while only 54 per cent of those commuting from Ciudad Real to Madrid had one (Menéndez et al. 2002b).

  New activities located in the small cities are based on metropolitan needs, are closely linked to transport, and require large land surfaces, looser environmental restrictions and low levels of professional labour (Ureña et al. 2005a). Located between Ciudad Real and Puertollano, the first private international Spanish airport has been built, occupying 1,000 hectares and accessible directly by HSR. It is able to operate 24 hours a day, which is impossible near a metropolis. Also, 10 km north of Ciudad Real, a tourism development of 1,000 hectares based on golf courses, nature activities and 9,000 dwellings has been promoted by a private national developer. Both projects are struggling to achieve profitability objectives due to the financial crisis. These two activities were impossible before the HSR and use resources that are cheap locally but expensive in the metropolis.

- Local services are being ameliorated by high-level professionals who commute from the metropolis to universities and hospitals. The main challenge in these cities is to profit from this partial metropolitan integration while not becoming solely a place for metropolitan sub-products (Ribalaygua et al. 2004) and preventing metropolitan suction of local tertiary functions and regional distribution. As a consequence, HSR has begun to raise provincial[8] polarisation towards cities that have an HSR station, guiding and reinforcing investment in them (e.g., dwellings, Garmendia 2008).

---

8 Province: Spanish administrative division below regional administration.

Between 1980 and 2006 Ciudad Real became the main provincial commercial centre, with the number of commercial trips from different municipalities of its province increasing by 47.4 per cent. In 2001, the intermunicipal commuting towards Ciudad Real (53.9 per cent of intermunicipal commuters) more closely resembled the patterns of metropolises (59.4 per cent in municipalities integrated in metropolitan areas) than those of other small, isolated Spanish cities (45.9 per cent) (Garmendia et al. 2010).

Also in Vendôme, a nationwide insurance company is relocating its regional office from the provincial capital and creating a nationwide continuous training centre next to the HSR station. This move was also an effort to attract young, bright professionals who may not want to live in the provincial capital but may more readily commute from Paris.

•   The overall effects are greater if, prior to HSR, the cities were a long way from national transportation corridors. The effects are generally positive in tertiary cities and neutral or even negative in industrial cities (Ureña et al. 2005a).

In Ciudad Real and Puertollano, located 50 km from the nearest traditional national transportation corridor, 75 per cent of present HSR passengers to/from Madrid did not undertake similar journeys before the HSR, while in Lleida, located on a traditional national transportation corridor, the equivalent figure is only 30 per cent. The overall economic effects of inwards and outwards commuters are positive in the tertiary city of Ciudad Real but negative in the industrial city of Puertollano (Menéndez et al. 2002a).

HSR may help in attracting some new activities. For example, three software companies that employ local computer-science university graduates and students, which have their headquarters in Madrid, have opened offices in Ciudad Real as computer scientists are cheaper in Ciudad Real than in Madrid. Also, new university engineering and medical colleges have appeared, with a large percentage of their high-level faculty members and doctors commuting from Madrid. On the other hand, HSR may also help to maintain activities. This situation was the case in Vendôme, where some car component and precision instruments plants decentralised from Paris during the 1960s and were maintained during the 1990s rationalisation processes, while some other national plants were closed. The HSR meant that none of the plants were closed in Vendôme. Some of them even increased their research-type jobs[9] due to the easy Paris-Vendôme personal contacts.[10]

---

9   Thales Avionics, which went through a re-concentration and closure of some plants in France, decided to concentrate some of its research activities at Vendôme. Without the HSR, these activities would have closed at Vendôme and been carried out elsewhere. This situation is the case for at least two other medium/large enterprises. At present, 300 total research-type jobs exist in the Vendôme area.

10   Some arguments are from interviews with officials of the Communauté du Pays de Vendôme, Xavier Garnavault (Chargé de Mission au Développement Economique) and Marc Gazeau (Chargé de Mission au Aménagement de l'Espace).

b. Metropolitan reinforcement at half an hour's high-speed rail travel time   The implementation of different HSR networks reveals other uses and concepts of HSR, particularly more intermediate stations and mixed services using both HSR and traditional infrastructure to bring the benefits of HSR to more places. A very recent new concept of intra-metropolitan HSR is being established, which happens when HSR stations are located in/near small cities or suburban areas that are already integrated into metropolitan processes. It is happening particularly in the cases of Madrid, Paris and London. This new concept is not uniform but has different forms.

In the case of Madrid, three HSR stations are located in small provincial capital cities, on three different HSR lines, at the same range of distances from the metropolitan centre (between 60 and 90 km), and on the edge of the metropolitan periphery (Guadalajara, Segovia and Toledo, see Figure 7.2). They have a small number of intra-metropolitan HSR services, much smaller than normal suburban traditional rail services, which only connect each HSR station with a central Madrid HSR station.

In the case of London, all three HSR stations are on the same HSR line, two in suburban areas, one of which is near the centre and the other just outside the greenbelt (25 km from the centre). The third one is in a small city that does not have an important administrative role, located on the edge of the metropolitan periphery (100 km from the centre). They have a great number of HSR intra-metropolitan services, nevertheless still smaller than normal suburban traditional rail services, which connect the London central station with them, between them and other stations in the sub-region of two of the three HSR stations. See Ureña, et.al (2010) and Garmendia, et.al In Print.

Small cities within 100 km of a big metropolitan area are already quite integrated into it. HSR can increase their level of metropolitan integration through the establishment of a new transport infrastructure that usually will not connect the cities to other intermediate zones within the same metropolitan area, but will instead connect them directly with that area's centre (Ureña et al. 2005a) and also with distant cities.

There is evidence that HSR is reinforcing the metropolitan integration of small cities within areas already integrated into the metropolises, which are up to half an hour's HSR travel time away, or up to 100 km distance from the metropolitan centre (Ureña et al. 2009d, 2010 and Garmendia, et.al In Print). While HSR is crucial for frequent day-return travel at 200-km distances, HSR is not indispensable at 100-km distances because of other existing transportation means (suburban trains, buses, private car).

The existing HSR connections of these cities and suburban areas to the HSR network are shown in Figure 7.3 and certainly have different territorial implications:

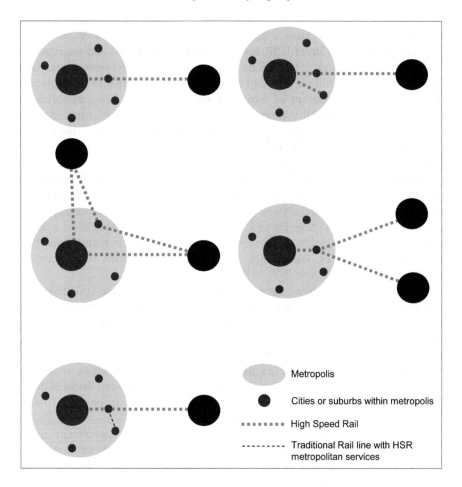

**Figure 7.3 Alternative HSR connections for small cities located close to a
            metropolis**

Source: Authors, based on Ureña et al. (2010).

1. Cities on an HSR through-line: the small city or suburb has a station on an
   HSR through-line that connects it to the centre of the nearby metropolis
   and to other distant cities and metropolitan areas. Examples include
   Guadalajara in relation to Madrid and Gerona with Barcelona in Spain (see
   Figure 7.2), Mâcon in relation to Lyon in France, and Stratford in relation
   to London in the UK.
2. Cities at the dead end of an HSR line: the small city or suburb has a station
   on a dead-end HSR line that connects it exclusively with the nearby
   metropolis. Examples include Toledo in relation to Madrid in Spain (see
   Figure 7.2) and Eskilstuna in connection with Stockholm in Sweden.

3. Cities on a tangential HSR through-line: the small city or suburb has a station on a tangential HSR through-line connecting distant cities, with no HSR connection to the centre of the nearby metropolis; the latter is done only through other transportation means. Examples include Charles-de-Gaulle, Marne-la-Vallée and Massy in relation to Paris in France.
4. Cities on several HSR through-lines: the small city or suburb is on an HSR through-line that connects with the centre of the nearby metropolis and where it branches off towards various distant cities and metropolises. Examples include Segovia in relation to Madrid and Tarragona to Barcelona in Spain (see Figure 7.2).
5. Cities on an HSR through-line with HSR services that serve the small city sub-region: the small city or suburb has a station on an HSR through-line that connects the centre of the nearby metropolis with other distant cities and metropolitan areas, and some HSR metropolitan services serve the sub-region of the small city, leaving the HSR line and serving other places through the conventional rail lines. Examples include Ebbsfleet and Ashford in relation to London in the UK and Calais in relation to Lille in France.

The first and fourth connection types often mean that the HSR station is not located in the centre of the small city or suburb but at a certain distance from its urban area in locations that are more conducive to the long-distance purpose of the HSR line and its technical requirements. The second type, in a dead-end position, normally facilitates a central location of the HSR station. The third type is seen in France, always located on the HSR by-pass of Paris. Finally, the fifth type needs the station to assure a connection between the HSR and the traditional rail infrastructure.

The issue advanced, in comparison with other transportation means, is under which conditions HSR could facilitate the development of these small cities or suburban areas as special sub-centres of the metropolitan area (with high-level office activities), with particularly good connections to the metropolitan centre and to other distant metropolises.

Relocation and location of economic activities and housing towards the metropolitan outskirts has taken place for a long time. In this outward process, metropolitan expansion has traditionally included small villages or towns, increasing their size and transforming them into suburban areas. These areas are characterised by late urban development due to a suburban process of metropolitan expansion/integration and by a low level of administrative and office activities. Only when these suburban places have grown in terms of population have they started to attract some of these high-level activities.

The further outward metropolitan expansion has also included cities that have played important regional roles (e.g., administrative capitals, university cities, public services, railway nodes). In the very big metropolises, such as London, this change happened some time ago; in other smaller or denser metropolises, such as Madrid, it is more recent (Bontje and Burdack 2005).

Some of these cities that have traditionally played important regional roles are now immersed in two processes: their traditional role, which polarises and serves a certain region (or province), and their new suburban role in relation to the metropolis, which means that some metropolitan activities may localise and/or re-localise in them. In this sense, the metropolitan role may facilitate the trivialisation of their previous functions. Being increasingly transformed into mere suburban places, it may facilitate industrial and logistic roles or it may facilitate the increase of their polarising roles as sub-centres of the whole metropolis. The factors that created their traditional regional importance may be very different from those that facilitate the new metropolitan roles.

Ureña et al. (2009c) argued that the question of whether the HSR facilitates the generation of metropolitan sub-centres may be relevant under certain circumstances:

- Cities with a good image (e.g., history, built environment) and high-quality public services (e.g., public administration, schools, universities).
- Within metropolitan areas already used for high-quality office and housing developments.
- Cities on other major national transportation networks (e.g., motorways, traditional rail, airports).
- Cities with central HSR stations and abundant medium- and long-distance HSR and conventional services, connecting them to all other parts of its metropolis – not only to its centre – and to the national system.

Studies of Spanish cities (Guadalajara, Segovia and Toledo in relation to Madrid and Tarragona in relation to Barcelona, see Figure 7.2) suggest that there has not been an appropriate metropolitan territorial strategy in the way the HSR has been laid out (central station of a through line). Instead, there has been a preponderance of the long-distance rationale of the HSR line (Bellet et al. 2008, Ureña et al. 2009c), diminishing the possibilities of creating metropolitan sub-centres.

Meanwhile, for the usefulness of HSR for metropolitan transportation, three variables must be considered: the HSR's capacity to serve parts of the metropolitan outskirts, the HSR's capacity to get to different parts of the metropolitan centre and the HSR station's locations on the metropolitan outskirts in these cities.[11]

The opportunities for the creation of new metropolitan sub-centres in the London area are greater than they are in Madrid because the HSR station locations are closer to the metropolitan centre in comparison to its size, the HSR connection types fulfil the long distance, metropolitan and local sub-regional services better, and the local station locations are more central.

---

11   The southeast/continental HSR line in England recently incorporated metropolitan HSR services that serve the London outskirts to/from a sole central station, while the HSR tunnel connecting the Madrid central-south and central-north HSR stations will allow metropolitan HSR services with two stops at the Madrid centre (Ureña et al. 2010).

Ureña et al. (2010) argued that, in London, there are HSR stations on all types of metropolitan peripheries, albeit on a sole/the same HSR line. Thus, decentralisation may happen in some of them; in Madrid, they are all too far away from the metropolitan centre and on different lines.

In the case of Madrid, the HSR stations (Guadalajara, Segovia and Toledo) have three different types of connections (see Figures 7.2 and 7.3) in three different corridors at the outer edge of the metropolitan periphery (around 60–70 km from its centre), too far away from the metropolitan centre to promote office decentralisation.

- Guadalajara (83,000 inhabitants, 60 km from Madrid) is already integrated into the metropolitan rail network and connected by two motorways. The HSR is a through station, type 1, with a peripheral location (8 km from the city centre) and no public transport connection. Guadalajara is a provincial capital, with neither a research university nor the image of quality. Today, there are no medium-distance (metropolitan) HSR services towards Madrid.
- Segovia (56,000 inhabitants, 63 km from Madrid by HSR) is connected to Madrid by a 93-km motorway. The HSR station is a through station, type 4, located 6 km from the city centre. Segovia is a provincial capital with mainly tertiary activity, a small private university, and has been declared a UNESCO World Heritage site. Today, there are medium-distance (metropolitan) HSR services to Madrid and Valladolid, plus long-distance trains.
- Toledo (82,000 inhabitants, 80 km from Madrid by HSR) is connected to Madrid by two motorways. The HSR station is a terminus station, type 2, located by the edge of the city centre but distant from offices. Toledo is a regional capital with high-quality services, a public university, and some small and low-technology firms, and is a very important tourism destination as it is also a UNESCO World Heritage site. Possible synergies between HSR and offices may appear because of the city characteristics and the station location, while the station characteristics (terminus) may be a negative fact, as Toledo is only connected by HSR with Madrid.

From this analysis of HSR-office location synergies, Ureña et al. (2010) found strong contradictions between the most appropriate corridors, cities and types and locations of HSR stations for office decentralisation, each HSR city having a mixture of positive, neutral and negative characteristics to produce synergies with HSR.

In the case of London, the metropolitan area is in much greater need of office decentralisation and reduction of inward commuting. The three HSR stations are through stations, two of them with transport services to their sub-regions (type 5 HSR station), which strengthens connections of the one small city and the two suburban areas with HSR stations to the metropolitan centre, with their sub-regions and with other more distant cities, in this case all of them foreign (France). The three stations are on one HSR line at different distances from the metropolitan centre, which may facilitate the definition of a more robust office decentralisation strategy. Nevertheless, attracting offices towards the east and southeast of the London metropolis would require changing the existing tendencies whereby the west has been the main destination of newer high-technology firms.

The following paragraphs synthesise each HSR station's and area's characteristics and its synergies with HSR.

- The Stratford HSR station is located in the London Borough of Newham (250,000 inhabitants, 36 km2), just northeast of the CBD at 9 km from the metropolitan centre. This suburban area will be redeveloped for and after the 2012 Olympics to allocate housing, offices and institutions. The HSR station is a through station, type 1. Stratford, due to the important planned redevelopment and urban transportation connections, may attract some offices of the type 'extension of the existing metropolitan centre'.
- Ebbsfleet HSR station is located in the Dartford and Gravesham urban area districts (155,000 inhabitants in an 8-km radius from the station), to the east of the metropolitan area, just outside the Green belt. The distance to the centre of London is 37 km. It is a mixed suburban area of industry, quarries and housing, with no offices. The HSR station is a through station, type 5, servicing the sub-region with a big commuter car park, and, in general, there are good transport connections. Office decentralisation seems more difficult in Ebbsfleet, and if any takes place, it might be 'new highly concentrated activity in specific peripheral areas not too distant from the metropolitan centre'.
- Ashford (70,000 inhabitants) is a city located in an important metropolitan and international corridor and has traditionally been the location of the main railway junction for the southeast. Its distance to central London is 88 km. It is a low-density housing and rural area, with no university, quality services or administrative roles. The HSR station is a central through station, type 5, serving the sub-region with mixed HSR services and also with abundant conventional rail services. Office decentralisation at Ashford may be quite unlikely, although it has recently been designated as a Growth Area by the South East Plan (2009).

7.4.2 Re-Articulation of Medium-Sized Cities to the System of Metropolises

HSR studies have considered the parallels between air and HSR transport (Plassard 1991), but Ureña et al. (2009d) conclude that, while air and HSR transport have similar consequences for the metropolises in lowering functional distances and generalised travel costs, they have rather different consequences for large intermediate cities because inter-metropolitan air services do not add benefits for intermediate cities. HSR services are also useful for intermediate cities because a percentage of them, between 20 and 70 per cent, stop at these intermediate cities (Figure 7.4).

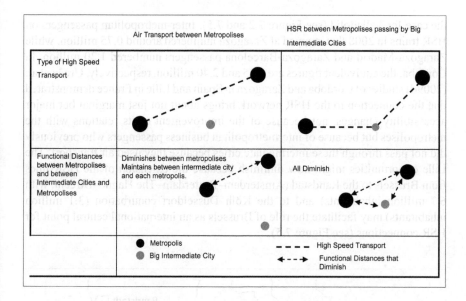

Figure 7.4 Air and HSR transport between metropolitan areas
Source: Authors, based on Ureña et al. (2009d).

While inter-metropolitan air transport has only a minor impact on the intermediate cities' transport accessibility, HSR significantly improves the interconnectivity between big intermediate cities and metropolises by considerably reducing travel times (Figure 7.4).

HSR offers these big intermediate cities two new advantages: improving their accessibility to several metropolises and improving their accessibility to intermetropolitan relations. A significant proportion of passengers who previously travelled between metropolises without passing through these intermediate cities by air now travel through these big intermediate cities by HSR. Ureña et al. (2009d) showed that the number of intermetropolitan passengers on HSR services stopping at big intermediate cities represents on average around 50 per cent of those passengers travelling between big intermediate cities and metropolises.

Studies undertaken shortly after the HSR was established suggest a small HSR capacity to facilitate the absorption and distribution of activities from metropolises to big intermediate cities (Mannone 1995, Burmeister and Colletis-Wahl 1996, SETEC 2004) and that HSR's improvement of overall accessibility in these big intermediate cities was small, given that these cities already concentrated numerous transport infrastructures and that in this context it was generally thought that new transportation investments generally bring only marginal benefits (Plassard 1991, Vickerman et al. 1999a).

In Spain, there are two cases, Zaragoza between Madrid and Barcelona and Córdoba between Madrid and Malaga and Seville, and in the future it will also be the case for Valladolid (see Figure 7.2 and 7.5). Inter-metropolitan passengers on HSR trains in 2008 that stopped at Zaragoza numbered around 0.75 million, while Zaragoza-Madrid and Zaragoza-Barcelona passengers numbered 1.20 million. In Córdoba, the equivalent figures are 1.25 and 2.40 million, respectively. Ureña et al. (2009d) studies of Córdoba and Zaragoza in Spain and Lille in France demonstrated that the connection to the HSR network brings about not just marginal but major accessibility changes, not because of the improvement of its relations with the metropolises but because of intermetropolitan business passengers who previously did not pass through these intermediate cities because they used air transport. The Lille opportunities might now diminish because the extension of the HSR lines from Brussels to the Randstad (Amsterdam–Rotterdam–The Hague–Utrecht, with 6.7 million inhabitants) and to the Kölh–Dusseldorf conurbation (3.1 million inhabitants) may facilitate the role of Brussels as an international central point for HSR connections (see Figure 7.5).

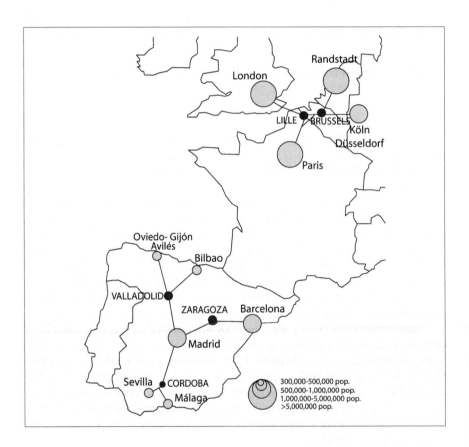

Figure 7.5 Zaragoza, Córdoba, Lille and Brussels HSR networks
Source: Authors.

Some of these large intermediate cities have been located within major transportation corridors over history, with many important economic and personal transactions passing through them in Spain. The twentieth century changed their transport connections in two ways: motorways strengthened their links with the intermetropolitan corridors, but air transport resulted in most intermetropolitan business trips not passing through them, thereby weakening their connectivity. In other cases big cities were historically at the dead end of transport corridors until HSR transformed them into stopping-off points in the centre of a network (e.g., Lille in France). HSR connectivity tends to overcome their traditional isolation from national and international transportation networks, significantly improving their location advantages (see Figure 7.5).

The percentage of intermetropolitan HSR services actually stopping at large intermediate cities is a key factor that determines the HSR contributions to these cities, being a clear measure of their levels of connectivity to intermetropolitan relations. As intermetropolitan HSR services aim to be as competitive as possible with air passenger transport, HSR travel time must be below three hours, in which case passengers divide themselves equally between HSR and air, and preferably under two and a half hours, in which case 65 per cent of passengers prefer HSR (Ureña et. al. 2009d). The HSR network lay-out, whether it makes stopping at the large intermediate cities feasible, and the travel time between metropolises together determine the possibility and practicality of a stop in these big intermediate cities. Table 7.4 shows the percentages of intermetropolitan HSR services actually stopping at Córdoba, Lille and Zaragoza and their travel times when stopping and when non-stop.

The network allows the London–Paris service to pass through Lille station, but the travel time of the direct London–Paris HSR service (2 h 20 m) and the high percentage of same-day return passengers leave little flexibility for a stop at Lille. On the other hand, the Brussels–London service has shorter travel times (1 h 50 m non-stop and 2 h 06 m when stopping at Lille), which allow a greater margin for stopping there (66 per cent of intermetropolitan services stop at Lille). The direct Brussels–Paris service travels through Lille's eastern periphery along a station-free by-pass, making a stop impossible (see Figure 7.5 and Table 7.4).

Zaragoza's southern HSR direct line allows Barcelona–Madrid HSR services to pass through without stopping. Furthermore, the travel time of the non-stop intermetropolitan service (2 h 43 min) leaves little flexibility for an additional stop at Zaragoza (25 per cent of intermetropolitan services stop at Zaragoza). In Córdoba, however, the HSR infrastructure sends all HSR services through the central station, and the 2 h 20 m travel time when stopping at this intermediate city increases the percentage of HSR intermetropolitan services stopping there to 80 per cent (see Figure 7.5. and Table 7.4).

In short, both network lay-out and travel-time flexibility determine HSR's potential to attract intermetropolitan passengers to large intermediate cities and are useful indicators for understanding the rationale behind the cities' HSR services.

Table 7.4 HSR services through big intermediate cities in 2008 (Madrid (Md), Seville (Se), Córdoba (Co), Málaga (Ma), Barcelone (Ba), Zaragoza (Za), London (Lo), Lille (Li), Brussels (Br), Paris (Pa))

	Córdoba		Lille			Zaragoza
New inter-metropolitan HSR passengers through intermediate cities	1,760,000		17,500,000			3,160,000

Intermetropolitan HSR services

	Md-Se	Md-Ml	Pa-Lo	Lo-Br	Pa-Br	Md-Ba
HSR services	Md-Se	Md-Ml	Pa-Lo	Lo-Br	Pa-Br	Md-Ba
Travel time of direct services	2h 20m	2h 40m	2h 20m	1h 50m	1h 22m	2h 43m
Travel time stopping at intermediate city	2h 30m	3h 00m	-	2h 06m	-	3h 00m
Total number of services (one way)	15	9	13	12	19	12
Percentage stopping at intermediate city	80%	55%	0%	66%	0%	25%
Intermetropolitan passengers on HSR services stopping at intermediate city (estimate)	1,250,000		3,200,000			750

Big Intermediate City relations with Metropolis

	Md-Co	Se-Co	Ml-Co	Lo-Li	Br-Li	Pa-Li	Ma-Za	Ba-Za
Services	Md-Co	Se-Co	Ml-Co	Lo-Li	Br-Li	Pa-Li	Ma-Za	Ba-Za
HSR travel time	1h 46m	45m	57m	1h 20m	34m	1h 02m	1h 26m	1h 39m
Passengers big intermediate city – metropolises (x1000)	1,300	0.6	0.5	0.45	0.466	4,700	1,600	0.603
Specific big intermediate city-metropolis HSR service	0	8	0	1	4	19	8	0

Source: Authors, based on Ureña et al. (2009d).

Ureña et al. (2009d) also showed that these large intermediate cities are starting to attract more metropolitan activities than previous scientific literature had suggested:

- Meetings of metropolitan professionals that used to take place in metropolises, which became even more likely if companies already had facilities and decision-making personnel in the large intermediate cities.
- Mid-level business and technical consultancy firms carrying out metropolis-related work, reducing wage and office costs while maintaining their close connections to several metropolises via HSR.
- Urban tourism and congresses, scientific meetings, seminars and related events.

Thus, these large intermediate cities started to play a more important role in the national system of cities, the most relevant factors being travel time and number of inter-metropolitan HSR services that stop in these large intermediate cities, synergies with other city developments, political weight, degree of concentration of HSR and other transport infrastructures, number of metropolises in the range of 300 km connected by HSR, size and the quality of their singular public services.

7.4.3 New (Previously Isolated) Transportation Nodes

Modern transportation infrastructures (motorways, HSR, airports and ports) have rigid criteria for being laid out on the territory (e.g., slopes, curvatures, deep waters, noise) and can have problems finding appropriate paths or areas that are sufficiently 'empty' to be laid out without disturbing existing activities. Often, the crossing points of these infrastructures (nodes) may have very good long-distance transportation capacities but are located far from important local places and may occur in previously isolated places.

In Spain, the planned HSR and motorway networks will facilitate the appearance of four new possible transportation nodes in previously isolated areas that are sparsely populated and far from the main urban areas (Figure 7.2): Ciudad Real–Puertollano, Cuenca, Badajoz–Mérida–Cáceres and Zamora. All of them are expected to gain two new motorways and HSR service.

Ciudad Real–Puertollano is an interesting case of a transportation node in a previously isolated area, 200 km from Madrid and Córdoba, sparsely populated and a bi-polar sub-region with HSR. There are two central HSR stations, one in each city (Table 7.2), with central locations that are very convenient for attracting professionals and economic activities (see Section 7.3). A third HSR station will be built by the new airport (Figure 7.6). This sub-region was previously distant from the main Spanish transportation corridors (50 km to both motorway and traditional rail) and is becoming a privileged meeting place of high-speed and high-capacity transport infrastructures, including two motorways, north-south and east-west (Madrid–Toledo–Andalucía and Valencia–Lisbon), which have the

Ciudad Real–Puertollano stretch in common and have direct access to both urban areas and the airport. This stretch also includes the conventional Madrid–Alcázar–Manzanares–Badajoz railway, with direct passenger and freight access to both cities and the airport (see Figure 7.6).

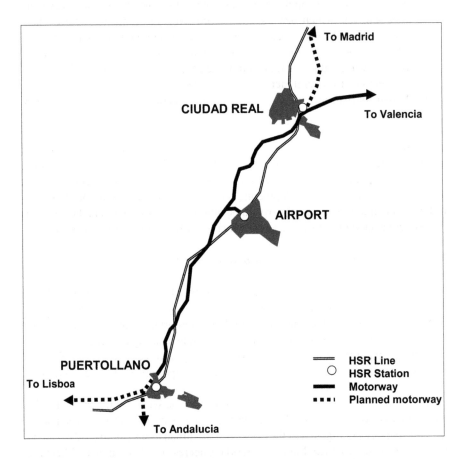

Figure 7.6 The Ciudad Real-Puertollano transportation node
Source: Authors, based on Ureña and Coronado (2009a).

The above case poses a new, interesting territorial situation of a possible multimodal transport node that is distant from conurbations but is well adapted to long-distance travel and to local needs. The more efficiently these transport nodes are laid out to have immediate access to the different transport modes and to the main local activities (e.g., urban centres, universities, hospitals, business estates), the more chances they have to compete with the big city hubs (Ureña and Coronado 2009a).

These new transport nodes, which include a diversity of high-speed transport modes, drastically reduce travel times and open up possibilities for new economic and social relations. They can collaborate with distant destinations via airports or HSR and with closer destinations via motorways or conventional rail.

The long distance requirements of HSR may produce more situations like that described for Ciudad Real–Puertollano, where isolated areas, thanks to HSR, reach high accessibility levels from nearly nothing. The question to research in the future is whether this situation may occur elsewhere or if it is only a consequence of a quite particular case where a private airport was built near a metropolis (Madrid).

7.4.4 Collaboration between Small Distant Cities

Prior to HSR, day return travel was feasible between any two distant national metropolises through air transport, and it was also possible between most small cities and some distant national metropolises through a combination of ground and air transport. However, in most cases it was not feasible to do so between two distant small cities.

Progressively, the Spanish HSR network is establishing stations in a greater number of small cities (around every 100 km in 1992 and now even at shorter distances). This change is opening up possibilities of day return travel and new economic and social relations between some small distant cities, mainly when they are located along the same HSR line.

These long-distance small-to-small relations depend on connection options and HSR configurations (end-of-line, through or crossing point). End-of-line cases will only have as many services as local demand will support, while services in through and junction stations could be more numerous than locally demanded (Ureña et al. 2006b).

This new perspective is similar to what happens with electronic relations between small and distant firms. Prior to HSR and the Internet, most relations were polarised from territorial, social and economic points of view, almost always through big entities (metropolises or large firms); thus, activities located in small cities tended to relocate to metropolises. Currently, electronic communications allow direct small-to-small connections and new economic relations between small firms in an equal-to-equal relationship (Dupuy and Geneau 2007). With HSR, the argument is similar: there is less need to use the metropolises for the relations between small distant cities, and thus the territory could become less polarised and more decentralised.

Currently, day-return trips between distant, small Spanish cities have become possible through HSR. Considering small HSR cities more than 350 km apart (Figure 7.2) and HSR travel between 7.00 and 23.30 hours, the following day-return trips are possible:

- Lerida–Ciudad Real, 670 km apart and staying 7 hours at destination.
- Antequera–Ciudad Real, 350 km apart and staying almost 10 hours at destination.
- Calatayud–Puente Genil, 700 km apart and staying almost 3 hours at destination.
- Tarragona–Guadalajara, 500 km apart and staying 7 hours at destination.

It is still too early to know how much this possibility will develop because small, distant cities with HSR have only existed since 2003. In any event, there are some signs that it is already happening; for instance, there are some new collaborations between Lleida and Ciudad Real (Ureña and Coronado 2009a).

7.5 Conclusions

The HSR network was initially thought to strengthen relations between distant metropolises; nevertheless, it is also useful for smaller and closer cities. The HSR network and services between distant metropolises were initially simple and straightforward but are becoming more complex as the number of stations increases and as the types of services become more diversified. HSR medium-distance services were first established in Spain and are crucial for some unexpected territorial effects.

The Spanish experience shows that the most relevant interurban spatial implications of HSR take place in medium-sized and small cities where HSR has produced major changes in accessibility. On the other hand, station location is playing key roles not only in urban and agglomeration HSR effects (see Chapter 8) but also in interurban effects. Station location is more crucial for workplaces than for residential locations, for small cities than for bigger ones, if accompanied with other synergic strategies and when stations are central.

The HSR decisions in most of the Spanish spatial situations that have been described are taken on the basis of short-term transport demand/supply criteria rather than including territorial or urban planning ones as well. A bi-univocal relation cannot be established between HSR and the attraction of economic activities or the generation of urban developments, but certain types of lay-out can facilitate the latter.

Over and above the strengthening of intermetropolitan relations, HSR can increase the opportunities for big intermediate cities to play greater roles in the national system of cities, for small cities to interact with metropolises up to one hour's HSR travel time and with other distant small cities, and for previously isolated areas to become transportation nodes.

Lessons learned show that better results can be obtained by combining HSR national lay-out criteria (minimum distances, fewer stops, etc.) with the local ones (proximity and more connections).

Finally, the lessons learned in Spain must be considered cautiously in other countries with different spatial models (settlement system and demographic density) and patterns (travel behaviour, commuting distances) because HSR is most useful in polarised urban networks.

Chapter 8
The High-Speed Rail in Spanish Cities: Urban Integration and Local Strategies for Socio-economic Development

Carmen Bellet, Pilar Alonso and Aaron Gutiérrez[1]

8.1 Introduction

In Spain the conventional rail network has a different gauge (wide-gauge: 1.688 metres) to that used internationally (UIC: 1.435 metres) by the High-Speed rail network. Only a few trains are able to operate within both networks and therefore the High-Speed rail network essentially duplicates the historic one. If we add to this the limitations exhibited by Spain's conventional rail services in recent decades (closure of stretches of track, limited services, lines without electrification, poor management, etc.), it is possible to understand why the arrival of High-Speed Rail (HSR) has been seen as an opportunity to change the role of rail transport within the country.

Various European studies have already shown that the construction of new railway infrastructure is usually accompanied by significant urban development at the local scale (Van den Berg and Pol 1998a, Bruinsma et al. 2008). For many European cities, the arrival of HSR has formed part of an urban development project that has not only been capable of transforming the areas around stations but also of leaving its mark on the wider structure of the city. This has been clearly shown in such cases as Lille, Lyon and Rotterdam. Large-scale urban development projects have formed part of both urban promotions and marketing initiatives and have also served as catalysts for operations of urban regeneration and transformation (Swyngedouw et al. 2005). Thus, as previously occurred with the initial arrival of the railway back in the nineteenth century, this new train service has fostered the emergence of a new city (Roth and Polino 2003).

In Spain the introduction of this new infrastructure has led to major urban changes which have been associated with three main factors. First, most of these HSR projects were undertaken within an expansionist phase of the property cycle. Second, the introduction of the HSR service offered an opportunity to overcome some of the historical problems associated with the integration of the railway within the city and was therefore seen as an opportunity to remodel the whole urban railway

---

1 Carmen Bellet and Pilar Alonso from the University of Lleida and Aaron Gutiérrez from the University Rovira i Virgili.

system. Third, it was possible to take advantage of the construction of this new infrastructure to deal with inherited, or previously unresolved, urban problems, even though the majority were not directly related to railway infrastructure. The combination of these three factors has produced some of the most important urban renewal developments that have ever been undertaken in Spanish cities.

The first part of this chapter analyses the urban transformations that have resulted from the arrival of the HSR in Spanish cities. The expectations for socio-economic development associated with the HSR are usually high, but in reality many never materialise; or when they do, the changes that result are slower and less intense than expected. Various studies have shown that the HSR can dynamise important aspects of local socio-economic structures, but this does not imply that it is able to automatically generate economic growth (Facchinetti-Mannone 1995, Van den Berg and Pol 1998a). Along these lines, it is possible to affirm that, thanks to improvements in accessibility, the HSR may accompany or enhance territorial dynamics that are already underway. However, having said that, it is also important to stress that the arrival of the HSR service is unlikely to induce or create new dynamics out of nothing (Bellet et al. 2010a).

It must be remembered that what are often referred to as the structural effects of a particular transport infrastructure cannot be isolated from, or considered without reference to, a series of other factors: the territorial context in which it is located; the characteristics and dynamics of its place; and/or the actions and measures undertaken by the agents that act in the local environment (Bellet et al. 2010a). The importance of the opportunities for new accessibility that the HSR service offers will be all the greater when the actions and strategies undertaken at the local level are coherent, comprehensive and dynamic. These strategies and actions cannot be improvised; it is important to have a clear, city–territory project, with medium and long term visions and coordinated actions involving agents who normally act at the local scale (Dematteis 1995).

The second part of this chapter (Section 8.4), analyses this set of actions carried out by local agents in order to take the fullest advantage of the arrival of HSR services.

8.2 Networks, Nodes and Places: the Impact of the Arrival of the High-Speed Rail on Urban Development

The introduction of new infrastructure inevitably has a spatial effect on the local territory. This is all the more so when it is a piece of transport infrastructure, because as well as the changes generated by its very construction, it also substantially modifies the conditions of spatial accessibility. These transformations are all the more important when this transport infrastructure needs to be integrated within a more-or-less consolidated urban environment. Studies of the introduction of HSR services in cities usually focus their interest on a very specific scale: the station and the neighbourhood in which it is located, whether this has been newly created or generated through renewal (Van den Berg and Pol 1998a, Bruinsma et al. 2008).

This type of study analyses the redevelopment of the areas around the railway station, highlighting the dual role of the station as both a transport node and a place able to generate a strong urban centrality (Bertolini and Spit 1998).

To fully understand the consequences of integrating a new railway service in a city it is necessary to work on at least three different scales: the local scale (urban agglomeration or municipal area); the station neighbourhood, and the station itself. This is especially so in many Spanish cities because planners have taken advantage of the arrival of HSR to rethink the whole railway system and to improve the integration of this infrastructure within the city (Bellet and Gutiérrez 2011). In Spain, it is still difficult to qualify the integration of the railway within the city as satisfactory (Capel 2007, Santos 2007). Degraded station neighbourhoods, tracks and infrastructure trapped within the urban fabric that act as barriers and railway spaces that lack functionality, are frequently found in the centres of Spanish cities. Historically speaking, urban planning and railways seem to have largely ignored each other. This helps us to understand why railways have often been seen as an urban nuisance in this context and why new projects to implement HSR have tended to propose radical or *hard solutions* when integrating the new train within the city: such solutions often imply covering stretches of urban track or proposals for new external lines.

Projects to introduce HSR in Spanish cities have mainly involved combining two types of action: transforming the existing railway system and developing urban projects involving the area around the station with the aim of giving the station greater urban centrality. We will analyse both types of action in Sections 8.2.1, 8.2.2 and 8.2.3.

8.2.1 Transforming the Railway System (I): Integration at the Agglomeration Scale

Remodelling the railway system of a city has an inevitable impact on its urban structure. Changes to the railway system tend to increase its efficiency, improve its integration within the city, and reduce the previously mentioned barrier effect (Bertolini and Spit 1998, Santos 2007).

Covering the tracks and other rail facilities is seen as the most desirable option in cases of city-centre interventions. In almost all such cases planners take advantage of the remodelling of the railway to move railway facilities that have become trapped within the urban fabric (such as technical and freight facilities and railway repair workshops) out to the edge of the city. These actions free centrally located space that can then be used for urban development projects associated with new centrality and which will attract advanced tertiary sector activities (Van den Berg and Pol 1998a, Bruinsma et al. 2008). In this way, at the local scale, projects to accommodate the new train service can become urban development projects capable of modifying the physical and functional structure of the whole area (Bellet et al. 2010a).

When trying to integrate new infrastructure into an existing urban environment there are a number of *soft solutions* (including: the treatment of fringe areas, increasing permeability, constructing crossings at different levels, and adapting to local topographic conditions) and *hard solutions* (such as covering stretches of track and building external lines) between which to choose. When accommodating HSR in Spanish cities hard solutions have tended to prevail (Bellet and Gutiérrez 2011).

Building an external line, which distances the station and the railway from the urban fabric, is difficult to reconcile with providing a means of passenger transport that bases its efficiency on the central location of its stations (Troin 1995). The option of covering track has been one of the most popular solutions used in the major and medium-sized Spanish cities that have received HSR services at central or city-edge stations. Both of the hard rail integration options treat the railway as an urban nuisance whose effects need to be palliated and require important levels of investment. ADIF, the Spanish railway administrator, is usually reluctant to accept such costly solutions. As a result local authorities are often called upon to establish capital holdings to develop and co-finance projects that involve the remodelling of railway systems and urban development projects around stations; examples of this include: Zaragoza Alta Velocidad 2002, S.A.; Valladolid Alta Velocidad 2003, S.A.; Valencia Parque Central Alta Velocidad 2003, S.A., etc. These companies try to take on these major urban development projects by adding funding from local and regional institutions and capital gains from the sale of land to the capital provided by ADIF.[2]

8.2.2 Transforming the Railway System (II): the Location of Stations:

As in other works relating to other European contexts (Hall 2009), in Spain the new HSR services have tended to give priority to connections between the main metropolises (Gutiérrez 2004). In Madrid and Barcelona, plans were initially presented to construct various central HSR stations which were destined to become large intermodal transport centres. As we shall see below, the changes in the railway systems in these major metropolises will generate important processes of urban renewal at central locations, but the HSR will also present great opportunities for other large urban centres such as Seville, Valencia, Malaga and Zaragoza, each of which has over 500,000 inhabitants (see Figure 8.1 and Table 8.1). In the first three cases central railway station locations have been preferred, as has the displacement of some railway facilities to the urban periphery and the promotion of the centrality of the area around the station. As we shall see later, in Zaragoza it was decided to close the old central station, create a new intermodal station at a city-edge location, build a completely new HSR by-pass line and displace freight activities to a new, peripheral location. This resulted in a large amount of urban renewal and has had an important impact on the overall structure of the city.

---

2   Even so, it is important to highlight the fact that in Spain, unlike in other contexts, public capital has been the main driving force behind these companies, with the participation of private capital being almost non-existent (Bruinsma et al. 2008).

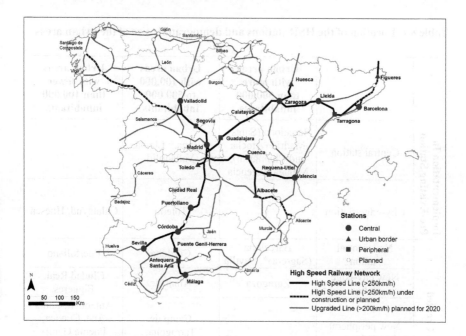

Figure 8.1 Current state and plans for the implementation of the HSR network in Spain

Source: Authors based on data from ADIF: the Administrator of Railway Infrastructure.

As can be seen from Figure 8.1, in Spain strong local and regional pressure has resulted in the HSR network also being extended to include some medium-sized and small cities: examples include Cuenca, Segovia and Camp de Tarragona (Gutiérrez 2004, Bellet and Gutiérrez 2011).[3] The creation of numerous intermediate stations along HSR lines demonstrates a major territorial sensitivity in what could be called the second generation of HSR in Europe.[4] The logic of this regional and territorial vision seems to have prevailed in the planning of the railway network undertaken in Spain during the 1990s and in the first decade of the twenty-first century (Ureña et al. 2009c).

---

3   Local pressure to maintain the network produces situations such as that observed on the Madrid-Lisbon line where many stations have been inserted in order to serve the maximum number of points in the regions of Castilla-La Mancha and Extremadura.

4   After the French experience, whose first HSR network was structured by the great metropolitan poles, in the 1990s, a more territorial vision seemed to emerge, with the introduction of more intermediate stops (Troin 1995, Ureña et al. 2006b).

Table 8.1   Location of the HSR stations and demographic size of the urban areas

		Urban areas with more than 500,000 inhabitants	Urban areas with 100,000 to 500,000 inhabitants	Urban areas with fewer than 100,000 inhabitants
Implementation In Pre-Existing Station	Central station	Barcelona (Sants), Madrid (Atocha and Chamartín), Málaga, Valencia	Girona,* Lleida, Valladolid	
	City-edge station		Toledo	Calatayud, Huesca
Newly Created	New central station	Barcelona (Sagrera)*, Sevilla	Córdoba	Puertollano
	New city-edge station	Zaragoza	Albacete	Ciudad Real, Figueres
	New peripheral station		Camp de Tarragona, Guadalajara	Antequera-Santa Ana, Cuenca, Puente Genil-Herrera, Requena-Utiel, Segovia

Note: *Arrival of HSR planned for the end of 2012 or beginning of 2013.
Source: Authors based on demographic data from the 2009 register of local population (Ruiz 2010).

The major investment required to position HSR services in central locations and the travel time that can be lost between the largest metropolises as a result of doing so largely explain the peripheral locations of stations in medium-sized and small cities and in less densely populated territories (see also Chapter 7). In this respect the criteria for HSR line efficiency have influenced the choice of many final locations (Ribalaygua 2006b). This is evident with a good number of French stations (Vendôme, Mâcon-Loche, Le Creusot, Haute Picardie, Arbois, Marne-la Vallée, Satolas, Valence, etc.) (Facchinetti-Mannone 2005) but also with some Spanish stations: Puente Genil–Herrera, Antequera–Santa Ana, Segovia, Camp de Tarragona, Cuenca and Requena–Utiel. In the case of peripheral stations external accessibility is a key question but not always one that is easy to solve. The problem is even more difficult in polynuclear rural territories and those with low population densities, which explains why Chapter 9 of this book has been specifically dedicated to this question.

However, in contrast to the French cases, in Spain many medium-sized cities (Valladolid, Cordoba and Lleida) and some smaller ones (such as Puertollano) already have HSR stations at central locations, while others (such as Girona) will soon have them.

In some other cases the arrival of HSR will take place at stations located on the edge of cities. Ciudad Real, Calatayud, Albacete, and the previously mentioned case of Zaragoza provide examples of this variation. A further example is Figueres, in the north-east of the peninsula, near the French border; for the moment, this is a provisional station receiving cross-border services from Perpignan.[5] In the cases of Ciudad Real and the future Figueres station, new stretches of track have been constructed parallel to the population nuclei in which the new stations are located (providing HSR and conventional rail services) generating notable urban renewal processes. In Calatayud and Zaragoza, advantage has also been taken of part of the previous conventional railway infrastructure.

8.2.3 Urban Development Around Stations and Central Areas

Urban development projects around stations normally have the aim of creating urban centrality that takes advantage of the fact that the station is both a transport node and a central place (Bertolini and Spit 1998).

In cases in which it is possible to take advantage of the existing railway infrastructure to receive new HSR services, urban development projects tend to focus on the redevelopment of the whole station area, creating intermodality and promoting centrality. Traditional station neighbourhoods and old railway spaces, which are more or less centrally located, are then reconverted into multifunctional spaces through important urban renewal operations. These renewal projects are usually based on powerful architectural designs, highly diverse land uses with a major presence of advanced tertiary sector uses, and multimodal transport nodes (Van den Berg and Pol 1998b, Bruinsma et al. 2008).

The best known examples include: the great Euralille project in Lille (Menerault and Barré 2001, Moulaert et al. 2001); the transformation of the area around St. Pancras in London (Bertolini and Spit 1998, Haywood 2009, Imrie 2009); the central station in Rotterdam and the change in the functions of its surrounding area (from industrial to multifunctional uses) (Pol 2008, Trip 2008); and the new station and powerful business district of the South Axis of Amsterdam (Louw and Bruinsma 2006, Debrezion and Willigers 2008, Bruinsma 2009).

According to Pol (2002), in these urban developments, local agents tend to invest in four main elements: the node, the place, spatial quality, and image. Investment in nodes usually focuses on: improving the station (especially with regard to its transport function), guaranteeing good (internal and external)

---

5   These services run through the Pertús tunnel, under the eastern foothills of the Pyrenean mountain range that separates France from Spain. The Perpignan–Figueres stretch came into service in December 2010, though the high-speed-line to Barcelona has yet to be completed. In Figueres, a provisional station has been built on the new stretch of the high speed line that runs along the edge of the urban nucleus.

accessibility and promoting intermodality. In such cases, the objective is to reinforce the role of the nodal function and to improve its connectivity with other transport networks (Bertolini and Spit 1998). Investment to promote greater centrality implies the creation of infrastructure and services and taking other measures required to attract new uses and activities to the zone. Investment in the urban fabric tends to concentrate on improving the quality of the urban environment around the station and above all the surrounding buildings and public spaces. Finally, it is also important to stress that local agents use the arrival of HSR as an important urban marketing tool. These four elements tend to be present in all urban local development strategies associated with HSR projects and help to promote *centrality*.

As we shall see later when we examine station-area redevelopment projects, in Spain non-railway private uses have tended to occupy the land around stations both densely and intensively. This contrasts starkly with the general practice in France, where attempts have been made to conserve much of the original railway land. This Spanish practice may, however, have repercussions, as the options for future rail projects may be limited. Furthermore, in Spain a good deal of the new land made available by railway redevelopment schemes has been dedicated to residential uses that do not contribute to the centrality bestowed by the transport node (Ribalaygua 2004, Ureña et al. 2009d). Residential uses have been the main protagonists in the urban development projects undertaken in Cordoba, Seville, Zaragoza and Ciudad Real. These are projects that have either been completed or which are now quite advanced. Residential uses have also been the main protagonist in the partially completed development around the new peripheral station of Guadalajara and they are also predicted to play an important role at the peripherally located Camp de Tarragona station (Bellet and Gutiérrez 2011) (see Table 8.1).

In Spain it is only in the largest metropolitan agglomerations (Madrid and Barcelona) and some of the major cities (particularly Zaragoza) that there are plans to locate amenities and advanced tertiary sector activities around HSR stations that may help to reinforce the centrality of these locations. The strong presence of residential uses can be explained by the fact that the projects in question were planned and carried out at times that coincided with a property boom that was particularly associated with the housing sector in Spain. We have already mentioned how projects for accommodating the HSR in Spain have tended to favour harder solutions for integrating rail services within cities, which require important levels of investment. These choices were originally influenced by the capital gains expected from the sale of urban land, following the freeing of former railway land (and the subsequent displacement of old railway activities to new locations on the urban periphery), which were expected to cover most of the project costs. However, the present economic crisis, which has hit the property sector particularly hard, has produced serious doubts about the future of many of these urban development projects. In many cases, including those of Valladolid, Zaragoza, Madrid and Barcelona, complex rail and urban development operations have effectively been paralysed as a result of the crisis.

8.3 The Introduction of the High-Speed Rail System into the Urban Environment: Rail Transformations and their Impact on Urban Structure

As previously mentioned, in many cases, the introduction of the HSR in the urban environment has implied reshaping the urban railway system (Bellet and Gutiérrez 2011). In each case the proposed reshaping has influenced railway-related issues but has also brought changes to the structures, forms and landscapes of the cities and territories that have received this infrastructure. In this section we should underline the fact that there is a clear relationship between the transformation of the new railway system introduced into the territory by the arrival of the HSR and its spatial effects or impacts. To this end we have tried to relate three variables: the level of transformation of the railway system; the spatial scale affected; and the magnitude of the urban development operations in question (see Table 8.2). The relationship between these three variables produces three different situations which we shall further consider in the next section:

- Firstly, in those territories in which a completely new rail system has to be constructed in order to introduce the HSR, its spatial impact tends to cause significant changes to the overall urban structure and may even affect its sub-regional structure.
- Secondly, in cases in which the HSR project has been implemented through less deep-seated transformations of the original railway system, the most intense spatial impact usually occurs at the local scale and affects specific areas that are subjected to intense processes of renewal. In such cases the arrival of the HSR can be used as an opportunity to redefine the relationship between the city and the railway. For this reason the HSR has become the driving force behind many important urban development projects.
- Thirdly, there are the smaller-scale railway and urban development projects. These projects basically involve adapting the existing station in preparation for the HSR, improving the integration of rail infrastructure within the existing urban fabric, and – in some case – reinforcing centrality.

Table 8.2 Level of transformation of the railway system and urban change in HSR Spanish cities

Level of transformation of the railway system	Spatial scale associated with the introduction of the HSR	Urban development operations	Type of HSR station	Spanish examples
(1) New railway system	Metropolitan or regional	Possible development of new urban land	A/ New station on the periphery	Camp de Tarragona, Cuenca, Guadalajara, Segovia, Requena-Utiel, Antequera-Santa Ana and Puente Genil-Herrera,
		New urban structure	B/ New city-edge station	Ciudad Real and Figueres
(2) Transformation of the railway system	A/ Impact on the structure of the whole urban area	Large-scale urban redevelopment operations	Central station (new in some cases). Tangential in the case of Zaragoza.	Valladolid and Zaragoza
	B/ Basically around the station	Urban redevelopment projects around the station		Madrid (Atocha and Chamartín), Barcelona (Sants and Sagrera), Valencia and Sevilla
(3) Redevelopment of the station area without modifying the railway system	Around the station	Variable (either small-scale or no operations around the station)	Central station. City-edge station in the case of Albacete, Calatayud and Toledo.	Malaga, Cordoba, Lleida, Calatayud, Puertollano, Toledo and Albacete.

Source: Authors.

8.3.1 The Construction of a new Railway System with Peripheral or City-Edge High-Speed Rail Stations

In some specific cases, and especially in those of small and medium-sized cities, the introduction of the HSR is often associated with the construction of a new urban railway system. In these spatial contexts the criteria for using the HSR line to unite the largest metropolitan poles impose their needs on the logic of the existing urban/territorial structure (Vickerman et al. 1999a, Gutiérrez 2004). New HSR stations must therefore be located along the line and this implies the creation of new peripheral or city-edge stations. In the case of peripheral stations this deployment model is often developed in isolation from that of the pre-existing conventional railway network and to the detriment of intermodality.

The new peripheral and city-edge stations act as new metropolitan nodes that can capture travellers from a wide territory (see Chapter 9). Providing these locations with adequate access is one of the main challenges facing this type of station. Having said that it is also important to stress that the results achieved in this respect have varied enormously; they have largely depended on specific territorial contexts and on the measures, or actions, undertaken by local agents (Bellet et al. 2010a).

When these stations are located on the urban periphery this usually offers the advantage of large swathes of land available for development. In France HSR stations located on the urban periphery have, in some cases, favoured new developments and activities in their immediate surroundings and especially those involving advanced tertiary sector activities. Nevertheless, and as previously mentioned, in Spain most of the land developed (or earmarked for development) has been destined for residential uses (Ureña et al. 2009d).

We should also stress that not all of Spain's peripherally located HSR stations are the same, nor do they all respond to the same spatial logic:

- The most frequent situation in the case of small or medium-sized cities is for the station to be located 5 to 10 km from the city centre. This is the case with the peripherally located HSR stations near Cuenca, Guadalajara and Segovia.
- A second scenario is the creation of a peripheral station in a territory with a low density of population, which is often in a rural environment that lacks any major urban polarity. In these cases the location of the HSR station on a stretch of high speed line allows the possible creation of a new centrality within a weakly polarised territory. This is the case with Antequera–Santa Ana, Puente Genil–Herrera and Requena–Utiel.
- Finally, the third case is that of the Camp de Tarragona station. This serves a relatively small metropolitan region with around 400,000 inhabitants which is characterised by the scattered nature of its population within a polynuclear urban system. The station is located on a stretch of track on the Madrid–Barcelona HSR line and lies to the north of the two main urban poles in the region: it is 10 km from Tarragona and 15 km from Reus.

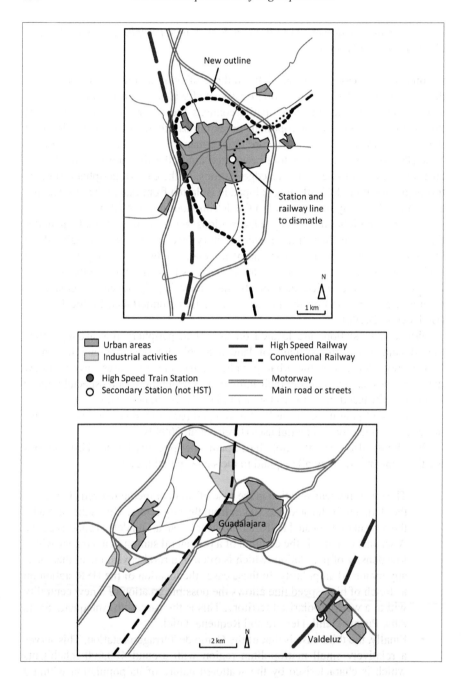

Figure 8.2 The HSR in Figueres and Guadalajara
Source: Authors.

In the case of Guadalajara, on the Madrid–Barcelona HSR line, the technical logic of the infrastructure has clearly prevailed over any territorial logic. In fact an urban development project was approved after the decision to create a new peripheral HSR station; this project has therefore generated a new territorial scenario. The Guadalajara–Yebes HSR station (which came into service in 2003) is located about 8 km from the urban centre of Guadalajara (see Figure 8.2). In fact, the city and the station are also separated by topographical and environmental barriers which make it difficult to imagine any possible physical link between the city and the new station area.

An important property development was planned for the area around the new HSR station, including the possible construction of a completely new small city: Valdeluz. The initial urban development plan foresaw the construction of 9,500 housing units in four phases which were to house 30,000 people; there were also plans for industrial and tertiary sector activities and for the provision of amenities (including a golf course). From its inception this project was intimately linked to the existence of the new HSR station and to the fact that Madrid would be only 20 minutes away by the new train service. However, the property project has not come up to expectations and there are currently only 453 inhabitants (data source: National Institute for Statistics, 2009). Furthermore, the project has not been built as originally planned, particularly with regard to the provision of associated services and amenities. To date, the use of the new HSR station has been rather limited, largely because the centre of Guadalajara houses a conventional railway station which already offers very good connections to Madrid.

The Camp de Tarragona station is located on the Madrid–Barcelona HSR line which came into service in December 2006 (see Figure 8.3). It is located between two small nuclei (La Secuita and Perafort) in an intermediate space that forms part of an extended and rather dispersed urban system that lies 10 km to the north of Tarragona and is 15 km from Reus. The creation of this new HSR station forms part of a much wider railway strategy for this territory. As well as the Camp de Tarragona station, this project also foresees a new intermodal station to the south of Reus airport, which will be located within the Mediterranean HSR corridor.

Accessibility has become one of the main problems of the Camp de Tarragona HSR station. The local access roads present notable shortcomings and there is a rather restricted supply of public transport. Furthermore, it is very difficult to structure the supply of public transport due to the large number of (small and scattered) nuclei to which services must be provided. As a result there are plans to create an interurban tram/railway network at some time in the future (*Tramcamp*); this will make use of part of the area's conventional railway network. Around the new station plans have been projected for a significant level of land development (about 85 hectares) for social housing (950 housing units) and for activities associated with the knowledge society and new technologies.

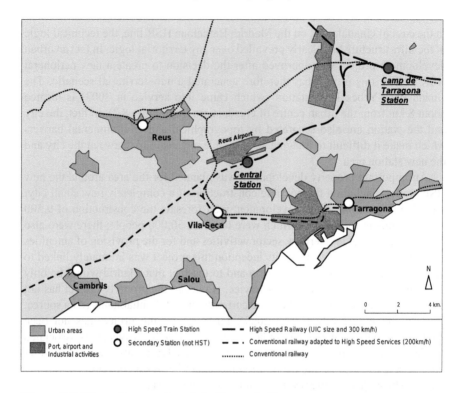

Figure 8.3 The railway network in Camp de Tarragona
Source: Authors.

In other cases, the construction of a new railway system has occupied sites on the edge of the main urban nucleus of the territory. This has already occurred in Ciudad Real and will be the case in Figueres. When this happens the construction of the HSR system is generally accompanied by the dismantling of centrally-located traditional railway infrastructure (conventional railway lines within the urban stretch of the system, old railway stations, freight stations, etc). In Ciudad Real this operation has already been completed. In Figueres the conventional centrally-located railway infrastructure has not yet been dismantled and remains operational, but this system is not connected to the new (provisional) HSR station. The new Figueres HSR station (which, in the near future, will provide both HSR and conventional services) is located on a new line that runs along the western edge of the city. Such displacements can help to overcome historical barriers that were previously created by railways crossing these cities (see Figure 8.2). They also offer a good opportunity to consolidate a new urban structure.

In Ciudad Real the construction of the new railway system was completed in 1992 and became a major instrument for urban development and planning. The new stretch of railway track, which runs around the edge of the city, involved the closure of the original station and the dismantling of the centrally located railway infrastructure that had been in service since 1861. The construction of the new external line made it possible to free centrally located land (17.5 Ha) from railway uses, remove railway barriers and create a completely new urban structure (Bellet 2000b, González et al. 2005). Through a project which was approved in 1992, the old railway land in the centre of the city was redeveloped with residential uses (900 housing units), an urban park and a new road network. This urban project led to improved connections between the centre and south of the city. Even so, there was a lack of provision for local needs and the newly available land around the HSR station was not effectively organised to help consolidate its new centrality (Ureña et al. 2001, Ribalaygua 2005).

In Figueres, a new external line has been constructed to the west of the city but, at least for the moment, this is only for HSR services. A provisional station has also been built on this stretch of track to house new services and provide connections with France (which came into service in December 2010).[6] In the future, when the old central railway infrastructure (which is now only used for conventional rail services) has been dismantled, the new intermodal station – whose station is 2.5 km from the old one – will provide all rail services (HSR and conventional). The new stretch of track and the future intermodal station will therefore be the motors behind a process that will bring important changes to the existing urban structure. This will also imply the total disappearance of railway land in the centre of the city. On the edge of the city, and around the new station, there are plans to generate a new urban centrality that should help to regenerate one of the most run down parts of the city. There are also plans to build a *Rambla* (tree-lined walkway) that will connect the new station to the centre of the city.

8.3.2 The Transformation of the Railway System as a Motor for Major Urban Redevelopment Projects

In major urban nodes (metropolises and very large cities) the HSR has taken advantage of much of the existing railway system to reach into the centre of cities. In general these interventions have tended to centre around: the construction of external by-passes and/or the completion of rail rings; the relocation of spatially extensive railway uses (workshops, railway freight areas, etc.) to the edge of the city; the conversion of railway terminals into through-stations; the conversion of stations into intermodal centres; and the creation of areas of urban centrality.

This is, or soon will be, the case in cities such as Madrid, Barcelona, Valencia, Seville, Zaragoza and Valladolid. Although the introduction of HSR will produce

---

6   These services run through the Pertús tunnel and under the eastern foothills of the Pyrenean mountain range that separates France from Spain. The Perpignan–Figueres stretch came into service in December 2010, though the high-speed-line to Barcelona has yet to be completed. In Figueres, a provisional station has been built on the new stretch of the high speed line that runs along the edge of the urban nucleus.

uneven results in terms of urban development, these actions – which imply major transformations to existing railway systems – usually have a major impact on the urban structure. In contrast, actions that prepare the system to receive the HSR service without excessively modifying the existing set up tend to have a smaller impact upon urban structure, and urban change tends to be much more centred on and around the station area itself.

The station becomes a dynamising element for its immediate surroundings and the driving force for urban renewal that may be more or less intense, according to each specific case. For this to happen, the station – as well as the new (advanced tertiary and housing) uses created around it – may be subject to a series of physical and functional transformations that are not necessarily directly linked to transport services; these include hosting business and leisure activities.

The HSR has therefore become a major tool of urban planning and development that can drive important processes of urban change. Railway transformations reinforce city projects, help to boost historical centralities, structure neighbourhoods and/or act as motors for the development of areas of new centrality. Financing these large-scale urban development projects has tended to depend on the income associated with the sale and reuse of former railway land. As a result, the recent property cycle crisis may call into question the viability of some unfinished and currently planned projects.

The examples of Zaragoza and Valladolid are particularly interesting because they are cases in which both the transformation of the urban railway and the associated urban development actions have had an impact upon the whole urban structure. In Zaragoza the introduction of the HSR infrastructure (which arrived in October 2003) has directly affected 114 ha of centrally located and city-edge land.[7] The displacement of the freight station, now located to the west of the city, and the new railway by-pass (for HSR and conventional services), which was built to the south for through traffic, have permitted the construction of the new intermodal Zaragoza-Delicias station. This intermodal station has also received conventional rail services from the former central station, which has now been dismantled (see Figure 8.4). The area around the old station (9.7 ha) has been the subject of an intensive urban renewal project, with the interventions undertaken having made it possible to pursue a wide range of ambitious urban development strategies: eliminating railway barriers in the eastern part of the city; creating a mixed-uses area for promoting the information society and new technologies on the site of the former station; opening the city towards the river; providing the city with large areas of open space; and adding important urban amenities (Alonso and Bellet 2009, Ureña et al. 2009d).

---

7   In 2002, a limited liability company, called Zaragoza Alta Velocidad, was set up with public capital provided by Spain's Ministerio de Fomento and the local administrations. This company has been responsible for transforming the railway in Zaragoza. Its objectives are to manage the urban development of former railway land destined for reuse and to construct new infrastructure. The initial budget for the project was € 661 million, though the final cost has already exceeded € 1,200 million. This, together with the economic crisis, has made financing the project very difficult.

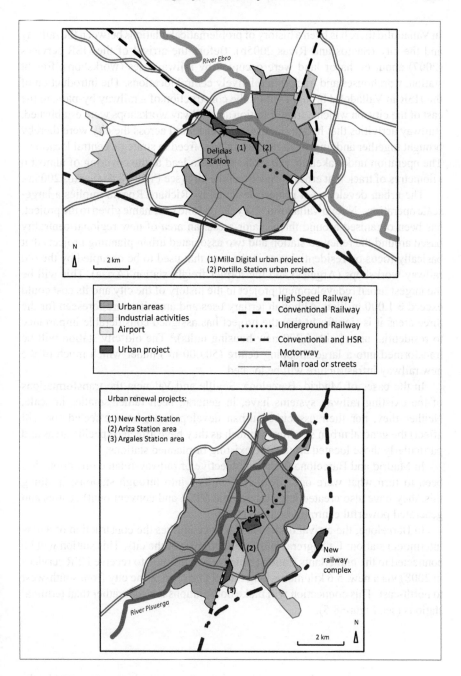

Figure 8.4 The HSR in Zaragoza and Valladolid
Source: Authors.

In Valladolid there has been a history of problematical relations between the railway and the city (Santos and Rivas 2005b). Before the arrival of the HSR services (2007) about 66 ha of land were occupied by railway uses (workshops, freight station, warehouses and tracks) in relatively central locations. The introduction of the HSR in Valladolid brought with it the construction of a railway by-pass, to the east of the city, on which a freight station and railway workshops were established. Railway activities that had previously been scattered across the city were thereby brought together and improved, while land was freed in strategic central locations. The operation undertaken in Valladolid will also lead to the covering of almost 6 kilometres of track that cross the centre of the city (see Figure 8.4) (Santos 2005a).

The urban development project designed by Richard Rogers implies a large-scale operation. 'Nuevo Valladolid' (New Valladolid), the name given to the project, has been organised around three major areas: an area of new regional centrality based around the renewed station and two associated urban planning projects that basically focus on residential uses in the area that used to be occupied by the old railway workshops (Argales) and the former freight station (Ariza). This will be the largest urban redevelopment project in the history of the city and its cost could exceed € 1,000 million. Although tertiary uses and amenities are foreseen for the three areas it is significant that the project has assigned considerable importance to residential uses (with 6,200 new housing units).[8] The old city station will be transformed into a large shopping centre (50,000 m^2) under which much of the new railway infrastructure will be located.

In the cases of Madrid, Barcelona, Seville and Valencia the transformations of the existing railway systems have, in general, been rather smaller in scale. Neither they, nor their associated urban developments, have affected (or will affect) the general urban structure as much as they have affected specific areas and particularly those located around the existing or planned stations.

In Madrid and Barcelona the main objective of railway-related operations has been to turn what were once dead-end stations into through stations; in doing this, they have also created large intermodal (HSR and conventional) centres and generated powerful centralities around them.

In Barcelona, the arrival of the HSR service implies the construction of a new intermodal station: La Sagrera, in the northern part of the city. This station will be connected to the main Sants station (which was renovated to receive HSR services in 2008) via a new, 5.6 kilometre-long tunnel that crosses the city from south-west to north-east. This connection will make both stations through rather than terminal stations (see Figure 8.5).

---

8   The idea is to largely finance this operation through the income generated by the sale of railway land which is currently dedicated to residential uses. The economic forecasts for the project were initially based on the price of land during the property boom. These must now be substantially reduced, which may endanger much of the initial project.

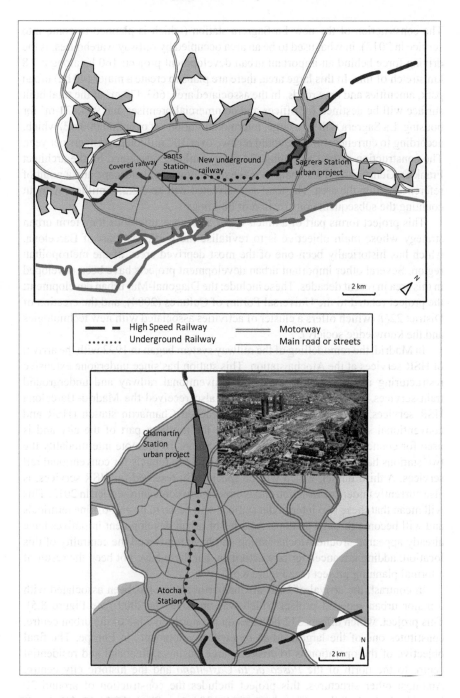

Figure 8.5 The HSR in Barcelona and Madrid
Source: Authors.

The construction of the new La Sagrera station (which is planned to come into service in 2012), in what used to be an area occupied by railway warehouses, is the driving force behind an important urban development project: 160 ha along a 3.8 km stretch of line. In this large area, there are plans to create a major (40 ha) urban park, amenities and new roads. In the associated area, 663,479 m² of the total built surface will be destined for offices and commercial premises and 994,421 m² for housing. La Sagrera will be a large, intermodal station (of over 260,000 m²) which, according to current estimates, could receive over 100 million passengers per year. The construction of two adjoining (34 floor) buildings designed by the architect Frank O. Gehry should also help to make this a powerful landscape and a point of reference within the area. The total sum invested will be € 2,250 million, without counting the subsequent construction of buildings.

This project forms part of a much wider and more ambitious long term urban strategy whose main objective is to revitalise the north-east part of Barcelona, which has historically been one of the most deprived areas of the metropolitan region. Several other important urban development projects have been developed in this area in recent decades. These include: the Diagonal-Mar urban development; the project related to the Universal Forum of Cultures (2004); and the creation of District 22@ (which offers a cluster of activities associated with new technologies and the knowledge society).

In Madrid, the remodelling of the railway system began in 1992 with the arrival of HSR services at the Atocha station. This station has since undergone extensive restructuring in order to receive HSR, conventional railway and underground train services. Since 2003, the station has also received the Madrid–Barcelona HSR services. In 2007 the HSR service reached Chamartín station (HSR and conventional services), which is located in the northern part of the city and is used for connections with the north-west of Spain. To promote intermodality the two stations have since been connected by two 7 km tunnels for conventional rail services. A third tunnel, which will be specifically reserved for HSR services, is also currently under construction and is expected to come into service in 2012. This will mean that these two intermodal stations will cease to be end-of-line terminals and will become through stations. A series of urban development initiatives have already appeared around Atocha station and have reinforced the centrality of this location, adding advanced tertiary activities, but these have not been the result of a formal planning project (see Figure 8.5).

In contrast, the arrival of HSR at Chamartín station has been associated with a major urban renewal project which was approved in 2009 (see Figure 8.5). This project, which affects 312 hectares on the northern edge of the urban centre, constitutes one of the largest urban renewal developments in Europe. The final objective of the operation is to create a large business, financial and residential centre to the north of the *Paseo de la Castellana* and the historic city centre. Amongst other structures, this project includes the construction of around 20 iconic high-rise buildings. The plan assigns 120 ha to offices, 16.5 ha to hotel uses and another 16.5 ha to commercial activities. There are also plans to construct

17,000 new housing units. The total investment required for this ambitious urban development was initially projected at around € 11,100 million.[9]

The project also includes the construction of the new Chamartín station, the restructuring of the public transport network to provide the station with greater connectivity and improvements to its road access. As a result a considerable increase in the number of travellers using this station has been forecast and it is expected to replace Atocha as the busiest railway station in Madrid.

In Valencia the introduction of the HSR service (in December 2010) has implied a transformation of the existing railway system. The new HSR services will be based in a new central station which will be located next to the present *Estación del Norte*. The new intermodal station will be a through instead of an end-of-line station. This change will be achieved through the construction of a new tunnelled stretch that will connect the station to the Mediterranean corridor (Valencia–Barcelona line) to the north of the city. This railway project also contemplates covering 9 kilometres of track within the urban trajectory. The transformation of the railway system will also bring with it the relocation of workshops and freight warehouses to the south of the city. This Central Park project will make it possible to carry out a 65.6 ha urban renewal project in a central location. This operation will produce a large (23 ha) park, a new central boulevard and various new squares and gardens (10 ha). The operation also foresees the construction of 630,000 m² of buildings dedicated to residential and tertiary uses, and 506,000 m² for new amenities. The total investment for the transformation of the railway system will be around € 804 million.

8.3.3 Minimal Transformation of the Railway System and Urban Redevelopment Project centred on the Station Area

This section analyses cases in which the introduction of the HSR system has not been accompanied by any significant transformation of the existing railway system and where there has only been a reduced impact in terms of new urban development. In these cases this spatial impact has generally affected only a small area around the station. This type of project has mainly been seen in small and medium-sized cities such as: Cordoba, Puertollano, Calatayud, Lleida, Malaga and Albacete and will soon take place in Girona. In the majority of these situations planners take advantage of the pre-existing railway infrastructure and try to improve its integration within the urban fabric. They also almost always opt to cover a stretch of track within the urban trajectory and to partially or totally remodel the station and its immediate surroundings. The most frequent objective in such projects is that of getting the station to act as a revitalising element for the surrounding area. To this end these projects tend to provide the station, or its surroundings, with new

---

9   Of the 312 ha in the project, 200 ha came from railway land, of which 140 ha will be destined for other uses.

activities: leisure, business, services and/or tertiary sector specialities.[10] In some developments the aim is also to generate a new urban centrality or to reinforce a previously weak centrality. Other objectives include promoting processes of urban renewal and providing greater architectonic and urban quality.

In Lleida, which is on the Madrid–Barcelona line, the HSR service was first received at the historic central (conventional) railway station in 2003. As a result, the station and its surroundings have become the basis of an important urban transformation. An urban redevelopment project for the station area (14.3 ha) was approved in 2003. It had the following objectives: to eliminate the railway barrier by completely covering the track running through the city centre; to increase connectivity by building two new bridges; to consolidate the centrality of the station by making it an intermodal node and providing it with leisure, business and tertiary spaces (91,000 m²) (Bellet 2002). It is planned to dedicate much of the space freed by covering the track to new tertiary uses; these should give this area greater centrality. The main uses currently being considered are: a *Vialia* shopping and leisure complex (5,000 m²); a new shopping centre (17,000 m²); and two office towers, with 15 and 21 floors, respectively, which will serve as iconic elements within this new space (see Figure 8.6). Near the station a new Conference and Congress Centre has been built and the Lleida Trade Fair has been extended in order to further support the station project and reinforce the functional centrality of this area.[11]

In Cordoba, which is on the southern Madrid–Seville–Malaga HSR line, the arrival of new services (in 1992) allowed several railway transformations to be undertaken: the covering of lines crossing the urban centre (3.7 kilometres) and the relocation of railway warehouses to the urban periphery. These changes have supposed the elimination of old railway barriers and the conversion of former centrally located railway land (43.4 ha) into various uses: housing, amenities, shopping activities, a park and a boulevard. This project was the subject of quite intense debate and much expectation in the three decades prior to the arrival of the HSR service. The project made it possible to create the largest area of urban redevelopment in the city and to develop the city towards an area that had previously been delimited by the urban barrier created by the railway. However, the uses that have since been developed (which have basically been residential) have not helped to reinforce the centrality provided by the station (Ureña et al. 2009d).

---

10   The stations at Albacete and Malaga already have Vialia shopping and leisure centres (as will those of Lleida and Valladolid, in the near future). These centres will have average sizes of between 5,000 and 13,300 m², except Malaga, where the projected shopping centre will have a total surface area of 35,000 m². The main shareholder in these shopping and leisure centres will be the Spanish rail operator RENFE.

11   These interventions have taken place within the framework of a strategy developed by local agents to take advantage of the arrival of the HSR and aimed at positioning Lleida as a leading conference and congress centre.

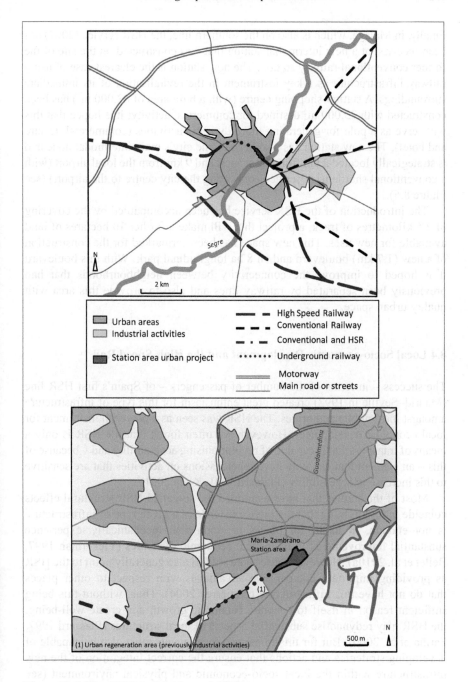

Figure 8.6 The HSR in Lleida and Málaga
Source: Authors.

Finally, in Malaga, which is also on the southern line, the HSR service (2007) has been received at a new intermodal station that was constructed on the site of the former conventional railway station. The new station is the clearest case of using railway infrastructure as a key instrument in the revitalisation of its immediate surroundings. A station-shopping centre (with a built area of 63,000 m^2) has been constructed with 35,000 m^2 destined for commercial activity; it is hoped that this will serve as a pole for generating more dynamic activities (commercial, leisure and hotel). The new station has also become the city's main intermodal node and is strategically located 2 km from the seaport and 9 km from the local airport (with a conventional shuttle train service connecting the city centre to the airport) (see Figure 8.6).

The introduction of the HSR service has been accompanied by the covering of 2.5 kilometres of track, a project that will make a further 10 hectares of land available for new uses. This new space has been earmarked for the construction of a new (1.7 km) boulevard and an 8 ha longitudinal park. With this boulevard it is hoped to improve the connectivity between neighbourhoods that had previously been separated by railway lines and also to provide this area with quality urban space.

8.4 Local Socio-economic Development and the High-Speed Rail

The success – in terms of the number of passengers – of Spain's first HSR line (Madrid–Seville in 1992) created great enthusiasm for this type of infrastructure amongst local public authorities. The HSR was seen as a powerful instrument for local economic development. However, we often forget that the HSR is only a means of transport that is capable of revolutionising accessibility and – because of this – an element that can only have repercussions on activities that are sensitive to this increase in accessibility (Plassard 1991, Klein 2001).

Most of the studies that have examined the so-called HSR structural effects coincide in highlighting that the mere existence of a given type of infrastructure is not enough, in itself, for places to, somewhat mechanically, experience substantial improvements in their local economic dynamics (Vickerman 1997, Bellet et al. 2010a). However, these same studies also generally point to the HSR as providing important comparative advantages with respect to other places that do not have this infrastructure (Gutiérrez 2004). Thus, without this being sufficient reason in itself to generate economic growth and create well-being, the HSR may redynamise substantial aspects of local structures (Plassard 1997, Fariña et al. 2000). But for this to happen local agents must also be capable of developing strategies and actions that ensure the correct integration of the new infrastructure within the local socio-economic and physical environment (see Chapter 9). They must also adopt appropriate measures to take advantage of new opportunities associated HSR services.

Nodal infrastructure such as that associated with HSR services should therefore form part of a series of (material and immaterial) elements that, by acting within the local territory, allow opportunities for socio-economic development (Dematteis 1995). According to these approaches, the so-called structuring effects of a given infrastructure can neither be isolated nor considered separately from the context in which they are located (Bellet et al. 2010a). Any analysis of the effects of the HSR service should therefore take into consideration the characteristics and organisation of the space in question – both before and after the introduction of the new railway services – and also the strategies developed by the different agents to take advantage of the new infrastructure (Albrechts and Coppens 2003, Garmendia et al. 2008).

8.4.1 The Socio-economic and Spatial Effects of the High-Speed Rail over Time

It may be expected that, with the arrival of the HSR, changes in local socio-economic dynamics and structures would be almost immediate, but in the majority of cases such changes take considerably longer. French academic literature, which is based on considerably more experience of this infrastructure than examining Spain, suggests that it may be necessary to wait over 20 years before being able to realistically evaluate the new socio-economic dynamics and spatial impact associated with the HSR service (see also Chapter 7).

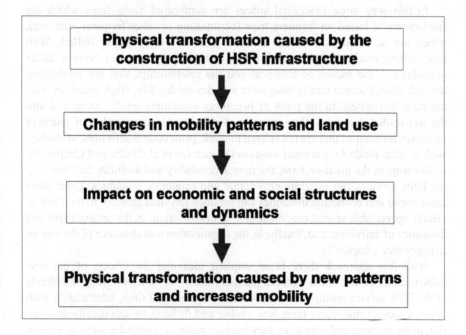

Figure 8.7 Socio-economic and territorial effects of HSR over time
Source: Authors based on Bellet et al. (2010a).

As we have already seen in the previous part of this chapter, the first – and two of the most important – changes that occur are physical and associated with the construction of the infrastructure: new lines, electrification, viaducts, new stretches of track, etc., which must be integrated into the territory. As commented in the previous section, the spatial impacts associated with the introduction of HSR infrastructure are not always the same and vary according to the importance of the rail changes and urban development projects related with the arrival of the new train service.

The transformation of the image of the city is almost immediate and comes with the announcement of the forthcoming infrastructure. A city that has HSR services becomes better known and impregnated with an image of modernity associated with the new means of transport. For this reason many cities take advantage of the arrival of this new infrastructure to reinforce and/or consolidate their internal and external images through marketing campaigns.

However, the most immediate change associated with the arrival of the HSR service is the revolution in mobility. There is an almost immediate increase in the number of rail trips and in relations with nearby metropolises and/or with other territories connected via the rail corridor (Fröidh 2008).This brings with it the capture of other trips that would previously have been undertaken using other modes of transport and also the induction, or creation, of new movements (see Chapter 6).

In this way large functional spaces are configured along lines which are fundamentally based on frequent trips (commuting or other frequent relations), which are no longer continuous in space (Ureña 2006b, Bellet 2010c). With time, labour market areas expand. Later, as high speed services become better consolidated, the means of transport and the relationships that are established through them become totally integrated into day-to-day life. High speed services are then 'trivialised' to the point of becoming something totally integrated into the day-to-day dynamics. One example of this is when the number of journeys increases for reasons that are not related to work, professional activities, or studies, such as trips made for personal motives (Menéndez et al. 2002a and Chapter 6). In this way, in the medium term, the new accessibility and mobility facilitated by the HSR services can generate new social and economic dynamics. Later these same social and economic dynamics can produce physical changes in the form of clearly appreciable spatial modifications: in urbanisation; in the arrangement and dynamics of activities; and, finally, in the organisation and structure of the city or territory (see Chapter 7).

With this approach there is an implicit idea that the effects of the new infrastructure do not finish with the inauguration of the line. Normally the effects of the HSR service multiply and grow with the passing of time, interrelating with other processes that make them less visible and difficult to specifically analyse. But, in the medium and long term, they become associated with the socio-economic framework of the city and with its territorial repositioning (see Chapter 7).

8.4.2 Local Development and Strategies Associated with the High-Speed Rail

The capacity of the HSR to turn itself into a instrument for development depends on a variety of factors, amongst which we should underline the following: the characteristics of the infrastructure and services; the correct integration of the infrastructure within the territory; and the level of coherence between the physical integration of the infrastructure and the city model/project agreed and defined by the social agents that interact in this territory. The train can only become a dynamising element when there is a solid project for the city and its territory and when it is possible to define and implement the strategies required for the HSR to fit into that project (Bellet et al. 2010a).

Faced with the arrival of the HSR social agents (both public and private) usually react relatively quickly, deploying certain accompanying measures and actions at the local scale. Generally speaking the measures and actions taken are not only aimed at trying to integrate the new infrastructure but also at taking advantage of the centrality generated by the station and the new accessibility provided by the train. These strategies or measures may be assigned to one of three large groups of measures: planning, management and promotional measures (Van den Berg and Pol 1998, Ribalaygua 2004).

a. *Planning measures* This type of measure is preferably proposed before the arrival of the new train. Above all, these strategies seek to integrate the new infrastructure within the local environment in the most appropriate way possible by:

- ensuring coordination and coherence between the HSR project and urban and territorial planning
- alleviating the possible negative effects of its physical implantation
- promoting the added value associated with the 'centrality' around the station, mainly through providing tertiary activities
- introducing improvements in internal and external accessibility from/to the station.

As mentioned in the previous section the introduction of the HSR in Spain's urban environment has made it possible to redefine the relationship between the city and the railway, particularly with respect to its integration within the urban fabric and the reuse of old railway spaces.

In Spain, Zaragoza is one of the cities that have most intensively developed previous planning measures associated with the physical introduction of HSR infrastructure. The territorial and strategic plans approved and undertaken in this city since the 1990s have not only sought to ensure the correct integration of the new infrastructure within the urban fabric but also to use the arrival of the HSR as an instrument for urban transformation and a driving force for socio-economic revitalisation. The arrival of HSR was supposed to contribute to the foundations of the twenty-first century city (Alonso and Bellet 2009). The first studies to analyse the introduction of HSR services in Zaragoza coincided with a debate that centred on a new Strategic Plan for the metropolitan area (1998) and the drafting of a City Master Plan (2001). This coincidence paved the way for the major (physical and economic) urban transformations which have been carried out in the city over the last decade.

The confluence of these (strategic and urban development) plans, the arrival of the HSR in 2003, the celebration of the International Water Exhibition in 2008 and other associated urban projects have formed part of a very important push to change the external image of the city.

As well as the urban centrality projects that we referred to in Section 8.3, which were directly associated with the transformation of the city's old railway system, we should also refer to several other urban projects (see Figure 8.4).

The most important project aimed at bringing economic change to the territory has been the PLAZA Logistics Platform, which is located in the south-west of the city, next to the new railway bypass. This is one of the largest logistics platforms in Europe (1,282 ha) and is located next to the airport and to a future second HSR station. The objective of PLAZA is to offer logistics operators well-equipped land and excellent accessibility to multimodal transport (road, rail and plane) services.

Another project that would encourage urban change, the Digital Mile project, is based on former urban railway land located between the new and old railway stations (see Figure 8.4). Its objective is to set up a City of Innovation and Knowledge and to promote the introduction and development of ICT (Information and Communications Technologies) through the creation of a digital corridor. This site will see the construction of automated housing units, companies and amenities, under a common approach based on activities related to new technologies and the knowledge society.

Another important project is related to the promotion of trade fairs and international events. As well as increasing the number of congresses that it hosts, Zaragoza has also prepared a special area for trade fairs on the banks of the River Ebro. This area, which has already hosted the 2008 International Water Exhibition, is near the new intermodal station. There are also plans to host another international exhibition focusing on horticulture, gardening and landscaping (ExpoPaisajes) in 2014.

These projects have helped to change the economic base of a city which has been historically associated with industrial activity and in particular with the car and agri-food sectors. The restructuring of the railway in Zaragoza with the introduction of the HSR has presented an opportunity to consolidate a new urban structure and to provide the city with a new economic base.

b. Management measures Among these measures the most relevant are those aimed at managing the mobility generated by the HSR and taking advantage of the station's vocation for centrality. These tend to be related to:

- Accessibility and intermodality: the coherent and coordinated management of (internal and external) flows, the conversion of the station into a modal exchange centre, etc. Issues related to accessibility were the first to be planned and implemented.
- Development of the land and/or project around the station. This relates to land that tends to be destined for specialised tertiary sector uses and activities.

Segovia (with 57,874 inhabitants in 2009) provides a good example; accessibility and mobility questions were planned when HSR services were about to be introduced.

When the HSR reached Segovia in 2007 the city effectively moved nearer to Madrid. By train it is now only 25 minutes from the metropolitan capital and 30 minutes from the regional capital of Valladolid. A new toll motorway and dual carriageway have also respectively improved road communications with Madrid and Valladolid. These new rail and road connections have effectively put an end to the historic isolation suffered by Segovia. With this new HSR infrastructure Segovia has effectively become immersed in the metropolitan dynamics of Madrid (Bellet et al. 2010b).

However, the peripheral location of the HSR station, which is about 5 kilometres south-east of the city centre, is a problem that local government still had to address. The most important challenge has been that of guaranteeing a good level of accessibility and connectivity between the station and the city centre and the immediate territory. According to ADIF data for 2009 the station handles around 1,500 passengers every day. To make the station more accessible a new road connection was constructed to improve and facilitate communications between the station and the city centre. To guarantee better accessibility and connectivity once the HSR services begin the local authorities have provided a shuttle bus service to connect the city directly to the HSR station in 20 minutes; this is a service that fits in with the train timetable. Two urban bus lines currently connect the city centre and the HSR station and transport between 50 and 60 per cent of the passengers who use the station (Bellet 2010c).

Passengers who access the HSR station by private car quickly occupied the 250 parking places available, so the number was increased to 400.

The possibility of establishing a tram system to connect the city to the surrounding municipalities was considered but ultimately rejected. It will be more complicated to establish exchanges with other modes of transport, such as bus and conventional train services, as they are located in the urban centre and distant from the HSR station.

Many of the challenges posed by HSR are logically related to the management of mobility and the new accessibility. These challenges are, if anything, all the more important in the case of peripheral HSR stations where there are generally problems of accessibility and difficulties in providing an efficient public transport service.

c. Measures for promoting and improving urban image   As well as the previously
mentioned measures and actions, many cities and territories have taken advantage
of the HSR to undertake marketing campaigns that are directed at both local
and external populations. The old style of campaign, which was essentially
aimed at potential tourists, has now given way to actions that are increasingly
complex and that cover a wide range of areas. Amongst these it is possible to
highlight campaigns related to urban marketing and tourism promotion and to the
creation of new land and services that will favour the introduction of economic
activities associated with the new economy (culture and innovation, research and
development, logistical activities, advanced services, and ICT, amongst others).
At present these campaigns favour external promotion and may even play an
important role in the economic revitalisation of some territories.

These measures are related to the process of recruiting economic activity and
using the HSR as a means of attracting investment and linking the image of the
city to the modernity that is associated with the new train services.

One example of how these measures have been used is provided by the city of
Lleida. This intermediate city (with 141,576 inhabitants in 2009) is the main urban
centre in a wider territory whose economic activity is based on the agri-food sector.
The new HSR services have been received at the historic central station which has,
as explained in Section 8.3, already been extensively transformed. The HSR has
effectively relocated this city, placing it only 115 minutes from Madrid and 70
minutes from Barcelona. From the very first moment the city was conscious of the
importance that the HSR could have for its image and development and that of its
surrounding territory. A year before HSR arrived, the local administrations and the
Chamber of Commerce and Industry promoted a new strategic Plan specifically
based on the HSR. Some of the measures contemplated by the Plan have already
been put into effect (Bellet 2002). Amongst them we should mention the change of
the station's name: it has now become Lleida-Pirineus (Lleida-Pyrenees) station.
The Pyrenees brand has been included in an attempt to boost the image of the city
as a doorway to the mountains that lie two hours to the north of the city, which form
part of an environment rich in natural wealth and tourist attractions. Paralleling the
arrival of the high speed train, an external promotional campaign was initiated and
measures were taken to increase local self-esteem. The resulting '*Lleida smuack*'
and '*Lleida t'estimo*' (Lleida, I love you) campaigns had quite a significant impact
at the national level, with one of the first adverts in the campaign specifically
referring to the arrival of the high speed train.

The arrival of the HSR service usually has a direct impact on tourist activity
within a given territory; it affects flows, product sales, services and the orientation
of tourism offers. Most of the Spanish cities that have received HSR have –
amongst its first effects – experienced a notable increase in visitors (Bellet et al.
2010a). However, the arrival of the new train in the city of Lleida has – above all
– been noted for the increase in tourism associated with meetings and congresses.
While in 2003 there were 124 events of this type, by 2009 there were 321. The
increase in activities related with the tourism of meetings and congresses has also

been boosted by the construction of parallel amenities and service facilities for the organisation of these events. A new 35,000 m² Congress and Conference Centre (2009) has been built close to the railway station which is also connected to the city's main exhibition and trade fair centre.

Another local urban project that has been given extra impetus since the arrival of the HSR service is Lleida's Food Science and Technology Park, a consortium involving Lleida City Council and the University of Lleida which was created in 2005. The Science Park seeks to become one of Spain's main scientific and technical platforms for the agri-food sector, and also a reference at the European level, by taking advantage of the local territory's traditional economic specialisation. Better external accessibility is fundamental for the majority of the activities that are based at the park; HSR should therefore make an important contribution to its consolidation (Bellet et al. 2010a).

We should conclude this section by underlining that when the HSR service arrives local agents tend to initiate a series of actions and strategies that typically include:

• Improving internal and external accessibility and promoting intermodality.
• Managing mobility at and around the new transport node.
• Creating or reinforcing urban centralities, which are usually closely associated with the station.
• Economically empowering the territory specifically affected by the arrival of the HSR service. This applies to existing activities and also to the development of new ones.
• Improving the physical environment and the quality of life within the local territory.

Finally, we must stress the importance of coordinating the introduction of the HSR service with strategic and territorial local planning. In this way it is possible to guarantee the complementarity of the different actions and to appropriately integrate the new infrastructure and services into local development policies.

8.5 Conclusions

As occurred with the introduction of conventional rail services at the end of the nineteenth century, the introduction of the High-Speed Rail (HSR) service in Spanish cities has engendered major urban transformations and redevelopment projects. This has made the introduction of HSR an efficient instrument for urban development and one that has been capable of transforming the physical structure of the city. There have been three basic reasons for this:

• Firstly, the introduction of HSR infrastructure in Spanish cities has presented a great opportunity to overcome some of the historical problems associated with urban railway integration. In this sense, it is possible to take advantage of the arrival of HSR to transform the whole railway system. This action also introduces the opportunity to improve the integration of railway spaces in the urban fabric and to overcome the traditional barrier effects that some railway installations have when they are absorbed by urban growth. However, in the face of this new and historic opportunity to improve the relationship between the railway and the city, instead of considering *soft integration* options for HSR, in Spain, local authorities have, more often than not, chosen *harder solutions*: such as covering large stretches of urban track and/or building new external lines. These *hard solutions* for integrating HSR infrastructure within the city are not only complex but also call for important levels of investment.

- Secondly, cities have taken advantage of the arrival of the HSR service to solve previously unresolved urban development problems that, in many cases, have little or no relation with the train.

- Thirdly, a large proportion of projects for the introduction of the HSR were drawn up at a time of great expansion in the property cycle in Spain and this has had a number of important consequences. Firstly – and as previously mentioned – very expensive projects were proposed that recommended *hard solutions* when integrating the railway within the city. Secondly, land released from previous railway uses in the centre of the city has become densely occupied. This implies that the renewed railway installations will have very little space available for future expansion. This situation is particularly easy to understand in the case of large metropolises and large urban centres where the pressure of high land prices is greatest, but it is difficult to understand in the case of less dense nuclei. A third consequence is that many of the future land uses in the area around the station are destined for housing. This was either the result of a response to a good moment for residential property coinciding with the expansionist phase of the property cycle or to uses being destined for amenities and public services as a result of pressure from the local population.

The combination of these three factors has resulted in some of the most important urban redevelopment projects that have ever been undertaken in Spanish cities. As we have already seen in the cases of Zaragoza and Ciudad Real, these transformations have, on occasion, implied important changes to the existing urban structure and similar changes are foreseen in the cases of Valladolid and Figueres. No less important have been the urban redevelopment projects associated with the introduction of HSR infrastructure in Madrid and Barcelona. However, the arrival of the economic and property cycle crisis has paralysed many of the urban development projects that were supposed to accompany these railway transformations. As a result some projects, which at one time were highly valued and regarded as strategically important for their cities, have now been seriously compromised.

This chapter has also highlighted the relationship between the extent of the transformation of the railway system following the arrival of the HSR service and its spatial impact on urban/territorial structure, form and landscape. Firstly, in territories in which a completely new railway system has been introduced, the spatial impact derived from it tends to cause major changes to the existing urban and/or territorial structure. The construction of completely new stretches of track also tends to imply the construction of peripheral or city-edge stations. In the case of peripheral HSR stations, the most important challenge facing local policy makers relates to accessibility. It should be stressed that in Spain there are relatively few peripheral stations and that most of them are clearly linked to a main urban nucleus (Cuenca, Guadalajara or Segovia). A second situation is the creation of a peripheral station in a territory with a relatively low density of population; this often corresponds to a rural environment lacking any major urban polarities (Antequera-Santa Ana, Puente Genil-Herrera and Requena-Utiel). The Camp de Tarragona station represents a third situation: a peripheral station that is located within a polynuclear urban system (Reus-Tarragona). When an external line and a new station are built at a city-edge location (Ciudad Real and Figueres), the whole urban structure is transformed. In such situations, advantage has generally been taken of the dismantling of the central railway infrastructure and its relocation on the new, peripheral line. This produces important urban renewal processes in the centre of the city and also changes to the general urban structure.

Secondly, it is possible to group together cases in which the HSR service has been introduced through the (more or less far-reaching) transformation of the existing railway system. In these cases, the most intense spatial changes usually occur at the local scale and affect specific spaces that are perceived to be subjected to intense renewal processes. This would correspond to the cases of large metropolises (Madrid and Barcelona) and some major urban agglomerations (Seville, Valencia, Zaragoza and Valladolid). In these cases the interventions undertaken have mainly focused on the conversion of end-of-line stations into through stations; the construction of rail bypasses and rail rings; the freeing of railway land in central locations; and the construction (or adaptation) of large intermodal stations. These are actions of very intense renewal that have produced quite densely occupied spaces.

Thirdly, and finally, there are the cases in which smaller scale railway and urban development actions have been undertaken. The majority of these correspond to the introduction of the HSR service in smaller and medium-sized cities (Albacete, Calatayud, Cordoba, Lleida, and Malaga). These interventions have basically focused on improving the integration of the railway infrastructure in the immediate vicinity of the station. In certain cases, these actions also form part of a more general strategy to revitalise the urban environment nearest to the station.

The arrival of the HSR in Spain has also generated important expectations for the socio-economic development of the cities and territories that it has reached. However, the majority of analyses carried out have concluded that the presence of the HSR is not a sufficient condition in itself to mechanically produce substantial improvements in the socio-economic structures and dynamics of cities. The train only offers new opportunities for accessibility that should be exploited at the local scale. To do this, cities and territories often undertake different types of policies and actions, which can be summarised in three groups:

- Planning measures aimed at integrating the new infrastructure into the environment as efficiently as possible.
- Management measures aimed at managing the mobility generated by the HSR and taking advantage of the station's vocation for centrality.
- Promotional measures that seek to take advantage of the arrival of the HSR to carry out urban marketing campaigns.

Finally, it is important to underline the importance of coordinating the introduction of the HSR service with strategic and territorial/urban planning. Only in this way is it possible to guarantee the complementarity between different actions and to appropriately integrate the new infrastructure and services into local development policies. This makes it possible to convert the arrival of HSR into a powerful instrument for urban renewal and provides the foundation for the city of the twenty-first century.

Chapter 9
High-Speed Rail and Regional Accessibility

Ángela de Meer, Cecilia Ribalaygua and Elena Martín[1]

9.1 Accessibility and High-Speed Rail

9.1.1 The Influence of High-Speed Rail on the Configuration of New 'Functional Structures'

Each city (and its surrounding territory) is composed of a spatial physical support (land, streets, roads, open areas, buildings, utilities, nature, etc.) and a functional structure (activities, population, relations, etc.). Thus, it is not possible to completely perceive an urban process without understanding both the spatial and functional variables. As indicated by Terán (2002),[2] the need to analyse the territory and the city from these dual viewpoints means that we have to understand the historic dynamics and the flows that appeared on the formal urban-territorial structure.

The arrival of the new railway system foreshadows obvious changes in the territorial and urban structures reviewed in the previous chapters. Apart from these changes, and indeed as part of them, there are direct modifications in the general organisation of urban and sub-regional territorial access, specifically to the railway station. There is an alteration in what we will call 'the functional structure' of the city complementary to its physical (or morphological) structure.

Literature that has addressed the analyses of the effects of the high-speed rail (HSR) range from studies that review the effects of the railway on other means of transportation to those focused on the reorganisation of railway transport (Mannone 1995, Ureña et al. 2009d, Menerault 2006).

Studies about the impact of HSR accessibility on the transportation system have focused mainly on the reduction of travelling times between large cities (Bazin et al. 2009, Blanquart and Delaplace 2009). The improvements in accessibility of the cities served by HSR and the implications involved have also been widely demonstrated (Paris 1992, Mannone 1995, Vickermann

---

1   University of Cantabria.

2   'If we refer to the city as a force field in movement, which is constantly reorganising itself, or as the economic and social result of a combination of historical circumstances in dynamic interaction, we will be dealing with very clear ways of understanding the city, which are based on the consideration of the elements that generate the transformation and highlight the changing, transient and moving aspects of its nature'. Terán (2002).

1997, Givoni 2006, Cheng 2009), specifically the accessibility improvement peculiarities in small cities (Ribalaygua 2005, 2006b, Ureña and Ribalaygua 2008) or peripheral regions (Paris 1992, Meer and Ribalaygua 2008, Ribalaygua and de Meer 2009b) as opposed to the great beneficiaries of HSR, which are the large cities (Auphan 2002).

The improvement in the interconnections between cities has been mostly reviewed through merely functional aspects such as public transport (Troin 1997, de Rus and Nombela 2007, Nash 2009) and, to a lesser extent, from the double spatial and functional viewpoint (Van den Berg and Pol 1998a, Ureña et al. 2005a, 2006b, Ureña and Ribalaygua 2005b, Ribalaygua 2005, 2007, Bellet et al. 2010a). Station accessibility has also been analysed at the urban scale with physical and functional criteria (Rietveld et al. 2001, Park and Ha 2006, Chang and Lee 2008, Peters 2009), but there are fewer studies focused on the two main aspects of the functional structure: the reorganisation of the transport systems and the transformation of activities in the area.

On the other hand, the physical support has been studied from different viewpoints and scales, from the European one to that of the area around the station. The spatial hierarchy modifications have been analysed based on the reinforcement of regional poles (Troin 1997, Kamel and Matthewman 2008, Ureña et al. 2005a, 2009c). The transformation of space has been demonstrated in accordance with the new travelling times (Givoni 2006, L'Hostis 2009) and with the spatial redistribution of regional growth including the new station (Mannone 1995, Menerault 1998, Garmendia et al. 2008, Facchinetti-Mannone 2009). Moreover, the modification of the city centres (Mannone 1997, Ribalaygua 2010b) and the remodelling of the area around the station (Menerault 1997, Pol 2002, Peters 2009) have been described from functional and physical points of view.

This chapter reflects on the functional variables in cities served by the HSR, based on the results of the authors research[3] on the impact of HSR on Spanish cities (complementing the analysis of the physical support discussed in Chapter 8). This research studies between 2007 and 2010 the development of activities in cities with a HSR station through two kinds of work. The first type was field work that recorded the type of activity on the ground floor of the buildings in areas around the stations of all the intermediate Spanish cities which have had the HSR station for more than one year. The second was a survey on the activities developed in the surroundings of HSR stations (between 34 per cent and 39 per

3   Study financed, in its first phase by the Regional Government of Castilla la Mancha, and in the second phase, by the Fundación Logroño integración del Ferrocarril, 2003. Researchers from various disciplines collaborated in the study: architects (C. Mota, F. García, C. Ribalaygua); civil engineers (M. Garmendia, S. Díaz, J.J. Sánchez) and geographers (E. Martín La Torre, E.M. García de Villaraco and V. Romero) with the support of several town halls, technicians from local and supra-municipal administrations and with the external collaboration of C. Bellet and V. Mannone. The methodology is explained in detail in Ribalaygua et al. (2009a), and partial results are published in Ribalaygua and García (2010a).

cent depending on the cases) to analyse their location decisions and the influence of HSR on their working procedures.[4]

The functional urban structure as a result of the new railway   The HSR stations, considered as generators of flows, become strategic urban and territorial elements whether they are located in the urban fabric or outside the city. The arrival of the HSR has an initial direct impact on the renewal of the urban (or territorial) functional structure, which is moulded through the reorganisation of transport and the creation of new activities.

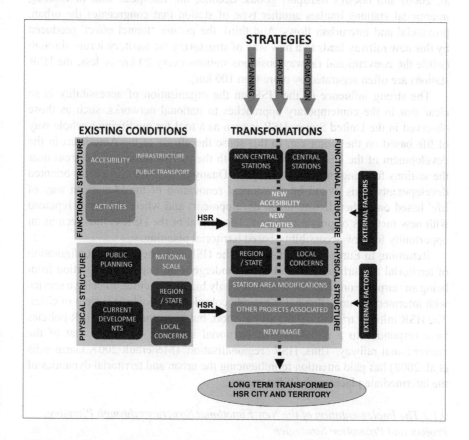

Figure 9.1 Transformation process along the arrival of the HSR
Source: Authors.

---

4   The survey was divided into five blocks: basic information on the company surveyed, spatial organisation of their market areas, the choice of the company's location, the displacements to other cities in the company's network, the HSR in the performance and location of their business. See: Ribalaygua et al. (2009a).

The reorganisation of the urban functional structure, therefore, will contribute to profiling the impact of the HSR on the city. External factors and two groups of actions, or strategies, intervene in this reorganisation: those aimed at mobility – in the different spatial scales and means of transport – and those aimed at the spatial distribution of activities (see Figure 9.1).

The territorial influence of the HSR inherits certain features of the conventional railway, although it has its own profile due to its operating conditions (speed, fare, reliability, etc.). First, the new train, unlike the conventional one, has customers who travel mainly for professional purposes (Klein 1992, 2003, Menéndez et al. 2006) and doesn't transport goods. Second, the European idea of creating intermodal stations implies another type of station that congregates the urban, provincial and interurban flows. And third, the greater 'tunnel effect' produced by this new railway leads to a new way of structuring the territory it runs through (while the conventional railway positions stations every 20 km or less, the HSR stations are often separated by more than 100 km).

The strong influence of the HSR on the organisation of accessibility is so clear that in the contemporary approaches to national networks, such as those observed in the United States, HSR is seen as a tool for modifying a whole way of life based on the motor car. In this sense the efforts of the Americans in the development of the HSR are combined with the reorganisation of the areas near the stations focusing on public transport (Duany et al. 2010), in transit-oriented developments. This would be a historical renovation of the 'American way of life' based on higher-density urban developments and where the car is replaced with new methods of public transport. The arrival of the HSR is thus seen as an opportunity for new accessibility-based territorial planning.

Returning to Europe, we can see that the HSR influence on the configuration of territorial and urban accessibility has undergone an important evolution from being an 'airplane on rails',[5] which linked only big distant cities, to being a service with intermediate stops that helps provide cohesion to the whole system of cities. The HSR initially tried to imitate air transport, but in recent decades HSR policies have responded to a philosophy of territorial irrigation more like that of the conventional railway. Thus, HSR 'regionalisation' (Menerault 2007, Garmendia et al. 2008) has paid attention to influencing the urban and territorial dynamics of the intermediate places with HSR services.

9.1.2 The Implementation of the New Functional Structures through Planning, Project and Promotion Strategies

Behind each modification of the functional urban or territorial structures there is a long administrative process, which is reflective and coordinated when done well. In order to understand the actions influencing location and accessibility decisions

---

5   Expression first used by Plassard (1992).

the heterogeneous strategies that have been developed at different times, and by different agents, are classified.

Based on the analysis of intermediate cities on French and Spanish HSR lines, strategies were classified in three blocks according to their nature (Ribalaygua 2005): Planning, Project and Promotion. This classification has been applied for the overall study of cases (Bellet et al. 2008, Paul 2008, García et al. 2010), although in this chapter it is used to analyse more specifically the strategies developed to transform the functional structures.

The first 'Planning' strategy is the process of making the HSR station's location coherent with the desired territorial and urban model. Only through this process will further developments be successful. The 'sustainable' location of the station will enable the creation of a reasonable public transport network and a coherent operation of the territory, but these types of concerted decisions only arise when there is a coordinated plan at a sub-regional scale.

Once the station has been located, the next planning strategy is to reserve the land around it to reinforce certain activities and the conservation of environmental or cultural values in the area, since this image of quality is in itself one of the differential values of the HSR (Plassard, 1992; Mannone, 1995; Troin, 1997). The next step is the articulation of the administrative process to create suitable infrastructures for station access, taking the regional and local scales into account. These measures also include the revision of old railway stretches and the search for conventional railway connections with the new HSR station.

The second 'Project' strategy is related to management and focuses on two objectives: management of transport and development of projects on the previously reserved land. The purpose of both is to extend the radius of influence of HSR around each station and thus optimise the territorial benefits of HSR investments.

Therefore, the local and regional transportation system must be reorganised at an early stage. It is common that consortiums, specific services, and above all, a great deal of flexibility are required to adapt the system to the specific features of the new HSR. The strategy must also involve the railway company so that HSR timetables, prices and frequencies match the needs of the territory. During this phase of the Project strategies, the land reserved by the sub-regional plan is managed. This stage needs studies about the best land use and land morphologies to the profile of the HSR traveller.

The third 'Promotion' strategy is of a marketing nature and tries to take full advantage of the HSR's potential. It is often necessary to promote the use of public transport in cities with stations that are not easily accessible, but it is even more important to promote certain economic sectors that are willing to connect with the HSR. The tourism sector stands out in this group (Paul 2008, Masson and Petiot 2009, Ribalaygua and García 2010a) as it is strongly reinforced by the image and access advantages of this new transport mode.

9.2 Urban and Sub-Regional Functional Structures. Variations according to the Location of the Station

The location of the HSR station is not only a determining factor in the reorganisation of the regional and local transport system but also a key item in the potential territorial centrality of the station's node, the generated flows, the attraction of investors to its surroundings, the energy and social cost used in their access, and its contribution to the desired territorial model.

There are as many solutions for territorial issues related to the location of HSR stations as there are urban and territorial structures, although their characterisation allows us to understand the variables that intervene in this process and to separate the factors that specifically affect the territorial functional structures. The literature on HSR stations location uses not only spatial criteria (Menéndez et al. 2006), but also connectivity to other transportation networks (Zembri 1992, Troin 1997, Preston et al. 2006, Nash 2009).

Among the widest location groupings, Klein (1992) describes five possible scenarios depending on the features of the cities and the location and connectivity of the station, in a classification that becomes more complex as a result of the territorial and accessibility variables, with respect to both HSR and other means of transport.

Pietri (1990) also establishes five groups depending on the local strategies developed, and finally reduces them to the three main possible locations (central, tangential and peripheral).

These classifications show the variety of solutions for the location of HSR stations. This chapter will analyse the factors that influence the functional structure from the viewpoint of the different locations. In this way, we distinguish between peripheral (or exurban) and urban stations; and within the latter, between central and tangential.

Each station location model has specific initial conditions as well as an ability to lean towards certain objectives. These differential factors are discovered in two stages of the process: some are related to the existing conditions and others to the development of the infrastructure and the modifications in the area (see Table 9.1).

The subdivision of the factors was carried out between urban and peripheral stations, as the activity factors are mainly differentiated through their relationship with the city centre. The availability of land or the organisation of transport also has a very different nature depending on whether the HSR station is urban or peripheral. Table 9.1 describes these differential factors of the functional structure.

Table 9.1　Differential factors of the functional structure

Phase	Main Aspects Of The Functional Structure Affected By The Hsr		Differential Factors Dependant On The Location Of The Station
Prior Conditions	Accessibility Conditions	Infrastructures	Interurban Scale
			Urban Scale
		Public Transport	Regional Network
			Urban Network
	Activity Conditions		Availability Of Land For New Activities
			Existence Of Prior Activity
After Arrival Hsr	Performance Of The Accessibility Of The Railway Service		Services
			User Profiles
			Area Of Influence
	Performance Of Activities		Consolidation Of Activities

Source: Authors.

For a more detailed analysis, the type of territory where the station is to be placed should also be considered. This analysis is mainly based on two criteria: whether it is a polarised territory and its population density. The station's capacity to attract activities and/or population, as a territorial node, depends on its capacity to attract regional flows, which to a large extent is determined by these existing conditions of density and whether it is a provincial or regional capital. This chapter will focus on the results of the urban environment scale analysis in Spanish HSR cities.

9.2.1 Prior Conditions of Accessibility

The conditions of accessibility prior to HSR cover two aspects: the status of the transport infrastructures and the management of the transportation service at the regional and urban scales. While the improvement of central stations means that regions already had this infrastructure and had developed urban transport systems for it, the new tangential or peripheral stations do not inherit these facilities and a large part of the work to be done is in developing them.

However, the qualitative value of the accessibility to the stations varies depending on the relative importance of public transport in the existing modal distribution. The influence of the other transport modes will be more relevant for stations that combine HSR with conventional trains or regional buses. The presence of these modes of transport in the HSR station increases the station's potential for accessibility by public transport.

The lack of economic activities besides tangential stations poses an added handicap to guaranteeing a minimum profitability when establishing public transport. Strong political and financial support is necessary, especially in the case of peripheral stations, not only for creating new access infrastructures but also for maintaining adequate public transport services.

The accessibility problems of the peripheral French stations of Mâcon, Vendôme and Le Creusot and of the Spanish ones of Guadalajara, Tarragona and Puente Genil, among others, are well documented and happened precisely because of their initial peripheral locations (Troin 1997, Menéndez et al. 2006, Meer and Ribalaygua 2008, Ribalaygua 2008).

On the other hand, the availability of land in peripheral locations has allowed the creation of new access roads to the stations, while this possibility is more limited in the urban context of the central or tangential stations. Therefore, the initial situation is that peripheral HSR stations generally have more land available for the creation of regional connection infrastructures (although more difficulties in the urban connection), while some urban stations have little space to improve or reorganise their accesses on a supra-municipal scale but have more facilities for the creation or extension of public transport services. Moreover, activities that make greater use of public transport and provide better opportunities for access are more frequently found around central stations (see the section dedicated to activities).

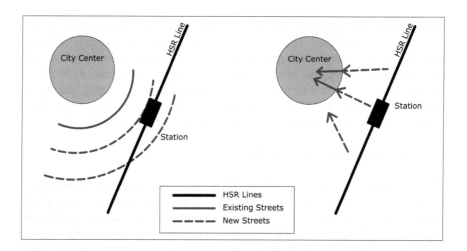

Figure 9.2 HSR accessibility models: tangential in Ciudad Real and radial in Segovia

Source: Authors.

Based on these existing conditions, the urban infrastructure that connects HSR stations with the city may respond to two models: tangential and radial towards the city centre (see Figure 9.2). The first case is evident at Ciudad Real, which created new infrastructure that is always tangential to the urban centre, and the second at Segovia, with a clearer desire to prolong the existing road system despite the long distances that separate it from the historical city centre.[6]

The different existing conditions of accessibility of the central, tangential and peripheral HSR stations will therefore lead to specific strategies. While the central stations focus on access to public transportation and coordination with other means of transportation on a regional or interprovincial scale, the peripheral stations overcome their difficulties through the availability of land for the creation of new territorial access infrastructures and large car parks. However, in the new generation of peripheral stations in France, this feature is adapted by locating the peripheral stations at communication nodes (regional conventional rail stations, motorway junctions, etc.) so that they can take advantage of a certain pre-existing accessibility on a provincial or regional scale. This is the case of the HSR station at Valence (Mannone 1995), which represent a renewal of the peripheral French model of strategic stations built in the territory that they serve (Ribalaygua 2005).

The Valence 'Rovaltain' Technological Park, located besides the combined station (162 hectares), was started with an inter-institutional association created in 1989 to accompany the development of the territory[7] (see Figure 9.3). There is a peripheral, combined HSR and conventional regional railway station located at a road junction. This position guarantees a wide connection area for the station, which extends beyond the municipal limits thanks to the supra-municipal management of the whole project and the developments associated with it.

9.2.2 Prior Conditions of Activity in the Station Area

The activity-conditioning factors in the surroundings of the station are determined by two aspects: the availability of land and the pre-existence of activity in the area. While in the case of the central stations there is barely enough room for growth, the peripheral stations can offer abundant land for new development. However, this lack of land in central areas is counteracted by the initial situation of their surroundings, normally with abundant tertiary and housing activities, given that the pre-existence of activities is a key factor in attracting new investments and by the possibility of renewing former central railway land. While attempting to attract new activities where there were previously none, the peripheral Guadalajara HSR station has not been able to consolidate the Valdeluz housing development (30.000 dwellings) which barely survives with a very small number of HSR services and commuters (Ribalaygua 2008). Nor has Mâcon in France had it easy in developing an industrial estate in the middle of the countryside beside the HSR station (Facchinetti-Mannone 2009, Ribalaygua et al. 2009a).

---

6   Both cases have been described through the historical analysis of the planning and management strategies with regard to the infrastructures created for the new high-speed railway station in Ribalaygua (2005).

7   The *Tertiary Park*, as a 10 ha services centre; *Parallel 45 park*, occupied by the 20 ha activity park which houses small industrial companies and the services sector; and the *Discovery Park*, dedicated to activities related to high technology and to sustainable development.

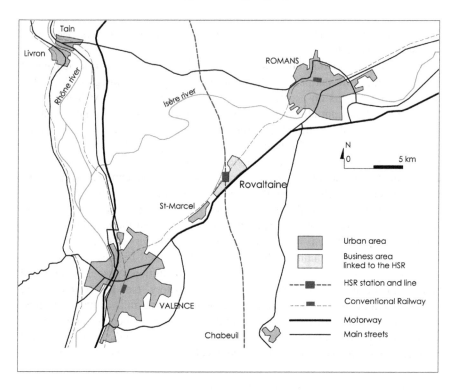

Figure 9.3 Technological park near the station of Valence, France
Source: Authors based on Ribalaygua (2005).

The importance of these aspects, related to those of accessibility, is also demonstrated in the study carried out on the activities in the areas surrounding the intermediate Spanish HSR stations (Ribalaygua and García, 2010a). The study interviewed companies in the areas surrounding the HSR stations about the factors that influenced their location decision. The results show that 28 per cent of the companies considered accessibility to the city to be very significant while for 13.9 per cent of them land availability was the main factor. Aspects such as the price of land or the cost of renting, the proximity to clients and suppliers, or even the quality of the urban environment were found to be of less importance.

It is significant that practically half of the premises (49.4 per cent) are dedicated to the creation of new businesses, which seems to indicate that their market may be aimed at the new HSR station. Independently of the connection with the HSR services, the new conditions of urbanisation and accessibility that come with the renewal of the conventional station into an HSR one or the creation of a new HSR station favour investment in purchasing or renting commercial spaces.

However, the number of premises used for the relocation of existing businesses is significantly lower, and the use of premises for the relocation of central offices already located in the HSR city is very low. This finding contradicts what was observed in the first studies carried out in France, where the station was used for the 'modernisation' of certain local companies and less so for attracting new businesses (Mannone 1995).

The difference between central and tangential locations is minimal in this case, while we can hardly report data regarding the location of peripheral stations in Spain because there is no activity in their surrounding area within a radius of 600 metres[8] (the area of reference in these studies).

The pre-existence of activity in the area surrounding a HSR station is so necessary that it has become a key factor in locating recent peripheral stations in France after a large number of failures in the 1980s and 1990s. Thus, a new location criterion for French exurban HSR stations emerged in 2001, when they began to be located at or near existing poles of activity. The Spanish stations of Guadalajara, Segovia and Antequera show no connection with the existing activities and, in cases such as Puente Genil and Tarragona, there is a minimal relationship with nearby activities.

In this sense, the strategies to be developed in the case of the central HSR stations are aimed at overcoming the shortage of land and implementing the potential that they have as an attraction point, continuing with activities already established in the city but with the understanding that the new railway is a stimulus for the renewal of the area.

The change in the profile of the passengers induces in many cases a reorientation of the market. We have recorded this in central stations such as Cordoba, but also in tangential stations that inherited existing conventional railway installations and stations. This is the case in Toledo, which has renewed activities in the area around the station alongside slow changes in its physical support such as buildings and streets (Guirao et al. 2008). Other cases such as Ciudad Real, which is also tangential, show the reorientation of previous activities, in this case industrial, making use of the favourable image and accessibility of the HSR to open up new and more specialised technological markets that replace the simply productive previous profile.

9.2.3 Performance of the Accessibility of the High-Speed Rail Service

There are also other functional aspects which are affected by the location of the HSR stations. A central HSR station implies a reduction in the HSR speed while proceeding through the urban area (usually along the urban conventional rail lines), but it also contributes to an increase in the number of HSR services that stop in these cities. Peripheral HSR station's locations allow a larger number of

---

8   A radius of 600 m was determined as the baseline for the study on the understanding that it is a walkable distance from any type of station, based on the prior analysis of other studies by Bertolinni and Spit (1998) 700m; Bourgeois et al. (1997) 600m; Menéndez et al (2006) 500 m and Bowes and Ihlanfeldt (2001) 400 to 600 m. See Ribalaygua et al (2009a) for a more detailed methodological discussion on this aspect.

HSR services to pass through without stopping. That is the reason why so many small cities wish, and fight, for a centrally located station instead of an exurban location (Guadalajara in Spain, with only 10 stopping services out of 46 that use its Madrid–Barcelona HSR line – this means that 36 HSR trains pass by – is a good example of this tendency).

We can also state that the location of the HSR station (central, tangential or peripheral) implies an initial tendency towards specific HSR patrons, with particular *areas of influence* that are initially different, regardless of whether these factors are later confirmed, or transformed, by the development of accompanying strategies. Peripheral stations' area of influence may be larger in terms of their easy access by car and parking facilities, while central stations depend to a greater extent on public transport. In this sense, peripheral stations may serve a regional territory while central ones will better serve their urban area and only other regional places when good public transport services are in place.

The Spanish experience, as well as that of other European countries, indicates that the magnitude of the HSR effect has little to do with 'having' a station but more to do with the type of existing rail services (prices, timetables, frequency and number of trains). In this sense, the larger the area affected by the HSR station, the larger the number of potential travellers and the more interesting the HSR offer. This finding means that a peripheral station, simply thanks to its location, may have in principle the potential for a larger regional clientele. However, it will need strong creative measures and management of its infrastructures to improve its real performance through the use of public transport and to achieve the level of urban accessibility of the central and tangential HSR stations.

On the other hand, the creation of *activity in the area* contributes to increasing the possibilities of connection as it will give more meaning to the public local or sub-regional transport services in peripheral stations. In the Spanish experience, the central stations already had activity when the HSR arrived. In some cases, the tangential ones did as well, and in no case did the peripheral stations have any. This activity factor is therefore related to the location of the station.

It does not necessarily have to be that way. The enlightening evolution of the French network (Pietri 1990, Mannone 1995, Ribalaygua, 2005) has led to the creation of activity parks in the areas surrounding the HSR peripheral stations, though only those that are linked to existing activities have been operating, as is the case of *Europôle Méditerranée de l'Arbois de Aix-en-Provence*, which was created seven years before the arrival of the new railway in 2001. Europôle is the first large European park (4,300 ha) dedicated to environmental research and monitoring. Most of the surface of the park (90 per cent) is green area, and the companies that are installed in it are laboratories with public participation involving relevant European companies seeking a quality environment. Other examples such as Rovaltain, in Valence, are also aimed at existing activities. The project, which is supported by the region of Rhône-Alpes, is located on a site recognised since 1992 as among the priorities of the Regional Territorial Organisation and Development Plan, and in 2005 it received the '*Gran Project Rodan-Alpes*' seal granted by the Regional Council to projects that promote sustainable development and international projection of the territories. Although it is part of a wide-ranging strategy, 50 companies of three types are already operating in it: branches and headquarters of environmental management organisations, services for companies and territorial entities that promote the park activities and affect the size of the catchment area.

With respect to the HSR users of urban stations, the use of the railway by the companies located in the vicinity of the HSR stations is significant. Of the companies consulted (Ribalaygua 2009a), slightly less than half (about 47.9 per cent) need to travel by HSR for business purposes, and only 20 per cent use the HSR as their main means of transport. The rest use other transportation alternatives, with the main one being the car (50.6 per cent), in regard to both central and tangential stations.

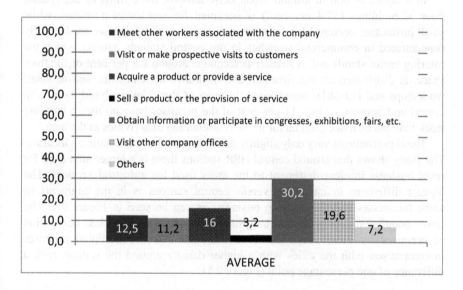

Figure 9.4 Use of HSR by companies located near a HSR station
Source: Authors.

The use of the railway, however, has very little direct effect on the commercial side of businesses as most travel on the HSR to 'obtain information, congresses, exhibitions, fairs' or to 'visit other company offices', and only 3.2 per cent used it to 'sell a product or provide a service'.

In the 1990s studies carried out through surveys of companies in France (Mannone 1995) showed that the HSR mainly transports 'grey matter'. The majority of passengers are business people, managers, high-level civil servants, university professors, etc.; in short, moderately to highly qualified professionals. This pattern is repeated regardless of the location of the HSR station or where the company is located within the city (Klein and Claisse 1997b, Klein 2003). In this case, the link is not different depending on the location, but there is a relationship between the profiles of the companies and workers that use the HSR and, therefore, an inclination towards a type of activity in the vicinity of the rail stop, as will be reviewed later.

9.2.4 Performance of Activities. The Effects of the Railway on the Development of Activities depending on the Location of the Station

The study carried out on the companies located near Spanish HSR stations concluded that there was practically no activity generated in the immediate vicinity of the peripheral stations. However, in the case of urban stations (central and tangential), the activity is much more apparent.

In a radius of 600 m around urban HSR stations, three fifths of the ground floor of buildings (57.4 per cent) is occupied for residential purposes, while small businesses occupy 18.2 per cent of it. These small businesses are basically concentrated in commercial stretches in the central stations, among which the catering sector stands out. A smaller percentage, around 2.5 per cent of the floor space, is distributed among financial and insurance activities, as well as small workshops and industrial warehouses. In most of the cities analysed, both with central and tangential sites, 11 per cent of the premises have no use, a building stock that can be a deciding factor in the reorientation of activities in the area.

These percentages vary only slightly depending on the urban station's location. The study shows that around central HSR stations there is a larger area used for retail business in clear detriment to the areas used for industrial services. The biggest difference in tangential versus central stations is in the segments of small businesses and the catering business, as can be seen in Figure 9.5. The lower population density around tangential HSR stations means less occupation of premises for these uses. Moreover, there are fewer unoccupied premises in comparison with the cities with a higher density around the station, with a difference of one percentage point (Figure 9.5).

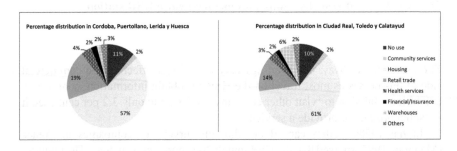

Figure 9.5 Comparison of the types of activities according to the HSR stations locations

Source: Authors.

9.3 Accessibility and High-Speed Rail in the Spanish and French Experience

9.3.1 Policies on Intermodality in Spain

Spanish accessibility and intermodal policies at HSR stations have evolved to a large extent based on European experience and guidelines. When the first Spanish HSR line was being built in 1990, the first European High-speed Network Director Plan (which established the priorities for the following 15 years) included scarcely any knowledge about the structuring capacity of the European HSR network. The expression of the EU policy that affected Spain was defined in the Communication of the Commission (directive 91/440/CEE), which presented the advantages of the network and the convenience of being integrated into supra-municipal planning. This beginning urge to coordinate the new system with the reorganisation of the regional and local functional structures for their optimisation; however, in Spain, the national guidelines point in a different direction when it comes to locating stations and making decisions on coordinating modes of travel.

Spain had barely inaugurated its first HSR line when the White Paper, 'Growth, competitiveness and employment. The challenges and ways forward into the twenty-first Century',[9] appeared. This work is a final step towards the integration of a global Trans-European network (TEN) and the incorporation of the three key factors now in force: interoperability, intermodality and sustainability.

The support for complementarity between means of transport in other official documents, such as the Essen List,[10] contrasts with the objectives of the first continental draft, which evidently intended to capture passengers from other transportation modes. This push was a firm move compared to the first drafts of the report 'Towards Trans European Networks: objectives and applications'[11] of 1989, in which transport reorganisation was barely mentioned.

The Spanish HSR network configuration is also affected by two new official documents that created coherence with European guidelines in matters of accessibility and intermodality: The 1999 European Territorial Strategy included the European high-speed network plans,[12] focusing on the idea of recovering lines

---

9 In the document, 60 per cent of the projects contemplated are aimed at the development of the high-speed railway, with four priority objectives: interoperability, intermodality, and promotion of intelligent and sustainable transport systems. Commission of the European Communities 1994.

10 Christophersen Group. 1995. *Report on RTE to the European Council of Essen.*

11 The report describes the projects and configuration difficulties in an incipient European network. The most relevant aspect of the report was that it brought to public attention the advantages of a European high-speed network, defending the technical and economic feasibility of the new railway. Commission of the European Communities 1989. *Towards Trans European Networks; objectives and applications*

12 The coherence between the scheme of the Trans European Working Group in 1990 and the contents of the *White Paper* made it possible to agree upon a network and the establishment of 14 priority projects, confirmed in December 1994 at the Essen Summit,

and adapting the speeds to the connection needs depending on the distance between poles. The new 2001 White Paper on Transport included a revision of the priority projects. The action programme proposed by the White Paper contemplated several priority issues,[13] but the one referring to the 're-equilibrium of transport modes' was the seed for the functional structures reorganisation dealt with in this chapter.

The National Strategic Reference Framework[14] shows the support for HSR and the importance given to the reorganisation of transportation, in coherence with the Strategic Transport Infrastructure Plan 2007–13. The priority of the EU is completing the Trans European Transportation networks and, especially, railway connections. Along the same lines, it is also a priority to increase the 'capillarity' in the European network links, improving the connections with the secondary or regional transport networks.[15]

In urban areas the strategic document expresses the need to promote clean and sustainable public transport modes and to develop and/or optimise intermodal platforms to guarantee a greater interconnectivity between HSR stations, conventional railway stations, bus stations and the underground network. The strategy also insists on the need to complement this action with greater coordination and with timetables and complementary tariffs.[16]

The connection of the HSR station with the nearby territory through public transport contributes to the configuration of intermodal nodes around the HSR stations, a strategic objective coherent with the European transport policy, as indicated by the European Committee of Regions.[17]

---

with a list of projects that are considered top priority, known as the Essen or Christophersen list. Committee of Territorial Development. 1999: ETS, European Territorial Strategy, Towards a balanced and sustainable development of the territory of the EU p. 75.

13   Eliminate bottleneck points, re-equilibrate the modes of transport, the quality of the service for the users and the management of the effects of the globalisation of transportation; White Paper. 2001. *European transport policy for 2010: time to decide.*

14   European Commission. General Directorate of Regional Policy. 2006. National Strategic Reference Framework. Fundamental strategic objectives with respect to Spain in the period of 2007–13. Final Version of 10 March 2006.

15   In this same sense, the intention is to 'improve the level of the traditional railways in order to guarantee the connection with the high-speed network and an adequate capillarity of the system, with respect to both the transportation of goods and of passengers. Support shall be given to the development of a model in the form of a matrix as opposed to the conventional radial model' European Commission. General Directorate of Regional Policy. 2006: 21.

16   European Commission, General Directorate of Regional Policy. 2006: 22.

17   For an effective and efficient transportation system, it is essential to integrate the different means of transport at local, regional, national and European levels. Integration is important for the economic development of the regions, whether they are peripheral or urban. Report of the Committee of the Regions on 'A strategy for sustainable transport for the regional and local entities and the European Union' CDR 255/97 end, Official Diary n° C 180 of 11/ 06 /1998, p. 0001.

The above policies make it clear that there is strong interest in intermodality and in supporting territories with difficulties in accessing HSR. In this sense two specific key aspects are addressed in this chapter:

- The reorganisation of the transport system when HSR arrives.
- The strategies aimed at favouring accessibility in low-density territories.

9.3.2 The Reorganisation of the Regional Transport System: the Case of France as a Reference Model

The reorganisation of the regional transport system in France, following the arrival of HSR, shows the value of developing measures that contribute to increasing the capacity of spreading accessibility, achieving more widespread benefits, granting access to the regional population and not limiting its effects to urban areas (Rodríguez et al. 2005).

With this in mind several reorganisations have been put into motion, some based on the railway system and others on the creation of new forms of managing and organising the different types of transport, with intermodality appearing as the best way of connecting HSR with the territory affected by the station.

The examples studied indicate that the best way of using the infrastructure depends on the actions and strategies developed around the HSR, that is, on the existence of a project to reorganise the regional transport model, in which the railway and the regional bus networks are organised around the HSR stations and complemented with on-demand transport systems.

Thus, for example, in Brittany (France), the reorganisation of the railway connections with other modes of transport following the arrival of the HSR shows an interesting experience. A system of intermodality was planned, and innovative transport, territorial and urban development projects were implemented. This includes the creation of parking spaces, '*Les parcs relais*', on the outskirts of the cities, which allow drivers to park their cars for free, take a train (HSR or conventional regional train) into the city centre and travel through the cities by underground, bus or bicycle, all of which is accomplished with a single ticket for all rail and bus transport.[18] These actions are reinforced in the territorial development plan (specifically in the *Schéma de Cohérence Territoriale*-SCOT) which proposes a change in the transport model by reducing car journeys, increasing the use of public or alternative transport systems (walking, bicycle) and linking the different systems (underground, regional conventional trains, bus, HSR).

The Rhônes-Alpes region can be added to this experience. Here, the main objectives are to improve the quality and capacity of the railway lines to facilitate access to the trains by all types of customers and to organise the train and bus timetables at regular intervals to facilitate their use. To support the regional rail network and to improve its services, the *Schéma Directeur Regional d'Accessibilité*

---

18 Ville de Rennes, 2005.

du Service de Transport for the Rhônes-Alpes region was approved in April 2008. Its objectives are to create a hierarchical network of stations and interchange poles to guarantee accessibility to the whole territory.

These projects to reorganise transport in France have been possible thanks to public actions at different levels. First of all, the State, through the two railway institutions (SNCF-*Société Nacional de Chemins de Fer* and RFF-*Réseau Ferré de France*), is improving the quality and capacity of the lines, electrify the regional railway network, improve access to the train, organise the train and bus timetables and improve the services at the stations. This is complemented by services enabling the passanger to book a taxi upon arrival on HSR, reserve a parking space in the outgoing station, to unify tickets if combining an air journey with the HSR, and to rent a car at the destination station, all of which contribute to a greater territorial penetration by the HSR.[19] On a local scale, in the definition of the proposed urban model (local plans), parking areas are reserved and intermodal public transport poles are created (rail stations, bus, underground and taxi). The municipalities are also developing local mobility plans to provide sustainable actions, a new model of transport based on a balance between the different modes, offering alternatives to the use of the car and access to the transport network as a whole. The reorganisation of regional transport following the arrival of the HSR calls also for Transport Services, Accessibility and Mobility regional plans in which the intention is to coordinate the different railway services (HSR and regional) and to support the HSR mixed services partially along the conventional lines (see Chapter 1) as a way of penetrating the territory with greater intensity.

Parallel to these developments, intermodal systems must be implemented to promote a better relation between rail transport and the local and regional bus network. To this end the stations and their surroundings must be conceived as interchange hubs for the different types of transport, with coordinated timetables and integrated management.

9.3.3 Supporting the Access to the Station in Low-Density Territories: Responsive-Demand Transport Systems

Unlike the improvement in accessibility to the cities that have HSR, it is much more difficult to connect stations with rural territories. The connection of stations with the nearby territory through public transport lines contributes, as we have seen, to fulfilling the European strategic objective indicated by the European Committee

---

19 According to the information of the French railway company (SNCF), it is possible to access the reservations centre of Taxis G7 by Internet or, if travelling in first class, through the conductor. The 'Resaplace' service or Internet can be used to reserve a parking space in the outgoing station. Plane and HSR tickets can be unified into a single ticket. Train Service plus car rental make the comfort of the train and the mobility of the car compatible (price for two days, 500 km, insurance, local taxes: 100.01 Euro). Train service plus hotel discounts are also offered.

of the Regions.[20] To do so the National Spanish Plan of Transport Infrastructures (PEIT)[21] includes among its guidelines the idea that a 'Real accessibility' to the territory is provided by the services offered and not only by the infrastructures. This means meeting the need for effective public access to the hubs of the high-performance networks. This 'capillary' access will be encouraged through inter-institutional coordination and adapting the infrastructures to these needs.

In the case of low-density territories, responsive-demand transport systems can be a useful tool, complementary to the regular services, Due to the difficulties encountered by certain social sectors in accessing services from less dense territories (Paulley et al. 2006)[22] this system is based on offer flexibility (Oña 2001, Oña et al. 2002). The key to its operation consists of responding to a specific demand in real time, which, in many cases, has led to more economically profitable and energy efficient solutions. New telecommunication technologies facilitate route organisation and real-time reservation systems, which are essential for low-density (demand) territories.

Responsive-demand transport systems are effective for rural areas (CERTU 2006) and for low-density urban peripheral areas. Although the number of experiences applied to HSR is still very low, there are a few examples. In France, Créabus is offered in Vendôme as a responsive-demand transport service, based on the use of microbuses. It is complementary to the conventional bus lines (VBus) and allows for personalised trips to all of the stops on the network. This program is a solution when trips cannot be made using conventional services or to prevent the circulation of buses with very few passengers (Centre de Transports du Loir-et-Cher 2007).

Lerida's subregional transport is managed by its 'Territorial Authority for Mobility' and complements the regular public services with others that have pre-established timetables but are based on the users' previous demands. This service has been implemented in areas where a regular service is not justified but in which there is a clear need for mobility, mainly for health, education or work purposes. This service is not necessarily linked to the HSR station.

The analysis of different European cases (Meer and Ribalaygua 2008) suggests that these responsive-demand services are suitable, using minibuses for territories that are not very large and taxis in the cases of very low density. For affluent commuters it would be desirable to have dissuasive car parks and to combine transportation of commuters with the distribution of mail, transportation of schoolchildren, etc. Moreover, the use of new telecommunication technologies is

---

20   Report of the Committee of the Regions on 'A sustainable transport strategy for regional and local entities in the European Union' CDR 255/97 end, Official Diary n° C 180 de 11/ 06 /1998, p. 1.

21   PEIT 2007–13, Document proposal. Action guidelines: 56,

22   Factors such as tariffs, the quality of the service and the economic level have considerable influences on the demand for public transport, as indicated by Paulley et al. (2006).

an essential tool in the organisation of this type of responsive-demand transport system as well as the inter-linking of information among transport modes.

9.4 Conclusions

New HSR stations influences spatial reorganisation on a two-fold scale: territorial and urban. On both scales, we find renewal strategies that modify the conditions of accessibility to the several nucleus. Following the arrival of the HSR new accessibility models are configured. They are defined in an early planning phase for the creation of new infrastructures (which includes reservation of land for new activities and protection of certain territorial values) and later phases involving the management of transport and development and promotion of projects that optimise the arrival of the new railway at each nucleus.

The city functional structure is typified by two factors that characterise the model in accordance with the type of location of the station: the 'degree of accessibility' achieved and the station's 'capacity to generate activity'.

Central stations have accumulated a long history of local, and often regional, transport infrastructures linked to the station that is reinforced with the arrival of the HSR, which becomes an important communication and transport centre. The opposite is true in the case of the peripheral stations, which have sufficient land to implement adequate access but do not have the capacity to maintain regular public transport services due to low and discontinuous demand.

The best use of the infrastructure depends on the characteristics of the mode itself and, especially, on the actions and strategies that are developed around the HSR; that is, it depends on the project to restructure regional transport, in a coordinated action among the agents. The arrival of the HSR in a region leads to the revision of the transport model with the aim of distributing its benefits, allowing access to the whole region and not limiting its effects to the urban areas.

Several systems have been implemented with this idea in mind. Some based on the railway mode and others on new management and organisation of the different transport modes in order to connect HSR with the rest of the transport network. In this sense, intermodality appears to be the best way of connecting HSR with low-density areas through conventional trains, public bus networks or demand-responsive transport systems.

Low-density territories specially need demand-responsive transport systems which, through very specific actions, connect these territories with the new stations.

Chapter 10
Economic Assessment of High-Speed Rail in Spain

Vicente Inglada, Pablo Coto-Millán, José Villaverde and Pedro Casares[1]

10.1 Introduction

High-speed rail (HSR) is currently the most significant mode of transportation in Spain. In 2010 Spain became the country with the largest HSR network in the European Union and the OECD. Nevertheless, the political choice to support the HSR does not correspond with the economic analysis that is necessary for any public investment policy. In objective terms public investment should be made if the cost-benefit analysis provides an adequate social rate of return.

At the end of 2010 the Madrid–Valencia link added 336.7 km of new HSR to the existing network coverage giving a total of 1,964 km in service (with speeds over 250 km/h), making the Spanish network the second largest in the world, behind China. Consequently Spain currently has more HSR than its neighbour France (1,872 km), or the world's pioneer in high-speed rail, Japan (1,875 km). However, fewer passengers are transported by the HSR in Spain compared to that of Japan (approximately 5 per cent of Japanese passengers) and France (approximately 10 per cent of French passengers).

In other words, in 2010 there were over 300 Million passengers in Japan and over 113 Million passengers in France, while in Spain the number of passengers during 2010 was scarcely over 14 Million.

According to Spanish government data, 64,000 million Euros had been invested in HSR lines as of the end of 2010. The result of this investment in the last decade has merely been the maintenance of the number of passengers (as in the rest of Europe, where the investment has been much lower). The number of passenger per Km in 2008 was 59,000 on the Paris–Lyon line (France) and 51,000 on the Köln–Frankfurt line (Germany), whereas on the Madrid–Barcelona line (Spain) this number was under 11,000 for its first working year. These data show inefficient utilisation of the capacity that was so costly to develop.

In Germany the government's choice was, generally, to modernise lines to enable speeds of 210–230 Km/h and to make passengers and merchandise rail services compatible (see also Chapters 1 and 2), which is referred to in Spain

---

1   Vicente Inglada from the Complutense University of Madrid and Pablo Coto-Millán, José Villaverde and Pedro Casares from the University of Cantabria.

as high performance. Using this German model in Spain would have required much less investment of resources and would have achieved a slightly smaller proportion of passengers and a great improvement in the proportion of transported goods. Nevertheless, the option chosen in Spain thus far has led to lines that do not even cover their usage costs. It will be crucial to determine whether the problem worsens or improves with each new line that is introduced into the service, that is, whether the traffic density is decreasing or increasing. Bel (2010) concludes that this density is decreasing, based on the observation previously made by, Thompson (1994), Haynes (1997), Van den Berg and Pol (1998a) and Givoni (2006) that the demand in small regions and cities is absorbed by larger, more economically dynamic cities, especially commercial and recreational cities. However, Coto-Millán et al. (2007) and Inglada et al. (2010) defend the opposite opinion, that is, the existence of network economies for the HSR in Spain.

In Spain, the Strategic Plan for Infrastructures and Transport (PEIT) (see Figure 1.6) has foreseen investments for the period 2005–20. Its goal is that by 2020, all of the provincial capitals will be connected to Madrid by HSR. With the financial crisis of 2008 public investment has been reduced in most areas in Spain, although the investment in HSR has not been significantly affected.

The decision to build the Madrid–Seville HSR line first rather than (as would appear more logical) the Madrid–Barcelona HSR line does not consider the criterion of social benefit from public investment. This result is demonstrated in Coto-Millán et al. (2007), based on the existence of network economies through its connection with the French railway network.

The European Commission (2008) and Albalate and Bel (2011) estimate that projects with fewer than 6 million passengers in the first year of service are only justifiable if the costs of construction are very low and the time savings are high. For medium costs and journey time savings, the minimum would be at least 9 million passengers in the first year (see also Chapter 2).

Among the numerous factors that moderate the social benefits of the HSR the volume of demand is the most relevant (Coto-Millán and Inglada 2002), and this determines the economic viability of each project. The objective of this chapter is to determine the minimum demand threshold that makes an HSR project economically viable in Spain. Using reasonable magnitudes of the influencing parameters in the profit and cost analysis, this threshold is estimated to be approximately 6.5 million complete trips. A complete trip (or passenger) is defined as a trip along the entire HSR line from start to finish, that is, with a trip length that is equal to the total length of the HSR line. It is obtained as a quotient of passengers-total in kilometres of the route and the total length of the HSR infrastructure. As described later, in all HSR routes, intermediate stations and even antenna-like extensions of the infrastructure introduce numerous trips that are shorter than the total length of the infrastructure.[2]

---

2   For example, in the case of the Madrid-Barcelona-French Border route, the average trip length is estimated to be around half the length of the infrastructure; therefore, the number

The delimitation of this social benefit threshold allows us to conclude that it is difficult for an HSR route in Spain to be profitable from an economic perspective, given that the results of the existing forecasts about the demand for different HSR routes suggest that this threshold can only be reached on the Madrid–Barcelona–French Border route (this implies taking advantage of the network economies once the Figueras–Perpignan section is in service and is extended to connect with the French HSR network, which is called TGV) and in some trunk sections, such as the Madrid–Valladolid section. This section provides a link or common core service for all the routes to the north (Galicia, Asturias, Cantabria, País Vasco and Castilla-León) from the centre and south of Spain and is another example of utilising network economies. In this sense the foreseen extension in the PEIT of the HSR (see Figure 1.6) of a network of more than 10,000 kilometres enables the positive potential economies to be accentuated. This can increase HSR demand more than proportionally as the network is extended and can improve the social benefits of the various routes, especially the trunk routes and those that link the network with France (the same may apply to Portugal).

The structure of this chapter is as follows. The second section addresses some basic Economic Analysis questions. The third section provides a description of the typology of the existing HSR demand. The fourth section analyses the basic characteristics of the HSR demand. The fifth section details the methodological framework that is used for the social evaluation of projects, combining the cost-benefit analysis technique with the internalisation and valuation of external factors of transport. The sixth section provides the values used for the parameters that are necessary to perform the simulations and undertakes a sensitivity analysis. The seventh section lists and analyses the results of the demand threshold, which delimits the positive social benefits of a typical HSR project in terms of diverse variables. Finally, in the eighth section, the most relevant conclusions are drawn from the results obtained.

10.2 Basic Economic Questions: What, How, and for Whom?

The question of what to produce can be addressed using consumer demand theory, and through aggregation, market demand can be generated.

The question of how to produce can be addressed using business theory. In their eagerness to maximise profit businesses end up generating the business offer, which leads to the market offer through aggregation.

The question of for whom to produce can be addressed by observing those who are prepared to pay a particular price for a certain product or service.

In social market economies governments can intervene in markets when there are failures related to the strategic policy of the economic agents, the existence of information asymmetries and problems of the assignation of property rights. In

---

of passengers on the route is approximately half the total number of passengers.

this third type of problems government action to alleviate the problems generated by an important external factor in transport, such as congestion, can be justified. Congestion can be observed from three perspectives: congestion in the passenger railway network itself, congestion in the passenger and goods railway network and congestion in other transport modes. Worldwide experience seems to indicate that the existence of HSR is due to the interest in correcting the external nature of congestion and achieving greater efficiency in France, Japan and Germany; only in the case of China does its existence seem to be due to political priorities.

It is well known that government action is not only justifiable from the perspective of the correction of market faults (that is, to generate the efficiency lost due to their presence), but it is also justified in actions that generate greater equality. The market model provides information about efficient assignations from a Paretian perspective, but not in terms of equality. Governmental action may be justified with the aim of favouring equality in such a way that territorial cohesion and regional development are the objectives that justify the HSR. From this point, and with a clearly defined political objective of equality, a cost and benefit analysis should be conducted on the social rate of return of public investments. If this social rate of return is not sufficient, other alternatives to the HSR project should be studied, including lower design speeds, combinations of passengers and freight transport and the re-use of existing railway infrastructure. If these alternatives are not viable from the perspective of social benefit, other projects should be pursued that help to provide citizens with greater equality. The construction of an HSR in Spain to connect the provincial capitals to the national capital, with an objective that is accepted as equitable, should comply with economic cost-benefit analyses that should be conducted for all public investments.

10.3 Analysis of the High-Speed Rail Demand

Given its relevance to the magnitude of the net benefit from the HSR, this section analyses the main characteristics of the HSR demand and distinguishes its two components.

The introduction of the HSR is associated with a significant reduction in the generalised cost or price of railway travel, generating an important volume of demand in this new transport mode. This reduction, which is produced in the non-monetary components of cost (time, comfort, etc.), produces two clearly differentiated effects on demand: 'induction' and 'substitution'. These effects correspond, respectively, to the trips that would not have occurred if the new service did not exist and the trips that would have existed using another mode of transport (see also Chapter 6).

Induction Effect

The component of HSR demand that is usually called 'induced demand' consists of all the new journeys. This 'generation effect' includes those travellers who had not previously undertaken the trip and the increase in the frequency of trips undertaken by people who were already travelling before the HSR was introduced into service. The magnitude of this component is particularly important in the case of the HSR. Therefore, as can be observed in Table 10.1, the average annual number of trips undertaken by the users of the Madrid–Seville route increases very significantly, from 11.1 to 15.2.

Table 10.1 Evolution of the frequency of trips on the Madrid–Seville route

	Before HSR	**After HSR**
Two or more per week	3%	6%
Once a week	6%	8%
Every fifteen days	7%	9%
Once a month	16%	16%
Once every three months	18%	16%
Less	30%	17%
Did not travel	21%	—
The first time	—	28%
Average number of trips a year	11.1	15.2

Source: Authors based on Inglada (1994).

Substitution Effect

The introduction of the HSR is associated with not only a significant reduction in journey time but also results in benefits to other components of the generalised cost of travel, such as safety and comfort. Based on a survey of Madrid–Seville HSR passengers, the relevance of these components among the preferences of the passengers are shown in Table 10.2. It can be highlighted that among the main reasons for choosing the HSR, comfort has a similar importance (29 per cent) to time (30 per cent) and is noticeably more significant than price (11 per cent). This result is especially significant within the group of air passengers, where the relative importance of comfort (31 per cent) is much greater than price (19 per cent), achieving a value that is similar to the sum of the 'traditional' components of the generalised cost of travel: price and time.

Table 10.2   Motives for choosing HSR in terms of other alternative transport modes. Madrid–Seville route (% of the long-distance segment)

	Car	Plane	Coach	Train	Total
Speed/Time	42	13	67	57	30
Punctuality	0	4	0	2	3
Comfort	35	31	13	19	29
Price	6	19	22	2	11
Novelty	3	11	3	9	9
Safety/Fear	10	6	0	0	5
City centre	0	4	0	0	2
Timetable	0	6	10	8	5
Others	4	6	5	3	6

Source: Authors based on Coto-Millán and Inglada (2003c).

Due to the high impact of the substitution effect, the introduction of the HSR produces significant effects on the demand for the transport modes that compete with it. In addition to the practical disappearance of the conventional train on the same routes, the introduction of HSR also causes an important decrease in air traffic; a 50 per cent reduction in air traffic occurs in the case of the Madrid–Seville route. In our case, we will use a substitution percentage of 40 per cent, which is the value obtained by Coto-Millán and Inglada (2003c) for the Madrid–Barcelona route. For travel by car, the decrease is less than in the previous cases, approximately 20 per cent for the Madrid–Barcelona route. Finally, in the case of coach travel, there does not appear to be a strong impact on the long-distance routes (11 per cent loss), given that both products are scarcely substitutable.

Therefore, it can be concluded that the introduction of the HSR produces a drastic change in the modal distribution of the demand, it being justifiable to talk about the transport market before and after the HSR. In this sense, it should be highlighted that the HSR has become the predominant mode of transport on the Madrid–Seville route, surpassing car travel and air travel in market share.

The initial demand for the route was determined before the introduction of the HSR using data from transport operators and mobility questionnaires. Based on the Madrid–Seville HSR results (Inglada 1994), the substitution and generation factors of the new travel demand were determined.

Analogous to the process of introducing a new product on the market, the potential national demand for the HSR is only achieved after a period of maturation. To estimate the demand evolution over this period, which has been estimated at four years, the frequently-used hypothesis that the evolution in the demand for a product is similar to the logistic curve is assumed. The estimation suggests that the demand reaches 50 per cent in the first year, 70 per cent in the second year,

90 per cent in the third year, and in the fourth year, all of the potential demand is achieved.

To evaluate the project and to apply the cost-benefit tool, it is necessary to determine not only the initial HSR demand but also its evolution over the period considered, disaggregated into its two components: generated and diverted traffic, as well as the revenues that are needed to assess the benefits produced by the trips generated.

To solve this problem it has been assumed that the demand for the HSR has an elasticity in terms of the Gross National Product that is equal to 1.4. This value is similar to the value obtained in air transport in Spain (Coto-Millán et al. 1997) and is in consonance with those obtained in other countries (Owen and Phillips 1987). Several scholars, including Bonnafous (1987), claim that the HSR is more like a plane than a conventional train.

10.4 Analysis of the High-Speed Rail Offer

As substantiated by the Madrid–Seville and Madrid–Barcelona routes, in the so-called high-speed offer in Spain, we can distinguish both the 'pure' HSR, which we distinguish as Long Distance (also called 'pure long-distance HSR'), and two other segments: shuttles (also called 'medium-distance HSR') and Variable Gauge (also called 'mixed HSR' services), which have specific characteristics (see Chapters 1, 6 and 7). The offer of these additional products enables a more efficient use of the infrastructure that capitalises on the excess capacity that exists in the Spanish HSR.

Table 10.3 shows the differentiating features of each of these segments for the Madrid-Barcelona route. This will be the model for the example considered in this work.

The essential discriminating factors between shuttles and long distance are the type of demand served and the price, whereas the variable gauge segment is differentiated from the others in its use of different rolling stock due to the need to use infrastructures with different gauges. Using part of the existing infrastructure over part of the trajectory along with the necessary gauge-change operation at the interchange means that the average speed, and therefore the reduction produced in the generalised cost, is less than that in other segments of the HSR offer.

A more detailed analysis shows that the shuttle segment, with low tariffs, new services with a greater offering of tourist-class seats and a predominant use of discounted ticket fares for frequent users, generates a railway demand for recurring day-return trips (commuters; see Chapter 6). This situation is a consequence of the reduction in the generalised transport cost (essentially, in time and price), which in turn produces a reduction in the price of a complementary area, such as housing. In fact, the shuttle segment is a high-quality suburban train that helps to increase the profitability of the costly HSR infrastructure.

Finally, the Variable gauge segment enables the same rolling stock to use the new line with UIC gauge and the conventional lines with the Spanish gauge. Thus, it is necessary to provide systems that allow the use of both types of gauge with a minimal time loss in the interchange between the two infrastructures.

Table 10.3 Discriminating factors of the Madrid-Barcelona HSR submarkets

	Shuttles	**Long distance**	**Variable gauge**
Routes	Barcelona–Tarragona	Madrid–Barcelona	Madrid–Soria
	Barcelona–Gerona	Madrid–Zaragoza	Madrid–Logroño
	Barcelona–Lerida, etc.	Others	Others
Material	Alsthom	Talgo and Siemens	Brava
Infrastructure	New high-speed lines	New high-speed lines	New and Conventional lines
Prices per passenger-km (cents Euro 2002)	8.11	10.82	9.32
Occupation level	0.60	0.65	0.60
Demand type	Suburban train with a high percentage of commuting trips	Long distance	Long distance

Source: Authors based on Coto-Millán and Inglada (2003c).

10.5 Cost-Benefit Analysis of the High-Speed Rail

The methodology used to evaluate the social benefit in the HSR cost-benefit analysis is a generalisation of the one used by Dodgson (1984). It is extensively described in De Rus and Inglada (1993, 1997) for the Madrid-Seville HSR case, in Coto-Millán and Inglada (2003c) for the Madrid–Barcelona–French Border case, and in Inglada (2010).

A summary of the basic points in relation to time savings is given next. As can be seen in Figure 10.1, for conventional train and coach users, the generalised cost (g_t), composed of the fare (p_t) and the value of total time spent on the trip ($g_t - p_t$), decreases to the generalised cost value of travelling by HSR (g_h). The benefits derived from this reduction can be expressed for each transport mode as $(g_t - g_h)q_t + 1/2(g_t - g_h)(q_h - q_t) + p_h q_h - p_t q_t - C_t + C_h$. This expression equates the areas of the rectangles $g_t b g_h e$ and $p_h f p_t j$ minus the net cost incurred to obtain these benefits (see Figure 10.1). This cost corresponds to the cost associated with the introduction of the HSR minus the savings generated by the suppression of conventional train and coach services.

Examining Figure 10.1 and ignoring who appropriates the excess, the social benefit can be obtained for the trips diverted from other transport modes through the time savings produced on introducing a faster mode of transport. Therefore, it is sufficient to calculate the travelling and accessing times reduction and multiply this by the time value.

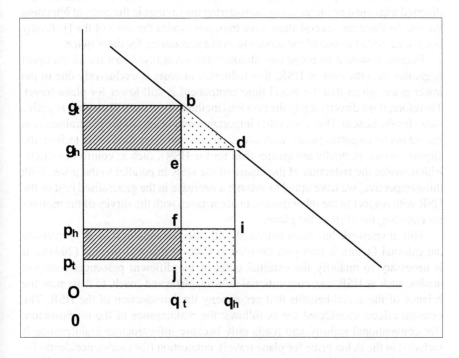

Figure 10.1 HSR benefits for passengers transferred from trains and coaches
Source: Authors.

For the trips generated, the total benefit produced is represented in Figure 10.1 by the area under the demand function (the trapezium bdq_hq_t) minus the area of the rectangle (edif), which represents the travel time and can be broken down into two elements. The first, which is represented by the rectangle (fiq_tq_h), is obtained through the income accrued from these trips $(q_h-q_t)\cdot(p_h)$. The second, represented by the triangle (bde), is half of the product of the difference of the generalised costs for the generated trips multiplied by the number of these trips $(q_h-q_t)\cdot(g_t-g_h)/2$.

Based on the survey conducted after the start of the Madrid–Seville HSR service, it was possible to distinguish among the trips generated due to the trips frequency increase (of previous users of other modes of transport) and truly new trips. For those who had previously travelled the generalised cost of the previous mode of transport was used as a reference, whereas for the new trips the weighted average of the generalised costs of the different transport modes was used. The weightings were determined from the survey's substitution effect data.

This methodology is valid for the conventional railway and coach, but it must be modified for the plane and the car. For the car the savings in resources in the diverted trips must be increased by considering the savings in the costs of operating the car. As there are several alternative transport modes the costs of the HSR only need to be added in one of the modes to avoid accounting for them twice.

Finally, it should be noted that although the generalised cost for air transport is greater than the cost of HSR, this reduction in costs is exclusively due to the lower price, given that the travel time component is still lower for plane travel. Therefore, if we directly apply the previous methodology, we will obtain a negative value for the benefit. However, other important components of the generalised cost should not be forgotten (along with adding access and dispersion times to/from the airports, which normally are greater than for the HSR), such as comfort or safety, which enable the reduction of the disuse of the HSR in parallel to the price. With this perspective, we have opted to assume a decrease in the generalised cost of the HSR with respect to the other modes, in accordance with the survey of the motives for choosing the HSR or the plane.[3]

This framework has been extended with the methodology used to evaluate the external factors in transport detailed in Coto-Millán and Inglada (2003b). It is necessary to quantify the external costs of the different passenger transport modes, such as HSR, car, conventional railway, plane and coach, to determine the balance of the social benefits that accompany the introduction of the HSR. The external effects considered are as follows: the maintenance of the infrastructure (for conventional railway and roads only because infrastructure maintenance is included in the ticket price for plane travel), congestion (for roads), accidents (for conventional railway and roads because they are considered negligible for the HSR and plane) and environmental effects (noise, pollution and climatic change for all modes of transport).

Similarly, all of the characteristic criteria for the evaluation of the projects social aspects have been used. These include shadow prices and tax exemption and are detailed in Coto-Millán and Inglada (2003c).

In summary, the total net social benefit (benefit-cost) of a HSR project is

$$\sum_{i=1}^{i=4}(t_i - t_h)q_t + \frac{1}{2}(g_a - g_h)\left(q_h - \sum_{i=1}^{4}q_i\right) + P_h\left(q_h\sum_{i=1}^{4}q_i\right) + \sum_{i=1}^{4}C_i + B_{exter} - C_h$$

Where i =1, ..., 4 = Bus, Conventional train, Plane and Car.

Therefore, the components of the total net social benefit are the following:

---

3   According to the evaluations given by the users and stated on the questionnaires, the generalised cost of the alternative modes has been extended to introduce other useful components: comfort, safety, etc. To do this, these costs have been multiplied by 1.8 for the car, 1.2 for rail travel, 1.15 for the coach and 1.5 for the plane.

- $\sum(t_i - t_h)q_i$: Sum of time savings X diverted trips in each mode
- $1/2(g_a - g_h)(q_h - \sum q_i)$: Generalised cost improvement for the generated trips (g_a = generalised cost before the introduction of the HSR)
- $p_h{}^*(q_h - \sum q_i)$: Income from the trips generated
- $\sum C_i$: Sum of the savings in each mode
- B_{exter}: External benefit (environmental, accidents, congestion and maintenance of infrastructure not considered in the prices)
- $-C_h$: Cost of HSR (infrastructure, maintenance and exploitation).

Table 10.4 shows the costs and benefits categories considered in the economic evaluation of a prototypical project. Therefore, we have not directly considered the macroeconomic, sector-related and regional effects that are analysed in depth by Álvarez and Herce (1993) and by Inglada (1993). These works illustrate the diverse macroeconomic effects produced during the construction of the infrastructure, which are common to all types of public investment. Among the positive effects, we can highlight the strong impact on the generation of employment, whereas other macro-factors, such as inflation and the balance of the public and exterior sectors, worsened. The strong pull effect on public investment is also well known, as is the effect of the transport sector on the other sectors. Nevertheless, in the case analysed here, it could be less than in other alternative projects, given that part of the incorporated inputs originate in other economies.

Table 10.4 Categories of costs and benefits considered in the evaluation of a prototypical HSR project

Costs	Benefits
Total Cost of the infrastructure, maintenance and exploitation (CT = I – R + MM + MI + E)	Total benefits (AT + RC + RCE)
Infrastructure (I)	Time savings (AT) of users from:
Residual value (R)	Other modes of transport
Mobile material (MM)	Trips generated
Maintenance of infrastructure (MI)	Reduction of costs (RC) in:
Exploitation (E)	Conventional railway
	Plane
	Coaches
	Car operation costs
	Reduction of external costs (RCE) in:
	Congestion
	Accidents
	Environmental
	Maintenance of the infrastructure

Finally, and from a regional equilibrium perspective, the benefit of the HSR introduction is evident for the corresponding territories, considering the peripheral situation of Spain with respect to the principal decision and production centres of the European economy. However, this effect is difficult to quantify, especially if the intention is to separate it from the benefit inherent in the transport time reductions generated by the HSR, which has been considered in this chapter (Nash 1991). Bonnafous (1987) describes the regional effects of HSR, indicating that the greatest impact has been produced in the Paris region and highlighting that some sectors, such as the hotel and catering industry, have declined.

Another category of benefits that were not included in the analysis is associated with the delay in public investment motivated by the traffic decrease on the alternative transport modes infrastructures. However, due to the strong expansion of transport infrastructures during the implantation period of the HSR, there will be an excess capacity in the alternative transport modes, which will drastically reduce the magnitude of this effect. Therefore, it has not been included in the quantification, with the assumption that it is part of the margin of error itself.

For example, as stated by Coto-Millán and Inglada (2003c), in the case of the Madrid–Barcelona route, the relative decrease in Madrid airport traffic due to the HSR would be very small[4] and would not be a decisive factor in the decision about a possible extension of this airport. Similarly, another benefit of the Madrid–Zaragoza–Barcelona HSR is the estimated approximately two-year delay in the required improvement of the Madrid–Zaragoza motorway as opposed to the alternative of maintaining the 'status quo'. Nevertheless, congestion on this motorway will not occur until ten years after the HSR project has finished, so its influence on the evaluation results will not be significant.

According to Coto-Millán and Inglada (2003c), the methodology for evaluating the costs and benefits is as follows.

Costs

Similar to any other product, the HSR costs can be classified as fixed, semi-fixed or variable, depending on the time frame considered. The fixed costs correspond to the construction of the infrastructure (in a wide sense) and its maintenance (although in the long term, these costs will probably evolve in parallel to demand). The semi-fixed costs correspond to the acquisition of rolling stock. Finally, the variable costs, or exploitation costs, are characterised by their high sensitivity to the evolution in travel demand. All taxes have been removed from each cost category.

A summary of the methodology used to quantify each of these cost categories is given next.

---

4   According to the estimations, the reduction in travellers in Barajas airport as a consequence of the introduction of the Madrid-Barcelona HSR will not be greater than 7 per cent.

Construction of the infrastructure The HSR infrastructure includes the line, such as the embankments, signalling, stations, rails and electricity. The total expenses and their distribution in time were obtained from the information available at the Spanish national railway institutions (ADIF and RENFE). The total cost of the 855 kilometres is 7,928.3 million Euros. Each kilometre of construction of the infrastructure cost 9.27 million Euros in 2002, which is the year that was used as a reference.

Maintenance of the infrastructure From the data included in the RENFE reports, the cost of maintenance of the infrastructure[5] is estimated to be 10.22 thousand Euros per kilometre. In the long term there will probably be a slight sensitivity of this cost to the level of demand. This effect has not been considered because it is assumed that it would be counteracted by a probable decreasing tendency of unitary costs of maintenance that is associated with the economies of scale generated by the extension of the HSR network.

Rolling stock From the information supplied by RENFE, the unitary costs of the three types of rolling stock considered are as follows:

   20.7 million Euros for long-distance trains
   9.6 million Euros for shuttle trains
   11.4 million Euros for variable-gauge trains

Obtaining the necessary rolling stock The methodology used to determine the required number of rolling units is as follows. In the long-distance case, the average capacity of the HSR trains (both Siemens and Talgo brands) is 361 passengers. An occupancy factor of 0.65[6] has been assumed, which is equivalent to 235 passengers transported per unit. Multiplying that value by the annual mileage of each unit in normal exploitation conditions (450,000 kilometres) indicates that 105.75 million passengers-kilometre per year will use the new train.

   For shuttles, an occupancy factor of 0.60 has been assumed. With their capacity of 238 passengers and based on the assumption that the train will travel 400,000 kilometres per year, it is necessary to introduce an additional train for every 57.12 million passengers-kilometre.

   For variable-gauge rolling stock, once again, based on an occupancy factor of 0.60, a capacity of 228 passengers per train and a standard mileage per year of 400,000 kilometres, a new unit is needed for every 54.72 million passengers-kilometre.

---

5   This value also includes other concepts such as conservation of the stations and superstructure. In the cost-benefit analysis, the corresponding VAT must be excluded.

6   This occupancy corresponds to the Madrid-Seville route that has been in service for 15 years.

It must be highlighted that ideal usage conditions or maximum efficiency in the incorporation of the new rolling stock has been assumed. Therefore, there are no discontinuities; the new units will be gradually incorporated when necessary, and the flow of expenses evolves in parallel.

Operating costs   This category includes all the costs derived from the HSR exploitation[7] and has been evaluated separately for both types of rolling stock. For long-distance rolling stock, the cost is 7.90 cents per passenger-kilometre, whereas for the other segments of the offer, it was 6.73 cents in 2002.[8]

Residual value   The rolling stock lifetime is considered to be 20 years, and a linear depreciation rhythm has been assumed during this period.

The Spanish Ministry of Public Works has studied the useful lifetime values for each of the various categories that comprise the infrastructure, which include rails, electrification and safety (Ministry of Public Works (MOPT 1991)). As an average of the various categories and sites, a value of 45 years has been estimated for the entire set of infrastructures. Therefore, after 40 years of use and assuming a linear depreciation, the residual value would be minimal, approximately 10 per cent of the value of the investment. Likewise, for a life period of 30 years, the residual stock value would be approximately 33 per cent of the initial investment.

Benefits

The methodology and the data used for the evaluation of the above-mentioned categories of the benefits are developed next.

Time savings   The first benefits category that accompanies the introduction of the HSR includes the time savings of the passengers who switch from other modes of transportation and new passengers. For each transport mode, it is necessary to determine the travel times from the origin to the destination (including the times to and from the station or airport) and the monetary values assigned to the total travel time. Likewise, to identify the savings that correspond to the trips generated, it is necessary to know the monetary costs of any transport mode that enables income to be derived.

---

7   Therefore, the categories of energy, personnel, maintenance of rolling stock and services, such as catering, video, etc., are included. We also opted to introduce 'extensive maintenance' in this cost, which is done every seven years.

8   In the cost-benefit analysis, it is necessary to subtract the VAT corresponding to the expenses in materials and services (a category that represents about 85 per cent of the total).

Table 10.5 Travel times on the Madrid–Barcelona route

Trip times Table 10.5 Travel times on the Madrid–Barcelona route	Car	Plane	Coach	Train	HSR
Journey time	5h 45'	55'	7h 35'	6h 35'	2h 35'
Access and dispersion time		1h 35'	50'	1h	50'
Total time	5h 45'	2h 25'	8h 25'	7h 35'	3h 25'

Source: Authors based on Coto-Millán and Inglada (2003c).

Trip times   Table 10.5 shows that the HSR is the second-fastest mode on the route after the plane, due not only to its high speed but also to its shorter access times. As shown in Table 10.3, the access times for HSR service are the shortest of all the transport modes, due to the central location of many the stations, the high punctuality, its optimal boarding facilities and several other factors.

Value of travel time   The modal monetary values of travel time in this work have used those supplied by the Spanish transportation administration, suitably updated and detailed in MOPT (1991). These values were used in De Rus and Inglada (1997) for the Madrid-Seville HSR route and in Coto-Millán and Inglada (2003c) for the Madrid-Barcelona-French border HSR route. These values are an average that corresponds to the various types of travel, and they take into account the main travel time as well as access and dispersion times. Table 10.6 shows the assumed values.

Table 10.6 Assumed Time Values (Euros 2002 per passenger and hour)

Car	Plane	Coach	Train
6.04	25.56	3.25	13.01

Source: Authors based on MOPT (1991).

Monetary costs   Table 10.7 shows the monetary components of the generalised cost for each mode of passenger transport that competes on the Madrid–Barcelona route. The HSR tariff is higher than any other transport mode, except for planes. In this case, if the maximum quality of the HSR is considered, its price is very close to that of the plane. These values are used to calculate the generalised cost of each transport mode, summing the monetary value of the modal total travel time. In this way, we can calculate the benefit that corresponds to the generated trips.

Table 10.7 Monetary costs of the various modes of transport, Madrid–Barcelona route (Euros 2002)

Car	Plane	Coach	Conventional train		HSR	
			1st Class	2nd Class	Business	Tourist
57.22	122.05	22.84	58	44	128.68	86.70

Source: Authors based on Coto-Millán and Inglada (2003c).

Reduction of the costs of alternative transport modes Another category of benefits that is inherent in the new product is the reduction in the costs of the alternative modes of transport: conventional railway, plane, coach and car.

Reduction of the costs of the conventional railway The intermodal substitution produced by the HSR is especially pronounced for the conventional railway, which becomes practically a marginal mode on the route.

To determine the corresponding reduction of costs, the structure of the average cost of production[9] of the daytime train is used, which is the mode that is most affected by the reduction. Of all of its components, the only one not included is half the cost associated with the category of stations. In contrast, the entire amortisation category has been incorporated, based on the possibility of the train being used on another transportation corridor.

Because the offer of long-distance conventional rail services practically disappears on this route, a unitary ratio of the cost per passenger-kilometre can be used to determine the total cost. This cost is obtained by applying to the average national value a coefficient that represents the differential of occupancy on this route with respect to the national average. This has been estimated to be 0.0385 € for the year 2002 per passenger-kilometre coming from the conventional train.

Reduction of the costs of the plane The displacement of travellers from air transport towards the HSR generates a reduction in the costs for air transport operators on the Madrid–Barcelona route. In this mode of transport, and in contrast to the conventional railway, the reduction in the offer (a reduction in the number of flights) is produced through a decrease in the average occupancy.

---

9   Therefore, the costs of central organisation, also referred to as structure costs, have not been considered.

For this reason, instead of being based on a unitary cost per passenger-kilometre, the methodology is based on the reduction in the number of flights to obtain the cost savings on the route, considering the average cost of a flight.

The unitary saving per flight has been obtained, removing part of the commercialisation and all the taxes from the total fixed costs, such as those corresponding to structure. The amortisation category has been maintained because the plane can be used on another route, as can be clearly understood in the case of the operator renting the plane. The final magnitude obtained is 0.1261 € per passenger-kilometre coming from the plane.

Reduction of the costs of the coach   The effect on the coach of the intermodal substitution produced by the introduction of the HSR generates cost savings in the operators through the reduction in the number of ticket sales. These savings were calculated based on the costs structure of a representative coach (MF 2010). It is important to emphasise that within the saved cost, all the components have been considered, even amortisation, given that there is a possibility (opportunity cost) of using this vehicle for another line in the medium term. Therefore, only the costs of the taxes category have been removed because it is assumed that the costs of structure or organisation are included in the data corresponding to discretional coach travel. The resulting savings from coach travel are 0.0319 € per passenger-kilometre.

Reduction of the costs in the car   In the case of private vehicles, unless they are rented, there is no possibility of substituting the initially foreseen displacement for another mode during the same period. Therefore, the categories that have the character of 'fixed' costs, such as amortisation and insurance, should not be included in the determination of the saving costs. The included part of the amortisation category is based on the MOPT (1991), where it is estimated that half of this category corresponds to the passage of time, whereas the other half is associated with the utilisation of the vehicle.

Continuing with this assumption, the structure of cost savings was obtained, eliminating the categories of fixed costs and taxes. The costs considered in each section and the specific methodologies applied are as follows: amortisation of the vehicle, maintenance, fuel consumption, oil consumption and tyre wear. The resulting overall savings are 0.0667 € per passenger-kilometre.

Saving of external costs   To evaluate the external costs, the values cited in Coto-Millán and Inglada (2003c) have been considered in this study and are shown in Table 10.8.

Table 10.8 Marginal external social costs per transport mode (Euros 2002)

	Environmental	Maintenance of infrastructure	Accidents	Congestion
Tourism	1.64	0.73	2.65	1.86
Train	0.52	2.28	0.15	0
Coach	058	0.14	0.68	0.32
Plane	2.14	0	0	0
HSR	0.43	0	0	0

Source: Authors based on Coto-Millán and Inglada (2003c).

10.6 Sensitivity of the Cost-Benefit Analysis Parameters

The simulations for the prototypical HSR project consider various parameters with the aim of conducting a rigorous sensitivity analysis. Based on empirical evidence, the parameters with the greatest influence on the project benefits are the following.

Discount Rate

To determine the final net benefit of the project, it is necessary to update the annual flows of profits and costs to the base considered year through a real social discount rate r. Thus, the present value (VAN) of the investment is as follows:

$$VAN = \sum_{t=1}^{n} \frac{B_t}{(1+r)^{t-1}} - \sum_{t=1}^{n} \frac{C_t}{(1+r)^{t-1}}$$

The project evaluation manuals of the transport infrastructure administration recommend using a social discount rate of 6 per cent in real terms. Likewise, this value has been used in other infrastructure projects (especially roads) conducted in Spain during the 90s. Riera (1993) uses ratios that are even greater (8 per cent and 10 per cent) for the economic evaluation of the Barcelona ring-motorways.

Nevertheless, the existence of favourable economic expectations since Spain's entry into the Economic and Monetary Union has resulted in the consolidation of real long-term low interest rates below 3 per cent. It thus seems logical to use a rate of 4 per cent for the real discount rate as a basic alternative in our evaluation of the HSR project.

Duration of the Project

Two project lifetime durations have been considered: 30 years and 40 years. The latter period seems particularly suitable given the project size and the experience with the Madrid-Seville HSR, and even more so considering that the use of a discount rate of 4 per cent penalises the net profits in future years to a lesser extent.

The evaluation is performed at stable 2002 prices. We assume that the relative prices of the various goods and services will be maintained during the project lifetime.

Economic Growth Rate

In the base scenario, the annual rate of growth of the GDP is assumed to be 3 per cent during the entire project. According to the opinions of many economic analysts, this value would correspond to the average potential rate of growth of the Spanish GDP, and it coincides with the growth rates average value over the last ten years. Alternatively, for the sensitivity analysis, two scenarios have been considered; these scenarios correspond to GDP growth rates of 2.5 per cent and 3.5 per cent, respectively.

The social profitability of the HSR is obtained by comparing the costs and benefits described previously, updated to the base year through the chosen rate of social discount. For each GDP rate of growth and other parameters, a demand value is obtained, from which the current value of the net social benefit is found to be positive.

10.7 Minimum Demand Threshold for Social Profitability

Minimum Level of Demand for Social Profitability

Figure 10.2 shows the costs and benefits of the prototypical project, updated to the base year with the real social discount rate of 4 per cent while assuming a duration of 40 years and a GDP growth rate of 3 per cent, which are the values chosen for the basic scenario. It can be observed that the costs and social benefits magnitudes of the HSR are sensitive to the levels of demand on the route.

Similarly, the slope of the benefits curve is noticeably greater than that of the costs. The cause of this weak sensitivity of costs to the levels of demand lies in the important weight of the fixed costs, particularly those that correspond to the infrastructure (Thompson 1994). Compared to the other transport modes, the HSR profitability is much more dependent on the traffic density on the route given that the offer of additional units of rail service incorporates a much smaller additional cost, due to a strong economy of scale effect. The disparity between the fixed and variable costs is higher for HSR than for road transportation, and it is even higher when compared to air transportation. The fixed costs of this new technology can be two or three times higher than those of road transportation. Moreover, these costs are incurred in the first years of the project, even before it comes into service, notably penalising its profitability.

Figure 10.2 shows the curves that correspond to the Net Present Value (NPV) of the social benefits and the costs depending on the traffic on the route, which is expressed as the number of complete passengers. Logically, due to the existence of important categories of fixed costs (that is, independent of the demand, whereas all of the categories of benefits are sensitive to it), the slope of the curve of the NPV of the costs is less than that of the benefits.

Figure 10.2 shows that the magnitude of the demand that corresponds to the cut-off point of the two curves where the NPV of the social benefits and costs coincide and which represents the minimum level of complete passenger traffic that makes the HSR project socially beneficial is 6.5 million complete passengers.

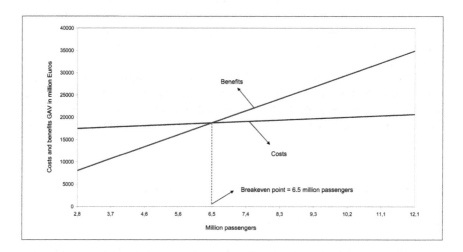

Figure 10.2 Evolution of costs and profits in relation to demand (Assumptions: Discount rate 4%, growth rate 3% and duration 40 years)

Source: Authors

Sensitivity Analysis

Table 10.9 shows the results of the simulations conducted to determine the sensitivity of the demand threshold that makes the HSR socially beneficial to the different values of the parameters. The parameters that were considered for the sensitivity analysis and their respective values are the discount rates (4 per cent and 6 per cent) and GDP growth (2.5 per cent, 3 per cent and 3.5 per cent). The values obtained for the demand threshold vary from 6.1 to 8 million complete passengers, with an average value of 7 million. The introduction of higher values for human life expectancy (1.5 million Euros) and for duration (60 years) slightly reduces the magnitude.

Table 10.9 Minimum volume of demand for HSR profitability (million equivalent passengers)

Discount rate	GNP growth rate		
	2.5%	3%	3.5%
4%	6.7	6.5	6.1
6%	8	7.6	7.1

Source: Authors

This social benefit threshold enables us to conclude that it is difficult for a section of HSR in Spain to be economically profitable. The results of all of the existing previsions of the demand on different HSR routes indicate that this threshold can only be reached on the Madrid–Barcelona–French Border route. This route will capitalise on the network economies once the Figueras (Spain)–Perpignan (France) section is introduced into service and the French HSR network is extended to Perpignan[10]. The HSR is also profitable in some trunk sections, such as Madrid–Valladolid, which provides a common link to the northern routes (Galicia, Asturias, Cantabria, País Vasco and Castilla-León) from the centre and the south of Spain. The HSR may also be profitable for some other trunk sections which are common for the Madrid-Valencia, Madrid-Alicante, Madrid-Murcia, Madrid-Sevilla and Madrid-Málaga See Figure 1.6.

For all of the previously mentioned reasons, transport planning and policy are at a crossroads and are confronted with a crucial challenge. However, the expansion of the HSR across Spain is now practically accomplished as a result of successive decisions by previous governments and cannot be reversed. However, the cost-benefit analysis economic evaluation of the various HSR routes shows that from the perspective of society as a whole, the HSR is only profitable on a few routes. What can be done in transport policy to escape this deadlock, using the criterion of maximum social benefit as a guide?

The answer to this question lies in the use of diverse complementary alternatives. For the routes where the foreseen HSR demand is less than the previously estimated social profitability threshold, an alternative to create profitability for the project would consist of the reduction of costs, particularly those that correspond to infrastructure, thus displacing the cost curve downwards, decreasing the minimum demand threshold and making the project profitable. In the routes with less potential demand, an example of this alternative is the utilisation of a part of the existing rail infrastructure, which would enable commercial speeds close to 200km/h to be reached through suitable improvements. The resulting reduction would be achieved in the infrastructure costs and in the other categories of external

---

10 Although it is currently the most commonly used route, its volume of traffic is not greater than 5 million complete passengers per year.

costs, such as environmental costs, with the drawback of less time savings. This approach has been adopted in the later extension of the HSR both in Japan and in other European countries (see Chapters 1 and 2), capitalising on part of the conventional network. In this way, the obstacle of the high cost of new pure HSR lines can be avoided.

Another alternative consists of the upward displacement of the benefits curve, thus decreasing the minimum demand threshold to make the project profitable. An example of this alternative would be the utilisation of the HSR to transport goods, which would generate an increase in several categories of benefits, including time savings and a reduction in the maintenance costs of the conventional road and rail infrastructures (which would be less necessary due to the reduction in traffic). An example is the section that links Tarragona with France in the Madrid–Barcelona–French border route, in which the transport of both passengers and goods is viable due to the geometrical characteristics of the design of the route.

Finally, in relation to HSR profitability in Spain, there are important synergies in terms of social benefits associated with the expansion of demand in the previously functioning routes for extending the network throughout the Iberian Peninsula. An example of the relevance of these network economies is described in Coto-Millán et al. (2007) for the Madrid–Barcelona–French border route, where the extension of the French HSR network to Perpignan might make this project socially beneficial, with a positive result for the NPV in the cost-benefit analysis. This effect of the network economies, which is common to the previously existing network, is especially clear in the trunk sections, such as Madrid–Valladolid.

10.8. Conclusions

The economic evaluation of Spanish HSR projects show that there are numerous factors that influence their profitability to a greater or lesser extent. Among these factors, demand is the most relevant given that this new mode of transport is characterised not only by its high speed (more than double the speed of the conventional railway) but also by the high cost of the infrastructure. Because its fixed-cost component is practically independent of the number of passengers, the infrastructure must have high volumes of demand to achieve an acceptable level of profitability.

Likewise, the profitability of HSR is sensitive to other parameters, such as the social discount rate, economic growth rate, project duration, and value of human life. The conducted simulations enable us to state that the traffic volume that delimits the social benefit threshold of each project is 6.5 million complete passengers, that is, trips that use the entire HSR line.

If this demand threshold is not achieved on the analysed route it would be necessary to consider alternative projects that have lower associated costs, particularly those that correspond to the infrastructure. An example of this is the utilisation of part of the existing rail infrastructure on the routes with lower potential demand, with a consequent reduction in the infrastructure costs and other costs categories, even though the benefits produced by the time savings would be smaller.

Another alternative consists of the utilisation of the HSR to transport goods, designing a high-performance network that would generate an increase in the diverse categories of the benefits.

Finally, important synergies in terms of the social benefits of extending the network throughout the Iberian Peninsula are associated with the expansion of demand in the previously functioning routes. This positive effect of the network economies is common to the previously existing network and can be clearly seen in the trunk sections, where diverse routes merge. Considering the benefit associated with these network effects, whose magnitude increases along with the extension of the HSR network, the demand threshold of 6.5 million complete passengers could be reduced in future projects.

Chapter 11
Afterthoughts: High-Speed Rail Planning Issues and Perspectives

José M. de Ureña[1]

11.1 Introduction

This book has shown that High-speed rail (HSR) not only has profound implications for passenger transportation but also substantially influences spatial development and planning issues, both on the interurban and urban scales. In addition, rapid transport has had a profound relation with modern forms of production and working procedures.

What was initially thought of as a mere transportation tool for long distance inter-metropolitan travel has been shown, over the years, to have a much more diversified role.

HSR alone may only modify the means and the frequency of travel, but accompanied by other local and regional initiatives, it can be a useful tool for spatial planning.

Thus, the balance between HSR upfront investments, running costs and usefulness cannot be analysed without considering both the transportation and the spatial planning perspectives.

11.2 Core versus Peripheral Areas, Big versus Small Cities

In the scientific literature there is debate regarding whether investments in transportation infrastructures are more beneficial to core or peripheral areas. These debates may be inconclusive because it has become clear that any transportation investment has implications in both of them. Furthermore, in each area the implications differ and are difficult to compare. Any transportation investment facilitates both centralisation and decentralisation; depending on the type of activities, some will tend to decentralise and others will tend to centralise.

It is rather difficult to add and subtract the consequences of these two tendencies. Therefore, it is difficult to conclude whether a transportation investment is more beneficial to the core or peripheral areas. These tendencies to centralise and decentralise depend not only upon the spatial situation and the type

1   University of Castilla La Mancha.

of transportation means but also on other aspects, such as the local initiatives and the prevailing socio-economic dynamics.

On the other hand, the regime of flexible accumulation requires a powerful system of transport and communications capable of efficiently integrate the different urban and territorial entities in order to reduce the durations of economic activities. The Spanish experience shows that HSR is able to improve accessibility of most places, but to a greater extent of some small cities that previously weren't well connected to the most important cities, but have intermediate positions between the bigger Spanish cities, thus facilitating their incorporation into the new accumulation regime.

11.2.1 Reinforcement of Large Urban Centres

From a transportation point of view the HSR network and services will tend to help the main urban centres reinforce their capacity to communicate with each other.

These main urban areas already have a high level of connectivity with the rest of the country (via air, road and rail); HSR reinforces this high-connectivity level. This book has explained that transport capacity between major distant urban areas was the primary reason for the implementation of HSR.

Long-distance HSR services mainly inter-connect metropolises. In Spain 74 per cent of these services do not have intermediate stops or have only one stop at a large intermediate city (cities of more than 0.3 million inhabitants) while two thirds of these HSR services do not serve any intermediate small city.

Four HSR lines (Madrid–Seville–Malaga, Madrid–Barcelona, Madrid–Valladolid and Madrid–Valencia) converge in Madrid, and a fifth line, which is planned for the near future (Madrid–Lisbon), will also do so transforming Madrid in the main beneficiary from the HSR network. The international HSR connection to France and the Mediterranean HSR line that will also be implemented in the near future will be beneficial for Barcelona, which will concentrate three HSR lines. No other Spanish city is expected to be served, in the near future, by more than two HSR lines.

This book has confirmed that HSR plays a relevant role in national inter-metropolitan passenger transportation. For instance, the number of passengers on air shuttle flights between Madrid and Barcelona has been halved, as many passengers are now using HSR instead. This role is more pronounced in countries that have a long tradition of HSR and a well-developed and interconnected HSR network.

HSR has not yet had a major role in international inter-metropolitan passenger transportation. The current usage of international HSR is not satisfactory, even though some of these cover similar distances (e.g., between two to t hree hours of HSR travel) and connect metropolises as large as those with success at the national level (e.g., Paris–London, London–Amsterdam, Paris–Amsterdam). This is an important issue because there are many other potential international interurban lines with similar distances in Europe (e.g., Madrid–Lisbon, Lyon–Milan, Berlin–Warsaw, Berlin–Copenhagen, Munich–Vienna) and because the EU is engaged in a large-scale promotion of a HSR Trans-European Transport Network (TEN). The present lack of success may be due to incomplete interoperability as well as time-consuming control and checking procedures (e.g., London–Paris, London–Brussels) that reduce the advantages of HSR compared to air transport.

In addition, whether or not travel along longer international HSR lines (e.g., Barcelona–Paris 1,200 km, Madrid–Paris 1,300 km, London–Marseilles 1,200 km, Paris–Roma) will become relevant remains to be seen. These trips require five or more hours of HSR travel time. The required investments for some of these inter-metropolitan international connections may be small because most of the lines have already been built by national HSR networks; thus, fewer passengers may be required for these HSR lines to be profitable.

11.2.2 Helping to Balance the National Spatial Development Patterns

This book has shown that HSR does not necessarily lead to dramatic changes in regional economics. However, it has also shown that cities with HSR stations at intermediate locations along HSR lines have been able to increase their economic activities. Governments could use HSR in these intermediate cities to modify the present concentrated spatial territorial pattern to a more polycentric one.

However, HSR only transports people, whereas motorways, conventional rail and aircraft transport both goods and people. Thus, the HSR implications are rather specialised, whereas other means of transport have more general territorial implications. In this sense, HSR has only minimal implications for industrial cities but may have stronger implications for tertiary cities.

As has already been mentioned in this book, the Spanish population is concentrated in the centre of the Iberian Peninsula (Madrid metropolis) and near the coast (between 500 and 700 km from Madrid). The Portuguese population is also concentrated along the coast. The three coastal strips (each approximately 60 to 100 km in width), i.e., the Mediterranean along the east, the Atlantic along the west and the Cantabric along the north, are composed of continuously distributed urban areas, with only a few less-populated areas. Inland, both in Spain and Portugal, the situation is almost the opposite, with a few populated medium-size urban areas, several small urban areas and many declining rural areas. See Figure 11.1.a.

Inland of the Iberian Peninsula there are at least four types of urban areas with HSR access. The territorial implications and opportunities for some of these areas have been explained in this book:

- One large city of more than 700,000 inhabitants
- Two medium-size cities of more than 300,000 inhabitants
- Several small cities with between 50,000 and 200,000 inhabitants
- Many very small cities or towns with under 50,000 inhabitants.

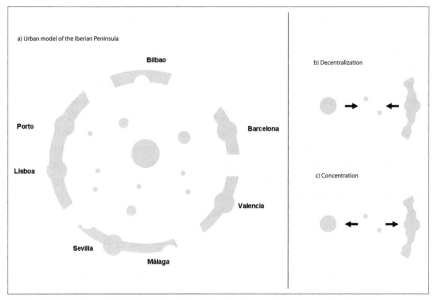

**Figure 11.1 A model of the Iberian Peninsula urban areas and of the
concentration/decentralisation processes**

Source: Author.

Despite the more dense population along the coast, HSR has increased accessibility
more inland compared to along the coastal stripes and Madrid. This is because the
main urban areas already had good road, rail and air connections with the rest of Spain,
unlike the less-populated inland areas. Therefore, the increased transport opportunities
offered by HSR were more substantial for inland cities than for the coastal areas.

Spanish inland urban areas that are, or will be, connected to the HSR network
are located between 200 to 300 km from both the centre of the country and the
coast. This means that 1 to 1.5 hours of HSR travel time would be required. This
book has shown that with these time intervals, HSR allows abundant daily return
travel, thus generating new mobility patterns and attracting activities. Therefore,
HSR presents opportunities for governments and private firms to decentralise
activities to these areas and also to re-concentrate activities at larger cities, because
with HSR it is possible to commute daily along this distance (see Figure 11.1.b).

What might the regional and/or national planning objectives for these areas
be, especially now that there are additional transportation tools to influence their
development? For each city (or groups of cities), the opportunities are different;
they depend on the characteristics of each city and on local initiatives.

One of the challenges may be to decentralise some national public activities
to medium-size and small inland cities. For example, a few years after the
implementation of the Paris–Lyon HSR line, the Interpol headquarters was
transferred from Paris to Lyon. In addition, two years before the second Spanish

HSR line was opened, the Logistics Military Academy was relocated to Calatayud, a small town with 12,000 inhabitants that is one hour from Madrid by HSR. Will it be possible to decentralise some other public activities to cities up to one and a half hours of HSR travel distance from the metropolises? Will it be possible to move the headquarters of these activities or only some of their more routine aspects? Could small cities up to one hour travel time from metropolises be developed into high-quality suburban metropolitan centres? Is this easier for larger cities than for smaller ones? Is this easier for cities that play a substantial regional role (e.g., regional capitals)? With HSR, all of this is more possible than before, but will governments use these opportunities?

Inland regions that only have several small cities at a distance along HSR lines present a different problem. It may be possible to allow several smaller cities to function as a single larger city (see Figure 11.2.a) using HSR if they are along the same line. This may allow these cities to play a greater role in the national system of cities. Under what circumstances, such as time distances between small regional cities and between each of the small regional cities and metropolises from other regions (see Figure 11.2.b), or such as small cities being along different HSR lines (see Figure 11.2.c) would HSR encourage the unification of these small cities or rather their separation by connecting them more easily to external metropolises?

Figure 11.2 Regional systems of small cities connected to HSR

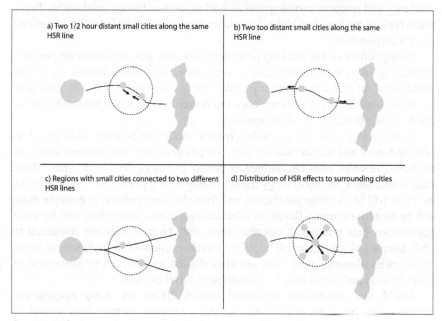

Source: Author.

A third challenge is to develop strategies designed to spread the opportunities opened by HSR to a wider regional territory (Figure 11.2.d). This book has explored the possibility of expanding HSR opportunities from cities with stations to wider areas around these cities and has discussed the needed reorganisation of public transportation to provide more service departing from new HSR stations.

11.2.3 A More Sustainable Territorial Structure

Another type of thought regarding HSR at the interurban scale draws attention to the long-term effects of a linear transport tool with distant stations, and the sustainability of the territorial pattern promoted by it. Originally, even though the HSR objective was to connect metropolises over long distances, stations were established in intermediate locations for security reasons. Later, unexpected HSR travel demand along shorter distances, and the objective of serving more regions, encouraged the creation of stations at closer intervals. This new 'long-distance' transportation tool has a very different territorial set-up than motorways, since the later have access points every few kilometres, facilitating a continuous linear development. HSR, on the contrary, may facilitate a long-term territorial structure of distant cities alternated with less populated areas because the distance between HSR stations would not facilitate a continuous linear urban area.

The present spatial distribution of activities and populations consists of polarised urban structures spread along enormous land surfaces due to road-motorway transportation. This model has led to an unsustainable situation in terms of energy and resource consumption as well as carbon dioxide production. These urban regions are based on highly interdependent areas and on intensive use of car/truck transportation.

On top, office sector working procedures are now less dependent on personal contacts by using telecommunication means (internet, mobile phones, etc.). This could allow for less commuting trips, both because the offices may not need to be so much concentrated at certain places and because persons will not need to be so much at their offices to continue working.

With these in mind, a polycentric territorial model can be envisioned, based on HSR transport and telecommunications, composed of more autonomous small- or medium-size cities each one located at greater distances from each other. These cities would allow for more energy friendly intra-urban trips (i.e. pedestrian, bicycle, etc.) and will be far from other cities and from the metropolises; in between there will be more rural areas. Based on telecommunications, these cities will be more autonomous than traditional suburban areas, and, because they are connected to HSR, people living in them will be able to travel occasionally or frequently to larger distant cities. Because these cities are more distant, it would not be convenient to travel by road and would only be convenient to travel by HSR.

Would this polycentric territorial model, based on more autonomous distant cities, be more sustainable that the traditional metropolitan sprawl in terms of energy and transportation consumption? The traditional metropolitan sprawl encourages many people to commute by automobile. In the HSR and telecommunication territorial model, the number of commuters would be smaller because each city would be more autonomous and would maintain an important percentage of their external contacts through telecommunication procedures, and those who had to commute longer distances would be encouraged to do so by HSR and not by automobile.

Where is the break-even point in terms of sustainability between these two territorial models?

11.3 Facilitating Urban Renewal

The increasingly rapid rate of change in our society and our economy requires equally rapid modernisation of our cities. For this reason, cities must find justification and financing for renewal processes. These processes are twofold: first, processes for reinforcing and extending central areas for office, commerce, residence, and city-wide community services; and second, processes of urban expansion for residence and production. HSR, which was originally thought of only as a new means of transportation, has also been shown to be an excellent catalyst for inducing or accelerating urban processes.

Most of these urban processes occur in the areas surrounding HSR stations, or they are associated with the re-use of the old railway station areas. In many cases, HSR can accelerate the progress of urban projects that have been in process for decades. In other cases, HSR can open new opportunities that had not been previously considered.

The Spanish experience shows that HSR has conveyed a sense of modernity as a marketing tool and has induced collaboration between different social and economic actors. The urban processes catalysed by HSR occur in parallel with the need to restructure the urban railway network.

This book suggests that there are abundant central urban redevelopment projects that have been built or envisioned in parallel with the implementation of HSR; it argues that in most HSR Spanish cities, local and national railway authorities prefer intensive or heavy central redevelopment projects to integrate conventional and new HSR railways in the city, instead of other alternative ways of doing so with less redevelopment (i.e., more soft projects). In France, redevelopment projects undertaken in parallel with HSR have been less intensive (e.g., less railway land was involved and more railway land retained its existing use and structure) and in addition, fewer tracks were put underground. One of the explanations for the degree of urban renewal in Spain may be that most of these projects have been built or envisioned in a period of economic expansion, with increasing housing and office prices. In this context, creating houses and offices on railway land was economically profitable. Due to the Spanish economic and housing crisis that began in 2010, some of these heavy redevelopment projects will likely be directly or indirectly slowed.

The most important aspect of these central urban projects, which are linked in time to HSR, is that most of them try to include objectives of overall urban renewal by strategically using the central urban railway land, which can be transformed in many cities. These overall city objectives include suppressing urban barriers, completing ring roads, expanding central office areas and creating large community service centres and congressional centres. The opportunity afforded by HSR and the redevelopment of conventional rail areas may not be available again for many decades (it has been more than a century since the last similar opportunity).

In some cases overall urban restructuring is accelerated by combining the HSR related projects with others which do not relate to railway, but that are envisioned together with the wave of change promoted by HSR. Even in some other cases the HSR enthusiasm is used to undertake urban changes that have nothing to do with the railway.

Spanish cases show that in a moment of economic expansion, central urban redevelopment projects induced by HSR have been implemented at a relatively rapid pace and have been economically viable. The Spanish case shows also that these central urban redevelopment processes very often generate modern urban areas in addition to the historic urban centres, generating a mixed combination of historic and modern urban forms and buildings that are very convenient for economic growth.

In the case of new stations located at the edge of the city or external to its urban area (termed peripheral or exurban stations in this book), the Spanish experience shows that urban expansion projects are generated in parallel with a new spatial idea or plan for the city or the sub-region. This happens much more often in small cities than in large cities. Most HSR stations in medium and large cities maintain a central location, whereas in small cities they are often peripheral. New stations located at the edge of the city are also more common when the urban railway system is transformed to a greater extent.

In many of these cases, urban processes occur only around the new HSR station in the periphery, whereas in some cases they occur both by dismantling central railway areas and by expansion in the periphery around the new HSR stations. The expansion developments with peripheral HSR stations have additional opportunities afforded by abundant land availability. However, the Spanish experience shows that peripheral infrastructure projects are implemented at a slower pace than central urban redevelopment projects. The peripheral projects also seem to be more unstable, depend, to a greater extent, on economic cycles and are not meeting expectations.

A question that should be asked is whether urban central redevelopments or peripheral expansions are more appropriate for smaller or larger cities. This question is relevant because, as has already been noted, small cities have a higher proportion of peripheral HSR stations, whereas medium size and big cities tend to have central HSR stations. Thus, urban processes induced by HSR in small cities will tend to be expansions, whereas in medium size and big cities they will tend to be central redevelopments. In this sense, are small cities capable of having two areas with office-type activities, i.e., traditional central areas and new peripheral areas built around new peripheral HSR stations?

11.4 Social Benefits of the High-Speed Rail

The socio-economic profitability of public investments is evaluated through several types of analyses, such as cost-benefit and input-output (De Rus 2009). In the case of HSR, there is a consensus that a positive rate of return through transportation advantages (e.g., time savings, security, new trips) will only be fulfilled when a new HSR line reaches a minimum transportation demand, i.e., between 6 and 9 million passengers per year under relatively favourable circumstances of construction costs and discount rates. Although very few new HSR lines meet this requirement, most national governments are engaged in establishing some type of HSR network.

New HSR networks are created to increase the capacity of interurban connections and to generate socio-economic development of cities and territories that they serve (Vickerman 2009). However, most analyses have concluded that the presence of HSR is not a sufficient condition for substantial improvements in the socio-economic structure and dynamics of cities. The train only offers new opportunities for accessibility. These opportunities must be exploited at the local level. To do this, cities and territories often undertake different types of policies and actions, as has been discussed in this book.

HSR is also viewed favourably due to lower external costs, such as accidents, noise, air pollution, and climate change, compared to car and air transportation. Campos et al. (2009a) argue that external costs for HSR are between one fourth and one half that of automobile and air external costs along distances between 300 and 1,200 km.

The global socio-economic transportation evaluation of the new Spanish HSR lines presented in this book concludes that given current construction and operating costs, a HSR line reaches a certain economic rate of return if it is used at least by 6.5 million passengers per year along its entire length. This book has also shown that none of the current Spanish HSR lines have achieved this benchmark. Nevertheless, HSR is generally viewed favourably by society.

In order to understand this dichotomy the overall evaluation of a public investment has to consider three additional aspects: the influence of new elements on the entire transportation network, less measurable spatial or social aspects, and a longer period of time for which profitability is calculated.

This book has suggested that as the HSR network becomes more complex, its new parts obtain higher rates of return because they increase the number of passengers over the entire network.

In Spain four small elements of the HSR network are currently being built. These elements will make the network much more interconnected, which will have the above-mentioned effect. The first of these elements is the Madrid urban HSR tunnel, which connects the south-east to the north lines, thus allowing through HSR services at Madrid and an HSR connection to the airport. The second element is the south-east connection about 40 km south of Madrid, which will allow south-east HSR services to avoid entering Madrid, thus allowing direct connections between Andalucía and Valencia regions. The third element is a complete southwest-southeast and northeast-southeast HSR line inter-connection located 90 km south of Barcelona. The fourth element is also an urban HSR tunnel, in this case in Barcelona, and will allow HSR services coming from inland areas to proceed towards France.

The overall evaluation of a public investment has to consider the implications of HSR not only on transport but also on urban and interurban aspects. These urban and interurban implications are rather difficult to synthesise in economic terms and are therefore difficult to include in traditional economic evaluation methodologies (e.g., cost-benefit analysis). Some authors suggest that these other implications have less impact than the transportation implication (De Rus and Nash 2009). Nevertheless, this book has clearly described the role of HSR in facilitating minor and major urban redevelopments and profound city changes, and it has also described significant interurban changes in HSR cities located in intermediate positions along HSR lines. These intermediate HSR stations result in much more than an apparent compensation for regions traversed by HSR. These urban and interurban implications are difficult to measure in terms that are comparable to transportation costs and benefits. In addition, they take much longer to appear that transportation changes.

Normally the economic viability of a public investment is evaluated in the context of a life cycle of a few decades (25 years or so). The real life cycle of a new transportation network is much longer than a few decades. In addition, changes in the transportation demand, due to new transportation infrastructures and services, appear rather quickly. New economic activities require more time to appear, and spatial changes require even more time. Thus, it is not clear what time periods should be considered. Territorial implications of HSR infrastructure should certainly be evaluated over a period that is much longer than 25 years.

In conclusion, the socio-economic profitability of HSR investments has to be evaluated considering a wide variety of elements, some of which are difficult to measure in comparable terms to the transportation costs and benefits and some of which have a longer life cycle.

Bibliography

Abler, R. F. 1975. Effects of space-adjusting technologies on the human geography of the future, in Human Geography in *a Shrinking World*, edited by R. J. Abler, D. G. Janelle, A. Philbrick and J. Sommer. North Scituate, MA: Duxbury Press, 35–66.

Adams, P. C. 1995. A reconsideration of personal boundaries in space-time. *Annals of the Association of American Geographers*, 85(2), 267–85.

Ahlfeldt, G. M. and Feddersen, A. 2010. *From periphery to core: Economic adjustments to High Speed Rail*. London School of Economics and University of Hamburg. [Unpublished] Available at: http://eprints.lse.ac.uk/29430. [accessed: 4 October 2011].

Aglietta, M. 1982. *A Theory of Capitalist Regulation*. Paris: Calmann-Levy.

Ajenjo, M. and Alberich González, J. 2005. La utilització de la variable població en els indicadors d'accessibilitat. Avantatges i inconvenients. *Documents d'Anàlisi Geogràfica*, 45, 149–468.

Albalate, D. and Bel, G. 2011. Cuando la economía no importa: auge y fulgor de la alta velocidad en España. *Revista de Economía Aplicada*. 55, 171-ss.

Albrechts, L. and Swyngedouw, E. 1989. The challenges for regional policy under a flexible regime of accumulation, in *Regional Policy at the Crossroad*. European Perspectives, edited by L. Albrechts, F. Moulaert, P. Roberts and E. Swyngedouw. London: Jessica Kingsley and Regional Studies Association, 67–89.

Albrechts, L. and Coppens, T. 2003. Megacorridors: striking a balance between the space of flows and the space of places. *Journal of Transport Geography*, 11, 215–24.

Alonso, M. P. and Bellet, C. 2009. El tren de alta velocidad y el proyecto urbano. Un nuevo ferrocarril para la Zaragoza del tercer milenio. *Scripta Nova. Revista Electrónica de Geografía y Ciencias sociales* [Online: University of Barcelone], XIII(281). Available at: http://www.ub.es/geocrit/sn/sn-281.htm [accessed: 24 December 2010].

Altvater, E. 1994. Ecological and economic modalities of time and space, in *Is Capitalism Sustainable? Political Economy and the Politics of Ecology*, edited by M. O'Connor. New York: The Guilford Press, 76–90.

Álvarez, O. and Herce, J. A. 1993. Líneas ferroviarias de alta velocidad en España. *Economía Aplicada*, 1(1), 5–32.

Anderson, A. 1986. The four logistical revolutions. *Papers of Regional Science Association*, 59(1), 1–12.

Aschauer, D. A. 1989. Is public expenditure productive? *Journal of Monetary Economics*, 23, 77–100.

—— 1989. Is public expenditure productive? *Journal of Monetary Economics*, 23, 177–200.

Auphan, E. 1992. Les gares TGV régionales: un exemple de contre-aménagement du territoire. *Hommes et Terres du Nord*, n° 1, 14–20.

—— 2002. Le TGV Méditerranée: un pas décisif dans l'évolution du modèle français à grande vitesse, *Méditerranée*, 1/2, 19–26.

Bailly, A. S. and Maillat, D. 1989. Servicios a las empresas y desarrollo regional. *Ekonomiaz*, 13–14, 128–37.

Bailly, A. S. and Coffey, W. J. 1994. Localisation des services à la production et restaurations économiques. Une analyse théorique. *L'Espace Géographique*, 1, 224–30.

Baradaran, S., and Ramjerdi, F. 2001. Performance of accessibility measures in Europe. *Journal of Transportation and Statistics*, 4 (2/3), 31–48.

Barcet, A., Bonamy, J. and May.et al. 1984. Les services aux entreprises: problèmes théoriques et méthodologiques. *Recherches Économiques et Sociales. La Documentation Française*, 9, 254–77.

Bauman, Z. 2000. *Liquid Modernity*. Cambridge: Polity.

Bavoux, J. J. 1997. *Les Littoraux Français*. Paris: A. Colin.

Bavoux, J. J., Beaucire, F., Chapelon, L., and Zembri, P. 2005. *Géographie des Transports*. Paris: Armand Colin.

Bazin, S., Beckerich, C. and Delaplace, M. 2006. La LGV Est-Européenne en Champagne-Ardenne: quels effets sur la cohésion territoriale champ ardennaise?/The eastern France European high speed railway in Champagne-Ardenne: which effects on territorial cohesion in Champagne-Ardenne?. *Revue d'*Économie Régionale and Urbaine, 2, 245–61.

—— 2007. *L'évolution des marchés immobiliers résidentiels dans l'aire urbaine de Reims: un effet de la Ligne à Grande Vitesse Est-européenne?* Paper to the Congress of the European Regional Science Association (XLVII Congress) and ASRDLF (XLIV Congress), Paris, 29 August – 2 September.

—— 2009. Desserte TGV et localisation des entreprises sur les quartiers d'affaires: nouvelle accessibilité ou nouvelle offre immobilière de bureaux? Le cas de la gare centre de Reims. *Les Cahiers Scientifiques des Transports*, n°56, 37–61.

Beauvais, J. M. 1992. À offre nouvelle, mobilité nouvelle? *Transports Urbains*, 74, 5–12.

Beauvais, J. M., Fouquet, J. Ph. and Assegond, Ch. 2007. *Recherche sur le Développement de la Grande Vitesse et de la bi-résidentialité. Rentrer chez soi chaque soir ou une fois par semaine?* Université François Rabelais: Beauvais Consultants.

Bel, G. 2010. Las infraestructuras y los servicios de transporte, in *La Ley de Economía Sostenible y las Reformas Estructurales. 25 Propuestas*. Madrid: FEDEA, 102–07.

Bell, D. 1973. *The coming of the Post-industrial Society, a Venture in Social Forecasting.* New York: Basic Books, Inc.
—— 1979. The social framework of the information society, in *The Computer Age: a Twenty-Year View*, edited by M. L. Dertousos and J. Moses. Cambridge, MA: MIT Press, 163–211.
Bell, M. E. and. McGuire, T. J. 1997. *Macroeconomic Analysis of the Linkages between Transportation Investments and Economic Performance.* National Cooperative Highway Research Program Report 389, Transportation Research Board, National Academy Press.
Bellanger, F. 1991. *Le TGV atlantique au Mans, à Saint-Pierre-des-Corps, à Tours et à Vendôme: opportunités, acteurs et enjeux.* Maison des Sciences de la Ville: Université de Tours.
Bellet, C. 2000a. L'impacta de l'alta velocitat en ciutats intermèdies. El cas de Ciudad Real, in C. Bellet (ed.), *Les oportunitats del Tren d'Alta Velocitat a Lleida.* Lleida: Pagès editors.
Bellet, C. (ed.) 2000b. *Les oportunitats del Tren d'Alta Velocitat a Lleida.* Lleida: Pagès editors.
Bellet, C. 2002. El impacto espacial de la implantación del tren de alta velocidad en el medio urbano. *Revista de Geografía*, 1, 57–77.
Bellet, C. and Llop J. M. 2005. El proceso del proyecto urbanístico y territorial del TAV/AVE en Lleida. *Ingeniería y Territorio*, 70, 82–87.
Bellet, C (dir.), Alonso, P., Casellas, A., Morell, R. and Gil, E. 2008. *Los efectos Socioeconómicos y Territoriales de la llegada del Tren de Alta Velocidad a Segovia.* Segovia: Ed. Caja Segovia.
Bellet, C. 2009. *The introduction of the high speed rail and urban restructuring: the case of Spain.* Paper to the EURA and UAA International Conference on Urban globalism and Urban change. Cityfutures 2009, Madrid. Available at: http://www.cityfutures2009.com/PDF/32_Bellet_Carmen.pdf.
Bellet, C., Alonso, M. P. and Casellas, A. 2010a. Infraestructuras de transporte y territorio. Los efectos estructurantes de la llegada del tren de alta velocidad en España. *Boletín de la Asociación de Geógrafos Españoles*, 52, 143–163.
—— 2010b. La integración del ferrocarril de alta velocidad en el medio urbano. El caso de Segovia-Guiomar. *Anales de Geografía de la Universidad Complutense de Madrid*, 30(1), 9–26.
Bellet, C. 2010c. Nuevas tecnologías de transporte y metropolización discontínua del territorio. El tren de alta velocidad en Segovia. *ACE-Arquitectura, Ciudad y Entorno* [Online: CPSV Polytechnic University of Barcelona], 12, 27–41. Available at: http://www-cpsv.upc.es/ace/Articles_n10/Articles_pdf/ACE_12_SA_11.pdf, [accessed: 12 September 2010].
Bellet, C. and Gutierrez, A., In press, 2011. Ciudad y ferrocarril en la España del siglo XXI. La integración de la alta velocidad ferroviaria en el medio urbano. *Boletín de la Asociación de Geógrafos Españoles*, 55 251-2796.
Bertolini, L. and Spit, T. 1998. *Cities on Rails. The redevelopment of Railway Station areas.* London: Spon Press.

Beyer, A. 2008. La capacité d´articulation des territoires, enjeu majeur de la grande vitesse ferroviaire européenne. *Bulletin de l'Association de Géographes Français: Géographies,* 85(4), 427–430.

Biggiero, R. 2006. Industrial and Knowledge relocation strategies under the challenge of globalization and digitalization: the move of small and medium enterprises among territorial systems. *Entrepeneurship & Regional Development,* 8, 443–4471.

Blanquart, C. and Delaplace, M. 2009. Innovations relationnelles, nouvelles offres de service et valorisation des nouvelles infrastructures de transport. Le cas de d'une plateforme multimodale et d'une desserte TGV. *Les Cahiers Scientifiques des Transports,* 56, 63–86.

Bleijenberg, A. 2002. *The driving Forces behind Transport growth.* Paper to the International Seminar: Managing the Fundamental Drivers of Transport Demand, Brussels, ECMT.

Blum, U., Haynes, K. E. and Karlsson, C. 1997. The regional and urban effects of high-speed trains. *The Annals of Regional Science,* 31, 1–20.

Boarnet, M.G. and Charlempong, S. 2001. New highways, house prices, and urban development: a case study of toll roads in Orange County, CA. *Housing Policy Debate,* 12(3), 575–605.

Bonnafous, A. 1987. The regional impact of the TGV. *Transportation,* 14, 127–137.

Bontje, M. and Burdack, J. 2005. Edge Cities, European-style: examples from Paris and the Randstad. *Cities,* 22(4), 317–330.

Borzacchiello, M. T., Nijkamp, P. and Koomen, E. 2010. Accessibility and urban development: a grid-based comparative statistical analysis of Dutch cities. *Environment and Planning B: Planning and Design,* 37, 148–169.

Bourgeois F., Barthelemy J., Liotard M. and Guyon P. 1997. *Les gares, locomotives du développement urbain? 1- Réflexion méthodologique à partir de cas français et étrangers. 2- Monographies: Lyon – Perrache, Marseille – Saint-Charles.* Paris: DRAST.

Boursier-Mougenot, I., Cattan, N., Grasland, C., and Rozenblat, C. 1993. Images de potentiel de population en Europe. *L'Espace Géographique,* 4, 254–333.

Bowes, D., y Ihlanfeldt, K. 2001. Identifying the impacts of Rail Stations on residential property values. *Journal of Urban Economics,* 50, 1–25.

Boyer, R. and Mistral, J. 1983. *Accumulation, Inflation, Crises.* Paris: Presses Universitaires de France.

Brewer, C. A. 1989. Colour chart use in map design. *Cartographic Perspectives,* 4, 3–10.

Brocard, M. D. 2009. *Transports et Territoires.* Enjeux et Débats. Paris: Ellipses.

Bruinsma, F., Pels, E., Priemus, H., Rietveld, P. and Van Wee, B. 2008. *Railway development Impact on Urban Dynamics.* Amsterdam: Physica-Verlag.

Bruinsma, F. 2009. The impact of railway station development on urban dynamics: a review of the Amsterdam South Axis project. *Built Environment,* 35(1), 107–21.

Burckhart, K., Martí-Henneberg, J. and Tapiador, F. J. 2008. Cambio de hábitos y transformaciones territoriales en los corredores de alta velocidad ferroviaria. Resultados de una encuesta de viajeros en la línea Madrid-Barcelona. *Scripta Nova* [Online], XII, 270(46). Available at: http://www.ub.es/geocrit/sn/sn-270/sn-270-46.htm [accessed: February 2011].

Burmeister, A. and Colletis-Wahl, K. 1996. TGV et fonctions tertiaires: grande vitesse et entreprises de service à Lille et Valenciennes. *Transports Urbaines*, 93, 11–16.

Bustinduy, J. 2006. El ferrocarril en la ciudad: evolución de los sistemas pasantes. *Ingeniería y Territorio*, 76, 54–61.

Cairncross, F. 2001. *The death of distance 2.0 : how the communications revolution will change our lives*. London: Texere.

Calvo Palacios, J. L., López, J. M., Pueyo Campos, A. and Alonso, M. P. 1997. Intégration des réseaux d'infrastructures en Espagne et développement régional: Aragon et Valence. *Revue de l'Économie Méridionale*, 45 (177–8), 151–80.

Calvo Palacios, J. L. 1998. Las llegadas del ferrocarril y ferrocarriles de alta velocidad a las ciudades. Generación del problema, velocidades del ferrocarril, poblamiento y planificación estratégica. *Revista Obras Públicas*, 45, 14–21.

Calvo Palacios, J. L. and Pueyo Campos, A. 2008a. *Demografía, Monografías del Atlas Nacional de España*. Madrid: Instituto Geográfico Nacional.

Calvo Palacios, J. L., Pueyo Campos, A. and Zúñiga Antón, M. 2008b. La réorganisation spatiale de peuplement en Espagne entre 1900 et 2007. *Sud-ouest Européen. Revue Géographique des Pyrénées et du Sud-ouest*, 26, 7–41.

Calvo Palacios, J. L., Jover Yuste, J. M., Pueyo Campos, A. and Zúñiga Antón, M. 2008c. Les nouveaux bassins de vie de la société espagnole à l'aube du XXIe siècle. *Sud-ouest Européen. Revue Géographique des Pyrénées et du Sud-ouest*, 26, 89–110.

Camagni, R. 2005. *Economía Urbana*. Barcelone: Antoni Bosch.

Campos, J., de Rus, G., and Barrón, I. 2009a. A review of HSR Experiences around the World, in *Economic Analysis of High Speed rail in Europe*, edited by G. de Rus. Madrid: Fundación BBVA, 19–32.

Campos, J. and de Rus, G. 2009b. Some stylized facts about high-speed rail: a review of HSR experiences around the world. *Transport Policy*, 16(1), 19–28.

Capel, H. 2007. Ferrocarril, territorio y ciudades. *Biblio 3w, Revista Bibliográfica de Geografía y Ciencias Sociales* [Online], XII(717). Available at: http://www.ub.es/geocrit/b3w-717.htm [accessed: 15 April 2010].

Carey, H. C. 1858. *Principles of Social Science*. Philadelphia: J.B. Lippincott.

Castells, M. 1995. *La Ciudad Informacional. Tecnologías de la Información, Reestructuración Económica y el Proceso Urbano Regional*. Madrid: Alianza Editorial.

—— 1996. *The Rise of the Network Society. The Information Age: Economy, Society and Culture*. Cambridge, MA; Oxford, UK: Blackwell.

—— 2000. *La Era de la Información. La Sociedad Red*. Madrid: Alianza Editorial.

Cauvin, C., Escobar, F., and Serradj, A. 2007. *Cartographie Thématique 1. Una nouvelle Démarche.* Paris: Lavoisier.

Centre de Transports du Loir-et-Cher. 2007. Créabus le transport à la demande. *Vendôme. Le Magazine de la Ville* [Online], 66, 10. Available at: www. vendome.eu [accessed: March 2009].

CERTU. 2006. *Le Transport à la Demande. État de l'art, éléments d'Analyse et Repères pour l'Action.* Lyon: Ministère des transports de l'équipement, du tourisme et de la mer.

Chang, J. and Lee, J. 2008. Accessibility analysis of Korean high-speed rail: a case study of the Seoul metropolitan area. *Transport Reviews,* 28(1), 87–103.

Chapelon, L. and Cicille, P. 2000. *Atlas de France. Volume 11. Transports et Énergie.* Paris: GIP RECLUS-La Documentation Française.

Charlton, C. and Vowles, T. 2008 Inter-Urban and Regional Transport, in Knowles, R., Shaw, J. and Docherty, I. (ed.) *Transport Geographies: Mobilities, Flows ans Spaces,* Oxford: Blackwell.

Chen, C. L. and Hall, P. 2010. The impacts of high-speed trains on British economic geography: a study of the UK's InterCity 125/225 and its effects. *Journal of Transport Geography,* DOI: 10.1016/j.jtrangeo.2010.08.010.

Cheng, Y. 2009. High-speed rail in Taiwan: New experience and issues for future development. *Transport Policy,* 17(2), 51–63.

Cheyland, J. P. 2007. Les processus spatio-temporels: quelques notions et concepts préalables á leur représentation. *Mappemonde,* 87(3), 21.

Coffey, W. J. and Bailly, A. S. 1992. Producer services and systems of flexible production. *Urban Studies,* 29(6), 857–68.

Colin, R. and Zembri, P. 1992. Vendôme et le TGV: un mariage surréaliste? *Transports Urbains,* 75, 19–24.

Comisión-Europea. 2001. *Libro Blanco. La política europea de Transportes de cara al 2010: la hora de la verdad.* Luxemburgo: Oficina de Publicaciones Oficiales de las Comunidades Europeas.

Coto-Millán, P., Baños-Pino, J. and Inglada, V. 1997. Marshallian demands of intercity passenger transport in Spain: 1980–92: An economic analysis. *Transportation Research (Logistics and Transportation Review),* 33, 79–96.

Coto-Millán. P and Inglada, V. 2002. *Parámetros determinantes de la Rentabilidad económica del Tren de Alta Velocidad.* Paper to the V Congreso Nacional de Ingeniería del Transporte, Santander.

—— 2003a. Innovación en el transporte: el tren de alta velocidad. *Economía Industrial,* 353, 83–8.

—— 2003b. Market failures: the case for road congestion externalities, in *Essays on Microeconomics and Industrial Organization,* edited by P. Coto-Millán, Germany: Springer-Verlag-Heidelberg, 22.

—— 2003c. Social benefits of investment projects: the case for High-Speed Rail, in *Essays on Microeconomics and Industrial Organization,* edited by P. Coto-Millán, Germany: Springer-Verlag-Heidelberg, 22.

Coto-Millán, P., Inglada, V. and Rey, B. 2007. Effects of network economics in high speed rail: the Spanish case. *Annals of Regional Science*, 41, 911–25.

Crozet, Y. and Musso, P. 2003. *Réseaux, Services et Territoires. Horizon 2020.* l'Aube: La Tour d'aigües.

Dalvi, M. Q. and Martin, K. M. 1976. The measurement of accessibility: some preliminary results. *Transportation*, 5(1), 17–42.

Daniels, P. W. 1985. *Services Industries. A Geographical Appraisal.* London: Methuen.

Daniels, P. W. (ed.). 1991. *Services and Metropolitan Development: International Perspectives.* Andover: Routledge.

—— 1993. *The Geography of Services.* London: Frank Cass.

De Cos Guerra, O. 2004. Valoración del método de densidades focales (Kernel) para la identificación de los patrones espaciales de crecimiento de la población en España. *Geofocus: Revista Internacional de Ciencia y Tecnología de la Información Geográfica*, 4.

De Courson, J., Remond E. and Jaquen, M. 1993. *Gares TGV et Urbanisme. Etude sur neuf Agglomérations des Impacts d'une gare TGV*, 3 vol. Paris: Ministère de l'Equipement, du logement et des Transport, SNCF.

De Mattos, C., Figueroa, O., Giménez i Capdevila, R., Orellana, A. and Yañez Warner, G. 2005. *Gobernanza, Competitividad y Redes: la Gestión de las Ciudades del siglo XXI.* Santiago de Chile: Instituto de Estudios Urbanos y Territoriales de la Pontificia Universidad Católica de Chile.

De Rus, G. and Inglada, V. 1993. Análisis coste-beneficio del tren de alta velocidad en España. *Revista de Economía Aplicada*, 3(1), 27–48.

—— 1997. Cost-benefit analysis of the high-speed train in Spain. *The Annals of Regional Science*, 31, 175–88.

De Rus, G. and Nombela, G. 2007. Is investment in high speed rail socially profitable? *Journal of Transport Economics and Policy*, 41(1), 3–23.

De Rus, G. (dir) 2009. *Economic Analysis of High Speed Rail in Europe.* Madrid: Fundación BBVA, Informes. Economía y Sociedad.

De Rus, G. and Nash, C. 2009. In What circumstances is investment in HSR worthwhile?, in *Economic Analysis of High Speed rail in Europe*, edited by G. de Rus. Madrid: Fundación BBVA, 51–70.

Debrezion, G. and Willigers, J. 2008. The effect of railway stations on office space rent levels: the implication of HSL South in station Amsterdam South Axis, in *Railway development. Impact on Urban Dynamics*, edited by F. Bruinsma et al. Amsterdam: Physica-Verlag, 265–94.

Dematteis, G. 1995. *Progetto Implicito. Il Contributo della Geografia Umana alle Scienze del Territorio.* Milan: Franco Angeli.

Dicken, P. 1986. *Global Shift: Industrial change in a Turbulent World.* London and New York: Harper and Row.

Díez, J. 1970. La jerarquía de las ciudades. *Ciudad y Territorio*, April-June (2), 13–34.

Dobes, L. 1998. *Externalities in the Transport sector. Key issues.* BTCE, Bureau of Transport and Communications Economics, information sheet 10.1.

Dodgson, J. 1984. Railways costs and closures. *Journal of Transport Economics and Policy*, 18(3), 219–35.

Dollfus, O. 1995. Mondialisation, compétitivités, territoires et marchés mondiaux. *L'Espace Géographique*, 3, 270–80.

Duany, A., Plateer-Zyberk, E. and Speck, J. 2010. Suburban Nation. The rise of sprawl and the decline of the American dream. *North Point Press.* New York.

Dupuy, G., Ribeill, G., Savy, M., 1985 Les « effets de réseau » des trains à grande vitesse, in *Les Aspects socio-économiques des trains à grande vitesse, Tome II*, edited by Ministère de L'Urbanisme, du Logement et des Transports, La Documentation Française, Paris, 685-669. Available at: http://temis. documentation.equipement.gouv.fr/documents/temis/7783/7783_2_7.pdf [accessed: April 2011].

Dupuy, G. and Geneau, I. 2007. Nouvelles échelles des firmes et des réseaux. Un défi pour l'aménagement. *Itinéraires Géographiques.* Paris.

Duranton, G. and Puga, D. 2002. *From Sectoral to Functional Urban Specialization.* Discussion Paper, 2971, revised version June 2003. London: Centre for Economic Policy Research (CEPR).

Echezarreta, M. 2005. *El lugar europeo de Retiro: indicadores de excelencia para administrar la Gerontoinmigración de ciudadanos de la Unión Europea en municipios españoles.* Albolote: Editorial Gomares.

Eicher, C. L. and Brewer, C. A. 2001. Dasymetric mapping and areal interpolation: implementation and evaluation. *Cartography and Geographic Information Science*, 28(2), 125–38.

Escalona, A. I. 1989. Tendencias actuales de la geografía del transporte: el análisis de la movilidad. *Geographicalia*, 26, 83–90.

ESPON, U. E. 2010. *First ESPON 2013 Synthesis Report. New Evidence on Smart, Sustainable and Inclusive Territories.* Luxembourg, European Union.

European Commission. 2008. *Guide to Cost-Benefit Analysis of Investment Projects.* Brussels: European Commission.

Facchinetti-Mannone, V. 1995. *L'Impact régional du TGV Sud*-Est. PhD-thesis. Université de Provence.

——— 2005. La nodalité des gares TGV périphériques. *Les Cahiers Scientifiques du Transport*, 48, 45–58.

——— 2009. *Location of High Speed rail Stations in French medium-size City and their Mobility and territorial Implications: central, peripheral and bis (both central and peripheral in the same city).* Paper to the International Conference City Futures in a Globalising World, Madrid, 4–6 June 2009.

Faiña, J. A., Fernández, J., Landeira, F., and López, J. 2001. La técnica de los potenciales de población y la estructura espacial de la Unión Europea. *Revista de Investigación Operacional*, 22(2), 1–10.

Fariña, J., Lamíquiz, F. and Pozueta, J. 2000. Efectos territoriales de las infraestructuras de transporte de accesos controlados. *Cuadernos de Investigación Urbanística-CIUr*, 29.

Faust, M., Voskamp, U. and Wittke, V. Eds. 2004._*European Industrial Restructuring in a global Economy: Fragmentation and Relocation of Value chains*. Göttingen: Soziologisches Forschungsinstitut Göttingen (SOFI) an der Georg-August-Universität.

Floyd, R. W. 1962. Algorithm 97: Shortest path. *Association for Computing Machinery*, 5, 345.

Flyvbjerg, B., Skamris Holm M. and Buhl, S. L. 2006. Inaccuracy in Traffic Forecasts. *Transport Reviews*, 26, 1–24.

Fröidh, O. 2003. *Introduction of regional high speed trains. A study of the effects of the Svealand line on the travel market, travel behaviour and accessibility*. Estocolmo: Universitets service US AB.

—— 2005. Market effects of regional high-speed trains on the Svealand line. *Journal of Transport Geography*, 13, 352–61.

—— 2008. Perspectives for a future high-speed train in the Swedish domestic travel market. *Journal of Transport Geography*, 16(4), 268–77.

García, F., Mota, C., Arizti, A. Schultz, A. and Ribalaygua, C. 2010. La transformación urbana de la alta velocidad ferroviaria. Ejemplos europeos, in C. Ribalaygua (ed.), *Proyectos Urbanos en torno a estaciones de Alta Velocidad Ferroviaria en Europa. Análisis de casos para la integración del nuevo ferrocarril en Logroño*, edited by Sociedad Mixta Logroño Integración del Ferrocarril 2003.

García, J. C. 2000. La medida de la accesibilidad. *Estudios de Construcción y Transportes*, 88, 95–110.

Garmendia, M. 2008 *Cambios en la estructura urbana y territorial facilitados por la alta velocidad ferroviaria, la línea Madrid-Sevilla a su paso por la provincia de Ciudad Real*. Unpublished PhD thesis, University of Castilla-La Mancha (UCLM), Ciudad Real

Garmendia, M., Ureña, J. M., Ribalaygua, C., Leal, J. and Coronado, J. M. 2008. Urban residential development in isolated small cities that are partially integrated in metropolitan areas by high Speedy train. *European Urban and Regional Studies*, 15(3), 265–80.

Garmendia, M., Ureña, J. M., Rivas, A., Coronado, J. M., Menéndez, J.M., Gallego, I. and Romero, V. 2009. High Speed Rail, a new mode of suburban metropolitan transport. *Urban Transport 2009*. Bologna. Italy: Wessex Institute of Technology.

Garmendia, M., Ureña, J. M. and Coronado, J. M. 2010. Long-distance trips in a sparsely populated region: the impact of high-speed infrastructures. *Journal of Transport Geography*, 19(4), 537–551.

Garmendia M., Ureña J.M. and Coronado, J.M. 2011. Cambios en la estructura territorial debidos a nuevas conexiones de alta velocidad en territorios aislados:

la provincia de Ciudad Real en España. *EURE Revista Latinoamericana de Estudios Urbano Regionales.* 37 (110), 89–115.

Garmendia, M., Romero, V., Ureña, J.M. de, Coronado, J.M. y Vickerman, R. In Print High-speed Rail Opportunities around Metropolitan regions: the cases of Madrid and London, *Journal of Infrastructure Systems (ASCE).*

Gaspar, J. and Glaeser, E. L. 1998. Information Technology and the Future of Cities. *Journal of Urban Economics,* 43(1), 136–56.

Gershuny, J. and Miles, I. 1988. *La nueva economía de los Servicios. La Transformación del empleo en las Sociedades Industriales.* Madrid: Ministerio de Trabajo y Seguridad Social.

Geurs, K. T. and van Wee, B. 2004. Accessibility evaluation of land-use and transport strategies: review and research directions. *Journal of Transport Geography,* 12(2), 127–40.

Geurs, K. T. 2006. Job accesibilty impacts of intensive and multiple land-use scenarios for the Netherlands' Randstad Area. *Journal of Housing auilt Eironment*[Occessed: January 2011].

Giddens, A. 1984. *The constitution of Society: outline of the Theory of Structuration.* Cambridge: Polity.

Gil, F. and Domingo, A. 2006. La complementariedad de la actividad de españoles y extranjeros: análisis sectorial y diferencias territoriales. *Papers de Demografía,* 308.

Gilli, F. 2002. Déplacements domicile-travail et organisation du Bassin parisien. *L'Espace Géographique,* 4, 289–305.

Givoni, M. 2006. Development and impact of the Modern High-speed Train: a review, *Transport Reviews,* 26(5), 593–611.

González, M. P., Aguilera, M. P., Borderías, M. J. and Santos, J. M. 2005. Cambios en las ciudades de la línea de alta velocidad Madrid-Sevilla desde su implantación. *Cuadernos Geográficos,* 36, 527–47.

Gourvish, T. 2010. The High Speed Rail Revolution: History and Prospects. Report to HS2 Ltd. Available at: http://webarchive.nationalarchives.gov. uk/20110131042819/ and http://www.dft.gov.uk/pgr/rail/pi/highspeedrail/ hs2ltd/historyandprospects/pdf/report.pdf [accessed: February 2011].

Graham, D. J. 2007. Agglomeration, productivity and transport investment. *Journal of Transport Economics and Policy,* 41, 317–43.

—— 2009. Identifying urbanization and localization externalities in manufacturing and service industries. *Papers in Regional Science,* 88, 63–84.

Grasland, C. 1991. Potentiel de population, interaction spatiale et frontières: des deux Allemagnes à l'unification. *Espace Géographique,* 3, 243–54.

Guirao, B. 2000. *El cálculo del tráfico inducido como herramienta en la planificación de las infraestructuras de transporte. Aplicación a la puesta en servicio de las nuevas líneas de alta velocidad en España.* Unpublished PhD thesis. Polyrtechnic University of Madrid.

Guirao, B., Menéndez, J. M. and Rivas, A. 2002. Les nouvelles lignes ferroviaires à grande vitesse en Espagne: Une opportunité pour l'analyse du trafic induit. *Transports*, 416, 3–12.

Guirao, B., Soler, F., González, N., Ribalaygua, C. and Coronado, J. M. 2008. Análisis de los impactos generados por la nueva línea de alta velocidad Madrid-Toledo sobre la demanda del transporte. *Estudios de Construcción y Transportes*, 108, 111– Fomento. ISSN: 1576–7108.

Gutiérrez, J. and Urbano, P. 1996. Accessibility in the European Union: the impact of the Transeuropean Road Network. *Journal of Transport Geography*, 4(1), 15–25.

Gutiérrez, J., Monzón, A. and Pinéro, J. M. 1998. Accessibility, network efficiency, and transport infrastructure planning. *Environment and Planning A,* 30(8), 1337–50.

Gutiérrez, J. 2001. Location, economic potential and daily accessibility: an analysis of the accessibility impact of the high-speed line Madrid-Barcelona-French border. *Journal of Transport Geography,* 9(4), 229–42.

—— 2004. El tren de alta velocidad y sus efectos espaciales. *Investigaciones Regionales*, 5, 199–221.

Gutiérrez, J., Gómez, G., García, J. C. and López, E. 2006. Análisis de los efectos de las infraestructuras de transporte sobre la accesibilidad y la cohesión regional. *Estudios de Construcción y Transportes*, 105, 215–39.

Gutiérrez, J. A., Mora, C., Gómez P., Jaráiz, F. J. 2010. Accesibilidad de la población a las aglomeraciones urbanas de la península Ibérica. *Finisterra, Revista Portuguesa* 9, 107–18.ISSN: 0430-5027.

Haesbaert, R. 2004. De la déterritorialisation à la multiterritorialité, in *Le sens du Mouvement. Modernité et Mobilités dans les Sociétés urbaines contemporaines*, edited by Bélin (ed.). Paris: Bélin, 69–79.

Hägerstrand, T. 1967. *Innovation Diffusion as a spatial Process*. Chicago: University of Chicago Press.

—— 1978. Survival and arena: on the life history of individuals in relation to their geographical environment, in *Timing Space and spacing Time. Vol. 2, Human Activity and time Geography*, edited by T. Carlstein, D. Parkes and N. Thrift. London: Edward Arnold, 2.

Hagget, P. 1972. *Geography: a modern Synthesis.* New York-London.

Hanrot, P. 1989. *Mise en évidence sur le cas du TGV Sud-est des modifications intervenues dans les pratiques de déplacement.* Seminar INRETS, 22.

Halbert, L. 2005. Les métropoles, moteurs de la dématérialisation du système productif urbain français: une lecture sectorielle et fonctionnelle (1982–99). *Bulletin de l'Association de Géographes Françaises*, 3, 279–97.

Hall, P. 2009. Magic carpets and seamless webs: opportunities and constraints for high-speed trains in Europe. *Built Environment*, 35(1), 59–69.

Hammadou, H. and Jayet, H. 2002. La valeur du temps pour les déplacements à longue distance: une évaluation sur données françaises. *Les Cahiers Scientifiques du Transport,* 42, 3–23.

Harris, B. 2001. Accessibility: concepts and applications. *Journal of Transportation and Statistics,* 4(2/3), 15–30.

Harvey, D. 1987. *Flexible Accumulation trough Urbanization: Reflexions on Post-modernism in the American City. Developing the American city: Society and Architecture in the Regional City* Yale School of Architecture.

—— 1989. *The Condition of Postmodernity. An enquiry into the Origins of cultural Change.* Oxford: Blackwell.

Haynes, K. E. 1997. Labor markets and regional transportation improvements; the case of high-speed trains: an introduction and review. *Annals of Regional Science,* 31(1), 57–76.

Haywood, R. 2009. *Railways, Urban Development and Town Planning in Britain: 1948–2008.* Aldershot: Ashgate.

Hillier, B. and Hanson, J. 1984. *The Social logic of Space.* Cambridge: Cambridge University Press.

Houée, M. et al. 1999. Évaluation de l'impact du TGV Nod-Européen sur la mobilité. Résultats de trois années du panel. Enseignements méthodologiques, Documents of SES, 168.

Illeris, S. 1989. *Services and Regions in Europe.* Aldershot: Gower.

Imrie, R. 2009. An exemplar for sustainable world city: progressive urban change and the redevelopment of King's Cross, in *Regenerating London. Governance, Sustainability and Community in a global City,* edited by R. Imrie, L. Lees and M. Raco. Abingdon, Routledge, 93–110.

Inglada, V. 1993. El Papel de las infraestructuras en la competitividad y el desarrollo económico. *Estudios Territoriales,* 1(97), 397–409.

—— 1994. Análisis empírico del impacto del AVE sobre la demanda de transporte en el corredor Madrid-Sevilla. *Revista de Estudios de Transportes y Comunicaciones,* 62, 35–51.

Inglada, V., Casares, P., Coto-Millán, Mateo, I. and Sainz, R. 2010. *Social Profitability Threshold of High Speed Rail.* Working Paper. University of Cantabria.

Innerarity, D. 2004. *La sociedad Invisible.* Madrid: Espasa-Calpe.

Innis, H. 1950. *Empire and Communications.* Oxford: Clarendon.

Isard, W., Bramhall, D., Carrothers, G. A. P., Cumberland, J. H. and Socholer, E. W. 1971. *Métodos de Análisis Regional: una Introducción a la Ciencia Regional.* Barcelona: Ariel.

Janelle, D. G. 1969. Spatial reorganization: a model and concept. *Annals of the Association of American Geographers,* 59(2), 348–64.

—— 1973. Measuring Human Extensibility in a Shrinking World. *The Journal of Geography,* 72(5), 8–15.

Janssen, B. and Hoogstraten. P. 1989. The "new infraestructure" and regional development, in *Regional Policy at the Crossroad. European Perspectives,* edited by L. Albrechts, F. Moulaert, P. Roberts and E. Swyngedouw. London: Jessica Kingsley and Regional Studies Association, 52–66.

Kamel, K. and Matthewman, R. 2008. *The non-transport Impacts of High-Speed Trains on Regional economic Development: a Review of the Literature* [Online Report]. Available at: http://www.locateinkent.com/images/assets/High%20 Speed%20Train%20Report%202008.pdf [accessed: March 2011].

Karst, T. Geurs, Bert van W. 2004. Accessibility evaluation of land-use and transport strategies: review and research directions. *Journal o.* doi:10.1016/j. jtrangeo.2003.10.005.

Kaufmann, A. and Desbazeille, G. 1974. *La Méthode du chemin critique: Application aux Programmes de Production et d'études de la Méthode P.E.R.T. et de ses Variantes.* Paris: Dunod.

Keeling, D. J. 2009. Transportation geography: local challenges, global contexts. *Progress in Human Geography* [Online], 33. Available at: http://phg.sagepub. com/content/33/4/516. [accessed: January 2011].

Kingsley, E. H. 1997. Labor markets and regional transportation improvements: the case of high-speed trains. An introduction and review. in special issue: The regional and urban effects of high-speed trains. *The Annals of Regional Science*, 31, 1, 57–76.

Kiyoshi, K. and Makoto, O. 1997. The growth of city systems with high-speed railway systems, in special issue: The regional and urban effects of high-speed trains. *The Annals of Regional Science*, 31, 1, 39–56.

Klein, O. 1991. Les espaces de la grande vitesse. *Les Cahiers Scientifiques du Transport*, 25, 117–128.

—— 1992. La logique de la grande vitesse et des liaisons entre agglomérations. *Transports Urbains*, 74, 17–24.

Klein, O. and Claisse, G. 1997a. *Le TGV-Atlantique: entre récession et concurrence-Evolution de la Mobilité et mise en Service du TGV-Atlantique: Analyse des enquêtes réalisées en septembre 1989 et septembre 1993.* Collection Études et Recherches: 7. Lyon: Laboratoire d'Économie des Transports du CNRS.

—— 1997b. *Le TGV-Atlantique et les évolutions de la Mobilité: entre récession et Concurrence.* Collection Études et Recherches: 7. Lyon: Laboratoire d'Économie des Transports du CNRS.

Klein, O. 1997c. Le TGV-Atlantique et les evolutions de la mobilite: entre crise et concurrence. *Les Cahiers Scientifiques du Transport*, 32; 57–83.

—— 2001. *Les horizons de la grande vitesse: le TGV, une innovation lue à travers les mutations de son époque.* PhD-thesis. Université Lumière, Lyon 2. November 2001.

—— 2003. Le travail métropolitain: un outil géographique pour révéler l'usage sélectif de la grande vitesse. *L'Espace Géographique*, 2(3).

—— 2004. Social perception of time, distance and highspeed transportation. *Time and Society*, 13(2–3), 245–63.

Klein, O. and Million, F. 2005. *La Grande Vitesse Ferroviaire, le Développement Socio-économique et l'aménagement des Territoires: Étude Bibliographique et Analyse des Expériences passées.* Direction Départementale de l'Equipement de la Charente.

Knowles, R. D. 2006. Transport shaping space: differential collapse in time-space. *Journal of Transport Geography,* 14, 407–25.

Kobayashi and Okumura. 1997. The growth of city systems with High Speed Railway system. *The Annals of Regional Science,* 31, 39–56.

Komei, S., Tadahiro, O. and Asao, A. 1997. High-speed rail transit impact on regional systems: does the Shinkansen contribute to dispersion? in special issue: The regional and urban effects of high-speed trains. *The Annals of Regional Science,* 31, 1, 77–98.

Kwang, S. K. 2000. High-speed rail developments and spatial restructuring: a case study of the capitn in South Korea. *Cities,* 17(, Issue 4), 251–62.

Le Bras, H. 1996. *Le Peuplement de l'Europe, La Documentation Française-DATAR.* Paris.

Le Breton, E. 2004. Exclusion et immobilité: la figure de l'insulaire, in *Transports, pauvretés, exclusions, Pouvoir bouger pour s'en sortir,* edited by J. P. Orfeuil. Paris: l'Aube, 115–47.

Lefebvre, H. 1974. *La Production de l'espace.* Paris: Anthropos.

L'Hostis, A. 2009. The shrivelled USA: representing time-space in the context of metropolitanization and the development of high-speed transport. *Journal of Transport Geography,* 17(6), 433–9.

Lipietz, A. 1986. New tendencies in the international division of labour: regimes of accumulation and modes of regulation, in *Production, Work and Territory,* edited by A. J. Scott and M. Storper. Boston: Allen and Unwin, 16–40.

López-Rodríguez, J., and Faiña, J.A. 2006. Does distance matter for determining regional income in the European Union? An approach through the market potential concept. *Applied Economics Letters,* 13(6), 385–90.

Louw, E. and Bruinsma, F. 2006. From mixed to multiple land use. *Journal of Housing and the Built Environment,* 21(1), 1–13.

Mandeville, T. 1983. The spatial effects of informational technology. *Futures,* 15(1), 65–72.

Mannone, V. 1995. *L'impact régional du TGV sud-est.* Thèse pour l'obtention du doctorat de géographie. 2 tomes, Université de Provence Aix-Marseille I.

—— 1997. Gares TGV et nouvelles dynamiques urbaines en centre ville: le cas des villes desservies par le TGV Sud-Est. *Les Cahiers Scientifiques du Transport,* 31, 71–97.

—— 2006. Gares exurbanisées et développement urbain: Le cas des gares TGV bourguignonnes. *Revue Géographique de l'Est,* vol. 46/1–2.

Marshall, T. 2009. *Infrastructure and Spatial Planning. France Working Paper.* Department of Planning Oxford Brookes University. Available at: http://www.brookes.ac.uk/schools/be/about/planning/projects/resources/frwpoctober2009.pdf [accessed: January 2011].

Martí-Henneberg, J. 2000. Balance del TAV en Francia. Enseñanzas para el caso español. *Ería* 52, 131–43.

Martin, J. C. and Nombela. 2007. Microeconomic impacts of investments in high speed trapain. *Annals of eg*/fulltext.pdf[accessed: January 2011].

Martínez Sánchez-Mateos, H. S. and Givoni, M. 2009. The accessibility impact of a new high-speed rail line in the UK-a preliminary analysis of winners and losers. *Transport Studies*, Unit School of Geography and the Environment [Online], Working Paper N° 1041. Available at: http://www.tsu.ox.ac.uk/pubs/1041-martinez-givoni.pdf [accessed: January 2011].

Martínez, H., Ureña, J. M., Coronado, J. M., Garmendia, M., Romero, V. and Solís, E. 2010. *Regional High-Speed Rail Services typology, demand and spatial implications*. Paper to the ERSA L Conference: High-Speed Rail as a new transport network. Sustainable Regional Growth and Development in the creative knowledge Economy, Jonkoping, August 2010.

Masson, S. and Petiot, R. 2009. Can the high speed rail reinforce tourism attractiveness? The case of the high speed rail between Perpignan (France) and Barcelona (Spain). *Technovation*, 29(9), 611–7.

Meer, A. de, and Ribalaygua, C. 2008. *High-Speed Railway: Impact on Regional Territorial Configurations*. Southampton, UK: CA BREBBIA: Wessex Institute of Technology. 169–79.

—— 2009. *High-speed railway and new territorial configuration at the regional scale*. Paper to the Conference: City Futures Intenational Conference 09, Madrid, 4–6 June 2009.

Menéndez, J. M., Coronado, J. M. and Rivas, A. 2002a. El AVE en Ciudad Real y Puertollano: notas sobre su incidencia en la movilidad y el territorio. *Cuadernos de Ingeniería y Territorio*, 2. Ciudad Real: Universidad Castilla La Mancha.

—— 2002b. Incidencias socioeconómicas y territoriales derivadas de la construcción y explotación de la línea ferroviaria de alta velocidad en ciudades de tamaño pequeño. El caso de Ciudad Real y de Puertollano. *Estudios de Construcción y Transportes*, 94, 29–54.

—— 2004. Les effects des navettes TGV sur les villes moyennes: le cas de Ciudad Real et Puertollano en Espagne. *Transports Urbains*, 106.

Menéndez, J. M., Coronado, J. M., Guirao, B., Ribalaygua, C. Rodríguez, J., Rivas, A. and Ureña, J. M. 2006. Diseño, dimensión óptima y emplazamiento de estaciones de alta velocidad en ciudades de tamaño pequeño. *Cuadernos de Ingeniería y Territorio, 7*. Ed. E.T.S.I. Caminos, Canales y Puertos, UCLM.

Menéndez, J. M. and Rivas, A. 2010. Caracterización de la movilidad de alta velocidad en relaciones de media distancia (Chapter 6), in *Final Report of the Research Project Alta Velocidad Ferroviaria, Intermodalidad y Territorio: Evaluación de las Oportunidades asociadas a su Implantación*. Spain: Ministerio de Fomento.

Menerault, P. 1996. TGV et transports ferres regionaux dans le Nord-Pas-de-Calais: analyse d'une politique publique locale. *Annales Les Pays-Bas Français*, 21, 45–62.

—— 1997. Dynamiques et politiques régionales autour du tunnel sous la Manche et du T.G.V. Nord. *Annales de Géographie*, 106(593), 5–33.

———— 1998. Processus de territorialisation des réseaux: analyse de la grande vitesse ferroviaire á l'échelle régionale. *Networks and Communication Studies NETCOM*, 12(1, 2 and 3), 161–84.

Menerault, P. and Stransky, V. 1999. La face cachée de l'intermodalité. Essai de représentation appliquée au couple TGV/air dans la desserte de Lille. *Les Cahiers Scientifiques du Transport*, 35, 29–53.

Menerault, P and Barré, A. (ed.). 2001. *Gares et Quartiers des Gares: signes et marges. Lille, Rennes et Expériences étrangères (Italie, Japon, Pays-Bas)*. Lille: Inrets (Actes col).

Menerault, P. 2006. *Les pôles d'échanges en France État des connaissances, enjeux et outils d'analyse*. Paris: Centre d'Études sur les réseaux, les transports, l'urbanisme et les constructions publiques.

———— 2007. El TAV en Francia en el marco de la red regional, in *Ferrocarril de alta velocidad y Territorio: actas de la I Jornada Europea Celebrada en Ciudad Real el 23 de marzo de 2006. Cuadernos de Ingeniería y Territorio, 10, dir. by C.* Ribalaygua. UCLM. Available at: http://www.uclm.es/cr/caminos/Publicaciones/Cuaderno_Ing_Territorio/Libros/cuaderno10/cuaderno10.pdf [accessed: March 2011].

Mérenne-Schoumaker, E. 2008a. *Géographie des Services et des Commerces*. Rennes: Presses Universitaires de Rennes.

———— 2008b. *Géographie des Transports*. Rennes: Presses Universitaires de Rennes.

Metz, J. 2004. Travel-time variable or constant? *Journal of Transport Economics and Policy*, 18, 37–42.

Ministerio de Fomento. 2005. *Plan Estratégico de Infraestructuras y Transportes 2005–20*. Madrid: Centro de Publicaciones del Ministerio de Fomento.

———— 2007. *Movilia 2006/2007*. Madrid, Ministerio de Fomento

———— 2010. *Observatorio de costes del transporte de viajeros en coach* [Online]. Available at: www.fomento.es [accessed: September 2010].

Ministerio de Obras Públicas y Transportes (MOPT). 1991. *Manual de Evaluación de Inversiones en Ferrocarril de Vía Ancha*. Madrid: Ministerio de Obras Públicas y Transportes.

MOPTMA, Ministerio de Obras Públicas, Transporte y Medioambiente. 1994. *Plan Director de Infraestructuras 1993–2007*. Madrid: Centro de Publicaciones del Ministerio de Obrte y Medioambiente. ISBN: 84-7433-993-6.

Módenes, J. A. 2007. Movilidad espacial: uso temporal del territorio y poblaciones vinculadas. *Papeles de Demografía*, 311, 34.

————2008. Spatial mobility, inhabitants and places: Conceptual and methodological challenges for geodemography. Movilidad espacial, habitantes y lugares: Retos conceptuales y metodológicos para la geodemografía. *Estudios Geográficos*, 69(264), 157–78.

Moles, A. and Romher, E. 1990. *Psicología del Espacio*. Barcelona: Círculo de Lectores.

Monzón de Cáceres, A., Gutiérrez, J., López, E., Madrigal, E. and Gómez, G. 2005. Infraestructuras de transporte terrestre y su influencia en los niveles de accesibilidad de la España peninsular. *Estudios de Construcción y Transportes,* 103, 97–112.

Monzón de Cáceres, A., López Suárez, E., Ortega Pérez, E. and Mancebo Quintana, S. 2008. *The use of accessibility measures to assess efficiency and equity effects of High Speed Rail projects: application to the case of Spain.* Paper to the 55th Annual North American Meeting of the Regional Science Association, Brooklyn, New York (United States), 19–22 November 2008. Available at: http://oa.upm.es/3122/1/INVE_MEM_2008_53285.pdf [accessed: March 2011].

Mora Aliseda, C., Domínguez Gómez, E. M., Gutiérrez Gallego, J. A. and Jaraíz Cabanillas, F. J. 2010. Accesibilidad de la población a las aglomeraciones urbanas de la península Ibérica. *Revista Portuguesa de Geografía,* 89, 107–18.

Morellet, O. and Marchal, P. 1997. Extension du réseau T.G.V. et évolution du trafic multimodal. *Les Cahiers Scientifiques du Transport,* 32, 27–34.

Moreno, A. and Escolano, S. 1992. *Los Servicios y el Territorio.* Madrid: Síntesis.

Morgan, K. 2004. The exaggerated death of geography: learning, proximity and territorial innovation systems. *Journal of Economic Geography,* 4, 3–21.

Moss, M. 1998. Technology and Cities. *Cityscape: a Journal of Policy Development and Research,* 3(3), 107–27.

Moulaert, F., Salin, E. and Werquin, T. 2001. Euralille. Large-scale urban development and social polarization. *European Urban and Regional Studies,* 8(2), 145–60.

Muller, M., Papinutti, M. and Reynauld, C. 1987. Cinq ans de diffusion des effets du TGV Sud-Est. *Les Cahiers Scientifiques du Transport,* 15–16, 127–150.

Murayama, Y. 1994. The impact of railways on accessibility in the Japanese urban system. *Journal of Transport Geography,* 2(2), 87–100.

Nash, C. 2009. *When to invest in high-speed rail links and networks?* International Transport Research Symposium, Madrid, November 2009. Available at: http://www.internationaltransportforum.org/Proceedings/Symp2009/2Nash.pdf [accessed: March 2011].

Nash, C. A. 1991. The Case for High Speed Rail. *Investigaciones Económicas,* XV(2), 337–54.

Nogales, J. M. and Gutiérrez, J. A. 2002. Análisis de accesibilidad a los centros de actividad económica de Extremadura mediante técnicas SIG. *Mapping Interactive,* 11.

Noyelle, T. 1985. *The shift to Services, Technological Change and the restructuring of the System of Cities in the Unites States.* Paper to the International economic restructuring and the territorial community, Viena, U. N. Industrial Development Organization, 1985.

O'Brien, R. 1991. *Global Financial Integration: The End of Geography.* London: Pinter.

OECD. 2002. *Impact of Transport Infrastructure Investment on Regional Development*. Paris: OECD Publishing.

Offner, J. M. 1993. Les 'effets structurants' du transport: mythe politique, mystification scientifique. *L'Espace Géographique*, 3, 233–42.

Ohnmacht, T., H. Maksim, et al., Eds. 2009. *Mobilities and Inequality*. Transport and society. Farnham: Ashgate.

Oña, J. 2001. *Política Europea de Transportes en zonas de baja densidad de población*. XXVII Reunión de Estudios Regionales, Madrid, 28–30 November 1–20.

Oña, J., Monzón, J. and Osorio, F.et al. 2002. *Nueva Metodología para la evaluación de un sistema de Transporte a la demanda*. V Congreso de Ingeniería del Transporte, Santander, 11–13 June 2002, 399–407.

Owen, A. D. and Phillips, G. D. A. 1987. The characteristics of railways passenger demand. *Journal of Transport Economics and Policy*, 21(3), 231–53.

Paris, C. 1992. The slow death of a Very Fast Train: government resistance to a privately funded transport innovation. *International Journal of Urban and Regional Research*, 16(4), 623–32.

Park, Y. and Ha, H. 2006. Analysis of the impact of high-speed railroad service on air transport demand. *Transportation Research (Part E: Logistics and Transportation Review)*, 42(2), 95–104.

Paul, D. 2008. *El Tren de Alta Velocidad en las Estrategias de Promoción Urbana. IX Coloquio de Geografía Urbana y Jornadas de Campo, Sevilla-Cadiz-Ceuta, 9–14 June*.

Paulley, N., Balcombe, R., Mackett, R., Titheridge, H., PrestoM., Shires, J. and White, P. Paulley, et al. 2006. The demand for public transport: the effects of fares, quality of service, income and car ownership. *Transport Policy*, 13(4), 295–306.

Peters, D. 2009. *The renaissance of inner-city rail station areas as a key element in the contemporary dynamics of urban restructuring*, Paper to the Critical Planning's 2009. Special Issue on Urban Restructuring.

Pietri, J. 1990. *Conséquences Économiques et Urbaines du TGV*. Paper to the III International Congress of the Association Mondiale des Grandes Métropoles. Metropolis' 90, Melbourne, 15–19 October 1990. Societé d'Économie Mixte de Massy, Massy, 255–324.

Plassard, F. and Cointet-Pinell, O. 1986. *Les Effets Socio-Économiques du TGV en Bourgogne et Rhône-Alpes*. Lyon: Laboratoire d'Economie des Transports.

Plassard, F. 1988. Le réseau TGV et les transformations de l'espace. *Annales de la Recherche Urbain*, 39, 112–116.

—— 1989. Les conséquences de la grande vitesse sur les déplacements d'affaires entre Paris et le Sud-Est. *Rail International,* January 1989, 91–100.

—— 1991. Le train à grande vitesse et le réseau des villes. *Transports*, 345, 14–23.

—— 1992. *The Relationship between Regional Policy and Transport and Communications Networks*. Paper to the European Conference of Ministers of Transport, Round Table, Lyon, 1992.

—— 1997. Les effets des infrastructures de transport, modèles et paradigmes, in *Infrastructures de Transport et Territoires*, edited by A. Burmeister and G. Joinaux. Paris: L'Harmattan, 39–54.

Pol P.M.J. 2002. *A renaissance of stations, railways and cities: economic effects, development strategies and organisational issues of European High-Speed-Train stations*. PhD-thesis. Delft: Delft University Press.

—— 2008. High-Speed-Train stations and urban dynamics: experiences from four European cities, in *Railway Development. Impact on Urban Dynamics*, edited by F. Bruinsma, et al. Amsterdam: Physica-Verlag, 59–77.

Potrykowski, M. and Taylor, Z. 1984. *Geografía del Transporte*. Barcelona: Ariel.

Preston, J., Larbie, A. and Wall, G. 2006. *The Impact of High Speed Trains on Socio-Economic Activity: the case of Ashford (Kent)*. Paper to the IV Conference: Annual Conference on Railroad Industry Structure, Competition and Investment, Universidad Carlos III de Madrid, 2006. Available at: http://163.117.2.172/temp/agenda/mad2006/papers/25.%20Preston.pdf

Preston, J. and Wall, G. 2008. The Ex-ante and ex-post economic and social impact of the introduction of high-speed trains in South East England. *Planning, Practice and Research*, 23(3), 403–22.

Priemus, H., Nijkamp, P. and Banister, D. 2001. Mobility and spatial dynamics: an uneasy relationship. *Journal of Transport Geography*, 9(3), 167–71.

Pueyo, A., Calvo, L. L., Jover, J. M. and Zúñiga, M. 2009. Les nouveaux bassins de vie de la société espagnole à l'aube du XXIe siècle. *Sud-ouest européen: revue Géographique des Pyrénées et du Sud-Ouest*, 26, 89–110.

Quinet, E. and Vickerman, R. 2004. *Principles of Transport Economics*. Northampton/Cheltenham: Edgar Elgar.

Rabin, G. 2004. Les *impacts économiques pour les villes et régions desservies. Proceedings of CESA (Conseil Economique et Social Alsace), TGV: 20 Ans d'expérience: Quels enseignements pour l'Alsace?* CESA (Conseil Economique et Social Alsace), 59–64.

Rada, J. F. 1989. Tecnología de la información y servicios. *Ekonomiaz*, 13–14, 62–99.

Raux, C., Mercier, A. and Ovtracht, N. 2008. Evaluation économique des politiques de transport et indicateurs d'accessibilité spatiale: l'apport des SIG. *Cybergeo: Européen Journal of Géographie, Systèmes, Modélisation, Géostatistiques*, 432.

Reques Velasco, P. and Rodríguez Rodríguez, V. 1998. *Atlas de la Población Española. Análisis de base Municipal*. Santander: Servicio de Publicaciones de la Universidad de Cantabria, CSIC y ESRI-España.

RFF (Reseau Ferré de France). 2005. *Bilan LOTI de la LGV Nord*. Paris: RFF.

Ribalaygua, C., Ureña, J. M., Menéndez, J. M., Rodríguez, F. J., Coronado, J. M., Escobedo, F., Guirao, B. and Rivas, A. 2002. Efectos territoriales de la alta velocidad ferroviaria. Estrategias para el planeamiento supramunicipal. *OP ingeniería y territorio*, 60, 74–83.

Ribalaygua, C. 2004. *Evolución de las estrategias de incorporación de la alta velocidad ferroviaria y sus efectos urbanísticos en ciudades medias francesas. Aplicación a los casos españoles*. PhD-thesis. Madrid: Universidad Politécnica de Madrid.

Ribalaygua, C., Escobedo, F., Ureña, J. M., Menéndez, J. M., Rodríguez, F. J., Coronado, J. M., Guirao, B. and Rivas, A. 2004. Alta Velocidad, integración metropolitana y proyectos territoriales. El caso de Ciudad Real y Puertollano. *Urban*, 9, 30–44.

Ribalaygua, C. 2005. Alta velocidad y ciudad: estrategias de incorporación de las nuevas estaciones periféricas francesas y españolas. *Cuadernos de Investigación Urbanística-CIUr*, 44, 134.

Ribalaygua, C., Sánchez, J. J., Coronado, J. M., Garmendia, M. and Ureña, J. M. 2006a. *Línea de Alta Velocidad Madrid-Barcelona: Primeros Estudios y Reflexiones sobre las Ciudades intermedias*. Paper to the VII Congress: Congreso de Ingeniería del Transporte, Ciudad Real (Spain), 14–16 June 2006.

Ribalaygua, C. 2006b. Nuevas estaciones periféricas de alta velocidad ferroviaria: estrategias para su incorporación a las ciudades españolas. *Colección Cuadernos de Ingeniería y Territorio, 5*. Universidad de Castilla-La Mancha, Ciudad Real.

Ribalaygua C. (dir.). 2007. Ferrocarril de alta velocidad y territorio: actas de la Jornada franco-española, in *Cuadernos de Ingeniería y Territorio, 10*. UCLM. Available at: http://www.uclm.es/cr/caminos/Publicaciones/Cuaderno_Ing_ Territorio/Libros/cuaderno10/cuaderno10.pdf [accessed: March 2011].

Ribalaygua, C. 2008. La nueva llegada del ferrocarril a la periferia urbana: ¿una amenaza o una oportunidad para la consolidación de un modelo de ciudad? *Ciudades. Revista del Instituto Universitario de Urbanística de la Universidad de Valladolid*, 11, 81–104.

Ribalaygua, C., Garmendia, M., Díaz, S., García-Villaraco, E., Sánchez, J. J. and García, F. 2009a. *Actividades en torno a Estaciones de Alta Velocidad: Metodología para su Estudio*. Paper to the XXI Congreso: Congreso de Geógrafos Españoles, Ciudad Real 27–29 October 2009, 605–619.

Ribalaygua, C. and de Meer, A. 2009b. Rural areas, high speed train accessibility and sustainable development, in *Sustainable Development and Planning I*, edited by Wit Press. Southampton, Boston, 375–89.

Ribalaygua, C. and García F. 2010a. *HSR Stations in Europe: new Opportunities for Urban Regeneration*. Paper to the ERSA L Conference: High-Speed Rail as a new transport network. Sustainable Regional Growth and Development in the creative knowledge Economy. Jonkoping, August 2010.

Ribalaygua, C. (ed.). 2010b. *Proyectos Urbanos en torno a Estaciones de Alta Velocidad Ferroviaria en Europa. Análisis de casos para la Integración del nuevo Ferrocarril en Logroño*. Edited by Sociedad Mixta Logroño Integración del Ferrocarril 2003.

Riera, P. 1993. *Rentabilidad Social de las Infraestructuras: un Análisis Coste-Beneficio*. Madrid: Civitas.

Rietveld, P., Bruinsma, F., Van Delft, H. T. and Ubbels, B. 2001. Economic impacts of high speed trains. Experiences in Japan and France: expectations in The Netherlands. *Serie Research Memoranda (Faculteit der Economische Wetenschappen at Bedrijfskunde)*, 20.

Rivas, A., Menéndez, J. M. and Coronado, J. M. 2002. *La Alta Velocidad Ferroviaria y su efecto sobre la movilidad en el corredor Madrid-Ciudad Real-Puertollano.* Paper to the V Congreso de Ingeniería del Transporte, Santander, 11–13 June 2002.

Rivas, A., Menéndez, J. M. and Guirao, B. 2004. *Nuevas pautas de movilidad en estaciones situadas en ciudades de tamaño pequeño como consecuencia de la puesta en servicio de trenes de alta velocidad.* Paper to the VI Congreso de Ingeniería del Transporte, Zaragoza, 23–25 June 2004.

Rivas, A. and Coronado, J. M. 2005. La movilidad de alta velocidad en estaciones situadas en estaciones de tamaño pequeño. *Ingeniería y Territorio*, 70, 52–57.

Rivas, A. 2006. *Servicios de alta velocidad en ciudades de tamaño pequeño. Caracterización de la demanda a partir de ocho casos estudiados en la red ferroviaria europea.* Unpublished PhD Thesis, University of Castilla La Mancha, Spain.

Rivas, A., Menéndez, J. M. and Gallego, I. 2006. *Caracterización de los viajeros de alta velocidad en desplazamientos inferiores a una hora. Los casos de París-Vêndome, Estocomo-Eskilstuna y Madrid-Ciudad Real.* Paper to the VII Congreso de Ingeniería del Transporte, Ciudad Real, 14–16 June 2006.

Rivas, A. 2008. *El Servicio de Alta Velocidad Ferroviaria entre Madrid y Toledo. Efectos sobre la Movilidad.* III Jornada de Alta Velocidad y Territorio, Universidad de Castilla la Mancha, 20 November 2008.

Rodríguez Rodríguez, V. and Warnes, T. 2002. Los residentes europeos mayores en España: repercusiones socioeconómicas y territoriales, in: *El nuevo orden demográfico (Monográfico de el Campo de las Ciencias y las Artes – 139)*, edited by P. Reques Velasco. Madrid: Servicio de Estudios del BBVA, 123–46.

Rodríguez, M., Novales, M. and Orro, A. 2005. Alta velocidad y territorio. Algunas experiencias internacionales. *Ingeniería y Territorio*, 70, 9.

Roger, V. 1997. High-speed rail in Europe: experience and issues for future development, in Special issue: The regional and urban effects of high-speed trains. *The Annals of Regional Science*, 31, 1, 21–38.

Rose, G. 1993. *Feminism and Geography: The Limits of Geographical Knowledge.* Cambridge: Polity Press.

Roth, R. and Polino, M. N. (ed.). 2003. *The City and the Railway in Europe.* Aldershot: Ashgate.

Ruiz, F. 2010. *Proyecto AUDES-Áreas Urbanas de España* [Online]. Available at: http://alarcos.inf-cr.uclm.es/per/fruiof *Transport Economics and Policy*, 41(1), 3–23.

Santos, L. 2005a. *Burgos y el Ferrocarril. Estudio de Geografía Urbana.* Valladolid: Editorial Dos Soles.

Santos, L. and las Rivas, J. L. 2005b. El proyecto urbanístico del AVE en Valladolid. *Ingeniería y Territorio*, 70, 2–7.

Santos, L. 2007. *Urbanismo y ferrocarril. La Construcción del Espacio Ferroviario en las Ciudades medias españolas*. Madrid: Fundación de los Ferrocarriles Españoles.

Schäfer A. and Victor D. G. 2000. The future mobility of the world population. *Transportation Research A*, 34(3), 171–205. Also published in: Lundqvist, L., Button, K. and Nijkamp, P. 2003. The Automobile – Classics in Transport Analysis 7, Edward Elgar Publishing LTd.

Scott, A. J. 1988. *New Industrial Spaces. Flexible Production Organization and Regional Development in North America and Western Europe*. London: Pion.

Serrano, R., Ureña, J. M., Pillet, F. and Coronado, J. M. 2004. Renovación y expansión urbana en Ciudad Real. Ejemplos de operaciones inmobiliarias de iniciativa privada entre mediados del siglo XIX y mediados del siglo XX in *Cuadernos de Ingeniería y Territorio, 3*. ETSI Caminos, Canales y Puertos, Universidad de Castilla La Mancha.

Serrano, R., Garmendia, M., Coronado, J. M., Pillet, F. and Ureña, J. M. 2006. Análisis de las consecuencias territoriales del AVE en ciudades pequeñas: Ciudad Real y Puertollano. *Estudios Geográficos*, LXVII(260), 199–229.

SETEC. 2004. *LGV PACA Etude relative aux Effets socio-économique et en terme d'aménagement: Volet 1, Analyse bibliographique des effets des LGV, Synthèse du fonds documentaire*. Setec Organisation. Available at: http://cpdp. debatpublic.fr/cpdp-lgvpaca/docs/pdf/etudes/etude_relative/LGV-PACA-EffetTerritoire-Volet4-juin04.PDF [accessed: April 2011].

Sheller, M. and J. Urry. 2006. The new mobilities paradigm. *Environment and Planning A: Planning and Design*, 38, 207-226.

Shen, Q. 2000. Transportation, Telecommunication and the Changing Geography of Oppoortunity, in *Information, Place and Ciberspace. Issues in Accessibility*, edited by D. G. Janelle and D. C. Hodge. Berlin: Springer-Verlag, 47–72.

Soja, E. W. 1989. *Postmodern geographies: the Reassertion of Space in critical social Theory*. London: Verso.

—— 1996. *Third Space: Journeys to Los Angeles and other Real-and-imagined Places*. Oxford: Blackwell.

—— 2000. *Postmetropolis: Critical studies of cities and regions*. Malden: Blackwell.

—— 2009. *Postmetrópolis: Estudios críticos sobre las Ciudades y las Regiones*. Barcelona: Proyecto Editorial Traficantes de Sueños.

Spiekermann, K. and Wegener, M. 1994. The shrinking continent: new time-space maps of Europe. *Environment and Planning B: Planning and Design*, 21(6), 653–73.

—— 2006. Accessibility and spatial development in Europe. *Science Regionali*, 5(2), 15–46.

Stanke, B. 2009. *High Speed Rail's Effect on Population Distribution in Secondary Urban Areas. An Analysis of the French Urban Areas and Implications for the California Central Valley*. Planning Report presented to the Faculty of the Department of urban and regional planning San José State University Master of urban planning. Available at: http://www.ca4hsr.org/wp-content/uploads/2009/10/Brian-Stanke-298-High-Speed-Rails-Effect-on-Population-Distribution.pdf [accessed: March 2011].

Suchan, T. A., and Brewer, C. A. 2000. Qualitative methods for research on mapmaking and map use. *The Professional Geographer*, 52, 145–54.

Swyngedouw, E., Moulaert, F. and Rodríguez, A. 2005. *The globalized City: Economic Restructuring and Social Polarization in European Cities*. Oxford: University Press.

Taede, T., Van Wee, B. and de Jong, T. 2003. *Road pricing from a geographical Perspective: a literature Review and Implications for Research into Accessibility*. Paper to the XLIII ERSA Congress, Jyväskylä (Finland). 27–30 August 2003. Available at: http://www-sre.wu-wien.ac.at/ersa/ersaconfs/ersa03/cdrom/papers/77.pdf

Tapiador, F. J., Mateos, A. and Martí-Henneberg, J. 2008. The geographical efficiency of Spain's regional airports: a quantitative analysis. *Journal of Air Transport Management*, 14(4), 205–12.

Tapiador, F. J., Burckhart, K., and Martí-Henneberg, J. 2009. Characterizing European high speed train stations using intermodal time and entropy metrics. *Transportation Research Part A: Policy and Practice*, 43(2), 197–208.

Tau. 1993. *Efectos urbanísticos y territoriales del tren de alta velocidad sobre las ciudades de Ciudad Real y Puertollano*. Unpublished, Ministerio de Obras Públicas, Transportes y Medio Ambiente. Madrid.

Terán, F. de. 2002. *Medio siglo de Pensamiento sobre la Ciudad*. Discurso de Ingreso en la Real Academia de Bellas Artes de San Fernando, Madrid, 17 February 2002.

Thompson, L. S. 1994. High-speed rail in the United States: why isn´t there more? *Japan Railway and Transport Reviews*, October, 32–9.

Thrift, N. 1996. New urban eras and old technological fears: reconfiguring the Goodwill of electronic things. *Urban Studies,*, 1463–93.

Tira, M., Tiboni, M., and Badiani, B.et al. 2002. *High Speed/high Capacity Railway and Regional Development: Evaluation of Effects on Spatial Accessibility. From Industriy to advanced Services. Perspectives of European Metropolitan Regions*. Paper to the XLII ERSA Congress: European Regional Science Association, Dortmund, 27–31 August 2002, 11.

Torres, M. C. 2003. La geografía de la sociedad de la información: ¿real o virtual? *Boletín de la Asociación de Geógrafos Españoles*, 35, 153–71.

Trip, J. J. 2008. Urban quality in high-speed train station area redevelopment: the cases of Amsterdam Zuidas and Rotterdam Central. *Planning Practice and Research*, 23(3), 383–401.

Troin, J. F. 1995. *Rail et aménagement du Territoire. Des héritages aux nouveaux Défis*. Paris: Edisud.

———1997. Les gares T.G.V. et le territoire: débat et enjeux. *Annales de Géographie*, 106(593), 34–50.

UK Department for Transport. 2010. *High Speed Rail*, Cm7827. The Stationery Office, London.

Ureña, J. M., Pérez, A., Coronado, J. M. and Rodríguez, F. J. 2001. Ideas para Ciudad Real. *Cuadernos de Ingeniería y Territorio*, 1. Ciudad Real: Universidad Castilla La Mancha.

Ureña, J. M., Menéndez, J. M., Guirao, B., Escobedo, F., Rodríguez, F. J., Coronado, J. M, Ribalaygua, C., Rivas, A. and Martínez, A. 2005a. Alta velocidad ferroviaria e integración metropolitana en España: el caso de Ciudad Real y Puertollano. *EURE Revista Latinoamericana de Estudios Urbano Regionales*, 92, 87–104.

Ureña, J. M. and Ribalaygua, C. 2005b. Le réseau ferroviaire à grande vitesse espagnol: état actuel d'avancement et d'appropriation par les villes desservies. *Transports Urbains*, 106, 3–10.

Ureña, J. M., Escobedo, F. and Serrano, R. 2006a. *Metodología e hipótesis para la evaluación de las consecuencias de la red de Alta Velocidad Ferroviaria en la organización territorial española*. Paper to the VII Congreso de Inerritorio-Estudios Territoriales (CyTET), 160, 213–32.

Ureña, J. M., Coronado, J. M, Escobedo, F., Ribalaygua, C. and Garmendia, M. 2006bc. Situaciones y retos territoriales de la Alta Velocidad Ferroviaria en España. *Ciudad y Territorio-Estudios Territoriales (CyTET)*, XXXVIII(148), 397–424.

Ureña, J. M. and Ribalaygua, C. 2008. Les villes espagnoles saisies par la grande vitesse ferroviaire: stratégies et projet (Chapter 2), in *Mobilité et Écologie Urbaine*. Paris: Descartes and Cie.

Ureña, J. M. and Coronado J. M. 2009a. *Changing territorial Implications of High Speed Rail in Spain: from individual Lines, Stations and Services to Networks*. Paper to the International Congress City Futures in a Globalising World, Madrid, 4–6 June 2009.

Ureña, J. M. 2009b. Grande vitesse ferroviaire Françaispagnole. *Revue d'Histoire des Chemins de Fer*, 39-2008/2, 111–25.

Ureña, J. M., Garmendia, M. and Coronado, J. M. 2009c. Nuevos procesos de metropolización facilitados por la Alta Velocidad Ferroviaria. *Ciudad y Territorio Estudios Territoriales*, LXI(160), 213–32.

Ureña, J. M., Menerault, P. and Garmendia, M. 2009d. The high-speed rail challenge for big intermediate cities: a national, regional and local perspective. *Cities*, 26, 266–79.

Ureña, J. M., Garmendia, M., Coronado, J. M., Vickerman, R. and Romero, V. 2010. New metropolitan processes encouraged by High-Speed Rail: the cases of London and Madrid. Paper to the *WCTR Congress*, Lisbon, July 2010.

Urry, J. 2007. *Mobilities*. Oxford: Polity Press.

US Department of Transportation. 2009. *Vision for High-Speed Rail in America*. U. S. D. o Transportation.

Van den Berg, L. and Pol, P. 1997. *The European High-Speed Train-Network and Urban Development. European Regional Science Association.* Paper to the XXXVII European Congress, Rome, 26–29 August 1997.

—— 1998a. *The European High-Speed Train and Urban Development. Experiences in fourteen European Urban Regions.* Aldershot: Ashgate.

—— 1998b. The urban implications of the developing European high-speed train network. *Environment and Planning C, Government and Policy*, 16, 483–97.

Varlet, J. 1992. Réseaux des transports rapides et interconnexions en Europe Occidentale. *L'Information Géographique*, 56, 101–14.

Vickerman, R. 1995a. Location, accessibility and regional development: the appraisal of trans-European networks. *Transport Policy*, 2(4), 225–34.

—— 1995b. The regional impacts of Trans-European networks. *The Annals of Regional Science*, 29(2), 237–54.

—— 1997. High-speed rail in Europe: experience and issues for future development. *The Annals of Regional Science*, 31, 21–38.

Vickerman, R., Spiekermann, K. and Wegener, M. 1999a. Accessibility and economic development in Europe. *Regional Studies*, 33(1), 1–15.

Vickerman, R. and Norman, C. 1999b. Local and regional implications of trans-European transport Networks: the Channel Tunnel Rail Link. *Environment and Planning A*, 31, 705–18.

Vickerman, R. W. 2007. Cost-benefit analysis and large-scale infrastructure projects: state of the art and challenges. *Environment and Planning B*, 34, 598–610.

—— 2008. Multi-level policy making in transport: the problems for border regions. *International Journal of Public Policy*, 3, 228–45.

—— 2009. Indirect and wider economic impacts of HSR, in *Economic Analysis of High Speed rail in Europe*, edited by G. de Rus. Madrid: Fundación BBVA, 89–118.

—— 2010. Myth and reality in the search for the wider benefits of transport, in *Applied Transport Economics: A Management and Policy Perspective*, edited by E. Van de Voorde and T. Vanelslander, Antwerp: De Boeck, 379–96.

Vinuesa Angulo, J. M. 2005. De la población de hecho a la población vinculada. *Cuadernos Geográficos*, 36(1), 79–90.

Virilio, P. 1991. *The Aesthetics of Disappearance*. New York: Semoitext(e).

Vries, J. de. 1987. *La Urbanización en Europa*. Barcelona: Crítica.

Warshall, S. 1963. A theorem on boolean matrices. *Association for Computing Machinery*, 9, 11–12.

Willigers, J., Floor, H. and Van Wee, B. 2005. *High-speed Railway Developments and corporate Location Decisions. The Role of Accessibility.* Paper to the XLV Congress of the European Regional Science Association: High-Speed Rail's Impact on The Location of Office Employment within the Dutch Randstad Area, Amsterdam, 23–27 August 2005.

Willigers, J. 2006. *Impact of high-speed railway accessibility on the location choices of office establishments.* Doctoral thesis Utrecht University. Available at:	http://igitur-archive.library.uu.nl/dissertations/2006-1019-200333/index. htm [accessed: January 2011]

Willigers, J., Floor, H., van Wee B. 2007. Accessibility indicators for location choices of offices: an application to the intraregional distributive effects of high-speed rail in the Netherlands. *Environment and Planning A*, 39, 2086–98.

Willigers, J. 2008. The impact of high-speed railway developments on office locations: A scenario study approach, in *Railway Developments. Impacts on Urban Dynamics*, edited by F. Bruisma, E. Pels, H. Priemus, P. Rietveld and B. V. Wee. Heidelberg: Physica-Verlag, 237–64.

Wolkowisch, M. 1973. *Géographie des Transports*. Paris, 4.

Zembri, P. 1992. TGV-réseau classique: des rendez-vous manqués? *Transports Urbains*, 75, 5–14.

Zembri P. and Varlet (dir.). 1999. *Réseaux de Communication et aménagement du Territoire: état de l'art des approches de la Géographie des Transports*. Final Report, Contrat GDR 903 "Réseaux".

Zembri, P. 2005. El TGV, la red ferroviaria y el territorio en Francia. *Ingeniería y Territorio*, 70, 12–19.

—— 2008. La contribution de la grande vitesse ferroviaire à l'interrégionalité en France. *Bulletin de l'Association de Géographes Français: Géographies,* 85(4), 443–60.

Zúñiga Antón, M., Pueyo Campos, A., Sebastián López, M., and Calvo Palacios, J. L. 2010. Estudio de la población en el atlas nacional de España. Variables relevantes para la ordenación territorial. *Revista electrónica Proyección* [Online], 9. Available at: http://www.proyeccion.cifot.com.ar/ [accessed: December 2010].

Index

Abler, R. F., 46, 251
accessibility, viii, 23–5, 34, 39, 43,
    45–7, 83–103, 159, 168, 170,
    188, 190–91, 202–3, 206, 260–63,
    272–3, 275,
    change (changes), 15, 24, 28, 35, 47,
        92, 98, 132, 154, 160, 216, 257
    HSR, viii, 15, 25, 47, 49, 53, 55, 92–3,
        95, 97, 132, 160, 164, 175, 189,
        197, 200, 203, 205, 207–8, 211,
        216, 256, 259, 261, 265, 267, 270,
        275
    improve (better, enhance, greater,
        improvement, increased, new,
        revolution, spread), 15, 24–5, 28,
        53, 84, 88, 91–3, 102–3, 117, 125,
        129, 132, 137, 142, 153, 159, 164,
        186, 188–9, 191, 193, 196–8, 200,
        213–14, 242–3, 249
    indicators, 91, 94, 96, 98, 276
    individuals, 15, 35
    policies (decisions, measures, plans,
        strategies), 23, 195, 200, 213–14,
        252
    potential, viii, 90–92, 94, 203
    region (territory), vi, 23, 25, 34, 39, 43,
        45, 47, 95, 197, 200, 205, 214–15,
        270, 275
    spatial, vii, 47–8, 53, 55, 102, 164,
        272–3
    urban (city, nucleus, station), 2, 49,
        53, 105, 125, 153, 159, 175, 191,
        198, 200, 204–6, 208, 216, 254,
        261, 267
Adams, P. C., 50, 251
ADIF (Spanish Administrator of Railway
    Infrastructure), xx, 8–9, 12–13,
    139, 166–7, 191, 229
Aglietta, M., 37, 251
Ahlfeldt, G. M., 26, 251

Ajenjo, M., 87, 96, 99, 251
Albacete, 10, 75, 92, 102–3, 136, 168–9,
    172, 183–4, 195
Albalate, D., 218, 251,
Alberich González, J., 87, 96, 99, 251
Albrechts, L., 40, 251
Alicante, 101, 139, 237
Alonso, M.P., v, xiii, 83, 97, 103, 163, 178,
    190, 251, 253, 255
Altvater, E., 42, 251
Álvarez, O., 227, 251
Amsterdam, 19, 26, 154, 169, 242, 254–5,
    257, 269, 273, 275
Anderson, A., 33, 251
Antequera (Antequera–Santa Ana), 10–11,
    75–6, 86, 92, 98, 102–3, 121, 123,
    136, 160, 168, 172–3, 195, 207
Arbois (Aix-en-Provence), 168, 208, 264
Aschauer, D. A., 24–5, 252
Ashford, 27–8, 135, 149, 152, 269
Atocha, 168, 172, 182–3
attract (attracting, attractive), 6, 7, 15, 50,
    53, 56, 77, 80, 107–8, 112, 114–15,
    118, 120, 123–4, 126, 129–30, 137,
    141–2, 146, 149, 152, 155, 157,
    160, 165, 170, 192, 202–3, 205,
    207, 244, 265
Auphan, E., 108, 134–5, 198, 252
axis (see corridor), 18, 43, 109, 112, 169,
    214–15, 255, 257

Bailly, A. S., 38, 252
Baradaran, S., 84, 252
Barcelona, vii, viii, xi, xii, 5, 7, 10–11,
    14–15, 20, 63–6, 71–3, 75–6, 86,
    92, 94, 97, 101–3, 111–13, 120–21,
    131, 136, 139, 142, 148–50, 153–5,
    166, 168–70, 172–3, 175, 177,
    180–84, 192, 194–5, 208, 217–19,
    222–4, 228, 231–2, 234, 237–8,

242–3, 250, 255, 261–2, 265–6,
269–70, 272, 275
Barcet, A., 38, 252
Barré, A., 169, 265
Bauman, Z., 34, 252
Bavoux, J. J., 83–5, 87, 144, 252
Bazin, S., 132–3, 197, 252
Beauvais, J.M., 55, 106, 252
Bel, G., 218, 251, 252
Belgium, 17, 21, 30
Bell, M. E., 36, 129, 253
Bellanger, F., 144, 253
Bellet, C., v, xiii, 56, 83, 97, 103, 134–6,
138, 144, 150, 163–7, 170–71,
173, 177–8, 184, 186–93, 198,
201, 251, 253
benefit, ix, xii, xv, 15, 20–31, 47–8, 53,
83–4, 103, 105, 114, 131, 133,
135, 138, 147, 152–3, 198, 201–
21, 223–30, 232, 234–9, 241–2,
249–50, 257–8, 270, 275
van den Berg, L., 132–4, 163–5, 169, 189,
198, 218, 275
Berlin, 18, 19–20, 243, 272
Bertolini, L., 132–3, 165, 169–70, 207,
253
Beyer, A., 208, 254
Biggiero, R., 48, 254
Bilbao, 5, 77–8, 101, 139
Blanquart, C., 197, 254
Bleijenberg, A., 43, 254
Blum, U., 56, 132, 254
Boarnet, M.G., 132, 254
Bonnafous, A, 105, 112, 223, 228, 254
Bontje, M., 149, 254
Borzacchiello, M. T., 56, 254
Bourgeois, F., 207, 254
Boursier-Mougenot, I., 99, 254
Bowes, D., 207, 254
Boyer, R., 36, 254
Brewer, C.A., 90, 254, 258, 273
Brocard, M. D., 83–5, 254
Bruinsma, F., 163–6, 169, 254–5, 257,
264, 269, 271
Brussels, viii, xi, 19–20, 27, 154–6, 243,
254, 258
Burckhart, K., 136, 255, 273
Burdack, J., 149, 254

Burmeister, A., 132, 134, 153, 255, 269

Cádiz (Cádiz-Jerez), 11, 73, 79, 101, 268
Cairncross, F, 42, 255
Calais, 131, 149, 265
Calatayud, 11, 75–6, 92, 94, 98, 102–3,
111–12, 136, 160, 168–9, 172, 183,
195, 245
Calvo Palacios, J.L., 56, 83, 84, 87, 89, 96,
99–100, 255, 269, 276
Camagni, R., 99, 255
Campos, J., 2–3, 55, 249, 255
capacity, 1, 4, 6, 17–19, 22, 26, 30, 41, 50,
56, 58, 68, 70, 88, 92, 94, 102, 125,
129, 141, 150, 153, 157, 189, 203,
211, 213–14, 216–17, 223, 228–9,
242, 249, 273
Capel, H., 165, 255
Carey, H. C., 99, 255
Casares, P., vi, xiii, 217, 262
Castells, M., 37, 255
Cauvin, C., 90, 256
Centre de Transports du Loir-et-Cher, 215,
256
CERTU, 215, 256
Chamartin, 168, 172, 182–3
Chang, J., 198, 256
Chapelon, L., 90, 252, 256
Charlempong, S., 132, 254
Charles de Gaulle (Roissy), xvi, 26, 149
Charlton, C., 2, 5, 256
Chen, C.L., 153, 256
Cheng, Y., 198, 256
Cheyland, J. P., 58, 256
China, 2, 20, 21, 217, 220
Cicille, P., 90, 256
city centre (see urban centre), 19, 27, 151,
165, 173, 182, 184, 186, 191, 202,
204–5, 213, 222
Ciudad Real, vii, viii, xvi, 11, 70–75, 77,
92, 94, 102–3, 109–12, 114, 116,
123–4, 130–31, 135–7, 142–6,
157–60, 168–70, 172, 176, 194–5,
204, 207, 253, 259–60, 265–6,
270–74
Claisse, G., 106, 108, 132–3, 209, 263
coexist, 4, 14, 36
Coffey, W. J., 37–8, 252, 256

Cointet-Pinell, O., 105–6, 132, 268
Colin, R., 138, 144, 256
Colletis-Wahl, K., 132, 134, 153, 255
comfort, 3, 6, 53, 121–2, 124, 126, 144,
    214, 220–22, 226
Comisión Europea, 85, 256
commerce (commercial), xvii, 1–6, 10, 63,
    146, 182, 186, 206, 209–10, 218,
    233, 237, 247
commuter (commuters, commuting,
    translocations), xi, xvi, 6, 27–8, 30,
    46, 57, 68, 77–9, 81, 106, 113–26,
    137, 145–6, 152, 205, 215, 223, 247
connect (interconnect, connected,
    connectivity, connection), viii, ix,
    xv, 2, 4–7, 9–11, 14–15, 17, 20, 22,
    24, 26–8, 34, 37–40, 46–51, 53,
    56, 63–4, 66, 68, 70, 73, 76–7, 79,
    84–8, 90–103, 108–11, 113–26,
    131, 134–42, 144–5, 147–55,
    157, 159–60, 166, 170, 175–7,
    180, 182–4, 186, 188, 191, 193,
    198, 201–2, 204–8, 212–14, 216,
    218–20, 242–6, 249–50
Cordoba, viii, xi, 7, 10–11, 64, 73, 75–7,
    79, 92, 102, 109, 111–12, 123, 136,
    153–7, 168, 170, 172, 183–4, 195,
    207
Coronado, J.M., v, xiii, 108, 113, 117,
    119, 129, 158, 160, 259–61, 265,
    269–72, 274,
corridor (see axis), vii, viii, xi, 4, 7–9, 12,
    14, 60, 63, 65–6, 75–6, 94, 97–9,
    102, 105–6, 110–14, 124, 129, 134,
    140, 144, 146, 151–2, 155, 157,
    175, 183, 188, 190, 232, 251,
de Cos Guerra, O., v, xiii, 55, 58, 257
cost (investment, invest), xv, 2, 7, 9, 12,
    14–15, 17, 20, 22, 28, 34, 46, 52–3,
    83, 86, 103, 106, 118–19, 122, 126,
    132, 134, 141, 144–5, 153, 166,
    168–70, 178, 180, 182–3, 192, 194,
    201–2, 205–6, 217–8, 220–21,
    223–35, 237–8, 241, 243, 249–50,
    253, 257–61, 267–70, 275
Coto-Millán, P., vi, xiii, 217–18, 222–4,
    226, 228, 231, 232–4, 238, 256–7,
    262

de Courson, J., 144, 257
Creusot (Le Creusot, Montceau-les-Mines,
    Montchanin), 105–6, 138, 142,
    144, 168, 204
Crozet, Y., 84, 257
Cuenca, 10, 66, 75, 92, 94, 102–3, 136–7,
    142, 145, 157, 167–8, 172–3, 195

Dalvi, M. Q., 84, 257
Daniels, P. W., 37–8, 257
Debrezion, G., 169, 257
Delaplace, M., 197, 252, 254
Dematteis, G., 164, 187, 257
Desbazeille, G., 86, 263
development around stations
    (redevelopment, urban renewal),
    26, 163–6, 169–70, 172, 175,
    177–8, 180, 182–4, 186, 190–91,
    193, 205–6, 247–9, 253, 268, 270,
    273
Díaz, S., 198, 270
Dicken, P., 43, 257
Díez, J., 100, 258
distance (km, kilometers, distant), 6,
    20, 26, 76, 97, 108, 121, 130,
    139–42, 144, 147, 149, 151–2, 159,
    200–201, 243–6, 250, 259
Dobes, L., 33, 258
Dodgson, J., 224, 258
Dollfus, O., 56, 258
Domingo, A., 60, 260
Duany, A., 200, 258
Dupuy, G., v, xiii, xv, 159, 258
Duranton, G., 38, 258

Ebbsfleet 149, 152
Echezarreta, M., 60, 258
economic activities (structures,
    development, dynamics, activity
    parks), 25, 137, 146, 151, 157,
    160, 163, 186–7, 190, 192–3, 195,
    208–10, 244–5, 269,
    high level activities (technological
        park, advanced services), 151, 273
    industrial (industry, cities, activities),
        134, 144, 207, 243, 273
    tertiary (cities, activities), 144, 151,
        157, 170, 243, 276

tourism, 201, 265,
efficient (efficiency), 2, 6, 14, 37–8,
    47–9, 53, 94–5, 103, 121, 126, 158,
    165–6, 168, 191, 193, 196, 212,
    215, 217, 220, 223, 230, 232, 242,
    261, 267, 273
Eicher, C.L., 90, 258
Escalona, A.I., 84, 258
Escobedo, F., 269–70, 274
Escolano, S., v, xiii, 33, 37–8, 84, 267
Eskilstuna, 148, 171
ESPON, U. E., 43, 258
Europe (European), v, vii, viii, xv, xvi, xix,
    1–2, 5, 7, 14–15, 17, 19–23, 31,
    43, 45, 58–60, 62–3, 83, 85, 105,
    107–10, 112, 123, 125, 130, 163,
    166–7, 182, 190, 193, 198, 200,
    208, 211–12, 214–15, 217–18, 228,
    238, 243, 251–2, 254–9, 261–2,
    264, 266–73, 275
European Commission, 212, 218, 258
evaluate (evaluation), v, xii, 15, 83–4,
    86–90, 96, 98, 102–3, 110, 118,
    187, 219, 223–4, 226–8, 230,
    233–5, 237–8, 249–50, 258,
    260–63, 269, 273,
extensibility: 50–51, 262

Facchinetti-Mannone (*see also* Mannone),
    V., 97, 135, 164, 168, 198, 205,
    258
Faiña, J.A., 99, 258, 264
Fariña, J., 144, 186, 259
Faust, M., 38, 259
Feddersen, A., 26, 251
feeder, 21–2, 26,
Figueres (Figueras), viii, 14, 168–9, 172,
    174, 176–7, 194–5, 219, 237
Floor, H., 275–6
Floyd, R.W., 86, 259
Flyvbjerg, B., 28, 259
France (French), viii, xiii, xv, xvi, 1, 2,
    4–5, 10, 14, 17–19, 21, 24–7,
    28–30, 97, 105–8, 112–13, 116,
    130–31, 135, 137–8, 141–4, 146,
    148–9, 151, 154–5, 167–70, 173,
    177, 187, 201, 204–9, 211, 213–15,
    217–20, 224, 231, 237–8, 242,

    247, 250, 252, 254, 256, 258, 261,
    264–6, 269, 271–2, 276
Frankfurt, 19–20, 26, 217
freight (goods transport), 25, 142, 166, 180,
    220, 239, 243,
frequency of travel, service, stations
    stops, etc. (frequent, frequently,
    frequencies, time table, number of
    services, infrequent), xi, 8–9, 12,
    25, 30, 51, 57, 106, 108–9, 113–15,
    117–26, 140, 134–5, 137, 140–43,
    145, 147, 165, 173, 183, 188, 201,
    204, 207–8, 221–3, 225, 241, 246
friction (of space): 34, 42, 46, 50, 53, 86, 96,
Fröidh, O., 55, 115, 118, 124, 132–3, 188,
    259

Gallego, I., v, xiii, 105, 259, 267, 271
García, F., 198, 201, 206, 259, 270
García, J.C., 83–4, 87, 99, 259, 261
García-Villaraco (García de Villaraco), E.,
    xx, 198, 270
Garmendia, M., v, xiii, 56, 129, 132–3, 136,
    138, 140, 144–7, 187, 198, 200,
    259–60, 265, 270, 272, 274
Gaspar, J., 51, 260
gauge, xv, 4, 7–8, 10, 12, 17–20, 130–31,
    163, 223–4, 229,
Geneau, I., 159, 258
Germany (German), xvi, 5, 17–21, 26–7,
    29, 30, 130, 138, 217–18, 220,
    256–7
Gerona (Girona), 148, 168–9, 183, 224
Gershuny, J., 37, 260
Geurs, K. T., 56, 260, 263
Giddens, A., 41, 50–51, 260
Gil, F., 60, 260
Gilli, F., 68, 260
Givoni, M., 56, 132–3, 198, 218, 260, 265
Glaeser, E.L., 51, 260
González, M.P., 171, 260
Gourvish, T., 17, 260
Graham, D.J., 25, 260
Grasland, C., 99, 254, 260
Guadalajara (Guadalajara-Yebes), viii, 66,
    70, 91, 92, 98, 102, 121, 135–7,
    147–8, 150–51, 160, 168, 170,
    172–5, 195, 204–5, 208

Guirao, B., 107, 113, 123, 127, 260–61, 265, 269–71, 274
Gutierrez, A., v, xiii, 136, 163, 165–7, 170–71, 253
Gutierrez, J., 47, 56, 83, 84, 87, 88, 89, 95–6, 99, 102–3, 132, 141, 166–7, 173, 186, 261, 267

Haesbaert, R., 84, 261
Hägerstrand, T., 50, 84, 261
Hagget, P., 84, 261
Halbert, L., 38, 261
Hall, P., 134, 166, 256, 261
Hamburg, 18, 20, 251
Hammadou, H., 97, 261
Hanrot, P., 112, 261
Hanson, J., 41, 262
Harris, B., 83, 87, 262
Harvey, D., 36–7, 41, 42, 50, 262
Haynes, K. E., 218, 254, 262
Haywood, R., 169, 262
Herce, J. A., 227, 251
Hillier, B., 41, 262
Hoogstraten. P., 39, 262
Houée, M., 106, 113, 262
house (household, warehouses), 126, 136, 175, 177, 180, 182–4, 205, 210, 247, 254
HSR (TGV, ICE)
    fares (price), xvi, 12, 115, 122, 125–6, 140, 201, 208, 224, 226, 231
    infrastructure
        gauge (change tracks with different), 4, 10, 18, 131, 223
        improved (adapted, upgraded), 4, 12–3, 138
        network (corridor, line, system, link, connection, except stations and urban railway system), vii, viii, xi, xv, xvi, 1–5, 10–12, 14–15, 17–23, 25, 29, 46, 49, 53, 55–6, 58, 60–66, 68, 75, 80, 89–90, 92–3, 95, 97, 99, 101–2, 105–10, 112–13, 125, 130–31, 133–5, 139–42, 147–9, 151, 154–5, 159–60, 167–8, 173, 175, 178, 184, 186, 188, 193, 199, 203, 208,

211, 217, 219, 223, 229, 231, 237, 239, 242, 244–5, 249, 261, 274–5
        new (purpose built, dedicated line, independent), 4–5, 8–9, 11, 13–15, 17, 22, 29, 80, 105, 107, 112, 117, 125, 133, 217, 238, 249
        tracks, 3, 5, 10, 28–9, 86
    integrated tickets, 214
    operators, 21–2, 46, 222
    passengers (demand, traffic, travellers, trips, users, potential travellers), vii, xi, xii, 7, 15, 25, 28–30, 46, 105–8, 110–11, 112–13, 115–18, 120–22, 124–6, 137–8, 146, 153–4, 186, 191, 208–9, 218–23, 236–7, 249
    plans (planning), viii, 13–4, 160, 167, 178, 189–90, 192, 200, 212, 219, 241, 248
    rolling and traction material (stock), 2–4, 19–20, 29, 131, 230
    services (offer, trains, not only in general as the introduction of the HSR), vii, xi, xvi, 1–8, 15, 30, 47, 49, 55, 115, 135, 138, 142, 152, 156, 203, 242, 250
        international, 21, 242–3
        long-distance (intermetropolitan), 6–7, 9–10, 12, 106, 109, 116, 118–21, 125, 131, 142, 145, 147, 150–52, 155, 157, 159, 223–4, 229–30, 242–3, 246
        medium-distance (regional), viii, xi, xvi, 6, 11–12, 27–8, 108–21, 125–6, 130–31, 142, 145, 150–51, 160, 223–4, 259
        mixed (variable gauge services), 2–4, 10–11, 14, 105, 131, 147, 149, 152, 214, 223–4
        pure, 9–10, 12, 130–31, 223
        short distance (suburban, intra-metropolitan), 7, 27–8, 116, 121–6, 142, 147–52, 259–60, 274
    speed, 2, 5–6, 10, 12, 14, 91, 118, 130, 134, 207, 220, 231

systems (models, approaches,
  concepts, second generation), vii,
  3–5, 17, 19, 21, 88, 90, 106, 108,
  113, 115–16, 118, 130, 137, 141,
  147, 167
travel purposes (motives, objectives,
  patterns), xi, 5–6, 9, 117, 119,
  121–3, 125–6, 130–31, 140, 222,
  244
travel time, 5–7, 19, 27, 43, 70, 105,
  108, 115–17, 120–22, 124–6, 130,
  133–5, 139–40, 142–3, 147, 155,
  160, 191–2, 221, 228, 230–31,
  243–5
Huelva, 73, 79
Huesca, 75–6, 92, 94, 102–3, 168

Ihlanfeldt, K., 207, 254
Illeris, S., 37, 262
Imrie, R., 169, 262
Inglada, V., vi, xiii, 107, 113, 132, 217–18,
  221–2, 224, 226–8, 231–4, 256–7,
  262
Innerarity, D., 41, 262
Innis, H., 33, 262
intermodality (connection, transport centre,
  intermodal, interchangers), 94
  conventional and HSR, 3, 94, 136, 149,
  HSR and airport, 157
  intermodal station, 166, 175, 177–8,
    180, 182–4, 186, 190–91, 195, 200,
    203, 211–12, 214, 216, 273,
  several HSR lines, 159,
international (internationally), xvi, 8, 12, 17,
  19–21, 27–8, 34, 38–9, 49, 132–3,
  135, 145, 152, 154–5, 163, 190,
  209, 242–3, 253–4, 257–6, 264,
  267–8, 274–5
Isard, W., 99, 262
Italy (Italian), 17–8, 21, 30, 259, 266

Janelle, D.G., 46, 50, 251, 262, 272
Janssen, B., 39, 262
Japan (Japanese), 1–2, 4, 17–8, 20–21, 26,
  106, 217, 220, 238, 267, 271, 273
Jover, J.A., v, xiii, 83, 255, 269

Kamel, K., 198, 263

Kaufmann, A., 86, 263
Kingsley, E. H., 55, 263
Kiyoshi, K., 56, 263
Klein, O., 47, 106, 108, 112–13, 132–5,
  186, 200, 202, 209, 263
Knowles, R.D., 1–2, 42, 46, 56, 256, 264
Kobayashi and Okumura, 134, 264
Koln, 19, 26, 154, 217
Komei, S., 56, 264
Kwang, S. K., 56, 264

land, xv, xvi, xvii, 7, 17, 21, 24, 26,
  28, 31, 34, 48–9, 55–6, 58–9,
  63, 79–80, 136, 141, 145, 166,
  169–70, 172–3, 175, 177–8, 180,
  183–4, 186, 190–92, 194–5, 197,
  201–7, 216, 246–8, 260, 263–4
land-use (land use), 21, 26, 28, 31, 34, 48,
  56, 59, 136, 201, 260
Le Bras, H., 58, 264
Lee, J., 198, 256
Lefebvre, H., 41, 264
Lerida (Lleida), viii, xiii, 10–11, 75–6,
  92, 94, 97, 102–3, 111–12, 135–6,
  142, 146, 160, 163, 168, 172,
  183–5, 192–3, 195, 224, 253
L'Hostis, A., 198, 264
Lille, viii, xi, 106, 113, 135, 149, 154–6,
  163, 169, 255, 266
Lipietz, A., 36, 264
Lisbon, 12, 103, 157, 167, 242–3, 274
Llop J. M., 135, 253
London, xi, 7, 19, 25–8, 134, 147–52,
  155–6, 169, 242–3, 251, 253, 255,
  257–8, 260–62, 267, 272, 274
López-Rodríguez, J., 88, 264
Louw, E., 169, 264
Lyon, xv, xvi, 1, 17–18, 26–7, 105–6,
  112–13, 144, 148, 163, 217,
  243–5, 254, 256, 263, 268

Mâcon (Mâcon-Loche), 106, 148, 168,
  204–5
Madrid, vii, viii, xi, xii, xiii, xvi, 1, 4,
  6–12, 14–15, 20, 26–7, 60, 63–6,
  70–73, 75–7, 79, 86, 91–2, 94,
  97, 101–3, 107, 109–14, 116–17,
  119–24, 130–31, 136–7, 139,

142–51, 153–9, 166–8, 170,
172–3, 175, 177, 180–84, 186,
191–2, 194–6, 208, 217–19,
221–5, 228–9, 231–2, 235, 237–8,
242–5, 249–50, 252–3, 255–62,
265–75
Maillat, D., 38, 252
Makoto, O., 56, 263
Malaga (Málaga), vii, xi, 10–11, 63–4, 73,
75–7, 79, 92, 101–3, 111–12, 121,
136, 139, 153, 156, 166, 168, 172,
183–6, 195, 237, 242
Mandeville, T., 37, 264
Mannone (*see also* Facchinetti-Mannone),
V., 105, 112–13, 132–3, 135, 144,
153, 197, 198, 201, 205, 207–9,
264
Marañón, M., v, xiii, 55,
Marchal, P., 97, 267
Marne La Vallée, 149, 168
Marseille (Marseilles), 7, 243, 254, 264
Martí-Henneberg, J., 255, 264, 274
Martín, E., vi, xiii, 197–8
Martin, K.M., 84, 257
Martínez, H., 111, 114, 265
Martínez Sánchez-Mateos, H.S., 56, 265
Matthewman, R., 198, 263
Masson, S., 201, 265
de Mattos, C., 84, 257
McGuire, T. J., 129, 253
Meer, A. de, vi, xiii, 197–8, 204, 215,
265, 270
Menéndez, J. M., v, xiii, 105, 109–10,
115–17, 123, 130–32, 135–7,
144–6, 188, 200, 202, 204, 207,
259, 261, 265, 269, 270–71, 274
Menerault, P., 4, 97, 134–5, 169, 197–8,
200, 265–6, 274
Mérenne-Schoumaker, E., 83–5, 266
metropolis (metropolitan), viii, xvi, 1–2,
5–7, 11, 15, 25, 31, 38, 49, 58, 60,
63, 65–6, 68, 70–72, 75–6, 79–80,
91, 94, 101, 108–10, 113, 115–17,
119–23, 125–6, 130, 132–3, 135,
138–57, 159–60, 166–8, 170,
172–3, 177, 182, 188, 190–91,
194–5, 241–3, 245–6, 253, 256–7,
259–61, 263–4, 268,

Metz, J., 43, 266
Miles, I., 37, 260
Million, F., 132, 134–5, 263
Ministerio de Fomento, xix, 44, 87–9,
91–3, 95, 97–8, 101, 108, 178,
265–6
Ministerio de Obras Públicas y Transportes
(MOPT), 230–31, 233, 266
Mistral, J., 36, 254
mobility, 34, 36–7, 43, 46, 53, 55–7, 70–71,
77, 79, 86, 105–6, 109, 114–16,
119, 125, 132, 191, 193, 200, 214,
222, 266, 272
effect on (generated, influence, change,
revolution), 109, 111, 113–16,
123–7, 188, 190, 196
HSR corridor (in cities with HSR) 106,
108
individual (personal, passenger), 6, 15,
44, 106, 125
medium-distance HSR, v, 109, 115
patterns (schemes, behaviours), 6, 56,
70, 77, 109, 113, 117–20, 124–6,
132, 244
plans (local plans), 214–5
potential (possibilities), 56, 77
to work, 57, 71,
Módenes, J.A., 96, 266
Moles, A., 50, 52, 266
Monzon (Monzón de Cáceres), A., 55, 84,
88, 89, 99, 261, 267–8
MOPTMA, 87, 94, 266
Mora Aliseda, C., 261, 267
Morellet, O., 97, 267
Moreno, A., 37–8, 84, 267
Morgan, K., 42, 267
Mota, C., 198, 259
Moulaert, F., 169, 251, 262, 267, 273
Muller, M., 108, 112, 267
Munich, 18, 243
Murayama, Y., 2, 47, 267
Murcia, 68, 139, 237
Musso, P., 84, 257

Nash, C., 198, 202, 228, 250, 257, 267
Netherlands (Pays–Bas), 17, 21, 260,
265–6, 271, 276
network economies, 218–9, 237–9, 257,

Nijkamp, P., 254, 269, 272
Nogales, J.M., 84, 267
Nombela, G., 198, 257, 264
Noyelle, T., 37, 267

O'Brien, R., 42, 267
OECD, 85, 217, 268
office, 6, 134, 137, 146, 149–52, 157, 182,
    184, 206, 209, 246–9, 257, 275–6
Offner, J. M., 133, 268
Ohnmacht, T., 46, 268
on demand transport, 213–15,
Oña, J., 215, 268
Oviedo (Oviedo-Gijón-Avilés), 77, 101, 139
Owen, A. D., 223, 268

Paris, xi, xiii, xv, xvi, 1, 7, 17–19, 25–8,
    105–6, 112–13, 142–7, 149, 155–6,
    197–8, 217, 228, 242–5, 251–2,
    254, 256–8, 261, 263–4, 266,
    268–9, 271, 273–4, 276
Paris, C., 197–8, 268
Paul, D., 201, 268
Paulley, N., 215, 268
Perpignan, xvi, 169, 177, 219, 237–8, 265
Peters, D., 198, 268
Petiot, R., 201, 265
Pietri, J., 144, 202, 208, 268
Phillips, G. D. A., 223, 268
Plassard, F., 5, 47, 105–6, 108, 112–13,
    129, 132–3, 141, 144, 152–3, 186,
    200–201, 268
Pol, P.J.M., 132–4, 163–5, 169, 189, 198,
    218, 269, 275
Polino, N.M., 163, 271
Potrykowski, M., 129, 269
Preston, J., 202, 269
Priemus, H., 132, 254, 269, 276
public transport (transportation), xv, xvii,
    22, 122, 138, 151, 175, 183, 191,
    198, 200–201, 203–5, 208, 212,
    214–6, 246, 268,
Puente Genil (PuenteGenil, Puente Genil-
    Herrera), 11, 76, 92, 102–3, 123,
    136, 160, 168, 172–3, 195, 204, 207
Pueyo Campos, A., v, xiii, 56, 79, 83, 96,
    99–100, 255, 269, 276
Puga, D., 38, 258

Puertollano, viii, xvi, 11, 70, 75, 77, 92, 94,
    102–3, 109–12, 114, 116, 123–4,
    130–31, 135–7, 142–6, 157–9, 168,
    172, 183, 265, 270–74
punctual (punctuality), 4, 6, 10, 122, 124,
    222, 231

Quinet, E., 132, 269

Rabin, G., 134, 269
Rada, J.F., 37, 269
railway, viii, 1, xx, 4, 19–22, 27, 30, 47,
    70–71, 85, 87–8, 90, 94, 97–8, 102,
    129–30, 149, 152, 158, 163–7,
    169–73, 175–8, 180, 182–4, 186–7,
    189–90, 193–5, 197, 199–201,
    203, 205, 207–14, 216, 218, 220,
    223, 226–7, 229, 232, 238, 247–8,
    252–5, 257–8, 262–5, 267–9, 271,
    273, 275–6
Ramjerdi, F., 84, 252
Raux, C., 87, 269
reliability (security), 3, 5–6, 27, 118, 124,
    200, 246, 249,
region (regional), vii, 4, 8, 10–11, 15,
    22–8, 33, 35, 37–40, 43, 45, 48,
    51–3, 56, 60, 63, 65, 67–8, 72–3,
    76–7, 80–81, 84, 87–8, 91, 94–5,
    98, 101–1, 113, 123, 130–6, 138,
    142, 144–7, 149–52, 157, 166–7,
    171–3, 180, 182, 191, 197–8,
    200–205, 208, 211–16, 218, 220,
    227–8, 241, 243–6, 248, 250,
    251–2, 254–5, 258–66, 269,
    271–6,
RENFE (Spanish Railway Company), xx,
    11, 110, 112, 130–31, 136, 139,
    184, 229
Requena (Requena-Utiel), 75, 92, 102–3,
    121, 136–7, 168, 172–3, 195
Reques Velasco, P., v, xiii, 55, 62, 66, 269,
    271
RFF (Reseau Ferré de France), 29, 214, 269
Ribalaygua, C., vi, xiv, 132–3, 135, 144–5,
    168, 170, 177, 189, 197–9, 201,
    204–9, 215, 259, 261, 265–6,
    269–70, 274

Riera, P., 234, 270
Rietveld, P., 198, 254, 271, 276
Rivas, A., v, xiv, 105, 108–10, 113–19,
    122, 124–5, 136–7, 144, 180, 259,
    261, 265, 269–71, 274
de las Rivas, J.L., 180, 272
Rodríguez, F.J., 265, 269–70, 274
Rodriguez Rodriguez, V., 60, 62, 66, 269,
    271
Roger, V., 56, 271
Romero, V., v, xiv, 129, 198, 259–60, 265,
    274
Romher, E., 50, 52, 266
Rose, G., 50, 271
Roth, R., 163, 271
Rotterdam, 154, 163, 169, 273
route, viii, xi, xii, 5–7, 17–20, 25, 27–9,
    53, 55–6, 80–81, 88, 90, 93–100,
    107, 109, 115, 117, 124, 126,
    129–30, 135, 215, 218–19, 221–4,
    228–9, 231–3, 235–9
Ruiz, F., 168, 271
de Rus, G., 255, 2–3, 28, 55, 132, 198,
    224, 231, 249–50, 257, 275

Sagrera (La), 168, 172, 180, 182
Santos, L., 135, 165, 180, 271–2
Sants, 168, 172, 180
Schäfer, A., 56, 272
Scott, A. J., 38, 264, 272
Segovia, viii, 10–1, 86, 91–2, 94, 97–8,
    102, 111–12, 121, 131, 136–8, 147,
    149–51, 167–8, 172–3, 191, 195,
    204, 207, 253
Serrano, R., 132, 144, 272, 274
SETEC, 132, 153, 272
Seville (Sevilla), vii, viii, xi, 1, 4, 6, 7, 9,
    10–11, 15, 20, 63–4, 70–77, 79, 98,
    101–3, 107, 109–13, 120, 123–4,
    130–31, 136, 139, 153, 156, 166,
    168, 170, 172, 177, 180, 184, 186,
    195, 218, 221–5, 229, 231, 235,
    237, 242, 259–60, 262, 268
Sheller, M., 35, 272
Shen, Q., 34, 47, 272
Societé Nationale des Chemins de Fer
    (SNCF), xv, 105–6, 214, 257
Soja, E.W., 41–2, 80, 141, 272

space-time relation (space-time)
    compression, 41–44
    convergence, 42, 43, 46, 50
    elasticity: 43
    experience: 34, 35, 41, 44, 45 50, 51,
        53
Spain (Spanish), v, vi, vii, vii, xi, xiii, xiv,
    xv, xvi, xvii, xix, xx, 1–2, 4–5,
    7–12, 14–15, 17, 20–21, 24, 26–8,
    30, 35, 44, 55, 57–68, 70–3, 75–80,
    83, 85, 87–91, 93–9, 107–9, 111,
    113–17, 119, 121, 125–6, 130–31,
    135–41, 143–6, 148–50, 153–5,
    157, 159, 163–96, 198, 201, 203,
    204, 206–8, 210–12, 217–20,
    223–4, 228–31, 234–5, 237–8,
    242–5, 247–9, 253, 256–7, 265,
    267, 270–71, 274
Spiekermann, K., 39, 43, 272, 275
Spit, T., 132–3, 165, 169–70, 207, 253
Stanke, B., 56, 272–3
station conventional and/or freight, viii, xvi,
    xvii, 3, 5, 10, 18–19, 26, 49, 71, 85,
    135, 147, 150, 165–6, 168, 175–8,
    180, 184, 186, 200, 205–7, 212,
    247, 254–5, 257,
station HSR, ix, xi, 3, 5, 6, 10, 15, 47, 49,
    65, 70–71, 75–7, 86, 89, 94–5, 97,
    99, 108, 114–15, 133–6, 141, 147,
    151–2, 155, 157, 160, 168, 171,
    176–8, 182–4, 189–90–2, 195,
    197–8, 200–201, 214–16, 229–30,
    232, 246, 269, 273–4
    area of influence (near, around,
        surroundings, by the, centrality,
        affected by), viii, xi, xvii, 49,
        75–6, 94, 102, 114, 116, 133, 138,
        143, 146, 163, 170, 178, 183, 186,
        189–90, 193–6, 198, 200–203,
        205–10, 213–14, 216, 246–7,
    access to, 115, 116, 135, 138
    big cities, 135, 248
    central (urban), xvii, 115, 135–8, 142,
        144, 147, 149–50, 155, 157, 160,
        166, 168–9, 172, 192, 202–5,
        207–10, 216, 231, 248,
    cities with (municipalities or towns),
        49, 53, 56, 70–72, 75–6, 91–2, 98,

102, 135–6, 144–5, 168–9, 198,
201, 246, 269
city edge (tangential), 136, 166,
168–9, 172–3, 176, 183, 195,
203–4, 207–10, 248,
intermediate (intermediate city), 22,
25, 26, 28, 125, 135, 147, 167,
198, 206, 218, 243, 246, 250
location (locating), ix, xi, xvi, 15,
28, 75, 114–15, 130, 134–8, 143,
150–51, 160, 166, 168, 173, 175,
199, 201–3, 207–11, 216, 258,
medium size cities, 126, 168–9, 173,
248, 258
peripheral (outside, exurban,
greenfield, distant,..), xvi, 28, 116,
135–8, 144, 149, 168, 170, 172–3,
175, 191, 195, 202–5, 207–8, 210,
216, 248–9
small cities (suburbs), 109, 115, 130,
135, 137, 141, 147–8, 151–2, 159,
168, 173, 248
Stransky, V., 97, 266
strategies (policies, marketing tool), 15,
21, 23–4, 26, 28, 132–4, 145,
150, 170, 175, 184, 189–90, 192,
196, 201, 205, 211–13, 216, 244,
247–8,
Stratford, 148, 152
suburb (suburban, suburbanisation), 4,
7–8, 10, 12, 38, 40, 52, 80, 110,
116, 121–2, 142, 147–52, 223–4,
245–6, 258–9
Suchan, T.A:, 90, 273
survey, 44, 225,
activities developed around HSR
stations, 198–9
households, 136
passengers (users of transport), 15, 27,
116, 135–7, 221–2, 225–6
transportation companies or
institutions, 209
Swyngedouw, E., 40, 251

Taede, T., 55, 273
Tapiador, F.J., 85, 94, 255, 273
Tarragona (Tarragona-Reus, Camp de
Tarragona,), viii, 10–11, 64, 75–6,

86, 92, 94, 102–3, 111–12, 121,
136, 138, 149–50, 160, 167–8, 170,
172–3, 175–6, 195, 204, 207, 224,
238
Tau, 144, 273
Taylor, Z., 129, 269
technology (technological), vii, viii, xv,
17–20, 34, 36–7, 41–4, 51, 53, 56,
100, 119, 131, 138, 151–2, 175,
178, 182, 190, 193, 205–7, 215,
235, 251, 259–60, 264–5, 267, 273,
Terán, F. de, 197, 273
Thompson, L.S., 218, 235, 273
Thrift, N., 51, 261, 273
Tira, M., 39, 273
Toledo, 10–11, 66, 73, 75–7, 92, 94, 102,
111–12, 121–2, 131, 136–7, 147–8,
150–51, 157, 168, 172, 207, 261,
271
Torres, M.C., 100, 273
track, 1–5, 7–8, 10, 12, 17–20, 22, 28–9,
163, 165–6, 169, 173, 176–7, 180,
183–4, 186, 188, 194–5, 247,
traffic, xv, xvi, 1, 17–21, 25, 27–30, 70,
91, 106–7, 109–10, 112–3, 115,
117–21, 124–6, 130, 145, 178, 218,
222–3, 228, 235–8, 259,
transport,
air (airport), xvi, 5–6, 21–2, 25–6, 31,
46, 86, 89, 91–2, 94–5, 97, 100–1,
112–13, 138, 140, 152–3, 155, 157,
159, 200, 222, 226, 228, 231–2,
235, 243, 249–50, 268,
road (highway, motorway, automobiles,
car, bus), xvi, 6–7, 21–2, 31, 46–7,
86, 88–92, 94–5, 100, 108, 112,
118, 122, 144, 147, 157, 159, 203,
213, 216, 222, 224–6, 231–3, 235,
243, 246–7, 249
conventional (traditional) rail, 4–7, 10,
12, 14, 22, 25, 30, 47, 118, 121,
124, 131, 137, 139, 147, 149–50,
159, 169, 176–7, 182, 184, 186,
200, 203, 205, 213, 216, 222,
224–6, 231–2, 238, 243, 247,
Trip, J.J., 131, 169, 273
Troin, J.F., 106, 112–13, 134–5, 138, 144,
166–7, 198, 201–2, 204, 273–4

United Kingdom (UK), xiv, 2, 17, 21, 23,
26–7, 29–30, 135, 148–9, 256, 260,
265, 274
urban (interurban, inter-urban) implications,
15, 135, 140, 250, 275
urban centre (see city centre), 114–16, 175,
182, 184, 191–2, 194,
Urbano, P., 56, 261
Ureña, J.M. de, v, vi, xiii, xiv, xvi, xix, 1,
5–7, 10–12, 27, 56, 117, 129–34,
138, 140, 144–8, 150–60, 167, 170,
173, 177–8, 184, 188, 197–8, 229,
241, 259–60, 265, 269–70, 272, 274
Urry, J., 34–5, 44, 272, 274
USA (US, United States), 2, 44, 200, 264,
267, 273–4

Valence, viii, 106, 168, 205–6, 208
Valencia, 10, 64, 67–8, 75, 91–2, 101–3,
136–7, 139, 157, 166, 168, 172,
177, 180, 183, 195, 217, 237, 242,
250, 255
Valladolid, viii, 10–11, 14, 60, 64, 75, 91–2,
94, 97–8, 102–3, 111–12, 117, 119,
136, 139, 151, 154, 166, 168, 170,
172, 177–80, 184, 191, 194–5, 219,
237–8, 242, 270–72
van Wee, B., 260, 273, 275–6

Varlet, J., 132, 275–6
Vendôme, 137–8, 142–6, 168, 204, 215,
253, 256, 271
Vickerman, R., v, xiv, 1, 17, 23, 25, 30, 84,
95, 102–3, 132, 135, 138, 153, 173,
186, 249, 260, 269, 274–5
Victor, D.G., 56, 272
Vinuesa (Vinuesa Angulo), J.M., 100, 275
Virilio, P., 41, 275
Voskamp, U., 38, 259
Vowles, T., 2, 5, 256
Vries, J. de, 65, 275

Warnes, T., 60, 271
Warshall, S., 86, 275
Wegener, M., 39, 43, 132, 272, 275
Willigers, J., 49, 55, 132, 169, 257, 275–6
Wittke, V., 38, 259
Wolkowisch, M., 129, 276

Zaragoza, viii, xi, xiii, xiv, 10–11, 14, 33,
60, 64, 75–6, 83, 92, 94, 97–8,
101–3, 111–12, 135–6, 139, 153–6,
166, 168–70, 172, 177–9, 189–90,
194–5, 224, 228, 251, 271
Zembri, P., 7, 97, 132, 135, 138, 144, 202,
252, 256, 276
Zúñiga Antón, M., v, xiv, 90, 255, 269, 276

For Product Safety Concerns and information please contact our
EU representative GPSR@taylorandfrancis.com, Taylor & Francis
Verlag GmbH, Kaufingerstraße 24, 80331 München, Germany.